North Korean Special Forces

NORTH KOREAN SPECIAL FORCES

Second Edition

JOSEPH S. BERMUDEZ, JR.

Naval Institute Press
Annapolis, Maryland

Library of Congress Cataloging-in-Publication Data

Bermudez, Joseph S.
     North Korean special forces / Joseph S. Bermudez, Jr. — 2nd ed.
       p.   cm. — (Special warfare series)
     Includes bibliographical references (p.   ) and index.
     ISBN 1-55750-066-5 (alk. paper)
     1. Korea (North). Chosŏn Inmin 'gun—Commando troops—History.
I. Title. II. Series: Naval Institute special warfare series.
UA853.K6B47   1997
356' . 167'095193—dc21

Printed in the United States of America on acid-free paper ∞
05 04 03 02 01 00 99 98   9 8 7 6 5 4 3 2
First printing

To my firstborn son, Shammah,
who has brought his mother and me
endless amounts of love and joy.

CONTENTS

Illustrations

PREFACE

This book began as a simple revision of my book *North Korean Special Forces,* published by Jane's Publishing Company in 1988. In the end, however, it turned out to be an entirely new book that shares only the form of its predecessor. The present book is not meant to be an all-inclusive study of the subject matter or a comprehensive study of the Korean People's Army itself. Like its predecessor, it compiles and summarizes the little open-source information available concerning one of the world's largest and most formidable special operations forces, the Korean People's Army special purpose forces.

Accuracy in any work dealing with the Korean People's Army, and especially its elite special purpose forces, is a matter of degree. A certain amount of the information in this volume will inevitably be incorrect. Other material may be misinformation disseminated by interested parties to serve their own purposes. Words like *probably, estimated, are believed to,* and *apparently* must appear frequently in any work of this type. The paucity of reliable information may have caused me to overstate the capabilities of special purpose forces for operations within the Korean Peninsula and underestimate their global capabilities (especially in the areas of foreign military assistance and terrorism).

Several conventions have been used to improve the readability of the book. I have endeavored to use the abbreviation *DPRK* to represent the Democratic People's Republic of Korea instead of the more popular *North Korea.* The term *Korean People's Army* and its abbreviation, *KPA,* are used to represent the *Chosen Inmingun* and the more commonly used *North Korean People's Army (NKPA).* The term *Fatherland Liberation War* is used by the KPA and in this book, instead of the more popular *Korean Conflict* or *Korean War.* The term *enemy* normally refers to an enemy of the KPA, typically the Republic of Korea, the United States, and their respective armies. The abbreviation *ROK,* instead of the more common term *South Korea,* is used to represent the Republic of Korea. Finally, the term *Chinese People's Volunteers* and its abbreviation, *CPV,* is used to identify Chinese Forces in Korea during the Korean Conflict, instead of *Chinese Volunteer Army (CVA)* or *Chinese Communist Forces (CCF).* This should not be interpreted as saying that these are the KPA's only potential opponents; they are not. The KPA's chances of accruing new opponents are especially good, considering the KPA's increasingly large commitments to combat operations in developing countries. Limitations of space have necessitated that much information regarding the KPA in general (e.g., history, tactics, and equipment) be excluded.

Few, if any, books are the product of one person, and this volume is most certainly no exception. Had it not been for the contributions and support of many people and organizations, some whom by necessity must remain anonymous, this volume would have been a mere shadow of its present self. I would like to extend my sincere thanks to the following people: Randy Baldini of the Naval Institute Press for his assistance in organizing and arranging the thousands of little details that go into producing a book of this nature; Anna Bermudez, my mother; Matt Brook; W. Seth Carus for his encouragement and assistance; Patricia Boyd for her patience and excellent editing of the manuscript; James R. Dennis; Mark Gatlin of the Naval Institute Press for his vision in publishing this book and his encouragement while I was writing it; Doug Ellice; Steven Glick; Rodney Graves; Howard J. Gunzenhauser, my father-in-law; Rebecca Hinds; Barry Hudson, who at the very end of this project did yeoman service by translating forty pages of defector interviews; David Isby; Lillian and Lydia Kouletsis; Linda O'Doughda; Sydney A. Seiler, author of *Kim Il-song 1941–1948: The Creation of a Legend, the Building of a Regime;* William Lewis of the National Archives and Record Center; Captain Raymond Yennello; the FOIA staffs at the Defense Intelligence Agency, U.S. Army Assistant Chief of Staff for Intelligence, and the U.S. Army ITAC (especially their North Korean analysts who had to review all my FOIA requests); and Steven J. Zaloga, who although he might not remember it, many years ago convinced me to start publishing the numerous works that I had written.

A unique note of thanks also goes to the "Lumber Road Gang," including Wayne "Red Dog" Cromwell; Thomas "High Boy" DiMisa; Michael "Mikey" Germaine; Thomas "Big Toe" Gill; Tom "Sweet Pea" Lillis; John "Big Mac" McDonald; Donald "Mumbles" Malone; Robert "Ode" Oderwall; Richard "Lotto Man" Oravitz; Joann "Red" Reale; Mike "Spike" Sullivan; and Paul "Yo-Yo" Yovino. I owe a very special debt of gratitude to both William "Mongo" Baynes and Chuck "Chas" Leo for their friendship, humor, and support. With companions such as these, ultimate victory is ensured, and there is no need to fear even the most menacing of antagonists.

My children, Shammah, Rebecca (Butterfly Sparkle Princess), and Micah, are deserving of note for their patience with a father who is enthralled with such a "weird" subject. Finally, there is my wife, Diane, without whose love and support I would not have been able to write this book. I'm still "madly, passionately, hopelessly" in love with her.

Thank you one and all.

North Korean Special Forces

Chapter 1

OVERVIEW

The point now is not whether a war will break out in the Korean Peninsula or not, but when it will be unleashed.

—*Kim Kwang Jin,* DPRK vice minister of defense, March 1996

The past ten years have witnessed the dramatic end to the Cold War and the dissolution, or transformation, of the vast majority of its rigid ideological and diplomatic institutions.[1] There remains, however, one last, almost intractable vestige of that era—the Democratic People's Republic of Korea (DPRK). For the United States, there are few regions in the world where political tension is potentially so volatile, or the threat of sudden, unintended war greater, than along the demilitarized zone (DMZ) that separates the Republic of Korea (ROK) and DPRK. Here the Korean People's Army (KPA), one of the world's largest armies, with over one million troops, stands prepared to attack and reunify the Korean Peninsula. A significant, yet poorly understood, aspect of this military threat is the KPA's special purpose forces. This force of approximately one hundred thousand troops represents one of the world's largest bodies of elite, specially trained soldiers and constitutes approximately 10 percent of the KPA's total peacetime strength.[2]

The term "special purpose forces" was coined by the United States in the 1970s to provide a single name for the elite, specially trained and uniquely structured group of KPA combat-related units. These units had been variously identified with names such as ranger/commando, light infantry, airborne, sniper, reconnaissance, amphibious assault, and others.[3] Differences between the various types of units are, by design, specific to their primary mission, training, and equipment. All special purpose forces units have the capabilities for ranger/commando, special-forces-type, unconventional warfare and special operations.[4] KPA doctrine

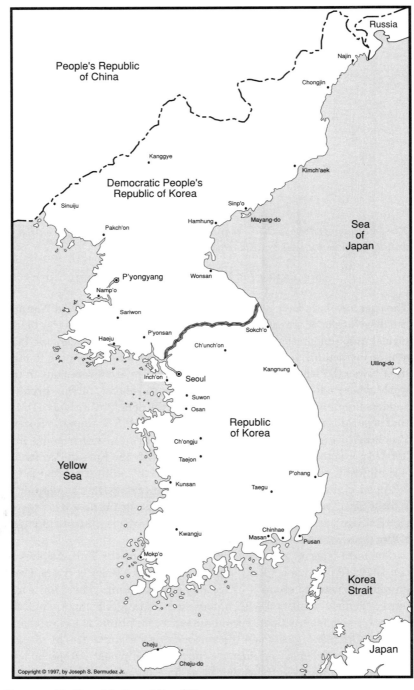

Democratic People's Republic of Korea.

calls for the integration of these units and their operations into all phases of combat operations.

Although they were influenced by both Soviet and Chinese World War II–era partisans/guerrillas and present-day elite forces, the KPA special purpose forces should be examined as a unique entity, and not as an extension or "mirror image" of current Russian and Chinese forces. All special purpose forces personnel are highly motivated, politically well indoctrinated, and well trained. The skills that the members of these units have—repelling, mountain climbing, swimming, martial arts, airborne instruction, demolition, and rigorous physical fitness—and their mental training, such as individual initiative, creativity, flexibility, and aggressiveness, are similar to those associated with elite units throughout the world.[5] Special purpose forces units are expected to continually seek the initiative, to turn all unforeseen events to their advantage, and above all, to achieve their objectives regardless of cost.

Complementing these elite troops is a large body of special operations trained intelligence operatives organized into four intelligence agencies subordinate to the Korean Workers' Party (KWP) Central Committee Secretary in Charge of South Korean Affairs. The KWP is the highest political body in the DPRK.

MISSIONS AND CAPABILITIES

The special purpose forces have the capability, training, and equipment to execute the following missions:

- Seizure or destruction of strategic/theater and global command, control, communications, and intelligence (C³I), missile, radar, and NBC (nuclear, biological, and chemical) warfare assets.
- Interdiction, seizure, or control of strategic targets (air bases, naval bases, port facilities, POL [petroleum, oil, and other lubricants] facilities, lines of communications, etc.) within rear areas.
- Raids against U.S. Air Force bases in Japan (Misawa and Yokota Air Bases) and on the island of Okinawa (Kadena Air Base) and conceivably against military installations in Hawaii and the continental United States.
- Seizure of critically important topographic features (mountain passes, tunnels, bridges, etc.) and civilian facilities (railroads, highways, power plants, etc.).
- Interdiction, seizure, and control of ROK/U.S. lines of communications, for the interdiction of reinforcements and supplies for forces deployed along the DMZ, and in advance of, or in support of, regular ground force operations.

- Targeting reconnaissance for DPRK weapons of mass destruction (e.g., ballistic missiles and chemical weapons).
- Covert delivery of biological weapons.
- Assassination or abduction of ROK political leaders and senior ROK/U.S. military commanders.
- Strategic reconnaissance and the provision of timely and accurate intelligence to the General Staff Department and corps commanders.
- Kidnaping and diversionary operations.
- Establishing military and political intelligence nets within the ROK and fostering the growth of guerrilla forces.
- Military training to foreign governments, revolutionary organizations, and terrorist organizations.
- Military assistance, training, and internal security for friendly governments and organizations (e.g., Nicaragua, Zimbabwe, Palestine Liberation Organization, and Burundi).

In addition to the aforementioned missions, special purpose forces have been trained and equipped to execute certain strategic defensive missions: the neutralization and destruction of ROK/U.S. special forces operating within the DPRK or the KPA rear areas, and guerrilla warfare within the ROK/U.S. strategic rear areas after an invasion. These missions and capabilities of the KPA's special purpose forces are roughly comparable with similar U.S. and Russian organizations (table 1-1).

A recent example of special purpose forces capabilities was the failed September 1996 Reconnaissance Bureau operation near the ROK city of Kangnung, where a *Sang-o*-class coastal submarine ran aground during an infiltration mission. Remarkably, two sniper brigade troops were able to successfully elude a massive (more than sixteen thousand ROK Army troops) cordon and search operation for 49 days before being located and killed. A third trooper eventually escaped back to the DPRK across the DMZ. It is a testimony to the KPA agents' training, skill, and determination. It is both tragic and ominous that twenty-three of the twenty-six Reconnaissance Bureau personnel involved in this incident accepted death rather then allow capture. This incident may be indicative of what to expect from these elite troops in wartime.

Another example was the October 1983 assassination attempt against ROK President Chon Tu-hwan (Chun Doo Hwan) in Rangoon, Burma. This operation was carried out by three Reconnaissance Bureau personnel, under the direction of the Liaison Department (now the Social-Cultural Department).[6] The implications of this act, and the potential for such acts in the future, are cause for concern throughout the international community. The more than one hundred DPRK embassies/diplomatic

Table 1-1

COMPARISON OF SPECIAL PURPOSE FORCES OF THE KPA, THE UNITED STATES, AND RUSSIA

KPA	U.S.	Russia
Light Infantry	Rangers	Raydoviki
Airborne and Airborne sniper	Airborne/rangers	Airborne/Raydoviki
Sniper	Special forces	GRU* troops/ Vysotniki
Amphibious sniper	Marines/SEALS	Naval infantry/ naval commandos

*GRU: Russian Chief Intelligence Directorate, General Staff.

missions, trading corporations, trade and aid missions, and military assistance and advisory teams located throughout the world provide safe havens for any such operations and pose a worldwide threat of DPRK support for insurgencies and terrorist activities.[7]

COMMAND AND CONTROL

Command and control of the DPRK's various special purpose forces is relatively straightforward and can be broken down into two broad categories—the military and the party.

The primary military policy-making body in the DPRK is presently the National Defense Commission, chaired by Kim Chong-il. This commission has held de facto control of military policies, their implementation, and the Ministry of the People's Armed Forces (MPAF) since April 1992. The MPAF consists of several bureaus and departments, the most important of which is the General Staff Department. This department, headed by the chief of the general staff, directly controls the KPA (which encompasses all military forces, including the navy and air force). Subordinate to the General Staff Department are the two organizations most responsible for the special purpose forces—the Light Infantry Training Guidance Bureau and the Reconnaissance Bureau. Additionally, the Korean People's Navy has two subordinate special purpose brigades, and several KPA corps have light infantry brigades. Thus command and control of all the military special purpose forces flows from the National Defense Commission through the MPAF to the General Staff Department. From here it flows in four directions: Light Infantry Training Guidance Bureau, Reconnaissance Bureau, Korean People's Navy, and the light infantry units subordinate to the various army corps.

The Korean Workers' Party is the most politically significant entity within the DPRK. Subordinate to its Central Committee, which is controlled by Kim Chong-il, are the National Intelligence Committee and the office of the Central Committee Secretary in Charge of South Korean Affairs (CCSKA). The National Intelligence Committee is also chaired by Kim Chong-il and serves as the primary national-level policy- and decision-making body for intelligence and security matters. The CCSKA controls four subordinate intelligence-related departments: Operations, Investigative, South–North Dialogue, and the Social-Cultural.[8]

STRENGTH, ORGANIZATION, AND DISPOSITION

During the past 30 years, the DPRK's special purpose force has undergone numerous and fundamental changes that have resulted in considerable

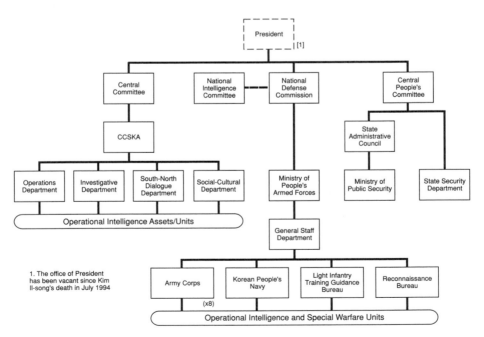

1. The office of President has been vacant since Kim Il-song's death in July 1994

Intelligence and special warfare command and control, 1996.

confusion about its strength and organization. U.S. intelligence estimates that this force has steadily expanded from 15,000 in 1970; 41,000 in 1978; 80,000 in 1984; and 88,000 in 1990 to its present strength of approximately 100,000. The force is apparently organized into twenty-five brigades and five reconnaissance battalions.[9]

These units are deployed throughout DPRK and are organized into five groupings (table 1-2):

- Brigades directly subordinate to the Light Infantry Training Guidance Bureau.
- Brigades and reconnaissance battalions subordinate to the Reconnaissance Bureau.
- Brigades subordinate to the Korean People's Navy.
- Brigades subordinate to KPA corps.
- Light infantry battalions, organic to some of the KPA's forward-deployed infantry divisions and brigades.

These organizations have approximately 15,000 operatives who are trained, and sometimes employed, for special operations.

INFILTRATION METHODS

The majority of the missions assigned to the special purpose units require a clandestine means of insertion. Infiltration operations are conducted at night or under cover of limited visibility. Most special purpose forces units will probably be infiltrated on the ground through the DMZ or front lines. Those units not attempting to infiltrate on the ground may be inserted by tunnel, air, or sea.

With the exception of the major land routes, the DMZ consists primarily of hilly or mountainous terrain, with slopes that restrict movement. Although this type of terrain is favorable for a conventional defense, it almost defies effective defense against irregular forces. The remote and inaccessible mountain regions provide cover and concealment, safe areas, and numerous routes for escape and evasion. The lowlands consist of numerous fields that have reverted to tall grass, weeds, thickets, and woods. Infiltration routes will typically include areas that are isolated, considered impassable (e.g., mountains and cliffs), boundaries between units, and areas where detection would be difficult. Infiltration will normally occur at night or during periods of limited visibility. Escorts (typically from the Reconnaissance Bureau, DMZ police battalions, or the CCSKA's Operations Department) who are thoroughly familiar with the area will usually assist the infiltration.

Table 1-2

PRESENT-DAY DPRK SPECIAL PURPOSE FORCES

Organization	Type	Brigades	Battalions	Manpower	Total
Army Corps	Light infantry battalion (division, brigade)		23	500	11,500
Army Corps	Light infantry brigades	11		3,500	38,500
Light Infantry Training Guidance Bureau	Airborne brigades	3		3,500	10,500
Light Infantry Training Guidance Bureau	Airborne sniper brigades	3		3,500	10,500
Light Infantry Training Guidance Bureau	Light infantry brigades	3		3,500	10,500
Korean People's Navy	Amphibious sniper brigades	2		3,500	7,000
Reconnaissance Bureau	Reconnaissance battalions		5	500	2,500
Reconnaissance Bureau	Sniper brigades	3		3,500	10,500
Total		25	28		101,500

Besides the conventional overland routes, special purpose forces personnel could be quickly and securely infiltrated in large numbers past the DMZ by using tunnels. There are presently four known, yet neutralized, tunnels and an estimated eighteen suspected active tunnels in various stages of completion along the DMZ.[10] Surveillance of the suspected tunnel exits continues, but their exact locations and the extent of construction are uncertain.

The second major means for insertion is by air. The majority of the Korean People's Air Force's (KPAF) large fleet of approximately three hundred An-2 Colt transport aircraft are earmarked to support operations by the special purpose forces. The KPAF also possesses an ever-increasing fleet of helicopters, which could be used to insert small special purpose forces teams. Most notable are the approximately eighty-seven Hughes MD-500D/E helicopters covertly acquired during the 1980s. These civilian helicopters, which have been disguised and armed as ROK MD-500 Defenders, pose a very serious threat. Reportedly, a few of these helicopters have already invaded ROK airspace.

The last means of insertion is by sea. Most of the Korean People's Navy (KPN) amphibious warfare craft and submarines are probably dedicated to operations employing the amphibious sniper brigades. These operations will undoubtedly make extensive use of the KPN's 23 *Namp'o*-class assault landing craft and the more than 135 *Kong Bang I/II/III*- and *Namp'o A/B*-class air-cushion vehicles. Additionally, small units of Reconnaissance Bureau and CCSKA personnel may be inserted by specially designed swimmer delivery vehicles, high-speed infiltration craft, *Yugo* midget submarines, or *Sang-o* coastal submarines. These four classes of craft are operated by the KPN, the Reconnaissance Bureau's Maritime Department, and the CCSKA's Operations Department.

EMPLOYMENT

There is little doubt that during any renewed hostilities on the Korean Peninsula, the KPA's special purpose forces will be actively employed from the very onset. Generally speaking, the division/brigade-level light infantry battalions will conduct unconventional warfare operations within 15–30 kilometers of the forward edge of the battle area (FEBA) and will be concerned with assisting the operations of their parent division. Operating in platoon- and company-sized units, the battalion will concentrate on targets of immediate tactical importance to isolate ROK/U.S. units deployed along the FEBA from their tactical rear. The light infantry brigades will conduct unconventional warfare operations in the area between 30 and 70 kilometers from the FEBA (i.e., out to the edge of the corps area of operations) and will be concerned with assisting the operations of the corps. Operating in platoon- and company-sized units, the brigade will concentrate on targets of tactical/operational importance to isolate ROK/U.S. units deployed along, and immediately behind, the FEBA from their operational/strategic rear. Operations beyond this will be the responsibility of the airborne, airborne sniper, amphibious sniper, and sniper brigades. The light infantry battalions and brigades also serve as a counter-special-operations force for the division and corps commanders, respectively.

The missions assigned to the three light infantry brigades directly subordinate to the Light Infantry Training Guidance Bureau are presently unclear. Available evidence suggests that their mission is a combination of the strategic defensive and counter-special-operations missions assigned to the airborne brigades and the strategic offensive mission to operate in the ROK/U.S. strategic rear by establishing a "second front."

Unlike the light infantry brigades and battalions, which have unconventional warfare operations as a primary mission, the amphibious sniper brigade's primary mission is to conduct offensive amphibious assault and special operations along the ROK coast. The brigades will engage in unconventional warfare operations as a secondary mission when and if the situation warrants.

The ability of the KPN to employ its two amphibious sniper brigades depends upon its amphibious lift capabilities. Realizing the importance of these units in a future conflict, the KPN has made considerable progress in increasing these capabilities since the late 1980s. At present the KPN has approximately 193 amphibious warfare craft and air-cushion vehicles, with an amphibious lift capacity of approximately fifteen thousand troops. This capacity easily exceeds the combined personnel strength for the amphibious sniper brigades. The KPA most probably plans to supplement the amphibious sniper brigades with additional special purpose troops or regular ground troops (especially armor, air defense, and artillery). In the event of renewed hostilities, the likely employment of the amphibious sniper brigades would initially include several operations:

- One strategic multi-battalion-sized landing on the west coast.
- Two battalion-sized operational landings on the east coast.
- Numerous company- and platoon-sized sniper/special operations landings.
- Special operations against U.S. facilities in Japan, Okinawa, and elsewhere.

In addition, if the DPRK leadership believed that the political situation warranted, they could once again institute a policy of calculated escalation. Such escalation could witness strategic/operational landings attempting to seize the ROK island of Ullung-do or more likely one of the United Nations–controlled islands of Paengnyong-do, Taech'ong-do, Soch'ong-do, and others. These operations would place both the ROK and the U.S. governments in an extremely difficult political position, especially if the United States were committed militarily in another region of the world (e.g., Bosnia, Iraq, and Iran). The ROK would either have to escalate, and risk full-scale war by attempting to recapture the island(s), or lose credibility by doing nothing.

The missions assigned to the Light Infantry Training Guidance Bureau's three airborne brigades are similar to those of the light infantry brigades. They will, however, be strategic/theater level in nature and be conducted farther from the FEBA (i.e., beyond the corps area of operations). More important, these units are given the task of securing and holding areas of strategic importance (e.g., mountain passes). The units also represent a significant part of the KPA's strategic reserves and have important counter-special-operations and counter-invasion missions.

The missions assigned to the three airborne sniper brigades are slightly different. These units are specifically targeted against ROK/U.S. air bases, air defense, and C³I assets. They will typically operate in small teams or companies.

The ability of the DPRK to employ these airborne brigades and airborne sniper brigades depends on the KPAF's lift capabilities. The KPAF currently possesses approximately 695 transport aircraft and helicopters capable of conducting airborne operations. Although these could theoretically airlift a total of 7,900 troops, a more realistic estimate would be 4,000–5,000 troops. Because of the importance of the three airborne brigades as a major portion of the strategic reserve forces and their vital rear area security mission, as well as the KPAF's limited airlift capabilities, it is doubtful that the equivalent of more than one or two airborne battalions will be employed for offensive operations during the initial stages of a renewed conflict. The remaining elements of these brigades may be employed when sufficient reserves become available to assume the rear area security mission (after approximately 30–60 days) and if the KPAF can maintain its airlift capabilities. The three airborne sniper brigades, however, will be utilized to the fullest from the very onset of a renewed war.

The primary missions for the elements of airborne brigades employed during the initial phases of a new conflict would be threefold. The brigades would support strategic and operational ground force operations by seizing and holding critical geographic features (e.g., mountain passes) or portions of the ROK infrastructure (e.g., tunnels and dams). A second mission would be the support of strategic and operational-level amphibious landings. Third, the brigades would establish a "second front" behind ROK/U.S. lines.

Missions for the airborne sniper brigades include the following tasks:

- Seizure or destruction of ROKAF/USAF–related facilities, especially air bases and C³I, and missile and radar sites.
- Seizure or destruction of strategic/theater C³I, and missile and NBC warfare assets.
- Targeting reconnaissance for DPRK weapons of mass destruction.

11

- The assassination or abduction of ROK political leaders and senior ROK/U.S. military commanders.
- Conduct special operations in Japan and Okinawa.

The Reconnaissance Bureau's three sniper brigades remain the DPRK's most elite special operations forces. Sniper brigade operations will typically be conducted in team-sized units. These teams will be inserted using the Reconnaissance Bureau's Maritime Department, CCSKA's Operations Department, or the KPAF, or by infiltrating themselves across the DMZ or ROK/U.S. lines. The sniper brigades have the capability, training, and equipment to execute a wide range of reconnaissance and special operations missions at the strategic/theater and global level. Such missions include the following:

- The seizure or destruction of strategic/theater and global C^3I, missile, radar, and NBC warfare assets.
- The assassination or abduction of ROK political leaders and senior ROK/U.S. military commanders.
- Special operations, including assassination or kidnaping of civilians, and diversionary operations.[11]
- Strategic reconnaissance and the provision of timely and accurate intelligence to the General Staff Department and corps commanders.
- Targeting reconnaissance for DPRK weapons of mass destruction (e.g., ballistic missiles and chemical weapons).
- Covert delivery of biological weapons.

SUMMARY

Since their inception, the DPRK's special purpose forces have undergone many changes and are presently assigned a wide variety of missions. The importance of these elite forces in the DPRK's strategic thinking, however, has remained constant. The DPRK leadership envisions a war of reunification taking place on two "fronts." The first "front" would be along the DMZ with the engagement of conventional troops; the second "front" would represent the warfare waged behind ROK defenses by these skilled warriors. The fact that 10 percent of the total KPA ground forces are comprised of these highly trained troops is a testimony to their potential importance. The large numbers of these highly trained troops, coupled with their extensive suprapeninsula activities, identifies the special purpose forces as significant contributors to the overall military capability of DPRK and a threat on the Korean Peninsula and beyond.[12]

Chapter 2

BIRTH, WAR, AND RECONSTRUCTION OF THE KOREAN PEOPLE'S ARMY, 1939–61

Our People's Army was founded with these patriotic fighters of the anti-Japanese armed struggle as its backbone and on the basis of revolutionary patriotic traditions and valuable experiences. For this reason, the Korean People's Army is the successor to the anti-Japanese guerrilla struggle.

—Kim Il-song, in *Selected Works*

The origins of the Korean People's Army (KPA) special purpose forces and unique unconventional warfare and special operations capabilities can be traced back to the roots of the KPA and the training of its leadership. During the fifty-eight years since the establishment of the Korean Volunteer Army in Yenan, China, and the fifty years since Kim Il-song assumed leadership, the KPA's unconventional warfare and special operations capabilities have continually evolved to produce today's special purpose forces. This evolution can be broadly divided into four periods:

1939–61: Birth, war, and reconstruction of the KPA
1962–68: Guerrilla war against the ROK
1969–90: VIII Special Purpose Corps
1990–present: Light Infantry Training Guidance Bureau

This chapter will focus on the birth, war, and reconstruction of the KPA.[1] Later chapters will address the remaining three periods.

The KPA evolved primarily from two distinct and competing political/military *bans* (power-holding groups or factions). The individuals who emerged as leaders from these groups, with their political ideals and combat experiences, provided the foundation upon which the KPA's present-day unconventional warfare and special operations capabilities were built. These two competing factions consisted of what have become known as the Yenan and the Kaspen factions.[2] The Yenan faction consisted of Koreans who generally supported Mao Zedong (Tse-tung) and had fought with the Communist Chinese forces during World War II and the Chinese Revolution.[3] The Kaspen faction was formed primarily from Korean partisans who fled from the Japanese to the Soviet Union, and a number of Soviet citizens of Korean ancestry. Some of these personnel served with Kim Il-song in the 88th Special Independent Sniper Brigade during World War II.

Aside from the Yenan and Kaspen factions, there were two additional major factions at this time: the Soviet faction, consisting of approximately three thousand Korean returnees from the Soviet Union, most of whom had been in the Soviet army; and the Domestic Faction, consisting of several thousand independent Communists and Communist partisans from both Korea and China.

YENAN *BAN*

The roots of the Yenan faction date to 1939, when an organization known as the Korean Volunteer Army (KVA) was formed in Yenan, China.[4] The two individuals responsible for the army were Kim Tu-bong and Mu Chong.[5] The army was then composed of thirty charter members and was commanded by Mu Chong. At the same time, a school was established near Yenan for training military and political leaders for a future independent Korea. By 1945, the KVA had grown to approximately 1,000 men, mostly Korean deserters from the Imperial Japanese Army. During this period, the KVA fought alongside the Chinese Communist forces, from which it drew arms and ammunition. After the defeat of the Japanese, the KVA accompanied the Chinese Communist forces into Manchuria, intending to gain recruits from the Korean population of Manchuria and then enter Korea. By incorporating local Korean self-defense groups the KVA reached a strength of approximately 2,500 men in September 1945. With this group, Mu Chong attempted to enter northern Korea through Sinuiju in late September 1945, only to be halted and have his group disarmed by the Soviet army. Reportedly, Mu Chong was told by the Soviet officers that he could not bring armed forces into Korea, but that the arms would be returned if he would take his group back into Manchuria and fight the Nationalists. Forced to accept the Soviet decision, Mu Chong returned to Manchuria and continued to strengthen his army. The Soviet attitude in this situation was motivated by their desire not only to assist Mao Zedong and the Chinese Communist forces in their battle against the Nationalists, but also to keep this well-equipped, well-trained, and politically indoctrinated force out of

Korea, thereby facilitating the consolidation of northern Korea's leadership within the hands of their own candidate, Kim Il-song, and his Kaspen faction. Kim had just returned to Korea in August 1945.

By October 1945, the KVA had grown to approximately five thousand men. A reorganization took place, which resulted in the army's being divided into three brigades and one battalion: the 1st South Manchurian Brigade, 3rd North Manchurian Brigade, 5th East Manchurian Brigade, and the Independent Battalion.

The Independent Battalion was to be stationed in Chinchon on the Darien Peninsula, but because of the advance of the Chinese Nationalist army in that area, this unit never materialized and the personnel later joined the 1st South Manchurian Brigade. In January 1946, the 5th East Manchurian Brigade was divided into the East Chilin and the Yenchi Brigades. Through continued efforts of Mu Chong and his followers, the KVA continued to expand. Additional local security groups were absorbed, and by April 1946, each brigade numbered approximately 5,400 men. During this period, the KVA participated in numerous small-scale actions against the Nationalist army.

In April 1946, the Chinese Communist armies in China and Manchuria underwent a considerable reorganization that resulted in the dropping of the title "Korean Volunteer Army." The units of the KVA became subordinate to the various area commands of the so-called northeast Democratic United Army. For example, the 5th East Manchurian Brigade became part of the East Kirin Peace Preservation Army. This army was in turn under the control of the Kirin military district. The purely Korean composition of the original army also changed after the reorganization, when Chinese and Mongolians were mixed into what were formerly Korean units.

Beginning in the late spring of 1946, the cadres for the newly forming Korean Peace Preservation Corps (i.e., KPA) began moving into northern Korea. The highest-ranking Korean officers of the Chinese Communist forces, members of the old KVA, and Koreans in the Soviet army were assembled in various training centers in northern Korea under the supervision of the Soviet army advisers to train the new recruits for the Peace Preservation Corps. Because of the exodus of so many leaders, the efficiency of the former KVA units dropped considerably. By the spring of 1947, the units, weakened by further officer transfers to northern Korea, were relegated to the line of communication role until they too were transferred into northern Korea to become part of the KPA. Despite the fact that the KVA officially passed out of existence in April 1946, the title, and those of the original KVA units, continued to be used until much later, possibly encouraged by authorities for security and morale purposes.

KASPEN *BAN*

The history of the Kaspen faction[6] is essentially the history of Kim Il-song, who until his death in 1994 was president of the DPRK, general secretary of Korean Workers' Party, and commander in chief of the KPA. The early life of Kim Il-song is surrounded with considerable confusion and debate. Most of this debate centers around his age, actual name, and accomplishments as an anti-Japanese partisan leader. Considerable research during the past ten years has gradually pieced together an authoritative account of his life and activities prior to 1950.[7]

■ KIM'S EARLY HISTORY, 1910–41
Kim Song-ju, now known as Kim Il-song, was born in P'yongyang in April 1912, the eldest son of a Chinese herbal doctor named Kim Hyong-jik.[8] As a young child his parents moved back and forth between Manchuria and Korea, resulting in his being educated in a mixture of Chinese and Korean schools. During the late 1920s he enrolled in the Yuwen Middle School in Jilin (Kirin), China. Here he supposedly joined a Communist youth organization known as the Rugil Association of Korean Students. It was also here, in 1929, that Kim engaged in his first anti-Japanese activities. He was subsequently expelled from school and was arrested and imprisoned by the Japanese. After his release from jail in 1930 he began following various bands of guerrillas in the Manchuria region. Also during this time, he changed his name to Kim Il-song (then a common practice among guerrillas). By early 1934 Kim had become a member of the Communist guerrilla forces known as the Northeast Anti-Japanese United Army (NEAJUA). Kim quickly worked his way up from a common soldier to commander of the 6th Division. The unit, comprising never more than three hundred troops, operated primarily along the northeast Chinese–Korean border, conducting raids against small Japanese-held villages and units.

In 1936 an organization known as the Korean Fatherland Restoration Association (KFRA) was established to create a united front organization of anti-Japanese Koreans operating in Manchuria. Subordinate to the KFRA was the Kaspen Operation Committee, named after a mountain in its operating area located on the Korean–Manchurian border. On 4 June 1937 Kim led a small group of partisans from the Kaspen Operation Committee on a raid against a small border village in Korea named Poch'ombo. Here they achieved a rare and notable victory by successfully defeating a small Japanese force before withdrawing back across the border. This much-celebrated victory subsequently became the source of the Kaspen faction's name.

As a result of increasing partisan activities in Manchuria and Korea during the late 1930s, the Imperial Japanese Army initiated a major antipartisan campaign that by the end of 1940 had effectively eliminated all such activities. During this campaign Kim and his surviving partisans were driven out of Manchuria and into Soviet territory. Despite having been forced out of China it is important to note that even at this early stage, news of Kim's activities and consequently his reputation (grossly embellished) were starting to be spread through Korea.

- THE 88TH SPECIAL INDEPENDENT SNIPER BRIGADE, 1941–45
Sometime during late 1940 Kim fled from Manchuria into the Soviet Union. Here he was arrested by Soviet border guards and placed in a camp with other survivors of the NEAJUA.[9] During the next year and a half, Zhao Baozhong, a former leader within the NEAJUA, reorganized the remnants of the NEAJUA under Soviet control. On 1 August 1942 the Soviet Far East Command's Reconnaissance Bureau established the 88th Special Independent Sniper Brigade with the survivors of the NEAJUA and appointed Zhao Baozhong as its commander.

The 88th Special Independent Sniper Brigade's primary mission was to collect intelligence on Imperial Japanese Army movements in Korea and China. It had a total personnel strength of six hundred to eight hundred men and women and was initially organized into a headquarters, headquarters staff, four battalions (1st, 2nd, 3rd, and 4th), and a signal unit. An independent Chinese language school and a separate accounting company were also attached to the brigade. Sometime later the unit was expanded by the addition of a mortar battalion, self-propelled artillery battalion, and an independent radio unit (sometimes identified as a battalion). Each of the four battalions consisted of two companies and a guard platoon. Each company consisted of three platoons. Kim Il-song commanded the 1st Battalion, which consisted of approximately two hundred personnel.

Even though it included battle-hardened former partisans and an extensive training regime, the 88th apparently conducted only a few operational missions during 1942–45. With the end of the war rapidly drawing near, the Korean members of the brigade were anxious to participate in the liberation of their homeland. In July 1945 the brigade was informed of its mission during the forthcoming attack on Japanese troops in Manchuria and Korea. When the invasion occurred, however, the brigade was held back, much to the dismay of the members of the 88th, apparently by the direct order of Joseph Stalin, who wanted the liberation of Korea to be a wholly Soviet operation. With the end of World War II, there was no further need for the 88th Special Independent Sniper Brigade. The unit was disbanded, and its members disarmed in August

1945. The Chinese members returned to China under the command of Zhao Baozhong, while the Korean members under the leadership of Kim Il-song were ordered to Korea to assist the Soviet occupation forces.

Notably, it was as members of the 88th Special Independent Sniper Brigade that Kim and his fellow Koreans received formalized training in special operations and intelligence collection. This training and their experiences as anti-Japanese partisans created an indelible mark upon their military thinking. Emerging from this new way of military thinking would be the KPA and its relentless commitment to unconventional operations and special purpose forces. An even more significant aspect of Kim's time in the 88th was that he forged lifelong bonds with his fellow Korean partisans. Almost all of them would subsequently play central roles in the establishment and maintenance of Kim's regime after the liberation of Korea. In the years following the Fatherland Liberation War (i.e., Korean War) these fellow veterans would become known as the "partisan generation."

■ RETURN TO KOREA AND CONSOLIDATION OF POWER, 1945–48
On 19 September 1945, while still a captain in the Soviet army, Kim Il-song returned to Korea through the port of Wonsan aboard the Soviet navy vessel *Pugachov*. Accompanying Kim was a group of approximately sixty supporters from the former 88th Special Independent Sniper Brigade. Kim kept his return to Korea as quiet as possible. After arriving in P'yongyang, he dispatched a number of supporters throughout the country (many operating undercover) both to gather information and to establish a popular base of power. Other supporters assumed critical positions throughout the Soviet occupation forces government, most notably in the security and police organizations. Kim himself initiated the process of ingratiating himself to the Soviet authorities, a process greatly facilitated by his previous service in the Soviet army with the 88th Brigade and his access to timely and accurate information from his supporters throughout the country.[10]

Through carefully planned and deftly executed plans, Kim gradually neutralized his political rivals and became the Soviets' primary candidate for leadership of Korea. With considerable Soviet assistance, Kim quickly moved to cultivate a friendship with Cho Man-sik, the leading Korean nationalist and the most respected non-Communist leader in northern Korea. After a somewhat labored beginning, Cho was eventually convinced that supporting Kim would present the best opportunity for Korea's future. Thus convinced, Cho introduced Kim at a liberation celebration in P'yongyang on 14 October 1945. The primary purpose of the celebration was to present Gen. Kim Il-song, the great partisan hero, to the public.

At this point, the largest and most influential Communist organization on the Korean Peninsula was the Korean Communist Party (KCP, popularly known as the Domestic Faction), headed by Pak Hon-yong. In August 1945 the KCP had organized itself into a Northern Branch and a Southern Branch to reflect the realities of Allied occupation. With continued Soviet support Kim quickly became popular. In December he secured the leadership of the Northern Branch of the KCP from Pak Hon-yong and his Domestic Faction. Six months later, on 23 June 1946, Kim broke away from the KCP and reorganized the Northern Branch into the North Korean Communist Party. Shortly thereafter he merged the North Korean Communist Party with the Yenan faction's New People's Party to form the Workers' Party of North Korea (WPNK). In response to these moves Pak, in November 1946, consolidated various Communist groups in the south into the Workers' Party of South Korea (WPSK).

Elections for members of the People's Committees of the WPNK were held in November 1946 and February 1947, and a People's Assembly was formed shortly afterward. A constitution was approved by the People's Assembly on 9 September 1948, as the People's Assembly became the Supreme People's Assembly, thus formally establishing the Democratic People's Republic of Korea. Kim Il-song was elected to the post of premier.

THE KANGDONG POLITICAL INSTITUTE

Although Kim was now officially the leader of the North Korean government, he did not by any means exercise absolute control. He was constantly engaged in power struggles with the many factions and subfactions vying for power and influence. An example of a struggle that directly impacted prewar guerrilla operations against the south was the conflict with the Domestic Faction led by Pak Hon-yong. Kim Il-song's move to secure control of the Northern Branch of the KCP in 1945 and then to break away from it in 1946 to form the North Korean Communist Party not only infuriated Pak but weakened Pak's political position considerably. Concurrent with these developments, ROK security forces were conducting a successful campaign against Communist elements, primarily Pak's forces, in the south. These two events forced Pak to leave the south. In October 1946 he established the headquarters of the WPSK in the port city Haeju, just north of the thirty-eighth parallel. Several months later he moved to P'yongyang. Although Pak and the Domestic Faction had been weakened by these events, they still exercised considerable authority. While Kim and Pak were both in competition for leadership of all the Communists on the Korean Peninsula, neither was strong enough to abandon or alienate the other. Both also desired to see

19

a united Korea under a Communist leadership. Not willing to surrender any further power to Kim, and in an effort to counterbalance Kim's establishment of the Security Officers Training Center in 1946, Pak established the Kangdong Political Institute (also called the Kangdong Political School) in Kangdong County, P'yongan-namdo, in September 1947.[11] The personnel who attended this institution were loyal to Pak Hon-yong and the WPSK and were drawn primarily from the young, idealistic Communist men and women from the south. At the institute, they took three- to six-month-long political and military courses that prepared them for guerrilla warfare operations in the south. Interestingly, while Pak was politically strong enough to establish this institute he was forced to accept So Ch'ol, a veteran of the 88th Brigade and supporter of Kim Il-song, as the overall director of military training.[12] During 1948–50, many graduates from this institute were dispatched to conduct operations in the south. The success of these operations varied considerably, however; their net effect was to prompt the ROK government into extensive anti-Communist operations. In June 1949, for a variety of reasons, the WPNK and WPSK merged to form the Korean Workers' Party (KWP). Kim Il-song became the new party's chairman, and Pak Hon-yong became its first vice chairman.

The Kangdong Political Institute was disbanded by the KWP in late 1949 after the abortive "September Offensive," in which 630 graduates were sent to the ROK in an unsuccessful attempt to precipitate a popular uprising. It is estimated that the institute trained approximately 2,400 personnel during its two years of operation. When the school was closed, Kim established the Hoeryong Cadres School (also called the Third Officers School) in Hoeryong to train KPA troops in special reconnaissance and partisan warfare tactics much as the 88th Brigade had been trained. This school was under the direction of O Chin-u, a veteran of the 88th Brigade. Approximately 4,000–6,000 troops, including the personnel for the 766th Independent Unit (see below), were trained at Hoeryong prior to the war.

BIRTH OF THE KPA

Aside from strong Soviet support, the most significant factor contributing to Kim Il-song's success in the numerous struggles to seize and maintain power was his control of the internal security and military apparatus. For example, one of the first organizations responsible for the maintenance of security within postliberation northern Korea was the Protection and Security Bureau. This bureau was established on 10 November 1945 and was headed by Ch'oe Yong-gon, a supporter of Kim Il-song and former member of the 88th Special Independent Sniper

Brigade. The unit was soon reorganized as the Security Bureau and would eventually become the Ministry of Internal Affairs.

Formal preparations for the creation of the KPA date to early 1946.[13] That year saw the establishment of the Security Officers Training Center.[14] This school was staffed by a mix of experienced Korean soldiers from both the Yenan and Kaspen factions as well as Soviet advisers. The mission of the school was to train the officers who would be utilized in the establishment of the KPA. Beginning in September 1946, graduates from the training center were supplied to the newly formed Public Security Officers Training Battalion Headquarters in P'yongyang.[15] The headquarters was commanded by Ch'oe Yong-gon and was organized into four departments: training, aviation, culture, and artillery. The two vice commanders were Mu Chong, a Yenan faction member and former commander of the KVA, and Kim Ch'aek, veteran of the 88th Brigade. An Kil, another former 88th Brigade veteran, served as chief of staff. Subordinate to the headquarters were three training centers, or divisions: the First, Second, and Third Public Security Officers Training Centers (or the 1st, 2nd, and 3rd Divisions), located at Kaech'on, Nanam, and Chinnamp'o, respectively. The 3rd Division was also known as the Surface Officers Training Center and would eventually become the Navy Headquarters.

During the next two years military training continued at an increasing pace, and the size of the security forces increased dramatically. This expansion was considerably aided, as previously noted, by large numbers of KVA veterans arriving from China. This first stage of the development process culminated with the official establishment of the KPA on 8 February 1948, with Ch'oe Yong-gon as the first minister of national defense. At this time the KPA's headquarters in P'yongyang controlled a central guard battalion; two infantry divisions, created out of the Public Security Officers Training Centers; an independent, mixed brigade; and embryonic air force and navy elements. The KPA's estimated personnel strength was then approximately 30,000. By the time of the KPA's invasion of the ROK in June 1950, the KPA consisted of ten infantry divisions, one armored brigade, and a few independent regiments and battalions. Its personnel strength had reached approximately 150,000–180,000. Additionally, there was a small air force and navy.

PARTISAN WARFARE VERSUS GUERRILLA WARFARE

Despite the Yenan faction's superiority in numbers, ideological indoctrination, and military experience, it could not secure a dominant position in the new government, because of the strong Soviet presence and the Soviets' support of Kim Il-song's Kaspen faction. The Yenan faction could, however, secure a number of prominent positions in both the new government and the army. This resulted in, among other things, a dual approach to unconventional warfare within the army, with the doctrine espoused by the Kaspenites generally being the more dominant.[16]

The Yenan faction's doctrine was based on Mao Zedong's *Guerrilla Warfare* and on experiences gained during the Chinese revolution.[17] Mao's concept, refined during his days in Yenan, placed heavy emphasis on the political indoctrination, education, and mobilization of the peasant class, with guerrilla leaders spending a great deal more time in organization, instruction, agitation, and propaganda work than they do fighting, for their most important job was to win over the people. "We must patiently explain," said Mao Zedong. "Explain," "persuade," "discuss," "convince." These words recur with monotonous regularity in many Chinese essays on guerrilla war. Mao aptly compared guerrillas to fish, and people to the water in which they swim. If the political temperature is right, the fish, however few in number, will thrive and proliferate. It is, therefore, the principle concern of all guerrilla leaders to get the water to the right temperature and to keep it there.[18]

Only when this political climate was right would the guerrilla leaders move into the active military phase, but the political aspect of the struggle remained the prime objective. The indigenous guerrillas of Pak Hon-yong's Korean Communist Party (South Korean Communist Party) operating in the south also tended to follow Mao's principles set forth in *Guerrilla Warfare.*

In comparison, the Kaspen faction's concept tended to minimize the political aspects of the struggle, emphasizing military operations based on the needs of the country and military. This concept, which best typifies today's special purpose forces operations, was based heavily upon the Soviet doctrine of partisan warfare in World War II. This Soviet doctrine called for the formation of small partisan units of 75–150 men and women within occupied areas to ferment unrest and provide intelligence. The basic combat formations of these partisan units were the company and the platoon. Their basic missions, usually carried out at night or from ambush, were to attack columns, concentrations of motorized infantry, dumps, ammunition transports, airfields, and railroad transports; to blow bridges and roads; to damage telephone and telegraph lines; to set fires in forests, stores, and transports; and to generally make conditions unbearable throughout the German rear.[19] This approach was strongly reinforced by both the experiences of the members of the 88th Special Independent Sniper Brigade and the belief among KPA and Soviet war planners that the war for national reunification would be short, thus negating the need for intensive guerrilla preparation in the south.

The net effect of these different approaches to unconventional warfare was manifest by how a particular unit would conduct such operations. The different approaches depended on the experiences and political orientation of the unit's commander and, to a lesser degree, the lower
ranks. Those units whose commanders were from the former Korean Volunteer Army and the Yenan faction tended to practice Mao's principles
of guerilla warfare, whereas the units whose commanders belonged to
the Kaspen faction, or who had been trained by the Soviets, practiced a
version of partisan warfare.

The time period of these activities was also a significant factor in
determining which doctrine was dominant. During 1945–47, guerrilla
operations conducted in the south by Pak Hon-yong's Korean Communist Party tended to be modeled after Mao's *Guerrilla Warfare,* with
heavy emphasis on political indoctrination. By 1947 these initial guerrilla activities were neutralized by ROK actions, and many guerrillas
were killed or forced to retreat to the north. Back in the north Pak Hon-
yong established the aforementioned Kangdong Political Institute to
train guerrillas for operations in the south. Although the trainees at this
institute had a guerrilla warfare mind set and political bias, they
received tactical training in partisan warfare. Thus, when they returned
to the south in 1948–50, their operations tended to be a blend of the two
doctrines. Concurrent with these developments was the establishment
and expansion of the KPA. Within the Soviet-trained KPA, partisan warfare was clearly the dominant doctrine for unconventional warfare. Even
with the return of the Korean Volunteer Army veterans from China and
their integration into the KPA, partisan warfare remained dominant
and, during the first two months of the Fatherland Liberation War,
guided unconventional warfare operations clearly. As the war progressed,
especially with the intervention of the Chinese People's Volunteers,
guerrilla warfare assumed predominance. Later, as the front lines stabilized and the KPA had time to reorganize, partisan warfare gradually
reemerged. At the time of the armistice agreement in 1953, both doctrines were in use, with areas under Chinese and KPA influence generally following their respective doctrines.

PREWAR GUERRILLA OPERATIONS

In 1946, after a brief period of political freedom accompanying the liberation of Korea, U.S. occupation authorities outlawed several antigovernment political organizations. Primary among these organizations was the
KCP, led by Pak Hon-yong, which was quickly forced by security operations to go underground. As noted, these activities forced Pak to leave the

south, move to P'yongyang in early 1947, and establish the Kangdong Political Institute. By the time the Republic of Korea was established on 15 August 1948, the WPSK had an estimated five thousand guerrillas and active supporters in the south.[20] Personnel in these units consisted of a varied collection of dedicated Communists, opportunists, bandits, and others. These were loosely organized into a wide variety of different-sized units lightly armed with former Imperial Japanese Army weapons. The units were concentrated in three primary areas: the T'aebaek-san area west of Kangnung and adjacent to the thirty-eighth parallel, the T'aebaek-san area southwest of Kangnung, and the Chiri-san area between Kwangju and Masan. Besides these concentrations, a few smaller groups were scattered around the country. The vast majority of all these units remained essentially inactive militarily until late 1948.

The first major guerrilla operation occurred on 3 April 1948 on the island of Cheju-do off the ROK's southern coast. Here guerrillas and their supporters initiated a series of antigovernment riots throughout the island. These riots and the ROK attempts to quell them would last until the end of July and resulted in the deaths of many civilians, Communists and sympathizers, and ROKA troops. The situation on the island remained relatively calm until 1 October 1948, when the remnants of the guerrillas attacked a police station in the fishing village of O Dung-ri. The ensuing fighting that lasted the reminder of the month resulted in losses of personnel on all sides and heavy property damage. In the end, however, all organized guerrilla elements were destroyed.

The events on Cheju-do were accompanied, on 19 October, by a mutiny of the ROKA 14th Infantry Regiment based in the port city of Yosu. This unit was being dispatched to reinforce ROKA units engaged in counterguerrilla operations on Cheju-do. Several enlisted men and NCOs of the regiment, led by a Korean Communist Party cell, mutinied and occupied the port and then joined with local sympathizers. Thus reinforced, they occupied the area around the port and moved into the city of Sunch'on. Here they established a provisional government, called on others to join them, and committed atrocities against civilians, police, and captured ROKA troops. Loyal ROKA and National Police units responded to the mutiny; in the ensuing battle hundreds of loyal troops, Communists, and civilians were killed. By the end of the month the rebellion was suppressed. Many Communist survivors escaped, however, and linked up with guerrilla units operating in the nearby Chiri-san region, providing these units with a critical infusion of well-trained troops.

These events were not isolated instances but rather the beginning of a general Communist offensive in the T'aebaek-san and Chiri-san regions. The objectives of these operations were to present the ROK government with a continuing threat to its internal security and to secure increased public support for the Communist cause. As secondary goals these operations sought to establish secure operating areas and to obtain supplies and recruits. The ultimate goal of this was the destabilization of the ROK government and the unification of the peninsula under Communist control.

In support of this general offensive the graduates from the Kangdong Political Institute began infiltrating into the ROK as organized guerrilla units beginning in November 1948. These infiltrations continued up until the beginning of the Fatherland Liberation War (table 2-1).

Between September 1949 and March 1950, over three thousand guerrillas were sent into the ROK, including more than six hundred graduates of the Kangdong Political Institute. Working together with Communist supporters in the ROK, the Kangdong graduates dramatically escalated the level of antigovernment activities. These activities were directed by two supporters of Pak Hon-yong who had remained in the south, Kim Sam-yong and Yi Chu-ha. These activities, however, were not successful, and most of the guerrillas and many of their supporters were arrested or killed during ROK counterguerrilla operations. One of the most damaging counterguerrilla operations resulted in the arrest of both Kim Sam-yong and Yi Chu-ha. The loss of these two dynamic leaders effectively eliminated any chance of a general uprising against the ROK government.

Initially, counterguerrilla operations were conducted by the ROK National Police. It quickly became apparent, however, that they were

Table 2-1

INFILTRATION INTO THE ROK BY GUERRILLAS FROM THE KANGDONG POLITICAL INSTITUTE

Date	Unit Size	Operating Area
14 November 1948	180	Odae-san
1 June 1949	400	Odea-san
6 July 1949	200	Odae-san
4 August 1949	200	Ilwol-san
12 August 1949	unknown	Myonchi-san
August 1949	40	Myonchi-san
20 September 1949	360	T'aebaek-san
28 September 1949	50	Kum Ok Chiri
6 November 1949	100	Pohyon-san
28 March 1950	700	Pohyon-san

incapable of dealing with all but the smallest guerrilla units. The ROKA was consequently called upon to augment the National Police and deal with the threat. The army, however, was ill prepared to deal with this threat because they lacked proper police or internal security training, equipment, and adequate manpower. Although there were some non-combat efforts to counter the guerrillas, such as an amnesty offer in November 1949, such endeavors were only marginally successful. The ROKA thus relied primarily upon rigorously enforced suppressive measures. Enforcement was draconian at times. Many innocent civilians were incarcerated, many died under interrogation, and in at least one instance, an entire village was massacred. Such measures did curtail guerrilla operations, especially during the winter of 1949–50, but the ROKA proved incapable of defeating the guerrillas. In fact, the increased level of guerrilla activity during 1949 had effectively denied the ROK authority over significant areas in the T'aebaek-san and Chiri-san regions. More significantly, these actions alienated segments of the population and resulted in a loss of public support for both the ROKA and the government. The ROK government realized the danger of this situation and in early 1950 established the combat police to relieve the ROKA of its internal security missions. Few combat police units, however, were operational by June 1950, when the DPRK launched its invasion.

Up until the winter of 1949–50, guerrilla operations were primarily directed against the ROKA, National Police, and ROK government objectives. The guerrilla operations, combined with an active propaganda campaign, not only kept public resentment of guerilla activities to a minimum but allowed for the development of genuine public support in some regions, most notably in the T'aebaek-san and Chiri-san regions and the eastern seacoast of Kangwon-do Province. The onset of winter, combined with increasingly successful ROKA interdiction and counterguerrilla operations, however, forced guerrilla units to raid rural villages and farms for food and clothing. This had the natural effect of eroding much of the good will that had been cultivated between the guerrillas and the people.

The winter weather and ROKA's counterguerrilla efforts also forced a compacting of guerrilla-controlled areas and the regrouping and reorganizing of guerrilla forces into larger units. In the months leading up to the war, the guerrillas never utilized their potential for large-scale and concerted operations, for several reasons. One reason was the arrest of Kim Sam-yong and Yi Chu-ha, whose leadership had been crucial in organizing the guerrilla forces. Another reason was that Kim Il-song did not want to see a successful uprising being conducted by guerrillas who were supporters of his political rival, Pak Hon-yong. Furthermore, the KPA leadership desired to maintain guerrilla strength as a "threat in being," which forced the ROKA to deploy its forces away from the thirty-eighth parallel, thus directly supporting the KPA in its forthcoming war. Inadequate communication capabilities among the various guerrilla concentrations also prevented effective coordination. Finally, the KPA leadership feared that increased guerrilla activities might precipitate even greater ROKA countermeasures, which could defeat the guerrillas and drive the public to support the ROK government.

In retrospect, probably the most significant military contribution of the prewar guerrilla operations was to force the redeployment of ROKA combat units away from the thirty-eighth parallel to conduct counterguerrilla operations throughout the ROK. Thus, on 25 June 1950, three infantry divisions of the ROKA were still deployed for counterguerrilla operations rather than along the thirty-eighth parallel, where they could have adequately defended against the invasion.

Ultimately, on the political level, these actions did not succeed in destabilizing the ROK government or in creating wide-scale support for Communism. They did, however, succeed in establishing a few regions within the ROK that where genuinely supportive of Communism. Additionally, as a result of the guerrilla and counterguerrilla warfare, several regions, while not sympathetic toward Communism, were not strongly supportive of the ROK government, either. For roughly the next half-century, the DPRK would attempt to exploit these regional sympathies.

From October 1949 until February 1950, guerrilla combat operations displayed sound tactical, weapons, and disciplinary training. The guerrillas operated in small groups and were frequently successful at luring ROKA and National Police units into isolated positions and then attacking them with superior forces. Raids were frequently and successfully carried out against communications and transportation facilities. Most guerrillas were well acquainted with their weapons (including machine guns and mortars), which they used effectively and with a minimum of ammunition wastage. They displayed high levels of morale and discipline under fire, as well as an intimate knowledge of the difficult terrain where they were operating, which they exploited to its maximum. Concurrent with combat operations, the guerrillas engaged in a widespread propaganda campaign explaining and justifying their actions.

Approximately two-fifths of the prewar guerrillas received specialized training within the DPRK. The remainder either received military training during World War II (with the Chinese or Japanese armies) or rudimentary training within secure areas of the ROK. For the guerrillas who were trained and organized within the DPRK, the next step was infiltration into the ROK. This occurred via two primary routes. The first was across the thirty-eighth parallel in isolated mountainous areas of the

T'aebaek-san mountains, most commonly in the eastern portion of Kangwon-do Province. The second, and more frequently employed, infiltration route was by sea. Guerrillas would embark at either Yangyang or the Wonsan area and be landed along the east coast of the ROK. A major port of entry for guerrilla groups was the ROK port city of P'ohang-dang, where there was a generally sympathetic attitude among the civilian population. Immediately prior to the war a few seaborne infiltrations also occurred along the west coast of the ROK. The staging area for these operations was probably Chinnamp'o.

On the eve of the Fatherland Liberation War there were an estimated 5,000 Communist guerrillas and supporters within the ROK. The core of these forces consisted of a group of well-indoctrinated and adequately trained and equipped guerrillas, numbering about 1,700 men and women. The majority of these were former ROK residents who were members of the KWP and had been trained at the Kangdong Political Institute. This core group was supported by a larger group of Communists and sympathizers who were either unarmed or armed with makeshift weapons. These were grouped into two broad categories: those who overtly worked with the guerrillas, and those who covertly worked with them. The latter group provided a channel for supply and reinforcement and operated as an effective intelligence service. In addition to these willing supporters, there were a few young men who had been kidnaped during guerrilla raids and pressed into service under threat of death or reprisals against their families.

These active, independent guerrilla units were deployed in three major concentrations. The first was located in the mountainous area north of the T'aebaek-san and along the thirty-eighth parallel, where a force of approximately two hundred guerrillas operated. Next was the mountainous area between the T'aebaek-san and the eastern seacoast of Kangwon-do Province. Located within this area were approximately eight hundred guerrillas. The third major concentration was approximately five hundred guerrillas operating in the southern part of the ROK in the mountainous Chiri-san region that straddled the provincial border between South Cholla and South Kyongsang Provinces. In addition to these major concentrations, approximately two hundred guerrillas operated in small bands scattered throughout the ROK.

The guerrilla units that had been trained and organized at the Kangdong Political Institute and had then infiltrated into the ROK were adequately equipped with U.S. M-1 and Japanese Type-99 rifles, plus a heterogeneous collection of other U.S., Japanese, German, and Czech small arms, including light machine guns and mortars. Ammunition for these weapons, however, was in short supply. Food, clothing, and shelter were acquired locally. The remaining guerrilla units were smaller, loosely organized, and more poorly armed and equipped. For these units, ammunition was extremely scarce.

Command and control of the guerrillas and Communist sympathizers operating in the south during the early years was generally exercised through Pak Hon-yong's WPSK. This control, however, would gradually be transferred to the KWP as the political landscape changed. By late 1949 control was firmly vested within the KWP's Liaison Department.

Concurrent with the development and operation of a guerrilla organization within the ROK, the Reconnaissance Bureau of the General Staff Department created and employed specialized reconnaissance units and agents. These units and agents were primarily assigned the collection of conventional military intelligence. Details concerning the prewar organization and operations of these units is presently unclear. Although the Reconnaissance Bureau dispatched agents into the ROK from the time of the bureau's establishment, the WPSK personnel were apparently the primary source of military intelligence during the years immediately following World War II. By early 1949, however, dedicated KPA reconnaissance units and agents had assumed much of this responsibility.

THE FATHERLAND LIBERATION WAR, 1950–53

▪ JUNE–SEPTEMBER 1950

In June 1950, as a prelude to the Fatherland Liberation War, guerrilla activity within the ROK declined to almost zero and, contrary to expectations, remained infrequent during the first days of the war.[21] On the other hand, KPA unconventional warfare operations were intensive from the very first hours of the invasion on 25 June and played a significant role in most operations. These operations initially displayed a considerable degree of cooperation between various units and controlling headquarters. This cooperation, however, would quickly deteriorate as units sustained casualties and advanced further from their supply centers. By August 1950, the majority of the highly trained independent army-level and divisional guerrilla units that had enjoyed considerable success during the early stages of the war were absorbed into regular KPA combat divisions as individual or unit replacements. Most notable were the operations of the 766th Independent Unit, which made a significant contribution to the successes of KPA operations on the east coast (see below).

For all the effort expended in training, supporting, and infiltrating the multitude of independent guerrilla units operational in the ROK prior to the war, they served a relatively minor role during the initial fighting. This was probably the result of the rapid advance of the KPA, the

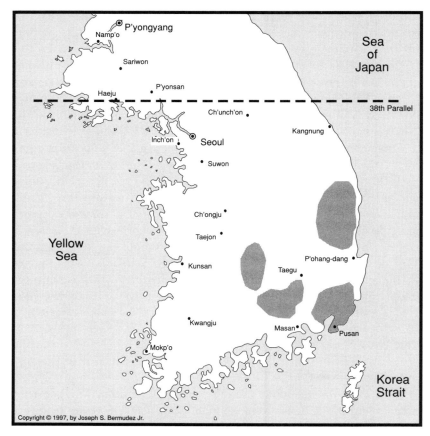

Guerrilla activity, 25 June–14 September 1950.

guerrillas' inability to sustain combat operations against regular United Nations Command (UNC) troops and to secure sufficient quantities of food, arms, and ammunition. When the war later turned against the DPRK, Kim Il-song would blame Pak Hon-yong for a lack of guerrilla support, since Pak had promised that two hundred thousand Communists would rise up in revolt against the ROK when the KPA attacked. One role in which the independent guerrilla units proved to be of considerable value was that of acting as local guides for advancing regular KPA units. Interestingly, guerrilla strength gradually increased during July and August as a result of both "victory enthusiasm" and pragmatic survivalism by essentially neutral civilians who joined the Communist cause.

As the KPA advance compressed UNC forces into the Pusan perimeter, guerrilla activities expanded notably. Although these activities were primarily the work of divisional guerrilla units and the survivors of the 766th Independent Unit, independent guerrilla units were also evident in many operations. Despite a desperate frontline situation, this increased guerrilla activity forced the UNC into action to protect its rear areas. On 19 July 1950, the Office of Coordinator, Protection of Lines of Communication, Rear Areas, was set up by the U.S. VIII Army. Its mission was to coordinate ROK and U.S. efforts to protect railroads, highways, and bridges. It also protected UNC signal communication units against sabotage and guerrilla operations. One of the first steps taken by this office was to form Korean police battalions. At first, one provisional ROK police company was assigned to the U.S. 24th and 25th Infantry Divisions, with the mission of procuring local guides, securing information on guerrillas, and familiarizing the respective commanding generals with local terrain conditions and road nets. After approximately two months, the ROK police companies were returned to the ROK National Police.[22] Guerrilla activities within the UNC rear areas continued until the Inch'on landing and subsequent breakout from the Pusan perimeter on 15 September 1950. At this point the character of guerrilla warfare changed.

At the beginning of the war, guerrilla and unconventional warfare operations were controlled through five distinct yet interrelated chains of commands. The KWP's Central Committee controlled all guerrilla units and Communist sympathizers through its Liaison Department. This department was responsible for all subversion operations against the ROK, including the collection of political intelligence. The personnel who manned this department were drawn primarily from former members of the WPSK. The Liaison Department exercised its control through two subordinate sections: the Guerrilla Guidance Section and Military Section. The Guerrilla Guidance Section (also called the People's Guerrilla Command) was responsible for all political aspects of the guerrillas and KWP within the ROK, including establishing overall political objectives, indoctrination and propaganda, training, ensuring the development and expansion of the KWP within the ROK, and so forth. The Military Section was operationally subordinate to the KPA's General Staff Department and was responsible for the military and operational aspects of the guerrillas and KWP within the ROK, including training and infiltration of agents, couriers, and guerrillas for operations within the ROK; communications with personnel and units dispatched to the ROK; and miscellaneous other support functions.[23] The KPA's Reconnaissance Bureau, the 560th Army Unit, was responsible for military reconnaissance and

espionage operations. It controlled a handful of specially trained reconnaissance battalions and agent teams. The reconnaissance battalions did
not operate as tactical formations, but rather as detached companies to
forward divisions. Next, most KPA infantry divisions formed organic, or
attached, guerrilla units. These units operated primarily as reconnaissance or ranger units rather than traditional guerrillas and were seldom
divorced from the parent unit. Finally, at least three units were specially
trained in unconventional warfare operations and were directly subordinate to the General Staff Department: the 766th Independent Unit and
the 945th and 956th Independent Naval Infantry Regiments.[24] These
units and their operational experiences during the Fatherland Liberation War formed the foundation upon which the KPA's present-day special purpose forces were built.

■ ■ *Independent Guerrilla Units*
As discussed previously, the efforts of Pak Hon-yong's Kangdong Political Institute and the KWP's Liaison Department established approximately 5,000 guerrillas, agents, and sympathizers operating within the

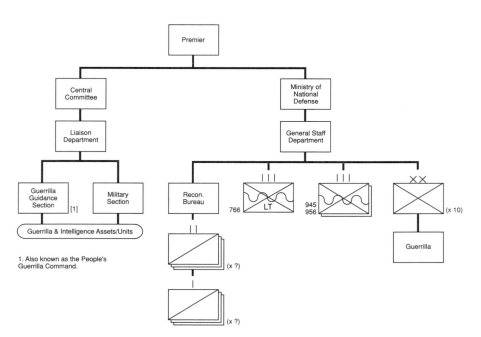

Unconventional warfare chain of command, 1950.

ROK at the start of the war, who were led by a core of some 1,700 specially trained personnel. The guerrillas were organized into a multitude of independent guerrilla units, the majority of which were loyal to Pak Hon-yong rather then Kim Il-song.[25] This ideological split, however, had no appreciable effect upon either their operations or their desire to reunify the Korean Peninsula under Communist control. While the units' personnel were predominantly southern Korean, the origins of other members were varied: there were former members of the People's Liberation Army (i.e., Chinese Communist Army), bandits, conscripted civilians, and ROKA defectors. It should be noted that some so-called independent guerrilla units were in reality simply groups of professional bandits exploiting a unique opportunity to obtain weapons and supplies and to extend their influence.

The independent guerrilla units varied considerably in their composition, strength, training, and efficiency. In general they comprised varying numbers of "battalions" and "companies," with one unit reportedly having twelve "battalions." Personnel strengths ranged from approximately fifty to up to a high of three thousand, reported for the Chiri-san organization, which was formed from elements involved in the October 1948 Yosu mutiny. All these units were loosely organized and lightly equipped. Once assigned an area of operations, they usually conducted operations at the discretion of the local commander. Few, if any, were known to have direct radio communications with higher headquarters; centralized control appears to have been limited. During the first two months of the war many independent guerrilla units received logistic support not only from local Communist sympathizers but reportedly from a mountain village in the area of Pohyon-san, located southeast of Kusan-dong (20 kilometers northeast of Taegu). There is, however, no evidence to suggest that a headquarters was located here.

▪ ▪ *Divisional Guerrilla Units*

Most KPA infantry divisions at the beginning of the war possessed an organic, or attached, guerrilla unit. The tables of organization for these units varied considerably among the various divisions.[26] Personnel for these units were selected from former Chinese-trained guerrillas and WPSK members who had escaped north. These troops were thoroughly trained in infantry as well as guerrilla tactics. The length and type of training for individual guerrilla units apparently followed no uniform schedule, although their curriculum was somewhat standardized. Training was generally divided equally between political indoctrination and guerrilla tactics, such as sabotage methods, intelligence collection, the procuring of supplies, and the selection of campsites. Infantry training evidently was not included, since many of the troops had received basic infantry training before assignment as guerrillas. Many units were apparently trained individually with the assistance of experienced instructors who had fought with the Chinese Communists. The units also used a manual entitled *Guerrilla Tactics*. Typical missions assigned to these units included the disruption of lines of communications supply; intelligence collection; the ambushing of withdrawing UNC elements and establishment of roadblocks; and, within unit capabilities, the taking of limited high-value objectives. To insure maximum coordination with the parent division, several portable radio sets were carried by each unit. In effect, the designation "divisional guerrilla unit" is somewhat of a misnomer since these units, insofar as tactics and cooperation with their parent divisions are concerned, functioned as divisional reconnaissance or ranger units.

KPA infantry divisions employed their guerrilla units intensively throughout the war. During normal combat operations, members dressed in standard KPA uniforms and carried the usual weapons. However, to reconnoiter towns, villages, and rear areas of UNC forces in daylight, members would wear civilian clothes or ROKA uniforms. These soldiers returned to the hills before dark and guided the main body back to the objective. In the approach to the objective, three scouts were sent out first, each approximately 5 meters apart. Companies were separated by 20–25 meters; platoons 15–20 meters; and squads, about 10 meters. After the attack, the guerrillas withdrew into the hills before daylight. At other times, guerrilla units mingled with refugees and infiltrated into UNC rear areas. At a predetermined point, they would separate from the civilian column and assemble their weapons, which had been hidden in oxcarts and bundles. After reconnaissance of the target was complete, the guerrillas launched an attack. Units were given specific missions and a specific time limit to accomplish each assignment. These units also provided guides for the infiltration of "enveloping units" behind UNC lines. There is no evidence that during the first two months of the war, any divisional guerrilla units were ever detached from their parent divisions for the purposes of either establishing or supporting indigenous guerrilla movements or operations.

■ ■ *766th Independent Unit*

As previously noted, with the failure of the 1949 September Offensive, the Kangdong Political Institute was disbanded and was replaced by the Hoeryong Cadres School. Under the direction of O Chin-u, the mission of the school was to train personnel for a new special unit in the tradition of the 88th Brigade.[27]

The 766th Independent Unit (also known as the 766th Independent Infantry Regiment, 766th Infantry Regiment, 766th Regiment, and 766th Guerrilla Unit) is believed to have been formed in July 1949 at Wonsan.[28] The core personnel for the unit were obtained by a reorganization of an entire infantry officers' class from the Hoeryong Cadres School, including instructors and students. From July 1949 until 12 June 1950 the unit, which was organized into three battalions, conducted basic and advanced training at Hoeryong. On 12 June, the 766th moved by rail to Munp'yong (5 kilometers north of Wonsan), where they were engaged in amphibious training under Soviet supervision until 22 June. The unit then moved by rail to the area north of the port town of Yangyang. Here the 766th was augmented by a number of independent guerrilla units, including the 15th, 27th, Nam Don Ue, and Namdo Guerrilla Units.[29] These attachments expanded the 766th to six "battalions" with a personnel strength of approximately 1,200–1,500.[30]

The 766th and attached units had the mission of establishing beachheads along the east coast in the rear of the ROKA in order to disrupt rear area communications and defenses (e.g., destruction of railroad tracks at crossings, bridges, tunnels, curves, and switches, and the disruption of telephone and telegraph service) and to provide intelligence. When this initial mission had been accomplished and contact had been established with the main body of the 5th Infantry Division, units of the 766th were assigned two additional missions. First, they were to act in the reconnaissance and ranger roles to assist the advance of the 5th Infantry Division. Second, elements were to infiltrate west and south through the mountains in the general directions of Pusan and Taegu as an ordinary partisan force and join other elements of the unit landed there.[31]

Prior to its commitment the 766th and its attached units operated under the direct control of the KPA's General Staff Department headquartered in P'yongyang, with which it maintained contact by radio. Available evidence suggests that once the war began, the 1st and 2nd Battalions maintained this subordination until the 766th was disbanded in mid-August. These two battalions also maintained close contact with the 5th Infantry Division. The 3rd Battalion of the 766th was apparently subordinated to the 5th Infantry Division at the beginning of the war. Little is known about the control of the various units attached to the 766th. It possibly mimicked that of the 766th's 1st and 2nd Battalions.

On 23–26 June, the 1st and 2nd Battalions boarded small merchant ships manned by the Korean People's Navy and conducted at least two amphibious landings in the ROK. The first landing area was near Nakp'ung-ni (10 kilometers south of Kangnung). From here the force moved inland after being attacked by ROKA units. This force subsequently moved north to support the attack on Kangnung. The second landing area was immediately south of the town of Chumunjin. Although there is some confusion over the operations of the 3rd Battalion during this time, it is believed to have fought alongside the 5th Infantry Division as it attacked south along the coast.[32]

The independent guerrilla units attached to the 766th Independent Unit had a more convoluted experience. The Nam Don Ue Guerrilla Force arrived in the Yangyang area in early June, where it was combined with the 15th Guerrilla Unit. On 21 June the combined force of four hundred or five hundred men left the Yangyang area for the port of Changjon (70 kilometers north of Yangyang). Two days later, the force boarded small ships for landings in the ROK. On 25 June the force landed at Imwonjin

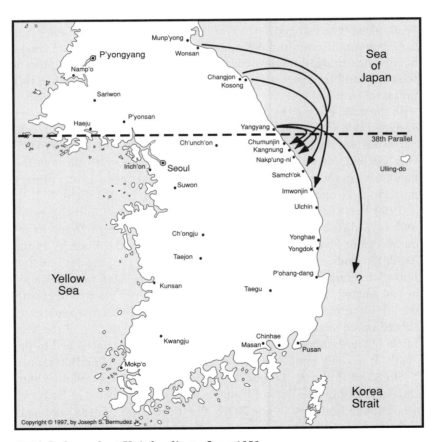

766th Independent Unit landings, June 1950.

(28 kilometers north of Ulchin) and reorganized itself into two units. It then proceeded southwest into the mountains toward Andong. The 27th Guerrilla Unit arrived in the Wonsan area on 21 June. The following day it boarded eight boats and sailed south to land at Mukko, near Kangnung. During the next two weeks it proceeded south toward Ulchin, where it arrived on 5 July. The Namdo Guerrilla Unit was formed at Yangyang on or about 18 June. On 23 June the unit, consisting of approximately two hundred men, moved north to the port of Kosong, were the unit was augmented by the addition of four hundred men. On or about 24 June, the unit embarked on four diesel steamers and landed in the Samch'ok area on the twenty-fifth. The unit proceeded south along the coast, arriving at Yonhae (14 kilometers north of Yongdok) on 1 July.[33]

The seaborne phases of these operations were relatively crude. Elements embarked on small coastal freighters (some of which were lightly armed) manned by the Korean People's Navy. They would then sail south under the cover of darkness, sometimes with an escort of P-4-class motor torpedo boats from the 2nd Naval Squadron based at Wonsan. Once the elements arrived at their destination, the actual amphibious landings were generally conducted in company-sized units (80–120 men each), using small power boats, fishing craft, and the like. Apparently, some troops even waded ashore or landed at the fishing piers of small villages.

In general the amphibious landings of the 766th and attached units proceeded smoothly and successfully. There was, however, one significant setback: "[On] the evening of the 25th there took place the most important surface engagement of the war. Northeast of Pusan PC 701 [an ROKN submarine chaser], Commander Nam Choi Yong, ROKN, encountered a 1,000 ton armed steamer with some 600 troops embarked, and sank it after a running fight. Since Pusan, the only major port of entry available for the movement of supplies and reinforcements to South Korea, was at this time almost defenseless, the drowning of the 600 was an event of profound importance."[34]

Given the known landing sites of other elements of the 766th and their missions, as well as the location of the sinking, it would appear that the ultimate objective of this unit was the port of Pusan. Had this landing been successful, and the port of Pusan interdicted even for a short while, the course of the conflict could have been significantly altered, because this was the primary point of entry for U.S. and UNC reinforcements.

The operations of the 766th were to clear the way for the advance of the 5th Infantry Division. At approximately 0500 hours on 25 June 1950, the 5th Division attacked across the thirty-eighth parallel down the main road that parallels the ROK's rugged east coast. This attack was supported not only by the amphibious landings of the 1st and 2nd Battalions of the 766th

Independent Unit, but apparently with ground operations by elements of the 766th. With the 766th leading, the 5th Infantry Division crossed the thirty-eighth parallel and entered Chumunjin without incident shortly before noon. Continuing the drive south, both units entered Kangnung the next day, after an all-night battle. With the 766th still leading the attack, both units continued south until they reached the approaches to Samch'ok. Here the 766th was joined by elements that had made an amphibious landing near the town. The reconstituted unit then proceeded into the hills. From there the troops, after changing into civilian clothes, infiltrated into Samch'ok, in order to gather intelligence. The division entered Samch'ok on about 5 July. On 9 July, after a large-scale engagement that involved the 766th only, the division and the 766th occupied Ulchin.

The 766th Unit, after undergoing a reorganization at Ulchin, infiltrated small units westward into the mountains with the mission of cutting communications between Pusan and Taegu, and P'ohang-dang. It continued to operate as the spearhead for the 5th, and later the 12th, Infantry Division, in the P'ohang-dang area for two months of intensive and costly fighting. On 17–19 August, both the 12th and the 766th, after having suffered serious losses, were reorganized. During this reorganization, the 766th was disbanded and its personnel absorbed by the 12th Division.

The view of these operations from the "other side of the fence" is interesting, as indicated in a letter dated 26 June 1950, to Gen. M. V. Zakharov, the deputy chief of staff of the Soviet armed forces, from T. F. Shtykov, Soviet ambassador to the DPRK:

On the very first day the DPRK navy made two landings on the coast of the Sea of Japan. The first landing party was in the Korio [Kangnung?] area and consisted of two battalions of naval infantry and around a thousand partisans. The second landing group was in the region of Urutsyn [Ulchin] and consisted of 600 partisans.

The landings took place at 5 hours 25 minutes and were carried out successfully.

The group of partisans took the city of Urutsyn [Ulchin] and a number of districts adjoining it.

The landings were carried out with a battle between warships of the People's Army and ships of the South Korean army. As a result of the battle one Southern trawler was sunk and one was damaged. The DPRK fleet had no losses.[35]

■ ■ 945th and 956th Independent Naval Infantry Regiments

Little is known about the 945th and 956th Independent Naval Infantry Regiments (also called Independent Regiments, Independent Infantry

Regiments, Marine Regiments, and Independent Marine Regiments).[36] The 945th is believed to have been established in July 1949 at Wonsan and was probably subordinate to the newly established Naval Head- quarters (also called the 599th Unit or 599th Army Unit) located at Chin- namp'o. The 945th probably received amphibious training under Soviet supervision in the Wonsan area prior to the war. Along with the 766th Independent Unit, the 945th was responsible for the amphibious land- ings along the ROK's east coast at the beginning of the war. Most sources indicate that the 945th landed in the wrong sector and proved ineffec- tive, but there is little additional information. It is conceivable that the 945th actually was the unit assigned to the Pusan landing and was sunk en route to its landing site. If this is correct, then the 945th proved "inef- fective" because it was destroyed. Regardless, the unit was disbanded in August 1950 and its personnel incorporated into the newly established 24th Naval Infantry Brigade (249th Brigade or 249th Army Unit).

The 956th Independent Naval Infantry Regiment was established in the west coast port city of Chinnamp'o in July 1949 and was subordinate to Naval Headquarters. Although little is known of its activities during the first two months of the war, it appears to have remained in the gen- eral area of Chinnamp'o and did not engage in offensive amphibious operations as had the 945th. Sometime in August 1950 the 956th was redesignated the 23rd Naval Infantry Brigade (239th Brigade or 239th Army Unit). At this time the battalions of the brigade were deployed from Chinnamp'o to Ongjin, Haeju, Kunsan, and Kwangju.

Interestingly, Kim Il-song placed significant importance on naval infantry units. Just one day after the war had begun, he sent a letter to Stalin requesting arms for the "formation of two divisions, 12 battalions of naval infantry and for the formation of security detachments." Two days later, Stalin responded that the establishment of new units should not be the main concern, but rather "to fill out the existing divisions and to increase their strength approximately to 12,000." The deteriorating war situation would, however, settle the question and postpone the estab- lishment of new naval infantry units.[37]

Airborne Capabilities

Although virtually nothing substantive is known concerning airborne capabilities, the Korean People's Aviation Association (later to become the Korean People's Air Force, KPAF) apparently began very limited para- chute training for its pilots sometime during 1946–47.[38] By early 1949 this capability was expanded with the construction of an airborne training center located in P'yongyang, on the west bank of the Tae-dong River, opposite the P'yongyang airfield. Reportedly, it was here that an estimated five or six hundred KPA personnel and KPAF pilots received parachute training. At present there is no evidence to suggest that an actual KPA paratroop unit was established during this period. There were no KPA paratroop operations during the Fatherland Liberation War.

■ September 1950–July 1953
With the success of the 15 September 1950 Inch'on landing and subsequent breakout from the Pusan perimeter, the complexion of unconventional warfare in the ROK changed. With its rear seriously threatened, its supply lines heavily interdicted, and its inability to rest and rehabilitate its weakened combat units, the KPA was in no position to fight a war on two fronts. The General Staff Department ordered a general retreat. This retreat, which started as an organized movement, quickly turned into a rout as many KPA units were cut off on their attempts to escape north. Unable to escape, many units and stragglers established their own guerrilla units or joined forces with existing KWP independent guerrilla units. Additional Communist sympathizers and KWP members also joined their ranks. The latter two groups typically furnished logistical support and performed espionage missions, while the former KPA personnel conducted guerrilla operations (e.g., raids and ambushes).

Whatever their motive, whether it was the accomplishment of true guerrilla missions or merely foraging for enough supplies to keep moving north to rejoin their units, these KPA guerrillas increased the tempo of operations within UNC rear areas. This pattern of activity moved perceptibly northward behind the advancing UNC forces. There was, however, enough continuous activity around the traditional strongholds within the ROK (e.g., Chiri-san) to indicate that the KWP's independent guerrilla units had not abandoned their efforts.

Increasing guerrilla activities, primarily from cut-off KPA units, during this time led UNC forces to divert large tactical units, divisions, or sometimes larger groups to secure rear areas. Since guerrilla forces typically possessed few, if any, heavy weapons, armor was frequently employed against them. By studying the movement of the guerrilla forces, UNC troops could sometimes block routes of withdrawal. Initially, platoon- and company-sized patrols were used to combat guerrilla forces, but these proved to be too small. Later, regiments and divisions were employed with good success. UNC operations would typically consist of deploying one battalion, organized for perimeter defense, along a suspected route of the withdrawal. Then the remainder of the regiment or division would encircle the area in which the guerrillas were known to operate, forcing the guerrillas to retreat into the predeployed battalion.

Command and control of these KPA units engaged in guerrilla warfare was exercised initially through the normal chain of command where it existed. When this was broken, the most senior officer available led the unit north to a predetermined rally point (which frequently shifted further north) until contact was reestablished. The intention of the vast majority of cut-off KPA personnel was to move north and regain KPA-held lines, then to reorganize and reequip. As the general war situation continued to turn against the DPRK (especially with the UNC's advance north of the thirty-eighth parallel), many cut-off KPA units were ordered to remain behind UNC lines and conduct guerrilla operations. Other units had no choice but to accept this role for survival. As this change of mission occurred, command and control over these cut-off KPA units passed to the KWP's Liaison Department and its subordinate Military Section (now designated as the 526th Army Unit) and Guerrilla Guidance Section.[39] Still other KPA units and personnel joined independent guerrilla units and operated under the control of the KWP.

The October 1950 intervention of China into the war with its Chinese People's Volunteers (CPV), and their Second Phase Offensive in November further changed the nature of unconventional warfare operations. With the KPA operationally ineffective and Kim Il-song sitting impotent in Kanggye, the Yenan faction, with the CPV's assistance, assumed a dominant position in the war. The CPV intervention allowed for the reorganization and reconstruction of the KPA to begin. The first concrete results of this reorganization were the deployment of the II and V KPA Corps (both understrength) along the eastern sector of the front. With regards to guerrilla warfare, several events occurred almost simultaneously. First, the CPV's concept of guerrilla warfare became more visible as the Chinese units brought with them their own guerrilla units. These units primarily conducted military operations behind UNC lines, and to a lesser degree attempted to win over the local populace and establish bases in the remote mountainous areas. Next, Kim Il-song and the KPA General Staff Department gave the guerrilla program a higher priority, for several reasons. One reason was that this was the only area in which the KPA was enjoying any success. Second, Kim had a natural affinity for the guerrillas based upon his personal experience. Third, tight control over the guerrillas would prevent Pak Hon-yong and the Domestic Faction from gaining any additional support or taking the credit for their successes. An indication of the importance attached to the guerrillas was that Kim Ch'aek, the DPRK vice premier and minister of defense, maintained close control over guerrilla training and activity until his death in January 1951. A further indication of its importance was given at the Third Plenum of the Central Committee held in Pyoro-ri in December 1950.[40] Here Kim Il-song examined the causes for the KPA's defeat during the first six months of the Fatherland Liberation War. Among the problem areas he identified was the lack of guerrilla warfare capabilities.

This increased emphasis upon guerrilla warfare witnessed both the KPA and the KWP initiating measures to tighten guerrilla organization and control. By the end of October 1950, approximately 2,800 KPA troops who had been cut off behind UNC lines were organized into the I Guerrilla Corps to conduct guerrilla operations within the ROK. With the UNC concentrated on the front lines, this reorganization continued with little interference, and soon five guerrilla brigades (1st through 5th) were established, each with ten to twenty "battalions" of approximately 100 men each. The combined strength of these KPA guerrilla units would soon reached an estimated 10,000 troops, the majority of whom were concentrated in the mountainous T'aebaek-san area (most heavily near Yongwol) in November–December 1950.

In addition to these KPA guerrilla units in the Yongwol area, there was the 10th Infantry Division. This unit was unique in that although it was cut off behind UNC lines, it was able to withdraw north while still maintaining its unit integrity. While the I Guerrilla Corps was concentrated around Yongwol in the ROK, the 10th Infantry Division sat astride the thirty-eighth parallel in the area bounded by Singye, Ch'orwon, P'yonggang, Inje, Yanggu, and Ch'unch'on. Here it successfully engaged in guerrilla warfare operations as an organized unit, denying the UNC freedom of movement in the region. For these exploits, the division was awarded the honorific title of "Guards."

To support these guerrilla units, most of whom were in desperate need of leadership and communication, the KPA and Liaison Department began to infiltrate small groups into the ROK. The groups were composed of couriers with orders for guerrilla commanders, signalmen with communications equipment, and officers and noncommissioned officers trained in guerrilla schools. It is believed that at least two general officers and their staffs were also infiltrated to the guerrillas. These infiltration efforts were considerably aided by the flood of refugees, which made proper UNC screening virtually impossible.

During November–December all these guerrilla units were placed under the operational control of the KPA's II Corps, which was advancing south as part of the CPV's Second Phase Offensive. The units would subsequently play an important supporting role in the combined CPV/KPA Third Phase Offensive in December 1950 and January 1951, more specifically during the KPA II and V Corps attack toward Andong on 7–22 January 1951. This attack witnessed heavy fighting, high casualties, and the highest level of guerrilla activity in the UNC rear since the war began. Apparently at this point, most of the cut-off KPA units that were engaged in guerrilla warfare operations, including the I Guerrilla Corps and 10th "Guards" Infantry Division, were absorbed back into the KPA as it advanced south.

A major objective of the Third Phase Offensive was the recapture of Seoul in January 1951. During the next two months, the KWP's Liaison Department established a headquarters to control guerrilla operations in Seoul and named it the Seoul Guerrilla Guidance Bureau. On 27 January, the department also established the Seoul Political Institute. Following the tradition of the Kangdong Political Institute, the mission of the new institute was to provide political indoctrination and specialized instruction for personnel to be dispatched behind UNC lines as agents or guerrillas. Both the Seoul Guerrilla Guidance Bureau and Seoul Political Institute were staffed by supporters of Pak Hon-yong.

These events were apparently accompanied by a reorganization of the guerrilla units that had not been absorbed back into the KPA. Initially, approximately 8,200 remaining guerrillas were reorganized into six separate branch units (1st Branch Unit, 2nd Branch Unit, etc.). Each branch unit had a specific mission and an assigned area of operations and was organized along military lines with anywhere from 600–4,000 men. The reality of the situation, however, resulted in units strengths varying from 80–7,150 men.

The primary missions of the branch units was the disruption of the UNC rear areas and the provision of intelligence. Communication and supply lines were attacked, villages were raided, and Communist propaganda disseminated. Food and ammunition were critical items, and desperate bands raided many villages out of necessity. Supplies were first gathered from sympathizers, and if this proved insufficient, they were supplemented by raids on farms or by the capture of UNC supplies. Hostages were also used to obtain contributions of food. Female guerrillas often purchased medical supplies at local markets. The practice of concentrating guerrilla forces in one area, however, increased the animosity of the local population toward the guerrillas, resulting in the brutal treatment of captured guerrillas. Guerrilla personnel were replaced as necessary with volunteers, kidnaped young men and women, hostages, and soldiers who infiltrated UNC lines.

The Military Section continually attempted to infiltrate not only personnel replacements but entire units south to reinforce the established branch units. For example, on 23 January 1951 the 4th Battalion of the 503rd Engineer Regiment, under the command of Maj. Pak Ki Ho, was

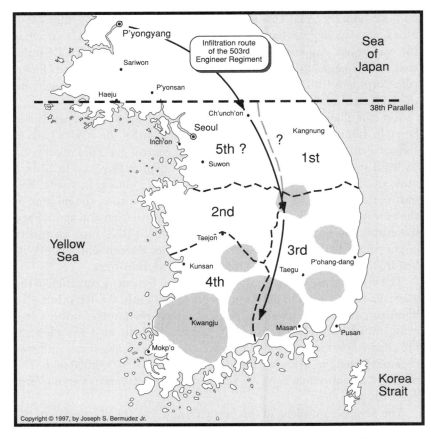

Guerrilla activity (shaded) and branch unit operating areas, 1951.

detached and departed P'yongyang for Ch'unch'on. At Ch'unch'on it was attached to the 6th Branch Unit, whose area of operations covered the Cholla-Namdo District situated in the southwest corner of the Korean Peninsula. The battalion was met by representatives of the branch unit near Ch'unch'on and, under their guidance, infiltrated through UNC lines on 10 February. It then proceeded toward the 6th Branch Unit's base around Chiri-san.[41]

Overlaid upon the more formal and military organization of the branch units, which were generally controlled through the Military Section, was the political structure and party organization of the KWP operating within the ROK, which was generally controlled through the Seoul Guerrilla

Guidance Bureau. This overlapping of organizations and responsibilities, by what was ultimately one headquarters—the Liaison Department—resulted in inefficient command and control and a plethora of unit and organization names and identities that confused UNC intelligence. The guerrillas in the field, however, were not greatly affected by this confusion.

On 25 January, the UNC began a general offensive across the entire front line. Accompanying this offensive, the UNC committed at least five divisions, including the U.S. 1st Marines and 7th Infantry and the 2nd, 5th, and 7th ROK Infantry Divisions, to counterguerrilla operations. With these activities the tide of battle turned against the KPA and CPV for the second time, and the number of guerrilla attacks and estimated strength declined rapidly. Other factors that contributed to this rapid decline in guerrilla activity were the severe Korean winter, which made resupply extremely difficult; endemic diseases, which the guerrillas were poorly equipped to deal with (in fact regular CPV and KPA units were also suffering from widespread typhus, cholera, and dysentery at the time); and an increasing number of desertions. By March 1951, UNC forces engaged in Operation Ripper recaptured Seoul, disrupting the Liaison Department's control over guerrilla operations and forcing the disbanding of the Seoul Political Institute. These events, combined with the aforementioned factors, resulted in total guerrilla strength's dropping from a January high of 37,500 to below 15,000. By the end of the month most guerrillas remaining within the ROK were avoiding combat in order to regroup, resupply, and conserve their strength. Continued counterguerrilla operations reduced total guerrilla strength to approximately 7,500 by mid-1951 and limited guerrilla operations to minor harassment and a fight for survival.

By this time UNC counterguerrilla operations had developed considerably with the addition of numerous ROK security battalions and the Korean National Police units to the battle. These two organizations fought the guerrillas in rear areas and were under the operational control of the ROKA. Both had the mission of guarding fixed installations and conducting counterguerrilla operations. ROK security battalions were attached to the T'aebaek-san command (which had the mission of guarding two strategic passes on main supply routes, the Tanyang and Munyong Passes) and to the Sonan command. The latter command was established in June 1951 at the insistence of the ROKA to combat guerrillas in the Sonan area. In addition to placing guards at VHF stations, which were prize targets for guerrilla raids, counterguerrilla measures extensively used wire, booby traps, and mines. Each rear-area organization had a standard operating procedure that it followed during a guerrilla raid. Security platoons rode railroad trains. Flatcars or gondola cars, carrying

NORTH KOREAN SPECIAL FORCES

machine guns and crews, were placed on the front and rear of some trains. Hospital trains had two gondolas in front, the first to explode any mines on the tracks. The second carried machine guns and crews. When a guerrilla unit attacked a village or installation, the National Police would respond immediately to pursue the attacking force. ROK security battalions did not. When a definite guerrilla force was located, the area was surrounded, and UNC air strikes were called in on the target. After the air raid, the National Police units cleaned out the area. Often such attacks were jointly conducted with the assistance of ROK security battalions. In addition to physically contacting the guerrillas, the National Police maintained agents in towns and provinces suspected of harboring guerrillas. Pamphlets guaranteeing safe conduct were distributed by land and air in the same areas to induce guerrillas to surrender.[42]

It should be noted that while counterguerrilla operations were making significant progress in reducing the guerrilla threat, these efforts also created occasional problems. This often occurred in areas in which the civilian population had generally supported the Communists prior to the war (e.g., Chiri-san, Pohyon-san). ROK counterguerrilla operations in these areas often met with indifference or resistance from the local population, which in turn resulted in harsher treatment by the counterguerrilla forces.[43] The harsher treatment itself would further alienate the civilians. These sentiments would last a long time and were a contributing factor for selection of certain operating areas by the KPA for its special operations during the 1960s.

With the stabilization of the front lines and increased UNC counterguerrilla operations taking their toll upon guerrilla forces, the KWP initiated a reorganization of the guerrilla command and support structure. On 31 August 1951 several political schools and training activities were merged into a newly established organization known as the Kumgang Political Institute (or Kumgang Political School), located at Odong-ri, Sohong-gun, Hwanghae-do. Like the Kangdong Political Institute and Seoul Political Institute before it, the mission of this new institute was to provide political indoctrination and specialized instruction for personnel to be dispatched behind UNC lines as agents or guerrillas. Topics taught included Communist theory, history of the Soviet Communist Party, history of the People's Democracy, world geopolitics, Fatherland Liberation War, geography, history of Korea since VJ Day, development of Communism in Korea, physical and military training, and guerrilla tactics. The greatest emphasis, however, was on political indoctrination. Many of the students were ROK prisoners of war and civilians held in custody by the KPA. Care was taken to train these recruits for duty in their former areas of residence, and to assign them there to recruit and organize additional guerrillas. As with the previous political institutes, the Kumgang Political Institute was staffed primarily by supporters of Pak Hon-yong.[44]

The change from fluid battlefield to stabilized front line, and the CPV and KPA commands' realization that total victory could not be achieved at this time, resulted in a further change in the nature of guerrilla operations within the ROK. All guerrilla units, while not completely abandoning their traditional military mission, were to now concentrate upon intelligence collection and political objectives. A document signed by Kim Il-song and KPA Chief of Staff Nam Il outlined the specific missions of the KWP guerrilla units as follows:

- Investigate the enemy situation in respect to industry with every means at your command and forward all information obtained.
- Carry out propaganda work effectively among the people; enforce the policies of the Democratic Republic of Korea; train the people to become active supporters of their own interests by explaining to them the aggressive tendencies of the U.S. imperialist and the traitorous deeds of Syngman Rhee's puppet group, thus fomenting disorder in enemy held areas.
- Take every opportunity to hinder enemy military action and to harass strategic enemy installations.
- Help to restore the People's government in "unliberated" areas as soon as possible.
- When a general offensive is launched by our ground and naval forces, Workers' Partisan Groups should assume leadership of the people and lead them in the struggle against the enemy.
- Cooperate with other guerrilla units in destroying bridges, railroads, and highways, thus restricting enemy activities.
- In liberated areas, the Workers' Partisan Group should change its function and become a Home Guard unit to maintain order and preserve peace.[45]

These orders were aimed not only at the preservation of the guerrillas themselves, but more importantly at the preservation, and expansion, of the KWP within the ROK.

In September and October 1951, guerrilla units in the southern region of the ROK concentrated themselves in the Chiri-san area. From here they mounted numerous raids to the north and east against UNC lines of communication and supply. A primary target was the railroad line running from Pusan to Seoul, which carried the vast majority of the supplies for the UNC. By November, as a result of a more stabilized front line and continued infiltration and support efforts by the Military Section, total

47

guerrilla strength increased slightly to approximately 8,200. This increasing strength was primarily located within the Chiri-san area and contributed to the upsurge in guerrilla activities.

Beginning in October, KPA units began to conduct numerous small amphibious raids along both coasts directed against UNC partisans and intelligence units.[46] Not only did these raids demonstrate reasonably good planning and implementation, they confirmed the beginnings of an amphibious capability. Small craft were massed without being detected, and operations were skillfully timed. Artillery support was well coordinated, and on at least one occasion the landing force reached shore without detection.[47] In several instances UNC forces were forced off these islands by these attacks.

By the end of 1951 a number of organizational changes had occurred, or were occurring, within the DPRK's intelligence and security agencies, which not only improved Kim Il-song's control, but more clearly delineated responsibilities. The three organizations primary concerned with intelligence and security organizations were the KPA's Reconnaissance Bureau, the KWP's Liaison Department, and the Social Security Department of the Ministry of Internal Affairs.

The Reconnaissance Bureau (the 560th Army Unit) was responsible for military reconnaissance and espionage operations designed to collect military-related intelligence concerning the ROK. It was organized into three detachments. The First Detachment was responsible for obtaining tactical information concerning UNC forces. It employed former ROKA officers who had been indoctrinated and trained in espionage work. Personnel were inserted by a specially trained escort team that led agents through the front lines. Three forward liaison posts were established at Hahyon-Ni, Changdo-ri, and Kosong to facilitate these operations. The Second Detachment was probably the elite of the military intelligence system. It consisted of a number of small teams of ten to twelve KPA officers and NCOs each. These teams were assigned both the collection of military intelligence and the establishment of intelligence networks within the ROK. The Military and Administrative Department handled normal military and administrative matters. The Reconnaissance Bureau also operated a few specially trained reconnaissance battalions. These battalions detached their organic companies to frontline corps and divisions. Their mission was to collect military intelligence within the respective corps and division areas of responsibility. Included within the Reconnaissance Bureau's responsibilities were special operations, including raids on high-value targets, kidnaping, and assassination.

The KWP's Liaison Department was responsible for all subversion within the ROK, including guerrilla operations, rather than the collection of intelligence. It was organized into approximately eight sections, the most important of which were the Military Section and Guerrilla Guidance Section (formerly the Seoul Guerrilla Guidance Bureau). The Military Section (526th Army Unit) was composed of KPA personnel and was responsible for escorting operatives into the ROK and then maintaining contact with and supporting them. The section accomplished these missions through its subordinate liaison offices located along the front lines (i.e., Western Liaison Office and Eastern Liaison Office). The Guerrilla Guidance Section was responsible for the control (ideological and tactical) and expansion of guerrilla and KWP groups within the ROK.

The Social Security Department of the Ministry of Internal Affairs was responsible for a wide range of internal security, counterintelligence, and propaganda missions. It was organized into five bureaus: the Civil, Political, Military Security, Industrial, and Foreign Bureaus. The Military Security Bureau would sometimes conduct agent operations within the ROK. The Foreign Bureau was responsible for conducting foreign espionage activities.

Command of the guerrilla organization operating within the ROK was still exercised through the KWP's Liaison Department and its subordinate Military Section and Guerrilla Guidance Section. This organization was now known as the Southern Guerrilla Army, or the Southern People's Guerrilla Corps. Its operational headquarters within the ROK was located in the Chiri-san area, and it had an approximate strength of 6,110 armed and effective guerrillas and many sympathizers. The original five branch units were now reorganized into four "guerrilla units" (i.e., 1st through 4th), each with a variable number of subordinate provincial parties or branch units. Each provincial party or branch unit was itself composed of a different number of county and town units. These county and town units were sometimes also referred to as parties and assumed the name of the locale in which they operated. In some provincial commands the units retained older identities as numbered divisions or regiments. Still others were independent or mobile units. Some of these units (e.g., the Lee Hyon Hang Unit) had a long history and objected to any particular subordination. They are believed to have been controlled directly by the Southern Guerrilla Army or Guerrilla Unit Headquarters. These, however, were relatively few in number. Until about mid-December, the Southern Guerrilla Army Headquarters was located in the Chiri-san area. As a result of Operation Rat Killer, however, the headquarters was forced to move to the Togyu-san area.

The increased guerrilla activity during October–November 1951 in the Chiri-san area resulted in the UNC's launching Operation Rat Killer, which began in December 1951. This operation was conducted in three phases, over a period of four months, by the ROK 8th and Capital Infantry Divisions. The first phase was directed against the Chiri-san area, the second against the Togyu-san area, and the third once again against the Chiri-san area. Operation Rat Killer lasted until March 1952 and caused the destruction of much of the organized guerrilla movement in the Chiri-san and Togyu-san areas. An estimated 8,000 guerrillas and sympathizers were killed or captured.[48] In the six-month period from December 1951 to June 1952, the total numbers of active guerrillas operating within the ROK fell from an estimated 8,200 to 2,400.

During the spring of 1952, the KWP Liaison Department's Military Section was reorganized and assigned a new code number, the 567th Army Unit. Whether this was an attempt to address the rapidly declining effectiveness of the guerrillas or simply a security measure is presently unclear.

Although dispersed and isolated, the remaining guerrillas constituted a nuisance to UNC rear area operations. In July the ROK 1st Infantry Division was pulled out of the front lines to conduct counterguerrilla operations. During the next three months the division claimed approximately three or four hundred guerrillas killed and an equal number captured. Small numbers of guerrillas continued to operate against the UNC rear. Their efforts, however, met with decreasing success because of continuing UNC counterguerrilla operations and because many of them were by this time reduced to tired, hungry, bandit groups struggling just to survive.

Sometime between December 1952 and March 1953, the power struggle between Pak Hon-yong and Kim Il-song came to a head when Pak's supporters attempted a military coup d'état. His supporters drew upon troops trained at the Kumgang Political Institute and members of the Liaison Department's 567th Army Unit. Although details are lacking, the coup attempt failed and Pak and his supporters were arrested. What followed was a purge of former WPSK members and supporters within the KWP (especially its Liaison Department), subordination of the Kumgong Political Institute to the Reconnaissance Bureau, and the deactivation of the 567th Army Unit. The mission of the 567th is believed to have fallen to either the Reconnaissance Bureau or Guerrilla Guidance Section.[49]

In spite of the guerrillas' poor condition, UNC counterguerrilla operations, and the failed coup attempt, guerrilla operations continued. One of the more unusual and sophisticated special operations, presumably conducted by the Reconnaissance Bureau, was the 13 May 1953 attempt to disrupt control tower communications at Taegu (K-2) airfield. An English-speaking voice broke into the ADF (Air Direction Finding) landing and vectoring frequencies and gave false instructions. All conversations were normal, and no foreign accent was detected. Disaster was averted when pilots realized that the instructions were false and changed frequencies

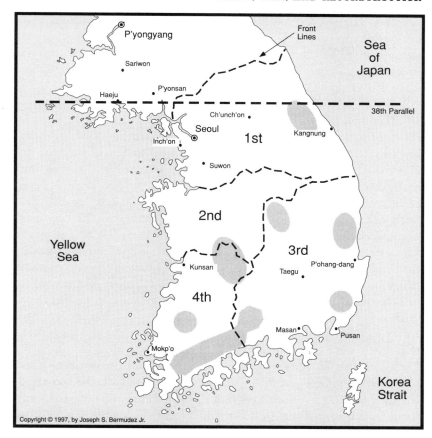

P'yongyang

Sariwon

P'yonsan

Haeju

Front
Lines

Sea
of
Japan

38th Parallel

Ch'unch'on

Seoul

1st

Kangnung

Inch'on

Suwon

2nd

Yellow
Sea

3rd

Kunsan

Taegu

P'ohang-dang

4th

Masan

Pusan

Mokp'o

Korea
Strait

Copyright © 1997, by Joseph S. Bermudez Jr.

Guerrilla activity (shaded) and branch unit operating areas, 1952–53.

to implement authorization procedures.[50] The last proven case of sabotage attributed to guerrillas during the Fatherland Liberation War took place on 15 June 1953, when a train was derailed outside of Pusan. The armistice agreement ending the war was signed on 27 July 1953.

▪ UNCONVENTIONAL WARFARE CAPABILITIES

Following the Inch'on landing and up to the signing of the armistice agreement, several units had built upon the unconventional warfare capabilities exhibited by earlier units, such as the 766th Independent Unit, 945th and 956th Independent Naval Infantry Regiments, and the divisional guerrilla units. Included among these units were the Reconnaissance Bureau, 10th "Guards" Infantry Division, and the 23rd Mechanized

Artillery Brigade. All these wartime units were viewed by the KPA as establishing the practical foundation upon which they built their special purpose forces. Of course, the KPA also always points to the 88th Special Independent Sniper Brigade and the guerrillas of the Fatherland Liberation War as the true inspiration.[51]

■ ■ *KWP Guerrilla Operations*
On the strategic level, the guerrilla operations controlled by the KWP's Liaison Department were a distinct disappointment to Kim Il-song and the KPA. Both had the strong belief, based upon the word of Pak Hon-yong, that as soon as the KPA crossed the thirty-eighth parallel, there would be a general uprising throughout the ROK and the war would end: "we all steadfastly believed the boastings of Pak Hon-yong that once we first occupied Seoul, then the 200,000 South Korean Workers' Party [WPSK] members who were hiding throughout South Korea would rise up and revolt, toppling the South Korean regime. . . . these words of Pak Hon-yong were one of the major factors in hardening Kim Il-song's resolve to invade southward."[52]

Ten years after the war, in a speech to KPA officers, Kim still expressed strong bitterness and disappointment over this matter: "Pak Hon-yong, the spy employed by the American scoundrels, exaggerated that there were some 200,000 underground party members in South Korea, with 60,000 in Seoul alone. Far from 200,000, by the time we had advanced to the Nakdong River Line, not even one uprising had occurred. If only a few thousand workers had risen in Pusan, then we certainly could have liberated [South Korea] all the way down to Pusan, and the American scoundrels could not have landed [in Inch'on]." [53]

This bitterness and disappointment should not be viewed as a general rejection of guerrilla warfare by Kim Il-song or the KPA; it was not. During the December 1950 Third Plenum of the Central Committee, held in Kanggye, Kim Il-song clearly placed the failure of the guerrillas in the ROK upon deficiencies in their ideological indoctrination, leadership, control, and support—not upon guerrilla warfare itself. The subsequent reorganizations of the KWP's Liaison Department were all meant to address these deficiencies in one form or another. By March 1951, the opportunity for the guerrillas to bring about a popular uprising had long passed.

On operational and tactical levels, the employment of the guerrillas can be viewed as having been somewhat successful. Their operations, or threat thereof, forced the UNC to dedicate tremendously disproportionate resources to combat them. When guerrilla operations were coordinated with regular KPA operations, the chances of success increased significantly. The areas in which the guerrillas achieved their greatest successes were the interdiction of UNC lines of communication and supply, and the collection of intelligence. It was these operational and tactical successes, combined with other wartime special operations successes, that would contribute to the development of light infantry units and the strategy of a "two-front war," as Kim Il-song would later explain:

> Deployment of guerrilla forces in the rear of the enemy defense line is necessary to undermine the mobility of enemy troops to tide over the unfavorable conditions created by the weak air force and mobility at our disposal, to scatter and destroy the enemy to strike at the enemy command headquarters and rear posts, to form a second frontier in the rear of the enemy defense line to cut off the retreat line of the enemy and to throw the enemy into confusion and fright. We failed [during the Fatherland Liberation War] to heed the tactical and strategic importance of guerrilla war and to wage a guerrilla war. [54]

• ■ *Reconnaissance Bureau*

Although few details are known concerning the wartime operations of the Reconnaissance Bureau it was obviously an elite organization that almost always accomplished its mission of infiltration and collection of military intelligence along the front lines. Its expansion and operations during the later part of the war clearly established the infrastructure for today's elite "sniper" brigades. As a good example of this, the infiltration organization (e.g., regional liaison posts/stations to control infiltration of the DMZ) employed by the First Detachment has remained fundamentally unchanged up till today. Other examples are numerous. The Second Detachment's use of small teams composed exclusively of ten or twelve specially trained KPA officers and NCOs has generally continued until today. The training, establishment, and employment of special reconnaissance battalions has led to the activation of larger reconnaissance units (e.g., the 17th Reconnaissance Brigade) and ultimately today's sniper brigades. Finally, the mission of collecting military intelligence and conducting special operations (e.g., raids on high-value targets, kidnaping, assassination) has not changed.

• ■ *10th "Guards" Infantry Division*

The wartime operations of the 10th Infantry Division, combined with the experiences with divisional guerrilla units, are viewed by the KPA as exhibiting the spirit of today's light infantry battalions and brigades.[55] Even postwar U.S. studies have remarked upon the 10th's performance:

> Late in 1950, the KPA 10th Infantry Division performed one of the most remarkable feats of the Korean War. Moving along mountainous

terrain, this division succeeded in infiltrating from the thirty-eighth parallel to within 30 kilometers of Taegu. Relying on the countryside for food and clothing and upon captured supplies for ammunition and medical facilities, this division was able to maintain its tactical integrity. As a result, it was able to keep the U.S. 1st Marine Division and ROK security forces occupied. Despite losses from constant attacks, the division continued to harass the UN forces and finally withdrew to its own lines at one-third of its original strength.[56]

A more detailed account of the 10th's operations between September 1950 and March 1951 is instructive. On 25 September 1950 the 10th Infantry Division was ordered to retreat north from the Pusan perimeter. It did so by first moving west through Kumch'on and then north through the T'aebaek-san while under attack by UNC forces. Unlike many other KPA infantry divisions the 10th remained a cohesive unit, albeit severely reduced in size and equipment. By November it had dispersed its subordinate units over a broad area astride the thirty-eighth parallel and bounded by Singye, Ch'orwon, P'yonggang, Inje, Yanggu, and Ch'unch'on. Here it engaged in guerrilla warfare operations as an organized unit. For these exploits, the division was awarded the honorific title of "Guards."

The division later consolidated itself near Hwach'on, just north of the thirty-eighth parallel, on or about 8 December 1950. The division participated in a limited attack against ROKA forces in the Ch'unch'on area and succeeded in advancing to the vicinity of Chongsyong-ni, where it was dispersed and again forced to withdraw but remained in contact in the Ch'unch'on area. During the latter part of December 1950, the division shifted east as part of the II Corps, under the command of Lt. Gen. Ch'oe Hyon, to the Yanggu area.[57] In the meantime the division had built up its strength to approximately four thousand troops. From this vicinity, in support of the combined CPV/KPA Third Phase Offensive, the division moved south through a break in UNC lines along the Inje–Wonju axis beginning in mid-December 1950. By 11 January 1951 the division had moved south to the Chech'on area, where it was engaged by elements of the U.S. 7th Infantry Division. It continued to move southward, avoiding contact where possible by skirting around major UNC troop concentrations and, by 25 January, was located in the area about 30 miles northeast of Taegu deep behind UNC lines. Meanwhile, UNC forces began to attack and close the gap in efforts to cut off II Corps. During this offensive all elements of II Corps, except the 10th Infantry Division, succeeded in escaping the trap, albeit with substantial losses. The 10th was cut off again and reverted to organized guerrilla tactics. In mid-March the division began to withdraw to the north in an attempt to rejoin the II Corps. During this withdrawal it was constantly engaged by UNC forces and its strength was reduced considerably. By the end of March the division was reduced to less than a thousand troops, but succeeded in regaining KPA lines as a cohesive unit. Subsequently, the division proceeded to the Ch'ongju area on the west coast, where it began reorganizing under the IV Corps as a mechanized infantry division.

▪ ▪ *23rd Mechanized Artillery Brigade*
Taken in combination with the early operations of the 766th Independent Unit and the 945th Independent Naval Infantry Regiment, the October 1951–March 1952 operations of the 23rd Mechanized Artillery Brigade can be viewed as providing the underpinnings for today's amphibious sniper brigades.[58]

As already noted, in August 1950, the 956th Independent Naval Infantry Regiment was redesignated the 23rd Naval Infantry Brigade at Chinnamp'o. The battalions of the brigade were then sent to the Ongjin, Haeju, Kunsan, and Kwangju areas. Following the Inch'on landing and subsequent UNC advance in September 1950, remnants of the brigade withdrew to the DPRK and began reorganizing and training in the Yongwon area northeast of Tokch'on. In mid-December 1950 the brigade, still understrength and poorly equipped, started advancing back to the Haeju area. Here it engaged in the coastal defense role of protecting the KPA western flank from UNC-controlled partisans and possible amphibious assault. Although the brigade was redesignated as the 23rd Mechanized Artillery Brigade in October 1951, it retained its mission of coastal defense.

Beginning in October 1951 and continuing through March 1952 the brigade engaged in what the UNC has called the west coast island hopping campaign. This consisted of numerous amphibious and shore-to-shore (i.e., movement across the mudflats) assaults on west coast islands held by UNC partisan forces intelligence units. The first major assault came on 9 October, when approximately six hundred troops, using sampans and other small craft, conducted an amphibious assault on the Korea Bay island of Sinmi-do. This initial assault force was later reinforced by troops arriving across the mudflats. As a result of these actions, the island was evacuated by UNC forces three days later. On the evening of 6 November, KPA units attacked and captured the small islands of Ka-do and Tan-do by amphibious assault. These islands were subsequently employed to provide artillery support and jump-off points for the successful 30 November amphibious assault on the island of Taehwa-do. These actions were accompanied by further shore-to-shore assaults, which seized six small coastal islands in Haeju Man. Between 16 and 18 December, a force of six hundred troops, believed to be from the 23rd, assaulted and captured two small islands east of Sok-to Island, at the mouth of the Tae-dong River. Following this last assault, UNC naval forces made a concerted effort to prevent any other such occurrences and successfully thwarted further attacks for several months. In March 1952, the 23rd attempted several assaults across the mudflats of Haeju Man against Yongmae-do, but these raids were unsuccessful because of overwhelming UNC naval firepower. With the failure of these assaults, the west coast "island-hopping campaign" essentially came to a close. In June 1952 the unit was redesignated the 23rd Infantry Brigade and concerned itself primarily with coastal defense until the end of the war.

POSTWAR POWER STRUGGLES AND REORGANIZATION OF ASSETS, 1953–61

With the signing of the armistice agreement on 27 July 1953 came several concurrent events that would provide the foundations for dramatic changes within the DPRK, the KPA, and the intelligence community. Kim Il-song immediately solidified his power base and affixed the onus of defeat on his rivals. The KPA and intelligence services initiated major reorganization and reconstruction programs. Last, the KPA military doctrine began a process of gradual Koreanization.

Kim Il-song's efforts to solidify his power base actually began in December 1952 with the failed coup d'état by Pak Hon-yong's Domestic Faction. Kim's efforts lasted through 1953, although Pak was not formerly tried and convicted until 1955. With the Domestic Faction dealt with, Kim turned his attention to the Yenan faction and, to a lesser degree, the Soviet faction. Because of the Kaspen faction's superior organizational positions he was able to purge many low-level officers and officials from both rival factions. This advantage over the Yenan faction could not be initially exploited fully, however, because of the popularity of some Yenanite leaders (especially within the military) and the presence of the CPV. This purge, nevertheless, gradually gained momentum, dramatically increased in late 1957, and peaked with the abortive 1958 coup d'état by Lt. Gen. Chang P'yong-san, a Yenanite.[59] After this purge and the withdrawal of the CPV later in 1958, the KPA and KWP were under the firm control of Kim Il-song and his Kaspen faction. By the Fourth Party Congress in September 1961, Kim had finally consolidated his power beyond dispute and had appointed his fellow partisans to almost all the important positions within the government and KWP.

Within the KPA a major reorganization and reconstruction program witnessed the demobilization of thousands of men and women from KPA service to enter into the economic development of the war-ravaged economy.[60] The program, which began in earnest in 1956, resulted in an overall reduction in KPA manpower strength, but not in combat capability. This paradox resulted from the streamlining of the command structure, consolidation and reequipment of combat units, and the return of the navy and air force personnel who were previously stationed, or training, in China and the Soviet Union.

By the end of 1957, the KPA had taken the first steps in reestablishing special warfare capabilities. It initiated a small amphibious training program and developed a limited capability to conduct amphibious operations and clandestine landings within the ROK. These activities could only be achieved by utilizing a small number of conventional Korean People's Navy amphibious warfare craft and approximately two thousand fishing craft, junks, and sampans. Personnel for these units may have been obtained from the deactivation of the GHQ-level 23rd Infantry Brigade in late 1957. It is believed that a few independent naval infantry units were established subordinate to the KPN during the late 1950s or early 1960s. During the early postwar years there was no evidence of any airborne training or capabilities, with the possible exception of routine pilot parachute instruction. Soviet-manufactured parachutes were the only items of airborne equipment known to have been available in the KPA, and these were in extremely short supply. By late 1957, this had changed and the KPA had reactivated the Paratroopers School at P'yongyang and had initiated small-scale training. Shortly afterward, the KPA established its first airborne reconnaissance battalions.[61]

The situation for intelligence and unconventional warfare units was somewhat confused, as competing CPV and DPRK military and intelligence commands remained actively engaged in operations against the ROK. The wide diversity of command headquarters was a by-product of the struggle for power within the government and the desire to maintain an intelligence-gathering capability within the ROK. During the years immediately following the armistice, attempts were made to reorganize operational units. As noted previously, with the purge of Pak Hon-yong in early 1953, the KWP Liaison Department's Military Section (then known as the 567th Army Unit) was disbanded in April or May of that year. Several months later, in the fall, the 992nd Army Unit was established, with new personnel to perform the functions of the 567th Army Unit. Then in late 1954 or early 1955, the unit code number was changed again, this time to the 869th Army Unit. These frequent changes in unit code numbers may have been the result of continued reorganizations of the unit or an attempt to confuse UNC intelligence agencies. During this turbulent period Maj. Gen. Cho In-ch'ol was the director of the Liaison Department. Along with these organizational changes within the Military

Section, it is believed that the few remaining guerrilla units operating within the ROK were gradually reorganized as party cells and reassigned a political subversion mission rather than a combat one. The Reconnaissance Bureau was greatly reduced in size as all non-KWP members were discharged or transferred, and the Fourth and Fifth Departments were disbanded. Immediately following the armistice agreement Maj. Gen. Pak Song-ch'ol was promoted to lieutenant general and appointed director of the Reconnaissance Bureau. Pak Song-ch'ol was a fellow veteran of the 88th Special Independent Sniper Brigade with Kim Il-song and during the war served as commander of the 15th Infantry Division. Pak was director of the Reconnaissance Bureau for approximately one year when in August 1954 he was appointed ambassador to Bulgaria. Although his tenure was short, it ensured that the bureau would remain an elite organization that followed in the tradition of the 88th.[62]

By the end of 1955 the DPRK's intelligence community had undergone further changes that eliminated many wartime components, reduced duplicate operations and capabilities, and more clearly delineated responsibilities. Although there was still some overlap of functions, the overall assessment was that the system was well planned and well coordinated. This basic organizational structure would remain essentially unchanged through the late 1960s. The intelligence community now consisted of the National Intelligence Committee, the Cabinet General Intelligence Bureau, KWP's Liaison Department, KPA's Reconnaissance Bureau, KPA's General Political Bureau, and the Social Security Bureau (formerly Social Security Department) of the Ministry of Internal Affairs.[63]

The National Intelligence Committee was chaired by Kim Il-song and was composed of what one defector called "professionals." It apparently was the overall policy-formulating body for all intelligence activities, which included unconventional warfare operations. It would establish overall intelligence objectives and delegate responsibilities to the intelligence community.

The Cabinet General Intelligence Bureau (also called the Secretariat's General Intelligence Bureau) was subordinate to the KWP's Central People's Committee. Chaired by Maj. Gen. Ch'oe In-dok, its primary members were Kim Il, Yi Chu-yon, Chong Il-yong, Kim Ch'ang-man, Pak Kum-ch'ol, and Pak Ch'ong-ae (almost all of whom were from the Kaspen faction). Additional members consisted of "professionals" and various administrators and directors. The Cabinet General Intelligence Bureau is believed to have been the central authority for coordinating and implementing the National Intelligence Committee's intelligence policy directives. The bureau exercised administrative control over all intelligence agencies, collected information from the other intelligence agencies, and disseminated finished intelligence products to all DPRK government agencies.[64]

The KWP's Liaison Department was concerned principally with political espionage and subversion of the ROK populace. It apparently exercised operational control over its own intelligence assets and those of the Social Security Bureau and the Reconnaissance Bureau. The department also conducted background investigations and assisted in training personnel for these intelligence units. It was organized into eight sections: Staff, Political and Indoctrination, Rear Services, Military, Guerrilla Guidance, Liaison, Technical, and Organization and Operations. The most important was the Military Section (the 869th Army Unit). Although the Guerrilla Guidance Section was still part of the Liaison Department, its organization and mission are unknown. With the exception of the Military Section, the Liaison Department was composed primarily of civilians. The Military Section was staffed by KPA personnel who were full members of the KWP. By 1955 the primary missions assigned to the Military Section were to train and escort agents into the ROK and assist agents already in the ROK by maintaining contact with the north. Secondary missions included maintaining a liaison with subversive elements in the ROK, establishing or reestablishing the KWP underground in the ROK, carrying orders to the ROK pertaining to the control of guerrilla and political operations, and

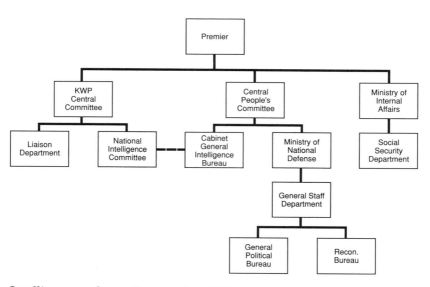

Intelligence and security agencies, 1955.

collecting political and social intelligence. The Military Section was orga-nized like the Reconnaissance Bureau, with a staff section and four liai-son offices (Kaesong, Western, Central, and Eastern) along the DMZ. These liaison offices each had approximately three subordinate indepen-dent direction units composed of military personnel who escorted agents to and from the ROK. The Kaesong Liaison Office had an additional three subordinate suboffices, reflecting the emphasis on activities in the west. Numerous agent units were deployed along the coast of North and South Hwanghae Provinces (i.e., the west coast). Because of the tremendous importance of nearby Seoul and the numerous advantageous routes to the south, most agents penetrated into the ROK from the this sector.[65]

The Reconnaissance Bureau (the 589th Army Unit) was responsible for military reconnaissance operations and espionage activities designed to secure military (and to a lesser degree, economic and political) intel-ligence concerning foreign military forces, particularly the ROK. It also provided military escorts for the intelligence units of the Liaison Depart-ment and the Ministry of Internal Affairs. This bureau was now orga-nized into just three departments. The specific organization and missions of the First and Second Departments are unknown, but are believed to be related to radio communications (e.g., monitoring UNC radio net-works, foreign broadcasts, and SIGINT). They also apparently provided guidance to tactical reconnaissance units of KPA infantry divisions and brigades, which now included an organic reconnaissance company. The DMZ police units may have evolved out of this cooperation. The Third Department, the 285th Army Unit, was responsible primarily for the selection and training of personnel assigned to escort detachments con-cerned with agent operations against the ROK. It consisted of a head-quarters and three regional, or "direction," offices located in the western (Kaesong), central, and eastern sectors of the DMZ. To handle the large amount of activity in the western section of the DMZ, the Kaesong office had two suboffices located at Kaesong and Yonan. The regional offices functioned as field headquarters, facilitating control of the numerous agent-escort detachments by the Reconnaissance Bureau or Third Department headquarters. The Third Department also maintained safe houses, where agents awaited infiltration, received training, were briefed or debriefed, and took cover while resting. The agent-escort field detach-ments, subordinate to the regional offices, were most probably the most important components of the Third Department. Most of these appear to have been concentrated between Kaesong and the west coast to take advantage of favorable routes into the ROK.[66]

The Social Security Bureau of the Ministry of Internal Affairs was responsible for a wide variety of internal security missions, including railroad security, counter-espionage, counterguerrilla operations, coastal and border security, and foreign espionage. Within the realm of its foreign espionage mission, the bureau conducted limited positive intelligence missions and maintained operatives in foreign countries primarily through its subordinate Foreign Security Bureau. The Foreign Security Bureau collected information and produced intelligence, conducted liaison with foreign embassies, monitored foreign broadcasts, and maintained wireless contacts with friendly intelligence agencies operating outside of Korea. It consisted of four sections: the south Korean and the Japan Sections, which gathered information and conducted subversive activities in the ROK and Japan; the Liaison Section, which maintained courier service with intelligence units and liaison with the Soviet, Chinese, Mongolian, Czechoslovakian, Bulgarian, and Rumanian embassies; and the Communications Section, which monitored all foreign broadcasts, maintained wireless contact with intelligence units outside the DPRK, and conducted SIGINT operations. By the mid-1950s the responsibilities for anti-ROK operations had been reorganized into two entities: the Anti– South Korea Operations Department and the Anti–South Korea Special Operations Unit. The latter unit evidently controlled its operations through its "Sinuiju Detachment," which had subelements in Peking (Beijing), Canton (Guangzhou), Hong Kong, and Japan. The Social Security Bureau employed high-level agents with special training and of unquestioned political reliability. The KPA frequently assigned personnel to the Social Security Bureau to assist with its agent activities.[67]

The Foreign Security Bureau apparently exercised control over the Chosen Soren (the pro-DPRK organization of Koreans residing in Japan). Sometime around 1960, Chosen Soren's central headquarters reportedly established covert counter–South Korea propaganda centers in the Japanese cities of Kobe and Tokyo. The primary mission of these centers was to smuggle revolutionary literature into the ROK and distribute it. In 1961, the security of these operations was compromised by Japanese security agencies, leading to the deactivation of these centers. Some of the personnel involved in these operations were subsequently trained in the DPRK and returned to Japan. Here they established individual intelligence networks known as "underground party operational bases in Japan," which were directly controlled by the DPRK (probably the Social Security Bureau). These networks probably continued to operate, unless compromised, throughout the 1960s.[68]

After the armistice agreement, infiltration of agents from all organizations into the ROK tended to be concentrated in the west, along the coast and through the Kaesong–Seoul corridor. It was also during this period that the Liaison Department, Reconnaissance Bureau, and Ministry of Internal Affairs established and operated several commercial trading companies to aid in the dispatch of agents, to carry information to and from the ROK, and to obtain funds to assist in the operation of their agencies. Although almost all these companies had headquarters within the DPRK, as time progressed, they would establish headquarters in Japan, Hong Kong, Macao, and a number of developing countries.[69]

The General Political Bureau, although institutionally subordinate to the General Staff Department, was directly controlled by the KWP's Military Affairs Committee. This shift in control was a relatively new development that grew out of the purges of the Yenan faction, when the General Political Bureau was deemed as having failed to control "reactionary elements" in the armed forces. The main functions of the General Political Bureau were to direct the political education, indoctrination, morale, and party activities of all service personnel, as well as conduct psychological warfare operations and propaganda activities against ROK/U.S. civilian and military personnel. The main subordinate bureaus included Organization, Statistics, Democratic Youth League, Propaganda and Instigation (agitation), and Enemy Affairs Guidance (psychological warfare). Under the guidance of the latter two bureaus, the General Political Bureau conducted limited special operations and maintained operatives in foreign countries.[70]

At the outset of the Fatherland Liberation War, KPA military doctrine was a subset of prenuclear Soviet military doctrine and heavily influenced by the principles of partisan warfare. The CPV's intervention in October 1950, plus the many Yenan faction supporters within the KPA, brought to prominence Chinese military doctrine and Mao's principles outlined in *Guerrilla Warfare* for the remainder of the war. The immediate postwar years witnessed the gradual Koreanization of these influences, accelerated by the withdrawal of the CPV in 1958 and the subsequent purging of the Yenan faction in the late 1950s. By this time, a Koreanized version of Soviet World War II doctrine, modified by KPA experiences during the war and containing a strong unconventional warfare element, had begun to emerge.

Kim Il-song had also begun to define the role of the KPA's emerging special operations forces. On 6 April 1958, he issued his "Instructions to Reconnaissance Troops" outlining the responsibilities of these elite troops:

(1) Reconnaissance troops must train under every type of weather and seasonal condition. They must undergo physical training night and day in the rugged mountain areas.

(2) Reconnaissance troops must constantly arm themselves with solid party ideology. Even when their lives are exposed to danger, they

must maintain solid ideology for the performance of their duties until the very end.

(3) Reconnaissance troops must respond to all physical training in order to strengthen their physical stamina.

(4) Reconnaissance troops must upgrade all levels of their duties to enable them to fight in the enemy's rearguard, and must promote themselves as operations officers.

(5) Reconnaissance troops must acquire the ability to bomb and destroy airfields, atomic guns, bridges, tunnels and locomotives.

(6) Reconnaissance troops must be able to operate airplanes, automobiles and trains.

(7) Reconnaissance troops must be able to operate ocean-going and river ships and boats, and be adept swimmers.[71]

It was also during the late 1950s that the DPRK embarked upon a concerted policy to develop international contacts with developing countries (e.g., Cuba, Indonesia, and Sri Lanka) and revolutionary groups (e.g., the Front de Liberation Nationale in Algeria). This involvement not only included financial assistance and the provision of weapons but included guerrilla warfare training within the DPRK. The training was apparently conducted by a number of KWP and KPA schools, under the joint guidance of the Reconnaissance Bureau, Social Security Bureau, and Liaison Department. Indicative of the importance attached to these new international relations was a 1961 statement by Kim Il-song: "We should continue our resolute struggle not only to consolidate our solidarity with international revolutionary forces, but also to isolate American imperialism and to crush its imperial policy. We should firmly unite with all the socialist countries, and at the same time we should support and solidify our unity with peoples of Asia, Africa and Latin America who are struggling to escape from the shackle of imperialism."[72]

The years 1958–61 were a time of tumultuous political change and vulnerability for the ROK. In mid-April 1960, massive rioting by university students over election irregularities forced the resignation of President Syngman Rhee's government on 26 April.[73] Rhee had been president since the founding of the ROK in 1948. His resignation was followed one year later in May 1961 by a coup d'état led by Gen. Park Chung Hee, which ousted Prime Minister Chang Myon's government. These events, and the DPRK's inability to effectively respond to them, would lead to significant changes within the DPRK and a reevaluation of anti-ROK operations.

Chapter 3

GUERRILLA WARFARE AGAINST THE ROK,
˙ 1962–68

The early 1960s were a time of heightened civil turmoil and vulnerability for the ROK. Large student uprisings forced the resignation of the Syngman Rhee government in April 1960, which in turn enabled the subsequent coup d'état by Gen. Park Chung Hee in May 1961. The DPRK's failure to effectively exploit these vulnerabilities resulted in a decision to both reorganize and modernize the KPA and to further reorganize the organizations involved in intelligence and anti-ROK operations.

RISE OF THE PARTISAN GENERALS

The first steps in this direction were taken during the Fourth Party Congress, held in September 1961. At this congress Kim Il-song successfully consolidated his power by securing the appointment of his fellow partisans to virtually all important positions within the government and the KWP. As most of these were active or retired generals they were collectively known as the "partisan generals." With this consolidation of power, the influence of the military become a dominant force in DPRK foreign policy.[1]

Within the KPA the partisan generals initiated a broad reorganization and modernization program. The goal was to move the KPA out of its prenuclear Soviet-styled organization and mold it into a modern fighting force (including the expansion of special operations capabilities) specially adapted to the Korean Peninsula and capable of quickly capturing the entire ROK. A major aspect of this program was the introduction of modern weapon systems during the next ten years, including T-54/55 tanks, FROG-3/5 battlefield support rockets, SA-2 surface-to-air missiles, MiG-21 fighters, Il-28 bombers, *Whiskey*-class submarines, and *Komar*- and *Osa I*-class fast attack craft.[2]

In response to the ineffective anti-ROK operations the partisan generals directed the purge of Pak Il-yong and Yim Hae, two of the few remaining Soviet faction members. More significantly, Pak and Yim had succeeded Maj. Gen. Cho In-ch'ol as directors of the Liaison Department. It was under their command that the unrest within the ROK had resulted in two changes of government with little foreknowledge or action by the Liaison Department. Yi Hyo-sun, a nonmilitary partisan, was appointed director of a new anti-ROK organization known as the South Korea General Bureau (also called the South Korean General Affairs Bureau, General Bureau of South Korean Affairs, Southern General Operations Bureau, Bureau of Overall Operations against the South, or General Liaison Bureau).[3] In this position Yi was responsible for coordinating all subversive and intelligence operations against the ROK and exercised direct control over the Liaison Department. At the same time, So Ch'ol was appointed director of the Liaison Department.[4] Under Yi and So's direction the Liaison Department was charged with establishing a revolutionary movement within the ROK. This mission was made extremely difficult by the virulent anti-Communist stance of the new Park government, the beginning of real economic growth in the ROK, and the strongly anti-Communist sentiment of the general population. Yi focused his primary attentions not on guerrilla warfare, but on political subversion and the establishment of a revolutionary movement. An additional obstacle he faced was that when Pak Hon-yong and his Domestic Faction were purged in 1953–55, the DPRK lost its corporate expertise on the ROK and the Communist movement within the south. Another complication was that many of Pak's former supporters within the ROK refused to cooperate with the KWP under Kim Il-song.

These events occurred against a background of deteriorating Soviet–DPRK relations and the heightened Cold War tensions between the Soviet Union and United States. By the Fifth Plenum of the Central Committee in December 1962, the Soviet Union had indicated that it would suspend military and economic assistance to the DPRK because of ideological differences. The Soviet stance was viewed as having "given in" to the United States rather than risk a military confrontation during the Cuban Missile Crisis. These changes in Soviet attitude toward the DPRK stunned the partisan generals, who now realized that despite its signing of the Treaty of Friendship and Cooperation in 1961, the Soviet Union might not come to the DPRK's assistance in case of renewed conflict on the Korean Peninsula. At the Fifth Plenum, Kim Il-song and the partisan generals responded to these developments. They reestablished the Central Military Committee under the KWP Central Committee to formulate overall military policy and direct the military forces, and they presented a new national security policy known as the "Four Great Military Lines." This policy has continued to influence DPRK national security policy until today. The Four Great Military Lines called for "the arming of the whole people, the fortification of the entire country, the training of all soldiers as a cadre force, and the modernization of arms."[5]

Two years later in February 1964, Kim Il-song explained the importance of strengthening the "three revolutionary forces" in order to bring about the reunification of the fatherland. These forces were the revolutionary force in the north, the revolutionary force in the south, and the international revolutionary force. Several events within the ROK the following year precipitated a more aggressive effort by the DPRK to strengthen "the revolutionary force of the south." The most significant of these events were the large-scale student demonstrations against the ROK government, the January ROK–U.S. agreement to dispatch ROKA combat troops to fight in Vietnam (they arrived in September 1965), and the June signing of the ROK–Japanese normalization treaty.[6] Beginning in July 1965, Yi Hyo-sun directed a substantial escalation of operations against the ROK. The number of infiltrators dispatched into the ROK increased dramatically, as did their aggressiveness. The underlying purpose of these operations was political subversion and creating the proper climate for establishing a revolutionary movement. Guerrilla warfare was not the present focus. It was believed that politically subversive operations, if carried out successfully, would draw the attention of the ROK government back to the Korean Peninsula and thus force the return of ROKA combat troops. If the DPRK could do so, it would achieve a major political victory for itself and receive credit for supporting the Viet Cong and People's Republic of Vietnam.[7] More significantly, Kim Il-song and the partisan generals also believed that such actions would fan the fires of revolution, which they believed were smoldering within the ROK, as demonstrated by the massive student demonstrations. The leaders in the DPRK hoped to avoid a repeat of their failure to capitalize on the student demonstrations in 1960–61. They hoped that this time, the fires of revolution would in turn lead directly to the collapse of the ROK government and the reunification of Korea, or to a call by "indigenous" people's revolutionaries for "assistance" from their brothers in the north. The KPA was honor bound to provide that assistance.

The suspension of Soviet military assistance from 1963 to 1965 had seriously impacted the KPA's modernization, expansion effort, and operational capabilities. Following the ouster of Khrushchev in 1964, relations with the Soviet Union improved, and negotiations for further assistance reopened. Military assistance resumed under agreements concluded in May 1965 and was expanded by further agreements in March 1967. The renewed influx of Soviet military assistance enabled the KPA to commence its delayed modernization program. Kim Il-song stressed the importance of this program at the second meeting of party delegates, held on 5 October 1966:

> We must strongly fortify the KPA with modern weapons and combat material. We must employ all means to modernize the weapons and make them more powerful based on the successes of ultra-modern science and technology. . . . In modernizing the KPA and developing military science and technology, we must fully consider the reality of our country with its numerous mountains and lengthy coastline. . . . We must develop and introduce military science and technology in accordance with the reality of our country and correctly incorporate old style weapons along with modern weapons.[8]

It is important to note Kim's emphasis on adapting technology and the modernization of the KPA to the realities of the Korean Peninsula, since this provided a major impetus to the development of the KPA's special warfare capabilities and units.

The dramatic change in the general level of active aggression against the ROK and United States was demonstrated on 28 April 1965, when two Korean People's Air Force (KPAF) MiG-17s attacked a USAF RB-47H from the 55th Strategic Reconnaissance Wing on a reconnaissance mission in international airspace. Although the RB-47 was damaged, there were no casualties.[9]

The two years from July 1965 through July 1967 witnessed a steady increase in the number of operations against the ROK. These subversive activities, while they did show a small measure of success (especially among college students), were simply not producing the results anticipated by the partisan generals. In fact, in many ways they were counterproductive as ROK/U.S. forces adapted new policies and measures that neutralized many of the successes, and as the ROK government increased its social welfare and anti-Communist programs in the rural areas of the country. The ROK/U.S. activities further limited the effectiveness of Yi's subversive efforts.

Although not immediately contributing to the DPRK's concerted efforts to infiltrate the ROK, the construction of infiltration tunnels under the DMZ was begun during this period (see appendix). These tunneling operations began slowly in the early 1960s and did not gain momentum until the late 1960s, with the ROK fortification of the DMZ. The engineer battalion of each infantry division deployed directly on the DMZ was assigned the task of digging two infiltration tunnels. For example, sometime during 1961–62 the engineer battalion of the 26th Infantry Division, then located in Yunan-gun, South Hwanghae Province, began construction on an infiltration tunnel by digging into the side of Yongkak Mountain. Technical and logistic assistance for these activities was provided by each army group's Engineer Department and the General Staff Department's Engineer and Rear Services Bureaus.[10]

REVOLUTION IN SOUTH KOREA

By the Fourteenth Plenum of the Fourth Central People's Committee of the KWP in October 1966, policy makers realized that the establishment of a realistic revolutionary movement within the ROK was not feasible under the current conditions and that such conditions could not be reasonably expected to occur unless a comprehensive policy based upon active guerrilla warfare was implemented.[11] In a speech given under a banner proclaiming "Revolution in south Korea," Kim Il-song announced the abandonment of the policy of seeking to unify Korea by peaceful means and the adoption of a new, more militant policy toward the ROK: "We must develop the revolutionary movement [in the ROK] at this time using a combination of methods involving all kinds of struggle, in correspondence to the objective and the subjective situation, political struggle and economic struggle, violent struggle and nonviolent struggle, and legal and illegal struggle."[12]

This speech would also form the basis for the KPA's new doctrines of "combined operations" and "two-front war," and emphasized the importance of guerrilla warfare and special operations. The combined operations doctrine called for the integration of guerrilla warfare operations with conventional KPA ground force operations. The two-front war doctrine called for the close coordination of conventional frontline operations with guerrilla and special operations deep within the ROK. The objective for both was to encircle and destroy the enemy on both the military and the political levels: "on this topic there are fundamental demands that require the establishment of regular warfare and guerrilla warfare as a two-part framework of fighting on the battlefield. . . . we are thoroughly opposed to the trend of guerrilla warfare being implemented carelessly so that a second strong battlefront cannot be formed . . . or the abandonment of powerful guerrilla activities that encircle and annihilate the enemy wherever he may be."[13]

The DPRK credited these new doctrines to a combination of Kim Il-song's military genius and the experiences of his guerrillas during the "anti-Japanese guerrilla struggle" of the 1930s. It would be more correct to assert, however, that the new doctrines were logically developed from the continued melding and Koreanization of conventional prenuclear Soviet military doctrine, "guerrilla warfare" and "partisan warfare" doctrines, and guerrilla warfare and special operations experienced during the Fatherland Liberation War.

By the Sixteenth Plenum of the Central Committee in July 1967, the DPRK was in a dramatically better position to take action against the ROK. It was now receiving substantial Soviet assistance, and dramatic improvements had begun within the KPA. The reorganization of intelligence and special warfare forces had now reached a point where they were considered capable of operations against the ROK. The partisan generals had lost patience with the limited results shown by Yi Hyo-sun's subversion operations and now decided to force the issue of revolution in the ROK in the manner they knew best, guerrilla warfare. Yi Hyo-sun and several other prominent officials, all nonmilitary partisans, were purged in an effort led by O Chin-u, a partisan and full Central Committee member.[14] Yi was specifically removed from his position as director of the South Korea General Bureau in July 1967 for his lack of success in establishing a revolutionary movement within the ROK. He was replaced by a partisan general, Ho Pong-hak. Ho quickly threw himself into his work, apparently wanting to demonstrate his capabilities and the correctness of the more aggressive strategy. Under his leadership, the Liaison Department and Reconnaissance Bureau would return to active guerrilla warfare and the Reconnaissance Bureau's special warfare capabilities would be expanded. Five months later in December, at the Fourth Supreme People's Assembly, Kim Il-song set the stage for what was to occur during the next two years:

> . . . the present situation requires us to conduct all our work in a more active, more revolutionary manner and subordinate everything to the struggle to accomplish the south Korean revolution by giving them support in their struggle and to reunify our country.[15]
>
> . . . In order to liberate the people of Korea and unify the Fatherland, the government of the republic will see to it that the people in the northern half are spiritually and physically well prepared to aid the south Korean people in a holy struggle to oppose America and save the nation and to actively usher in a great revolutionary upheaval.
>
> The people in the northern half of the republic must be well prepared ideologically to join the decisive struggle with the south Korean people in achieving the grand task of unifying the Fatherland if and when the struggle of the people in south Korea intensifies, the revolutionary situation becomes ripe, and our support is called for.[16]

Under the direction of Ho Pong-hak and the partisan generals, a dramatic change from political subversion to active guerrilla warfare occurred between July 1967 and July 1969. The changeover was designed to deliberately destabilize and precipitate the collapse of the

ROK government by direct confrontation, to drive a wedge between the ROK and the United States, to discourage foreign and domestic investment in the ROK, to weaken the general confidence in the ROK government, to actively establish and support a KWP within the ROK, and to create an environment favorable for a popular uprising in the ROK. These years have become known in the DPRK as the era of the upsurge-period tactics, or the era of two-front tactics for both war and peace. To conduct these operations the DPRK turned to a number of newly reorganized, or established, intelligence and special warfare units trained in guerrilla warfare, espionage, sabotage, terrorism, and subversion.

ORGANIZATIONAL DEVELOPMENTS, 1962–68

During the six years following the December 1962 Fifth Plenum of the Central Committee the DPRK conducted numerous dramatic organizational changes within its special warfare and intelligence assets.[17] Some of these were the natural continuation of efforts begun during the late 1950s. Other developments were, however, in direct response both to changing doctrines and to the decision to initiate a guerrilla war within the ROK. The intelligence community consisted of the National Intelligence Committee, KWP's South Korea General Bureau, KPA's Reconnaissance Bureau, and the Ministry of Public Security.

The Cabinet General Intelligence Bureau was dissolved and its functions and responsibilities were apparently assumed by the National Intelligence Committee and the South Korea General Bureau. Exactly how and why this occurred is unclear. The National Intelligence Committee remained as the primary national-level policy- and decision-making organ for intelligence and security matters. The South Korea General Bureau is believed to have been established in September 1961 to exercise overall responsibility for intelligence and subversive operations against the ROK. The Reconnaissance Bureau retained responsibility for military intelligence but received the expanded responsibilities for conducting special warfare and guerrilla operations. The General Political Bureau was refocused primarily upon political security within the KPA, although it retained its significant propaganda and psychological warfare responsibilities. Under the guise of these responsibilities, it conducted limited special operations against the ROK. In 1962 the Ministry of Internal Affairs was reorganized and the Ministry of Public Security was assigned many of the former organization's responsibilities for internal security and foreign espionage and subversive operations.

An integral component of the KPA reorganization and modernization program initiated during the early 1960s was the expansion of its special

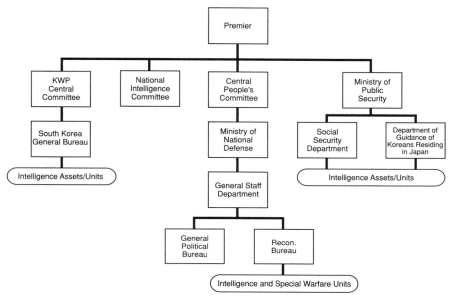

Intelligence and special warfare organizations, 1961–68.

warfare forces. These changes built upon the base of experiences established by their predecessors during the Fatherland Liberation War and in the late 1950s. The units that were established and the capabilities that were developed during this period provided a logical and significant step toward the development of the present-day special purpose forces. Although progress was initially slow, by 1965 notable advances were being achieved. These included the establishment of light infantry units, the reorganization and consolidation of amphibious units, and the establishment of dedicated airborne units. From an early stage, all airborne capabilities were apparently subordinate to the Reconnaissance Bureau (see below). By 1968 the KPA had established a significant special warfare capability equivalent to seven regiments/brigades (nine if the 124th Army Unit and foot reconnaissance stations are included).[18]

▪ SOUTH KOREA GENERAL BUREAU

In 1961–62 the KWP expanded and reorganized the Liaison Department. Out of these changes emerged the South Korea General Bureau, directly subordinate to the KWP's secretariat.[19] Although this new organization drew heavily upon the personnel and resources of the Liaison Department,

71

it brought together all KWP intelligence and active anti-ROK organizations under one central command. The South Korea General Bureau consisted of the Liaison Department, Culture Department, Intelligence Department, and Central Committee Political School. The mission of the bureau was the overall control of psychological warfare, espionage, and subversive operations against the ROK; the production of intelligence; and the guidance and coordination for the intelligence and unconventional warfare operations of the Ministry of National Defense and the Ministry of Public Security. The first person to head this powerful new bureau was Yi Hyo-sun.

■ ■ *Liaison Department*

The Liaison Department, which had been completely reorganized, retained its former responsibilities of recruiting, training, and dispatching intelligence and subversive agents to the ROK and Japan. It also took over several anti-ROK activities from the Ministry of Public Security (that is, from the Anti–South Korea Operations Department and Anti–South Korea Special Operations Unit) and possibly the General Political Bureau.

The department was now organized into at least seven sections: Headquarters, Organization (or Organization and Operations), Liaison, Communications (also called Technical), Personnel, Rear Services, and the South Korea Exhibition Hall. The former Guerrilla Guidance and Military Sections were disbanded, and the responsibilities for the support and infiltration of agents were incorporated into the Liaison Section. The former Liaison Offices were reorganized into a number of Sea Escort and Overland Escort Units. These escort units tended to complement the foot reconnaissance stations and sea escort unit of the Reconnaissance Bureau (see below), although there was some overlapping of responsibilities and jurisdiction. Liaison Department agents were usually trained in safe houses in groups of two or three by the instructors and agent handlers of the Organization Section. By the end of the 1960s approximately three hundred agents were annually trained and made available for operations by this section. Others agents were trained by the Central Committee Political School.

To insert and support its agents the Liaison Section not only employed its own sea escort and overland escort units, but also made use of the Reconnaissance Bureau's foot reconnaissance stations. By the late 1960s there were three sea escort and one or two overland escort units. The sea escort units included the 753rd Army Unit at Namp'o, the 755th Army Unit at Haeju, and the 632nd Army Unit at Wonsan. In addition to these, there was a similar sea escort unit subordinate to the Reconnaissance

Bureau, the 448th Army Unit (see below). Total sea escort personnel strength was estimated to be 2,500, of whom 900 men were escort agents and crewmen. The sea escort units operated a total inventory of approximately sixty-four vessels of two principal types to infiltrate the ROK. At least twenty were large, high-speed craft with a capacity of approximately 40 men, including the crew. Most of the remainder were slow, 20-foot motorized craft very similar to small ROK fishing boats. These small craft could pass undetected through the ROK fishing fleet and were thus used primarily for short, direct runs to deliver one to four agents or troops.

The specially built large, high-speed infiltration craft had the outward appearance of legitimate fishing trawlers to make their identification among a fishing fleet more difficult. They did, however, have certain distinctive characteristics. The craft were generally of about 50-ton displacement and were 18–21 meters long and 3.5–4.5 meters wide. This length-to-beam ratio distinguished the craft from the shorter, squatter fishing boats. Infiltration craft also had a low freeboard—approximately 1 meter—and a generally low profile, but a high bow. The hull design incorporated a distinctive splash rail below the bulwark to deflect water at high speeds. Without exception, the deckhouse was located aft, beginning approximately amidships, and featured a stepped-down after cabin. Although fishing gear was carried for deception purposes, infiltration craft presented a neat, trim appearance in contrast to the cluttered topsides of working trawlers. Another identifying clue was that seagulls were not attracted to infiltration craft as they were to trawlers. The predominant color of the infiltration craft was white, rather than the blue usually associated with civilian DPRK fishing boats. Although hull colors varied, the deckhouses of the infiltration craft were almost always white. While a few ROK fishing boats had radios or electronic navigational equipment, the infiltration craft mounted navigational radar and radios revealed by horizontal wire antennas rigged either between the single high mast forward and the mast aft, or between a forward mast and the deckhouse.

The infiltration craft were capable of speeds of 30–35 knots, whereas most fishing boats could only do 8–10 knots. At high speeds, the specially designed planing hull of the craft created a distinctive, wide rooster tail.

All infiltration craft were armed with a variety of weapons. A deck gun mount was usually positioned in the center of the bow section, another was positioned just aft the deckhouse, and sometimes there was a third one beside the deckhouse. The mounts, generally canvas covered, were easily readied for use. Typical armament aboard included one or two 12.7- or 14.5-millimeter heavy AA (antiaircraft) machine guns, a 45-millimeter antitank gun, three to four 7.62-millimeter light machine guns, five to ten

7.62-millimeter assault rifles, pistols for the crew and escort agents, and twenty to thirty hand grenades. Also frequently carried was an 82-millimeter B-10 recoilless antitank gun. Most weapons were carried below deck but were readily accessible and could be used very effectively against surface vessels, although not against fast-flying aircraft. A graphic example of the problems posed by these specialized heavily armed infiltration vessels occurred in mid-1969. On 13 June ROKN patrol boats intercepted and, after a six-hour-long battle, captured an even larger infiltration craft off the southeast coast of the ROK. It was a 75-ton vessel, powered by four engines, and with a maximum speed of approximately 35 knots. The vessel was disguised as a fishing ship and was armed with an 82-millimeter recoilless gun, four 40-millimeter guns, two 14.5-millimeter AA machine guns, three 12.7-millimeter heavy machine guns, two 7.62-millimeter machine guns, eight AK-47s, five pistols, and two RPG-2 grenade launchers. The ship also carried radar equipment.[20]

During 1968, as a result of the expanding overseas commitments in support of terrorist and revolutionary organizations, the Liaison Department established a Foreign Operations Section. This section was vested with the primary responsibilities of recruiting and training guerrillas in foreign countries and for screening guerrillas to be sent to the DPRK.[21] Although the Liaison Department was directly responsible for this section, the actual instructors appear to have been drawn primarily from the Reconnaissance Bureau, with the Ministry of Public Security performing a minor role. This system would eventually develop to the point where basic training was conducted overseas and advanced training within the DPRK. The foreign nationals sent to the DPRK were either first selected from the most promising of the overseas trainees or were processed at the request of a foreign country (e.g., the Soviet Union and Cuba).

■ ■ *Culture Department*

The Culture Department was responsible for conducting psychological warfare operations against the ROK. It was organized into eight sections: Peaceful Unification Propaganda, Publications, Publications Guidance, Reporters, Broadcast Guidance, Personnel, South Korea Research, and Chosen Soren Affairs. It published propaganda material and controlled the activities of the DPRK reporters dispatched to the Military Armistice Commission meetings. By publishing newspapers and controlling radio broadcasts, the department indoctrinated DPRK citizens on reunification and the situation in the ROK. The Culture Department also directed political and psychological activities toward Korean residents in Japan and analyzed the political, economic, social, cultural, and psychological situations in the ROK. Although the department was also responsible for some operations conducted by the Chosen Soren, overall control of the organization is believed to have rested with the Ministry of Public Security.

▪ ▪ *Intelligence Department*
The Intelligence Department was responsible for collecting and analyzing intelligence information concerning the ROK. In November 1966 Pang Hak-se was appointed the department's director.[22]

▪ ▪ *Central Committee Political School*
The Central Committee Political School (also called the Central Korean Workers' Party School, 695th Army Unit, and 695th Detachment) was apparently the successor to most of the responsibilities held by the Kumgang Political Institute.[23] During this period it underwent a dramatic expansion. The school was responsible for providing preliminary training to prospective agents, many of them former ROK citizens, who were to infiltrate the ROK and establish an underground KWP organization. Advanced and specialized, as well as mission specific, the training was conducted by elements of the Liaison Section. The school consisted of a unit headquarters and a system of training centers and safe houses, most of which were located near Sunan, north of P'yongyang. In addition to the Central Committee Political School it appears that two additional agent schools located in Ch'ongjin and Yangwon were established under the control of the South Korea General Bureau.[24] These were probably "branch schools," a collection of eight to sixteen safe houses located near one another.

▪ MINISTRY OF PUBLIC SECURITY
The Ministry of Public Security, which was responsible for a wide variety of intelligence, subversion, and internal security missions, also underwent organizational changes during this period.[25] Through its subordinate International Department (formerly the Foreign Security Bureau), it conducted limited positive intelligence operations in foreign countries. Apparently, the Anti–South Korea Operations Department and Anti–South Korea Special Operations Unit were disbanded and most of their anti-ROK responsibilities assigned to the Liaison Department and Reconnaissance Bureau. The Department of Guidance of Koreans Residing in Japan (Guidance Department) was responsible for all operations, including covert intelligence and subversion, concerning the Chosen Soren in Japan. The Chosen Soren is a legal, overt organization of pro-DPRK Koreans living in Japan. The Chosen Soren then had an estimated active membership of 80,000 and an additional 170,000, who were affiliated with its various front organizations. Operational responsibilities of the Guidance Department included Communist indoctrination,

training cadres, disseminating propaganda, supporting DPRK policies, smuggling, undermining Japan–ROK relations, insuring Chosen Soren's loyalty, and directing Japan-based anti-ROK agent operations.

- RECONNAISSANCE BUREAU
  Like other anti-ROK agencies, the Reconnaissance Bureau underwent significant reorganization and expansion during this period.[26] Although it maintained its traditional responsibility for the collection of military intelligence concerning the ROK and foreign military forces, this was now expanded to include the regular collection of economic and political intelligence on the ROK. Additionally, the bureau was assigned responsibilities for guerrilla warfare and special operations. Although the priority assigned to intelligence collection, guerrilla warfare, and special operations would vary from 1962 to 1968, depending on political priorities, the Reconnaissance Bureau itself would continue to expand in size, responsibilities, and capabilities. Subordinate operational units of the Reconnaissance Bureau during this period included three foot reconnaissance stations; the 448th Army Unit, which was a sea escort unit; the 17th Reconnaissance Brigade; the 38th Airborne Brigade; the 283rd Army Unit; and the 124th Army Unit. Additionally, there were six departments (Political, Intelligence, Special, Technical, Training/Plans, and DMZ Police); a Foreign Language College; and a Photography Staff Office.

- ■ *Foot Reconnaissance Stations and Sea Escort Unit*
  Among the many changes within the Reconnaissance Bureau during the 1960s was the reorganization of the Third Department into the Foot Operations Department. With this reorganization the three regional, or "direction," offices were reorganized into three foot reconnaissance stations. These were located and operated in direct support of the three army groups deployed along the DMZ. They were, however, under the operational control of the Reconnaissance Bureau. Their missions included conducting reconnaissance of ROK/U.S. positions along the DMZ; reporting on ROK/U.S. equipment, movements, and other activities; harassing and ambushing; and assisting agents infiltrating into the ROK. The foot reconnaissance stations were reorganized and expanded in 1968 to approximately nine thousand personnel.

  By the late 1960s, each foot reconnaissance station was organized similarly to the others, with a headquarters and three bases. Each base consisted of a small headquarters and ten reconnaissance companies. This organizational structure closely paralleled that of the 124th Army Unit.

  The foot reconnaissance stations normally utilized teams of three to five lightly armed and equipped troops who operated within the army groups' area of responsibility. Operations beyond this were assigned to the 124th Army Unit or South Korea General Bureau. The following incidents are typical of the operations conducted by the foot reconnaissance stations during this period.[27]

On 22 May 1967 two U.S. Quonset barracks were destroyed by satchel charges. Two soldiers were killed, and nineteen were wounded. The incident was the work of at least four demolition experts. Selecting a well-covered avenue of approach, they chose the barracks housing the most troops. They completed the operation without alerting any of the nine manned guard positions, and escaped.

On 28 August 1967 a force of nine or ten men attacked elements of the 76th Engineer Battalion compound located approximately 700 meters south of the DMZ and adjacent to the advance camp of the UNC component of the Military Armistice Commission. The attackers fired approximately three thousand rounds of automatic weapons fire from a ridge line 400 meters from the compound. Three personnel were killed and twenty-one wounded; three Korean civilians were also wounded. A quick ROK/U.S. reaction force deployed to the area received hostile fire. A second force was dispatched in armored personnel carriers, one of which hit an enemy mine, wounding two soldiers.

On 14 April 1968 a ³/₄-ton truck carrying four U.S. personnel and two KATUSA (Korean Augmentation to the U.S. Army) was ambushed en route from the advance camp to the Joint Security Area at Panmunjom. Of the six soldiers, four were killed and two were wounded. This coincided with a meeting in Hawaii between President Lyndon B. Johnson of the United States and President Park Chung Hee of the ROK.

Two ROK trains were derailed by explosive charges, probably TNT, a short distance below the DMZ, on 5 and 13 September 1967. These were the first such attacks on trains since 1953.[28]

The 448th Army Unit, located in Wonsan, was the only Reconnaissance Bureau sea escort unit positively identified during this period. It would seem reasonable, however, that subunits or other sea escort units existed on the west coast, most probably at Chinnamp'o or Haeju. The 448th was apparently organized from the Third Department agent-escort field detachments that had utilized small boats and fishing vessels for covert infiltration along the ROK coastline. The unit possibly had three subordinate boat teams. Like the sea escort units of the Liaison Department, the 448th was also equipped with the specialized agent infiltration crafts previously described. Unlike the Liaison Department, the 448th appears to have had operational control over, or have operated, a few midget submarines and swimmer delivery vehicles in the KPN's inventory. It may also have conducted operations using the KPN's two *Whiskey*-class submarines.

On 5 July 1965, ROK security forces located and captured a midget submarine that had been abandoned by its crew after becoming grounded on a mudflat during a receding tide at the confluence of the Imjin and Han Rivers. This three-man, 3-ton, 5.7-meter-long midget submarine was of crude construction and is believed to have been a one-of-a-kind vessel. The submarine may have belonged to the 448th Army Unit. After this submarine's failure, the KPN apparently came to realize that its indigenous design and production capabilities were inadequate for midget submarine development, and the KPN decided to purchase a Yugoslav midget submarine. The KPN acquired the submarine in the late 1960s via a covert operation that funneled the sale through Singapore, using falsified end-user certificates. The vessel was utilized as a pattern upon which the KPN began production, at the Yukdaeso-ri shipyard on the west coast, of the 20-meter *Yugo*-class midget submarine. Construction would continue from the late 1960s until the early 1980s. The *Yugo* had a crew of two and could carry four to six swimmers. Since the vessels had insufficient range to reach most of the ROK, they had to be launched and supported by "mother" ships.[29]

▪ ▪ *17th Reconnaissance Brigade*
It is believed that along with the reorganization of the Reconnaissance Bureau's Third Department into foot reconnaissance stations in the early 1960s, a new unit was established: the 17th Reconnaissance Brigade (17th Foot Reconnaissance Brigade). The brigade may have held the honorific title of "sniper" brigade at this time, but this is uncertain. The personnel for the unit were obtained from the former Third Department; the consolidation of a variety of Reconnaissance Bureau assets, which had been previously attached to the army groups deployed along the DMZ and their subordinate divisions; and the KPA's first airborne reconnaissance battalion (see below). The mission of the 17th Reconnaissance Brigade was to engage in guerrilla warfare in the ROK during wartime. Consequently, the brigade probably was not actively engaged in anti-ROK operations during this period. It did, however, supply personnel to both the 124th Army Unit and foot reconnaissance stations.

The 17th Reconnaissance Brigade consisted of approximately 9,300 troops and was organized into a headquarters; five reconnaissance battalions; and security, engineer, communications, and instrument reconnaissance companies. The reconnaissance battalion is believed to have been the primary tactical unit and was apparently capable of independent operations. Each reconnaissance battalion consisted of approximately 1,720 troops and was organized into headquarters (45 men); reconnaissance command company (71 men); five reconnaissance companies

(301 men each); and a reconnaissance heavy weapons company (99 men).[30] All elements, with the exception of the reconnaissance heavy weapons company, were equipped with light infantry weapons, including pistols, assault rifles, light machine guns, and antitank launchers. The reconnaissance heavy weapons company was equipped with 82-millimeter mortars. Communications and transportation equipment was available at levels beyond typical KPA infantry standards. Elements of the brigade were air mobile or parachute qualified or both. The brigade reportedly had enough parachutes to equip 500–600 troops, but was dependent upon the KPAF for airlift .

The estimated personnel strength of the 17th Reconnaissance Brigade was unclear, with estimates as high as 9,300, and as low as 4,000–5,000. The uncertainty stemmed from several factors: the actual organization of the 17th fluctuated significantly over time; the 38th Airborne Brigade was apparently established utilizing elements of the 17th; and during the late-1960s the 17th was apparently expanded and eventually used to form additional reconnaissance units.

▪ ▪ *38th Airborne Brigade*

Although the Paratroopers' School was reactivated in P'yongyang as early as 1958, available information suggests that it was not until the early 1960s that paratrooper training began in earnest. By 1962 the KPA had established at least one airborne reconnaissance battalion (approximately three hundred men) subordinate to the Reconnaissance Bureau and was regularly conducting small airborne training exercises. Either this battalion was reorganized into the 17th Reconnaissance Brigade, or personnel from it were incorporated into the 17th. Sometime around 1966, the KPA established its first brigade-sized airborne unit, the 38th Airborne Brigade. The cadre of personnel for this new unit was apparently drawn from the 17th Reconnaissance Brigade, and like the 17th, it was subordinate to the Reconnaissance Bureau.

By 1968 at least two airborne units had reportedly been established. One was the 38th Airborne Brigade, but the size and identity of the second is unclear. The second may have been a new unit formed with personnel drawn from both the 38th and 17th Brigades, or simply confusion over the status of the 17th Reconnaissance Brigade since elements of the brigade were air mobile and/or parachute qualified.

The organization and strength of the 38th Airborne Brigade during this period are unclear. By the late 1960s the brigade would consist of a headquarters, twelve airborne battalions of 500 troops each, a signal company, and small combat (guard platoon) and service support (medical and rear services) assets. Total troop strength was approximately 6,700.

KPAF airlift capability at this time was extremely limited (table 3-1). For example, in 1965, KPAF airlift capabilities were consolidated into a single transport battalion, headquartered at T'aech'on, which was directly subordinate to KPAF Command Headquarters. The battalion's estimated strength was twenty-six aircraft, including six Antonov An-2 Colts, eight Lisunov Li-2 Cab transports, and twelve Mi-4 Hound helicopters. This small unit had an estimated total lift capability of about 356 troops, or approximately one airborne battalion. This severely limited any significant offensive airborne capabilities. Another limiting factor was that the primary mission of these aircraft was governmental support and VIP transport.[31]

The KPAF understood the limitations of its airlift capability and sought to address it by purchasing light transports (An-2, Li-2, etc.) from Poland, the People's Republic of China, and the Soviet Union. For example, from 1965 to 1968, the KPAF received approximately fifty-five Y-5s (Harbin An-2 Colts) from China. These efforts slowly increased the KPA's ability to employ its airborne brigades.

■ ■ *283rd Army Unit and 124th Army Unit*
During the mid-1960s (possibly 1965) the Reconnaissance Bureau established the 283rd Army Unit to train and possibly dispatch personnel for clandestine and subversive operations within the ROK. The initial personnel for this new unit were drawn from the bureau's own foot reconnaissance stations. The lack of success encountered during these operations and those of the South Korea General Bureau were critical reasons for the subsequent purge of Yi Hyo-sun in July 1967. Even prior to this the KPA leadership had decided to redirect the Reconnaissance Bureau to active guerrilla warfare against the ROK. As a result of this new, more aggressive mission, the 283rd Army Unit was disbanded in early 1967 (March or April). The agent training bases and personnel of the 283rd were reorganized and redesignated as the 124th Army Unit.[32] The numerical designation 283rd Army Unit was then assigned to either the Reconnaissance Bureau itself or the element within the bureau responsible for the overall training and dispatch of unconventional warfare forces.

The 124th Army Unit was established in April 1967 with the intention that it would be the "main force" for reunification in the 1970s.[33] Its mission was to plan, train for, and conduct unconventional warfare operations against the ROK. Kim Shin-jo, a captured member of the 124th, stated that his unit was charged with infiltrating "deep within the enemy's rear to conduct reconnaissance, espionage, subversion, and sabotage, and to organize local sympathizers into an irregular fighting force."[34] Such operations were designed to lend credence to P'yongyang's

Table 3-1

KPAF AIRLIFT CAPABILITY, LATE 1960s

Aircraft	Est. Number	Est. Capacity (Troops)	Total Lift Capacity (Troops)
An-2 Colt	6	8	48
Li-2 Cab	8	16	128
Mi-4 Hound	12	15	180
Total	26		356

propaganda claim that the "people's revolution" was alive within the ROK and to create a revolutionary atmosphere. It was an elite unit in every sense of the word. Its cadre of personnel was drawn from the 283rd Army Unit, foot reconnaissance stations, and 17th Reconnaissance Brigade. It received specialized training and equipment for unconventional warfare. The following year, the 124th Army Unit underwent a significant expansion. By April 1968, it had been reorganized into a headquarters (with Staff, Political, Political Safety Training, and Rear Services Sections), five operational agent training bases, and a sixth base believed to be a replacement training center. Each operational base (believed to be identified as the First Base, Second Base, and so on) consisted of a headquarters and ten companies of approximately one hundred men each, for a total of five thousand troops. This organizational structure closely paralleled that of the foot reconnaissance stations.

Although the organizational life of the 124th Army Unit would be relatively short, it was dramatic. In 1968 it launched two high-impact operations: the abortive raid on the Blue House in January, and the landing of some two hundred heavily armed agents on the east coast of the ROK between October and December.

▪ ▪ *DMZ Police Companies*

The DMZ police companies are believed to have evolved out of the postwar operations of the Reconnaissance Bureau in support of the reconnaissance elements of KPA divisions deployed along the DMZ. By the early 1960s each division deployed along the DMZ had four to nine DMZ police companies to serve as the forward security element in lieu of the reconnaissance company normally found in a KPA infantry division headquarters. It is important to note that these were not traditional military-police-type units, but rather an elite melding of border guard and reconnaissance/commando-type units. Half of the DMZ police companies were on duty while the other half were in reserve. These companies rotated periodically, every two to six months. Although these companies operated under the supervision of the divisional reconnaissance section they are believed to have been trained and controlled by the Reconnaissance Bureau (possibly through the foot reconnaissance stations). Personnel for these units were probably drawn from the foot reconnaissance stations. If hostilities were resumed, DMZ police units would probably be absorbed into the Reconnaissance Bureau or serve as divisional reconnaissance units. Because of their familiarity with the terrain along the DMZ, personnel from these companies are believed to have sometimes acted as escorts for infiltrators from the Reconnaissance Bureau or Liaison Department.[35]

▪ ▪ *Foreign Language College*

The Reconnaissance Bureau is known to have had an element responsible for language training since the 1950s. By the early 1960s this element had developed into the Foreign Language College (also known as Foreign Language School, Foreign Language University, Am-Nok-kang College, or Amnok-gang [Yalu River] College).[36] This college, located in P'yongyang, was primarily responsible for training Reconnaissance Bureau and KPA personnel who were to be assigned to foreign operations. These personnel could be either an acknowledged member of the MND mission in the host country (e.g., military attachés and advisers) or those engaged in covert operations. A few students were not members of the MND and were assumed to be from the South Korea General Bureau or Ministry of Public Security. The majority of the instructor and administrative positions were filled by former members of other sections of the Reconnaissance Bureau.

Before 1964, Russian was the only category-one foreign language. English, Japanese, Chinese, and German were category-two languages. When active guerrilla operations began against the ROK, English and Japanese were elevated to category-one languages. This policy development led to the expansion of the Foreign Language College.[37]

Interestingly, at least three, and maybe as many as eleven, instructors in the English Department were U.S. defectors or POWs from the Fatherland Liberation War. These instructors concentrated on teaching the proper pronunciation of English and also doing a small amount of translation of English-language materials.[38]

■ KPA SPECIAL WARFARE UNITS

■ ■ *Light Infantry Units*

Between 1965 and 1968, the KPA began activating a new class of infantry units, the light infantry regiment.[39] To facilitate the establishment of these units, a single infantry regiment from the reserve division of each army group was selected and reorganized.[40] The regiment then received training and equipment for its new special and guerrilla warfare missions. The regiment consisted of approximately 1,300–1,800 troops and was organized into a small headquarters staff, a signal company, and three or four light infantry battalions. The units received minimal organic service support and no combat support assets. Each light infantry battalion consisted of approximately 300–450 troops and was organized into three companies.

The light infantry regiments were organized from their inception as special warfare units. They were responsible for conducting guerrilla warfare and special operations within the army group's area of responsibility. The concept for these units was to operate in much the same manner as had the 766th Independent Unit and divisional guerrilla units during the Fatherland Liberation War.

■ ■ *Amphibious Forces*

Throughout the late 1950s and early 1960s the KPA had only a limited amphibious warfare capability. Available craft were limited to fishing boats, junks, sampans, and a few conventional amphibious warfare craft. Changing doctrine and the increased activities against the ROK during the mid-1960s, however, necessitated that the KPA establish a viable amphibious warfare capability. This was accomplished by the acquisition of conventional amphibious warfare craft, the indigenous production of small, mechanized landing craft (LCM), and the gradual expansion of the few naval infantry units subordinate to the KPN.

BLUE HOUSE RAID, JANUARY 1968, AND OTHER OPERATIONS IN EARLY 1968

Several events in early 1968 demonstrated the intricacy of operations and the determination of DPRK special forces.[41] On 5 January 1968, in the city of Sariwon, a thirty-one-man assault team of the 124th Army Unit commenced final pre-mission training for a secret operation. Eight days later, the group was transported to the Sixth Base of the 124th Army Unit, near Yonsan. Here the members, all of whom were in their twenties, were briefed on their specific mission by Lt. Gen. Kim Chung-tae.[42] The mission was to assassinate ROK President Park Chung Hee at the presidential residence—the "Blue House"—in Seoul. More specifically, Lieutenant General Kim said, "Your mission is to go to Seoul and cut off the head of Park Chung Hee. You are to kill any others you find in the residence. . . ."[43] It was believed that the death of President Park would result in the outbreak of civil unrest, thus opening the way for "revolution in the south," the intervention of the KPA, and the reunification of the Korean Peninsula. On 17 January, the unit was transported to Kaesong (11 kilometers north of the DMZ), where its members received a final briefing by the commander of the 124th Army Unit, Col. Lee Jae-hyung. After supper, the unit was taken by bus to checkpoint 17 on the DMZ, where they changed into the ROK uniforms of the 26th Infantry Division and were armed with PPS-43 sub-machine-guns and hand grenades. Over their uniforms, they wore dark overalls. The group was met by two scouts (probably from foot reconnaissance stations or local DMZ police), who led them through the DMZ and returned.

The group moved through the U.S. 2nd Infantry Division sector that evening. During the daylight hours of 18 January, the group slept in an isolated wooded area. That evening they continued south past the 2nd Infantry Division headquarters at Camp Howze, camping on a forested mountain only a few kilometers away. At approximately 1500 hours on the nineteenth, the group was accidentally discovered by four local woodcutters, who were taken hostage. The woodcutters were detained for about 5 hours while the infiltrators displayed Communist propaganda material, praised Kim Il-song, and boasted that Korea would be reunified in 1968. They described themselves to the woodcutters as being part of a five-thousand-man KWP organization operating in the Kangwon-do and Kyonggi-do Provinces, the provinces bordering the DMZ.[44] They asked for details on the local military and police checkpoints and about the woodcutters' personal backgrounds and living conditions. Before releasing the woodcutters, the infiltrators threatened retaliation against their families and villages if they reported the encounter to ROK authorities. One of the woodcutters was given an inexpensive Japanese wristwatch to compensate for the loss of a day's work. The woodcutters, however, went directly to the ROK police, who contacted the ROKA and initiated counterguerrilla procedures.

In the meantime the group continued its movement south toward Seoul, using mountainous terrain whenever possible for its route to avoid detection. The infiltrators proceeded to an area approximately 5 kilometers north of Seoul, where they established a camp. On 21 January the infiltrators removed their overalls, cached all their supplies and equipment, except for sub-machine-guns and hand grenades, and proceeded in smaller groups to a rendezvous point 1.5 kilometers from the Blue House.

Posing as an ROKA counterintelligence unit returning from a mission, the reunited group brazenly marched in column formation toward the Blue House. At approximately 2200 hours that same day, the infiltrators were challenged by a member of the National Police. The policeman asked the lead soldier in the column for identification. The trooper replied they were an ROKA counterintelligence unit and continued on. The policeman became suspicious and waited until the last soldier passed his position, then attempted to grab him to check his identification. A firefight resulted in which two ROK civilians were killed and one ROKA soldier and three National Police members were wounded. During the fighting one infiltrator threw hand grenades at two ROK civilian buses. Throughout that night and all the following day, the infiltrators battled with the ROKA and National Police personnel. Some of the firefights occurred within 800 meters of the Blue House. During the initial stages of the activity, four commandos were killed and two captured, one of whom committed suicide by detonating a concealed hand grenade.[45]

Acting on information furnished by the second captured infiltrator, ROKA and National Police personnel searched and blocked the planned escape routes north of Seoul. During these operations, twenty-seven additional members of the assault team were killed or died of wounds and exposure. The remaining two were missing and presumed dead. Later, however, information obtained from other captured DPRK agents indicates that the remaining two commandos successfully returned to the DPRK. Of the ROK personnel involved in this incident, twenty-seven were killed and sixty-five wounded. Throughout this episode P'yongyang radio broadcasts reported that the "south Korean people had valiantly risen in their heroic struggle against the government."[46]

Concurrent with the Blue House raid, on 23 January, four KPN P-4 torpedo boats, aided by two KPAF MiG aircraft, attacked the USS *Pueblo* (AGER 2). They boarded the vessel and then towed her from the international waters of the Sea of Japan to the DPRK port of Wonsan. The *Pueblo,* an unarmed U.S. Navy SIGINT (signals intelligence) ship, had left Yokosuka, Japan, for her first operational mission on 5 January 1968. The mission was to sample the electronic environment off the east coast of the DPRK and to conduct surveillance of Soviet naval units operating in the Sea of Japan and Tsushima Straits. This mission became especially critical, given the unexpected Blue House raid and the possibility of either an ROK retaliation raid or an escalation of hostilities by the DPRK.[47]

Five months later, on 8 June, a small guerrilla unit consisting of approximately sixteen men believed to be from the 124th Army Unit, infiltrated into Songnae-dong, Ch'orwon-kun, in Kangwon-do Province, located in the central part of the ROK adjacent to the DMZ. The unit was quickly identified and neutralized by ROK counterguerrilla forces.[48]

MISSIONS ON THE EAST COAST, OCTOBER–DECEMBER 1968

Four months later, operations would once again intensify when the 124th Army Unit conducted the largest single infiltration operation since the Fatherland Liberation War.[49] Between 30 October and 2 November, on three distinct occasions, a total of 120 troops organized into eight operational teams were landed along the eastern coast of the ROK in the areas of Samch'ok and Ulchin. These fifteen-man operational teams were equipped with PPS-43 sub-machine-guns, hand grenades, radio receivers/transmitters, bona fide and counterfeit ROK currency (approximately three hundred thousand won per team), and propaganda literature. They were clothed in a variety of military uniforms, fatigues, and civilian apparel. Their mission was to infiltrate preselected isolated ROK villages and subvert the rural populace, revolutionize the people, establish a military intelligence network, and then return north across the DMZ.

Sometime prior to 30 October 1968, two subunits from the 124th were assembled at Wonsan harbor, on the east coast. Late that afternoon, one unit embarked in small coastal craft and proceeded south. After midnight, this unit conducted a landing at Kop'o beach, Puk-myon, in the Samch'ok–Ulchin area (virtually the same landing sites used by the 766th Independent Regiment during the Fatherland Liberation War). The unit quickly proceeded inland into the rugged T'aebaek Mountains and at 0610 hours on the thirty-first, reached the village of Chuin-ri. On the evening of 2 November, the second unit conducted a similar landing in the same general location and moved inland to the area of Sokhwai-ri. It should be noted that not only were these villages in remote and mountainous regions of T'aebaek-san, they were also the same areas in which KWP guerrillas operated during the Fatherland Liberation War and in which the local villagers had displayed some initial sympathy toward the guerrillas. In fact, the activities of the 124th Army Unit seem to have been focused on similar regions throughout the ROK (e.g., the mountainous area north of T'aebaek-san along the DMZ, the mountainous area between T'aebaek-san and the eastern seacoast of Kangwon-do Province, and the mountainous Chiri-san region).

Once in the villages the teams conducted political indoctrination and attempted to recruit followers by bribery and threats. Terror tactics included public execution of so-called traitors or reactionaries. In this operation, the infiltrators killed twenty-three ROK citizens with the double intention of creating fear and deterring the villagers from reporting

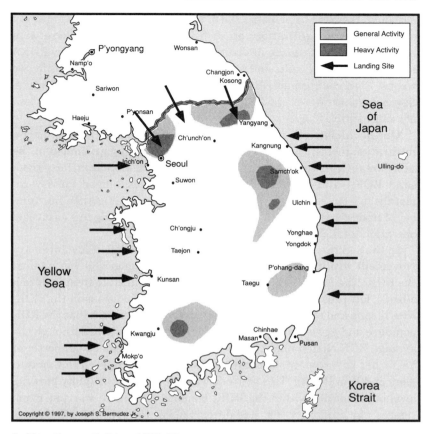

Legend:
- General Activity
- Heavy Activity
- ← Landing Site

Sea of Japan

Yellow Sea

Korea Strait

Copyright © 1997, by Joseph S. Bermudez Jr.

Infiltration activities, 1965–68.

their presence to ROK security forces. Villagers were forced to assemble for indoctrination and recruitment speeches. Communist banners were displayed, and villagers were coerced into filling out application forms for membership both in the KWP and in other Communist organizations. The infiltrators also distributed large amounts of real and counterfeit ROK currency. Contrary to what the members of the 124th Army Unit had been led to believe, the ROK civilians did not receive them as liberators. In fact, while not being outwardly hostile, the civilians were quite cool to DPRK propaganda efforts and quickly informed the ROK authorities. Aside from this propaganda activity, the 124th made a concerted effort to kill any ROK government officials, including postmen, whom they encountered.

Although they had been instructed to attack police stations and military outposts during exfiltration, no such incidents occurred. There were numerous firefights as the infiltrators sought to evade pursuit by ROKA and National Police units and to exfiltrate through the DMZ. Within two weeks, ROK counterguerrilla units had killed most of the infiltrators. Seven members were captured, despite orders to kill themselves instead of being captured alive, and 107 were killed.

One month later, during the period from 30 November to 2 December, infiltration teams from the 124th Army Unit were again landed in the same area. These too were eventually neutralized. More than forty thousand ROKA and National Police troops were mobilized for several months to isolate and neutralize all the infiltrators. Altogether, the number of troops that the 124th Army Unit dispatched during this east coast operation totaled nearly two hundred men.

In the end the DPRK failed in its efforts to establish a revolutionary movement within the ROK and then later in its guerrilla war against the ROK. The failure was not due to any lack of effort. It stemmed from a basic, but profound, misunderstanding of the conditions in the ROK. Kim Il-song and the partisan generals incorrectly believed that the ROK populace and government were ripe for active revolution. Although the average ROK citizen might not have been a wholehearted supporter of his or her government, the majority were totally opposed to Communism and Kim Il-song. This attitude was a result of the rapidly growing level of prosperity within the ROK, memories of brutal wartime experiences, the animosity that had developed between rural ROK citizens and the KWP guerrillas, and extremely broad and effective anti-Communist and counterguerrilla campaigns by the ROK government. The magnitude of this profound misunderstanding rivaled that of Pak Hon-yong's belief prior to the Fatherland Liberation War that two hundred thousand Communist sympathizers would rise up in revolt when the KPA attacked.

SOLIDARITY WITH THE PEOPLE OF ASIA, AFRICA, AND LATIN AMERICA

In October 1965, Kim Il-song reaffirmed his 1961 statement that the DPRK's struggle was not only one against the ROK and the United States but against imperialism anywhere in the world: "The Korean Workers' Party and the Korean people will make every effort to strengthen their solidarity with the peoples of Asia, Africa and Latin America in the future as in the past and will positively support their struggle against colonialism and imperialism."

It was during this period that the DPRK made continued progress in the development of contacts with developing countries and expanded its support for international terrorist and revolutionary organizations.[50] Most notable was the DPRK's involvement with the Front de Liberation Nationale in Algeria, the People's Liberation Front in Sri Lanka, the Sarawak Communist Organization in Indonesia, and the support for Palestinian (e.g., PLO and PFLP) and numerous African revolutionary groups. The training and support of foreign terrorists and revolutionaries, which up to this point apparently was handled ad hoc by several organizations, was reorganized in 1966. Training within the DPRK was placed directly under the control of the Reconnaissance Bureau, and training in foreign countries under the control of the Liaison Department and the International Department. To supervise the training within the DPRK and to meet the increasing demands of its own anti-ROK operations, the 695th Army Unit was expanded. This expansion was soon complemented by the establishment of two additional schools and several training bases. The number of foreign nationals who passed through these schools in the late 1960s is believed to have been approximately one or two thousand. Although this internal training was under the direct control of the Reconnaissance Bureau, the Liaison Department and the International Department also played significant roles.

Chapter 4

THE VIII SPECIAL CORPS, 1969–89

With the dramatic failures of the 124th Army Unit's operations on the east coast, Kim Il-song realized that the efforts to initiate active guerrilla warfare within the ROK were an abysmal failure. The ROK had responded vigorously to the threat by expanding its military and internal security forces to the point that the unification of the Korean Peninsula could now only be achieved by a renewed war, or a prolonged, covert, subversive effort. This realization led to the purging of the partisan generals, the reorganization of the special warfare and intelligence assets, and the reformulation of policy. Rather than guerrilla warfare, political subversion, with selected use of military special operations, now became the policy to be pursued against the ROK. This would be complemented by a dramatic increase in support for "international revolution" and the struggle against imperialism (i.e., revolution and terrorism) as an indirect means of striking at both the ROK and the United States.

These actions were accompanied by a further development in doctrine. The catalyst for this doctrinal development was a speech given by Kim Il-song at the Fourth Plenary Meeting of the Fourth KPA Party Committee in January 1969. Here Kim emphasized the "study of combining regular and irregular warfare, and of mountain warfare." He indicated that this would be a unique strategic approach based upon "light infantry units," which had the capability of conducting "all forms of combat." This was a pivotal point in the development of the KPA's special warfare forces. Up to this time special warfare units had guerrilla warfare as their primary mission above almost all other aspects. Now, however, these units would be responsible for a broader, more balanced range of unconventional and special warfare operations. Guerrilla warfare would no longer be emphasized to the detriment of other capabilities. Within the non-military anti-ROK organizations, prolonged political subversion and intelligence collection became the primary missions.

PURGE OF THE PARTISAN GENERALS

Despite the repeated failures in anti-ROK operations in 1965–68, the prominence of the partisan generals had continued to rise and had reached the point at which they had even begun to involve themselves in nonmilitary affairs. Kim Il-song, however, viewed the partisan generals with increasing concern. They had failed to undermine the ROK and almost brought the country into a war with the United States, a war that the DPRK was unprepared to fight. Kim undoubtedly also felt threatened by the growing popularity and power of his fellow partisans. At the end of 1968 he responded to this potential threat and purged the partisan generals.[1]

Although it is unclear exactly when this purge began, two dates stand out. The first was 11–16 November 1968 at the Eighteenth Plenum of the Central Committee. The second was 6–16 January 1969 at the Fourth Plenary Meeting of the Fourth KPA Party Committee. Apparently, the purge first began in late November 1968 in the midst of the embarrassing failure of the 124th Army Unit's operations on the east coast, peaked during the January 1969 meeting, and had run its full course by mid-1969.

Kim dispassionately pursued the purge with the critical assistance of O Chin-u, who had remained personally loyal to Kim since the days of the 88th Special Independent Sniper Brigade. It should also be remembered that just prior to the Fatherland Liberation War, O Chin-u was appointed director of the Hoeryong Cadres School (replacing the Kangdong Political Institute), which had trained selected KPA troops like the 766th Independent Unit in special reconnaissance and partisan warfare tactics.

This purge, however, was conducted in a relatively low-key manner with little of the public fanfare that accompanied previous purges. The reasons for this were twofold. First, Kim had spent the past ten years building up the partisan myth of which he was a critical player. Attacking the partisans publicly would mean opening himself up to a similar attack. Second, a number of the partisan generals had become quite popular and powerful. At the November 1968 meeting, O Chin-u began the purge by criticizing Ho Pong-hak and Defense Minister Kim Ch'ang-bong. Later, at the January 1969 meeting, O Chin-u directed the purge of the partisan generals in earnest, accusing them of a broad range of failures.

The generals were accused of four major blunders. First, they had neglected to incorporate the lessons learned in the Fatherland Liberation War and stressed only the purchase of advanced weapons and their integration into the KPA. These advanced weapons were considered unsuitable for the Korean Peninsula. Second, the generals had neglected to implement the policy of "fortification of the entire country" either by failing to construct tunnels or by sometimes constructing them in unsafe areas. Third, the generals were accused of squandering military supplies and resources. Last, they had attempted to form a clique within the military and had operated a number of units as a private army. O Chin-u specifically denounced Ho Pong-hak for "failing in organizational operations in the ROK, being unfaithful to the revolution within the [South Korea General Bureau], and creating factionalism and regionalism while 'running alone.'" Among the things that O Chin-u accused Kim Ch'ang-bong of were "opposing the inheritance of the revolutionary tradition, creating factions, and opposing the cadreization [sic] and modernization of the armed forces."[2] Kim Ch'ang-bong had readily introduced high-performance aircraft (e.g., the MiG-21 and Il-28), but had opposed the introduction of the low-performance An-2 Colt. More significantly, he was denounced for failing to establish a "separate light infantry force."[3] Such a force was to be specifically trained in mountain warfare in order to "pierce the heart of the enemy." He had failed to remember Kim's admonishment from 1962: "In modernizing the KPA . . . We must develop and introduce military science and technology in accordance with the reality of our country and correctly incorporate old style weapons along with modern weapons."[4]

Of course many of these charges were simple fabrications, or situations in which the partisan generals were directly following the orders of Kim Il-song himself. Some charges, however, were based upon fact. It appears that some of the partisan generals had developed significant loyalties among specific military or paramilitary organizations (e.g., Guerrilla Training Units). Kim Il-song, remembering Pak Hon-yong and the Kangdong Political Institute, clearly felt threatened by these developments. Another example was that many of the partisan generals had indeed concentrated on the acquisition of advanced Soviet weapons and the modernization of the KPA. This was accomplished at the expense of Kim Il-song's favored light infantry units.

Kim Il-song replaced the partisan generals with a few loyal partisan followers and a growing number of technocrats and young leaders who had been trained by the partisans. Defense Minister Gen. Kim Ch'ang-bong was replaced by Gen. Ch'oe Hyon, chairman of the KWP's Military Affairs Committee and a former partisan. Ch'oe was regarded as the DPRK's leading authority on guerrilla warfare, having commanded the 2nd Infantry Division and later the II Corps (under which the 10th "Guards" Infantry Division had fought) during the Fatherland Liberation War. In February, O Chin-u was himself promoted to the position of KPA chief of staff, replacing Gen. Ch'oe Kwang. Ho Pong-hak was replaced by Kim Chung-nin, a candidate member of the Central Committee and former director of the Culture Department.[5] For the next twenty years Kim's name would be synonymous with the DPRK's covert operations against the ROK. Other prominent partisans who were purged included Vice Premier Kim Kwang-hyop; Adm. Yi Yong-ho; Ch'oe Min-ch'ol, commander of the I Army Group; Chong Pyong-gap (Chong Byong-kap), commander of the III Army Group; Kim Cha-rin; Kim Ch'ang-dok and Kim Ch'ang-Ki (brothers of Kim Ch'ang-bong); Kim Jong-tae, commander of the Reconnaissance Bureau; Kim Yang-chun, commander of the VII Army Group; and Yu Chang-kwon, KPN commander. One of the last major personnel changes was the appointment of Kim Yong Ha to replace Sok San as the minister of public security. With this appointment, a clean sweep of the directors of the organizations and units involved in anti-ROK and special operations had been completed. It has never been disclosed exactly how many high-level officials were affected by this round of purges, but estimates range as high as 160.[6]

The purge signaled the end of the militant policy of the late 1960s and the implementation of a new policy based upon long-term political subversion and the diplomatic isolation of the ROK at the international level. Accompanying the dramatic changes in leadership were equally pivotal developments in the organization and responsibilities of the intelligence community and special warfare forces.

DECLINE IN OPERATIONS

By the beginning of 1969, a noticeable change had taken place in DPRK's tactics and operations against the ROK. Instead of sending large units on commando-type raids or to establish guerrilla bases, small two- to three-man teams of infiltrators were dispatched. The primary objectives of these missions were the establishment and expansion of KWP cells within the ROK and the acquisition of military and political intelligence.[7] Because the DMZ had been reinforced, almost all these infiltrations were now occurring by sea. Seaborne infiltration operations typically were staged out of Wonsan on the east coast, and Namp'o and Haeju on the west coast. Alternately, infiltration teams would embark at Namp'o; be transported to Tsingtao, in the People's Republic of China (PRC); rest there for approximately one week; and then attempt to infiltrate. The infiltration team would sail southward along the PRC coast and eventually eastward, across the Yellow Sea to the ROK.[8]

These infiltration operations would frequently lead to clashes with the ROKN and ROKA. Typical of these were the following encounters.

- On 8 June 1969, ROK coastal gunners sank an infiltration craft early in the morning, approximately 200 meters off Buk-pyong, on the east coast.[9]

- On 11 June 1969, a 75-ton high-speed infiltration vessel, probably from the 753rd Army Unit, disguised as a fishing ship, left the port city of Chinnamp'o. The vessel was heavily armed, with an 82-millimeter recoilless gun, four 40-millimeter guns, two 14.5-millimeter antiaircraft machine guns, and more. It first headed west into the Korea Bay and then south into the Yellow Sea. Its mission was to infiltrate ROK waters and retrieve a KWP agent named Kim Yong-ki on the island of Huksan-do, approximately 350 kilometers southwest of Inch'on. At approximately 2325 hours on 12 June, ROKN patrol boats intercepted the vessel. What followed was a six-hour-long running battle between the infiltration craft and ROK patrol boats and aircraft. The battle ended at 0600 the next day, with the vessel captured and fifteen of its crew dead. A search was initiated for any survivors or infiltrators who might have been put ashore. Three days later, ROK security forces located and killed six additional infiltrators.[10]
- On 24 September 1969, the ROKN destroyer *Pusan* sank a heavily armed infiltration craft from the 753rd Army Unit approximately 30 kilometers west of Huksan-do after a four-hour early morning chase. Approximately fifteen people aboard the 50-ton ship, including the crew, are believed to have drowned.[11]
- On 13 October 1969, ROKN and ROKAF units located and destroyed a high-speed infiltration craft from the 753rd Army Unit in the Yellow Sea north of Sohuksan-do, Sinan-gun, Cholla-namdo (an island in the extreme southwest section of the ROK).[12]
- Despite a general decline in intensity of anti-ROK operations the DPRK conducted one other hostile action of international significance during the late 1960s. On 15 April 1969, KPAF MiG-21 fighters attacked and shot down a U.S. Navy EC-121M aircraft operating out of Atsugi Naval Air Station, Japan. The EC-121M, with thirty-one personnel aboard, was conducting a Beggar Shadow (SIGINT) mission in international airspace over the Sea of Japan when it was attacked and shot down without provocation.[13] The exact reasoning behind this action is unclear. One source suggests that this may have been a deliberate but desperate attempt by the partisan generals to prove their military prowess and their importance to Kim Il-song.[14]

Another facet of the anti-ROK operations during the mid- to late 1960s was that the ROK responded to the increased overland infiltration by initiating the construction of a complex, integrated barrier system south of the DMZ (see appendix). It consisted of a 3-meter-high chain-link fence anchored in concrete, topped with concertina wire, and supplemented with minefields, ditches, and electronic sensing devices. Reinforced watch towers, concrete bunkers, and guard posts were established behind this fence and overlooking the most frequented infiltration routes. Thousands of acres of brush were cleared along roads and fences and around military positions within and adjacent to the southern boundary of the DMZ. In some places, chemical defoliants were used to control summer foliage.[15] This effective barrier system would influence future anti-ROK operations and force the expansion of seaborne infiltration capabilities.

EVOLUTION OF DOCTRINE

Concurrent with the purge of the partisan generals, the DPRK realized that it must further develop the doctrines of combined operations and fighting a two-front war. This development would move away from the heavy emphasis on guerrilla warfare and be based upon the combination of regular and special purpose forces. These units would be responsible for a broad range of unconventional and special warfare operations, with strong emphasis upon rapid infiltration and disruption of enemy rear areas through concealed movement: "lighter arms and faster foot pace."[16] The catalyst for this light infantry doctrinal development was a speech given by Kim Il-song at the November 1968 Eighteenth Plenum of the Central Committee in which he emphasized

> the activation of light infantry units, which are highly mobile for the conduct of effective mountain combat operations.
> . . . If three light infantry regiments had been operated on Mun'gyong gorge [Pass] during the Fatherland Liberation War the KPA could have driven the enemy to Pusan.
> . . . [While the DPRK] can manufacture large quantities of ordnance KPA personnel cannot be reinforced without limit. The activation of the light infantry units, therefore, is an urgent program.[17]

This speech echoed the concerns Kim had voiced at the Third Plenum of the Second KWP Central Committee held in Pyoro-ri in December 1950. In that speech, he had identified the lack of guerrilla warfare capabilities as a primary cause for the KPA's defeat during the first six months of the Fatherland Liberation War.

During the Fifth Party Congress in November 1970, Kim Il-song spoke of this revised doctrine:

> Our country has many mountains and rivers, and has long seacoasts. In the terrain of a country such as ours, if one takes good advantage of this kind of terrain, carrying out mountain and night combat with skill,

and correctly applying combinations of large scale warfare and small scale warfare, regular and irregular combat, even in the case of an enemy who is armed to the fingertips with the latest military technology, we can do a good job of annihilating him. The special experiences of the Struggle for National Liberation in our country bear this out, and, in the same manner, the Vietnam War of today also bears this out.[18]

Doctrinal changes continued. In 1972, the revised doctrines of combined operations and fighting a two-front war were further elaborated:

Our great leader has invented an exceptionally excellent policy enabling North Korean forces to strategically and tactically smash the enemy by either integrated [sic] or combining the following: large unit and small unit operations; the experiences of the guerrilla units and modern military technology; guerrilla and modern war tactics; strong guerrilla activities and national popular resistance.

The close integration of both the large and small operations is fully compatible with the tactical principles of the guerrilla units, which hit and destroy the enemy by employing concentration, dispersion, and swift mobility. This combination is a wise strategic and tactical policy which enables guerrilla units to constantly hold the initiative in their hands until the enemy is crushed.

This combination of guerrilla tactics and modern warfare tactics, and the integration of guerrilla activities and people's resistance is intended to mobilize the whole nation, organize all the people into combat forces, reinforcing the main standing regular forces, and have them strike and annihilate the enemy everywhere.

This is an excellent strategic and tactical policy which will make it possible to completely liberate the whole fatherland.[19]

These doctrinal developments formed the foundation of the KPA's doctrine today, especially that of the special purpose forces. Accompanying these developments were changes within the organization, composition, and control of the DPRK's intelligence and special warfare assets.

ORGANIZATIONAL DEVELOPMENTS, 1969–82

Beginning at the November 1968 Eighteenth Plenum of the Central Committee there began a number of dramatic organizational changes within the DPRK's intelligence and special warfare assets.[20] Although some of these may be viewed as the logical continuation of efforts begun during the mid-1960s, most were in direct response both to the changing doctrines and to the decision to halt the guerrilla war against the ROK. By 1969 the intelligence community would consist of the National Intelligence Committee, KWP's secretary in charge of anti-ROK operations, the Reconnaissance Bureau, and the Ministry of Public Security. Special warfare and guerrilla operations were now spread among three entities: the Reconnaissance Bureau, the newly established VIII Special Corps, and the army-group-level light infantry brigades.

The National Intelligence Committee remained the primary national-level policy- and decision-making organ for intelligence and security matters. The South Korea General Bureau was reorganized into a group of organizations directly subordinate to the secretary in charge of anti-ROK operations (SICARO). The SICARO oversaw all intelligence and subversive operations against the ROK. The Ministry of Public Security retained its responsibilities for internal security, some foreign espionage, and subversive operations. The Reconnaissance Bureau retained its military intelligence duties but now shared responsibilities for conducting special warfare and guerrilla operations with the newly established VIII Special Corps and army-group-level light infantry brigades. The KPA's General Political Bureau still maintained a very limited special operations capability associated with its propaganda efforts against the ROKA.

Clearly the most dramatic changes were within the KPA's special warfare forces. As noted, an entirely new command, the VIII Special Corps,

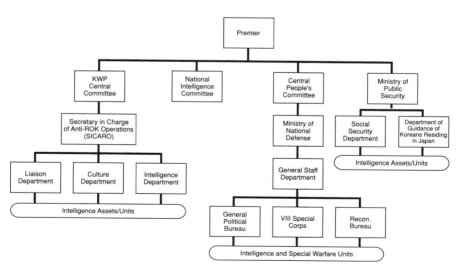

Intelligence and special warfare organizations, 1969.

was established to control KPA special warfare and guerrilla operations. This corps and its subordinate units built logically on the developments of the mid- to late 1960s, and unlike the slow-starting progress of the mid-1960s, the changes during this period occurred quite rapidly. These changes occurred within the context of a general reorganization of the KPA that began in June 1970.

Also of significance during this period was the signing of a military agreement with the PRC in September 1971 and the revision of the DPRK's constitution in 1972. The agreement witnessed a wide range of military sales from the PRC to the DPRK and cooperation in numerous military-related projects. As a result of the constitutional revision, the Ministry of National Defense became the Ministry of People's Armed Forces (MPAF).

This period also saw the beginning of Kim Il-song's efforts to ensure that his son Kim Chong-il would succeed him as the ruler of the DPRK. One of the more significant aspects of this effort occurred in 1980, when Kim Chong-il was elected to the KWP's Central Military Committee.[21] Following this appointment Kim Chong-il undertook a significantly more active role in military and intelligence affairs.

■ SECRETARY IN CHARGE OF ANTI-ROK OPERATIONS

With the purge of Ho Pong-hak, the South Korea General Bureau was reorganized into the office of the SICARO. The first person to hold the position of SICARO was Kim Chung-nin, a former director of the Culture Department. As SICARO, Kim was given a broad mandate to reorganize and supervise all anti-ROK assets and operations. He oversaw a wide range of organizational changes, including the following:

- Disbanding of 124th and 283rd Army Units.
- Establishment of the VIII Special Corps, which was to be responsible for special warfare operations.
- Disbanding of the foot reconnaissance stations.
- Establishment of the sniper and amphibious sniper brigades.
- Expansion of the light infantry regiments into brigades and the establishment of additional light infantry brigades.
- Reorganization of the 695th Army Unit.
- Establishment of the Research Department.
- Reorganization of the Culture Department into the Unification Front Department.
- Reorganization of the Intelligence Department into the General Affairs Department, and subsequently into the Research Department.

98   In addition, the SICARO directed and supervised subordinate agencies in the training of espionage and subversive agents and the production of intelligence. He also provided guidance and coordination for intelligence and unconventional operations of the Ministry of National Defense (Ministry of People's Armed Forces after the revision of the DPRK's Constitution in 1972), Ministry of Public Security, and the Chosen Soren. During the early 1970s the organizations directly subordinate to the SICARO included the Liaison, Culture, and Intelligence Departments.

▪ ▪ *Liaison Department*

The Liaison Department was responsible for positive intelligence and special and subversive operations within the political sphere. In this role it remained responsible for coordinating the recruiting and training of agents and dispatching them to the ROK and Japan. The department was organized into eight major components: Headquarters, Organization, Liaison, Communications, Personnel, Rear Services, the Central Committee Political School, and the South Korea Exhibition Hall.

With the establishment of the SICARO, the Central Committee Political School (695th Army Unit), which had previously been directly subordinate to the South Korea General Bureau, was reorganized and subordinated to the Liaison Department. The 695th continued to provide preliminary training to many prospective agents. The responsibility for advanced, specialized training, and accommodation of agents on standby for dispatch on specific missions was, however, taken away from the Liaison Section and organized into the 940th Army Unit.

The 695th Army Unit's headquarters and most of its branch centers and safe houses were located primarily near P'yongyang. It is estimated that the main training school could now handle about three hundred agent trainees at one time. Courses ranged from six months to four years in duration. The basic course of instruction generally included many subjects. Political indoctrination included the study of the basic tenets of Communist philosophy, the life of Kim Il-song, the history of the KWP and the background of the DPRK's anti-imperialist struggle. Tactical training included instruction in overland and seaborne infiltration techniques, methods of travel and disguise within the ROK, the establishment of hide-outs and equipment caches, and methods of escape and evasion. Operatives received general training in the study of ROK topography, marksmanship, weapons handling, self-defense, unarmed combat, communications and technical equipment training, and familiarization with ROK and U.S. military unit designations, insignia and equipment. Finally, students received physical conditioning training. Liaison Department agents with no specific occupational skills were frequently taught a vocation to enable them to secure a job after infiltrating. Training in welding, sheet metal work, sewing machine operation, and vending was reportedly provided. **99**

Advanced, specialized training for graduates of the 695th Army Unit and other selected individuals was provided by the 940th Army Unit. This unit operated a number of safe houses at various locations throughout the DPRK, although most were located in the P'yongyang area. Courses conducted by this unit were six months to two years in duration and included briefing and preparation of agents and agent teams for dispatch on specific missions. Agent teams lived alone, except for a housekeeper, and were permitted to leave the house only once a week. They were visited by instructors and other officials who inspected their progress. Safe houses were isolated so that agents knew only the members, operations, and training of their own team and, if captured, could not jeopardize other missions.

To support the infiltration of agents, the Liaison Section now operated four sea escort and two overland escort units. The four sea escort units operated from the port cities of Haeju (755th Army Unit), Namp'o (753rd Army Unit), Wonsan (632nd Army Unit), and Ch'ongjin (459th Army Unit). Additionally, there were two training centers for seaborne escort personnel, one at Taejong on the west coast, the other at Kosong on the east coast. The sea escort units continued to use a variety of specialized high-speed infiltration craft. It was also during the 1970s that a number of new classes of swimmer delivery vehicles and semisubmersible infiltration craft were either purchased or began development. The two overland escort units were assigned operations through specific sections of the DMZ. The 217th Army Unit (i.e., the IV and II Corps), based at Kaesong, operated through the western section, and the 250th Army Unit (i.e., I and V Corps), based at P'yonggang, operated through the central and eastern sections of the DMZ.

In September 1975 Chong Kyong-hui was appointed director of the Liaison Department. Previous to this she was deputy director of the Culture Department in 1973–74.[22]

■ ■ *Culture Department, Unification Front Department*
The Culture Department remained essentially the same as it had previously, with most of its responsibilities and operations intact. It was organized into nine known sections: Headquarters, Peaceful Unification Propaganda, Publications Guidance, Broadcast Guidance, Publications, Reporters, Chosen Soren (General Federation of Koreans Residing in Japan) Affairs, South Korea Research, and Personnel. Naturally, its psychological warfare and propaganda activities had to be adjusted to the new political policies and military doctrines. The Culture Department appears to have duplicated some of the propaganda and psychological warfare responsibilities of the General Political Bureau. There may also

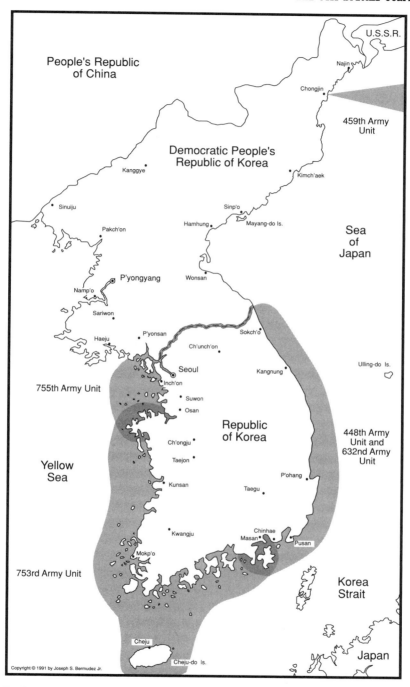

Seaborne escort operating areas, 1970s.

have been an expansion of the Chosen Soren Affairs Section's responsibilities. Until at least 1975, however, control of the Chosen Soren is believed to have been exercised by the Guidance Department of the Ministry of Public Security.

Since the DPRK had no formal diplomatic ties with Japan, the Chosen Soren continued to function as its semiofficial representative with the government of Japan and promote greater political, economic, and social interaction between the two countries. The organization also attended to the concerns of the Korean population in Japan and spread propaganda in the interest of the DPRK. More significantly, various DPRK agencies continued to utilize the Chosen Soren to conduct covert and overt intelligence and propaganda operations against the ROK. These operations were under the control of the SICARO through the Culture Department's Chosen Soren Affairs Section. The Ministry of Public Security's Department of Guidance of Koreans Residing in Japan (or Guidance Department) was responsible for all other activities. Within the Chosen Soren itself the Political Bureau was generally responsible for these operations. A handbook entitled *Counter-South Operations Guide* was prepared and distributed to Chosen Soren officials in the early 1960s. It provided general guidance on identifying, approaching, indoctrinating, and recruiting potential agents. The extent to which these activities were actively pursued is unclear. Many intelligence operations against the ROK during this period originated from Japan with Chosen Soren assistance. In 1972, twenty of the eighty-seven DPRK agents apprehended in the ROK had penetrated via Japan. In 1973, the number had risen to thirty-seven out of eighty. A further indication was the 1974 assassination attempt against ROK President Park Chung Hee by a Chosen Soren member, Mun Se Kwang. Mun was taken to the DPRK and apparently trained by the 940th Army Unit. He was then sent back to Japan to infiltrate the ROK and assassinate President Park. Additionally, throughout the 1970s the Chosen Soren continued to provide front companies and trading companies for DPRK intelligence and smuggling operations, including the support of international terrorists and revolutionaries.

It is believed that sometime during 1978, and at the direction of Kim Il-song, the Culture Department was reorganized into the Unification Front Department. The exact reasons for this reorganization are presently unknown, although it probably had something to do with the increasing levels of north–south dialogue at the time. To the responsibilities previously held by its predecessor, the new organization added overall control of all "North–South Dialogue."[23] At this time Yo Yon-ku was appointed director of the Unification Front Department. She would hold this position until the mid-1980s.[24]

▪ ▪ *Intelligence Department, General Affairs Department, Research Department*
Since the late 1960s, the SICARO's Intelligence Department was responsible for the collection of foreign intelligence and conducting overseas operations. From the early 1970s through at least 1975 it had been reorganized and was identified as the General Affairs Department. As the General Affairs Department, it is believed to have been charged with foreign intelligence operations and may have absorbed many of these missions from other organizations such as the International Department of the Ministry of Public Security. By the late 1970s, possibly 1976, it was reorganized and renamed the Research Department, possibly absorbing the Culture Department's South Korea Research Section. Exactly what prompted these organizational changes and the nature of the various responsibilities accompanying these changes are presently unclear. It is believed that Yim Ho-kun was appointed deputy director of this department by 1974 and director in 1978.[25]

▪ MINISTRY OF PUBLIC SECURITY, STATE SECURITY DEPARTMENT
The Ministry of Public Security remained responsible for a wide variety of internal security missions, including maintaining public order and investigating general crimes, counterintelligence, counter-espionage, providing security protection for high-ranking government and visiting foreign officials, and insuring the security of the nation's coasts and vital installations. The ministry's subordinate Department of Guidance of Koreans Residing in Japan remained responsible for overall operations concerning the Chosen Soren in Japan. Most intelligence, special operations, and propaganda operations concerning the Chosen Soren, however, appear to have been controlled through the Culture Department.

In June 1970 the ministry underwent a major reorganization. Although the details of this reorganization are limited, it evidently concentrated on two areas. First was the refocusing of the ministry's mission almost exclusively upon internal security. Second was the consolidation and subordination of all the DPRK's various paramilitary internal security forces under it. This was accompanied by the deactivation of a number of paramilitary organizations (e.g., Guerrilla Training Units).[26] These developments were probably an outgrowth of Kim Il-song's concerns over the popularity and power attained by the recently purged partisan generals. The development of a larger, more independent security force would serve as a counterbalance to anything like this happening in the future.

In 1973, the State Security Department was separated from the Ministry of Public Security and directly subordinated to the Central People's

Committee. It probably assumed the political security responsibilities formerly the jurisdiction of the Security Bureau of the Ministry of Public Security. As such it functioned as a "secret police." In this role the "Fourth Bureau" of the State Security Department reportedly conducted foreign operations, including the recruitment of operatives. The "Eighth Bureau" collected data on Koreans who repatriated to the DPRK from Japan. From the information it obtained concerning their relatives and friends still in Japan or in the ROK, the "Eighth Bureau" selected likely candidates for recruitment. It should be noted, however, that the State Security Department's primary mission was political security and the protection of the regime, not positive intelligence or special operations. Interestingly, with the establishment of the State Security Department as an independent agency it apparently assumed the Ministry of Public Security's duties of assistance to terrorist and revolutionary organizations.[27]

By 1975 the Ministry of Public Security had evolved into a comprehensive and powerful agency focused almost exclusively on internal security. The primary exception to this was its control over the Chosen Soren and possibly some limited foreign intelligence operations. The ministry was organized into a secretariat; five vice ministers (Rear Services, Public Security, Internal Security, National Security, and Forestry) who oversaw a varying number of subordinate bureaus; Department of Guidance of Koreans Residing in Japan; and a Political Bureau.

■ RECONNAISSANCE BUREAU

The Reconnaissance Bureau underwent a number of significant organizational changes from 1969 to 1982. Although it remained responsible for positive tactical and strategic intelligence within the military sphere, it would share the responsibilities for conducting special warfare and guerrilla operations with new organizations, the VIII Special Corps and army-group-level light infantry brigades. Additionally, the bureau exercised operational control over agents engaged in military intelligence activities and oversaw the training, maintenance, and deployment of guerrilla teams available for operation in the ROK. Although the Reconnaissance Bureau was directly subordinate to the Ministry of People's Armed Forces, Kim Chung-nin as SICARO exercised some indirect control over its peacetime operations against the ROK.

After an initial flood of organizational changes (including the disbanding of the 124th Army Unit and the foot reconnaissance stations) in 1969–70, the Reconnaissance Bureau was composed of seven departments, the Foreign Language College, and a number of operational units. The departments included Headquarters, Political, Intelligence, Special, Technical/Radio, Training/Plans, and DMZ Police. During the 1970s the seaborne elements of the Reconaissance Bureau are believed to have been formed into the Maritime Department. By the late 1970s, operational units included the 907th, 198th, and 448th Army Units and three sniper brigades (17th, 60th, and 61st).

▪ ▪ *124th Army Unit, 283rd Army Unit, and Foot Reconnaissance Stations*
The first units to be affected by the reorganization of the Reconnaissance Bureau were the 124th and 283rd Army Units, which were disbanded in 1969. Their personnel were utilized to establish the light infantry brigades of the VIII Special Corps.[28] The foot reconnaissance stations, which were reorganized and expanded in 1968 to approximately nine thousand personnel, were subsequently reduced during the latter half of 1969 to approximately three thousand in three foot reconnaissance stations. The personnel lost through this reorganization were funneled into the newly forming light infantry brigades. The three remaining foot reconnaissance stations were subsequently disbanded and their personnel utilized, in combination with former members of the 17th Reconnaissance Brigade, to establish two new sniper brigades.

▪ ▪ *907th and 198th Army Units*
The 907th and 198th Army Units were responsible for training espionage and subversive agents. The 907th Army Unit, headquartered at Tae-dong, was utilized to train ROKA personnel who had been abducted or who had defected to the DPRK. The 198th Army Unit operated safe houses in the P'yongyang area that were similar in function to those operated by the Liaison Department's 940th Army Unit and 695th Army Unit.

▪ ▪ *Maritime Department, 448th Army Unit, and 137th Squadron*
During the 1970s the operational and training seaborne elements of the Reconnaissance Bureau were formed into the Maritime Department (also called the Special Seaborne Operations Unit). This department exercised overall control of all the bureau's seaborne-related activities. The 448th Army Unit, headquartered at Wonsan, apparently was the Maritime Department's sole seaborne infiltration unit. In this role it operated a number of highly specialized swimmer delivery vehicles, midget submarines, semisubmersible and high-speed infiltration craft, and cargo vessels. The 448th had subordinate elements deployed on both coasts.

The production of the *Yugo*-class midget submarine continued throughout this period, and by 1980 production had reached about thirty. During the mid-1970s the KPN obtained a later class of a Yugoslav midget submarine in much the same manner as it had acquired the first. This boat evidently was used for experimental purposes and not as a design for the production of a new class of midget submarines within the DPRK. Using a combination of its experience gained in the production of the *Yugo* class, the KPN began design on its *41-Meter*-class submarine. Only one of these experimental SSAG 41-by-3-meter designs would be produced. It was launched during the early 1980s. It had a crew of about fifteen and was armed with two 533-millimeter torpedo tubes. Either because of its experimental mission or because of its possible design flaws, this vessel would spend the majority of its career tied up to a dock.[29]

Around 1980 the 137th Squadron (also known as the 137th Naval Squadron or 137th Combat Squadron) was established subordinate to the Maritime Department to serve as the headquarters and operational command of midget submarine infiltration operations. Up until this time the midget submarines were manned by, and under the control of, either the 448th Army or the KPN. These vessels, however, were used almost exclusively for Reconnaissance Bureau operations.[30]

▪ ▪ DMZ Police Companies

By the late 1970s the number of DMZ police companies attached to each KPA infantry division deployed along the DMZ had risen to approximately eight to twelve, depending upon the terrain. Personnel from these companies are believed to have continued to serve as escorts for infiltrators from the Reconnaissance Bureau or Liaison Department. Despite the reorganization of the Reconnaissance Bureau in the early 1970s its relationship with the DMZ police companies continued. The nature of this relationship, however, is unclear.

▪ ▪ Foreign Language College

The Foreign Language College continued its primary mission of language instruction during this period.[31] Courses of instruction could last for several years, depending upon the language and the requirements of the students' designated assignment. For example, the Russian course apparently could take a total of two years to complete (with prior language training).[32]

The activities of the former U.S. personnel who were new English Department instructors took several interesting turns. Between 1981 and 1985, two of them played leading roles in the DPRK propaganda movie *Unknown Hero*. Additionally, several by this time had married Korean women and started families.[33]

▪ ▪ Sniper Brigades

By 1969–70 the personnel strength of the 17th Reconnaissance Brigade had increased to an estimated 9,300. At this point the brigade underwent a dramatic reorganization. It was reduced in strength and organized along light infantry lines with a brigade headquarters, ten reconnaissance battalions, and small combat and service support assets. The brigade would also soon possess a small, specially trained element (perhaps company sized), which was specifically assigned "direct action" operations.[34] Gone were all heavy weapons and equipment. It was also about this time that the term "sniper" was frequently used to refer to this and the other soon-to-be-established brigades.[35] The term "sniper" was both an honorific referring back to the 88th Special Independent Sniper Brigade in which Kim Il-song had served during World War II and an indication of the intended special warfare nature of these units. For many years these new sniper units would still be referred to as reconnaissance or reconnaissance sniper brigades.

The personnel left over by the reorganization of the 17th were combined with the personnel from the disbanded foot reconnaissance stations to establish two new brigades: the 60th and 61st Sniper Brigades. These three brigades were deployed and operated in direct support of the three army groups (soon to be redesignated corps) deployed along the DMZ. In effect, the three brigades replaced the former foot reconnaissance stations. Each sniper brigade maintained the capability and responsibility of infiltrating its specific section of the DMZ. Elements of each brigade were airborne qualified.

The missions assigned to the sniper brigades included both intelligence collection and strategic special operations throughout the ROK and overseas. Published reports suggest that the DPRK established a special twenty-man "body-snatching" unit in 1975.[36] It is unclear whether this related to a Liaison Department or Reconnaissance Bureau unit.

▪ VIII SPECIAL CORPS

Probably the single most important event in the development of the DPRK's special purpose forces was the establishment of the VIII Special Corps (also known as VIII Special Purpose Corps, VIII Special Operations Corps, VIII Special Duties Army Group, Light Infantry Army Group, Reconnaissance Army Group, and 3729th Army Unit) in 1969. During the purge of the partisan generals, O Chin-u had criticized Defense Minister Kim Ch'ang-bong for failing to establish a separate light infantry force. Following the purge, one of the first things ordered was the establishment of a new special warfare organization known as the VIII Special Corps to exercise overall control of KPA special warfare and guerrilla operations. Some evidence suggests that the VIII Special Corps, headquartered at Tokch'on-up, was from its inception subordinate to the Reconnaissance Bureau since much of its manpower was drawn

107

from the bureau. Whether or not this was correct, the corps was soon made directly subordinate to the General Staff Department.

As part of the reorganization of the Reconnaissance Bureau, the 124th and 283rd Army Units were disbanded and their personnel utilized to establish the new light infantry brigades. The first of these new light infantry brigades were themselves subordinated to the newly established VIII Special Corps. This initial cadre of elite troops was augmented by the addition of the 38th Airborne Brigade. The VIII Special Corps would continue to expand throughout the 1970s. By the late 1970s the term "special purpose forces" was coined to describe those DPRK units that possessed ranger/commando- and special-forces-type capabilities, as well as capabilities for unconventional warfare and special operations. There are considerable differences of opinion concerning the composition of the special purpose forces at that time. Declassified contemporaneous intelligence documents indicate that the ROK estimated fourteen light infantry brigades and one airborne brigade, while the U.S. estimated eleven light infantry brigades and five airborne battalions. Based on recently declassified documents and defector interviews it would appear that by 1978, these forces consisted of fifteen brigades: the VIII Special Corps, which had expanded to include four light infantry brigades and three airborne brigades; three sniper brigades under the Reconnaissance Bureau; three light infantry brigades attached to the I, II, and V Forward Corps; one light infantry brigade attached to the IV Corps; and a single amphibious sniper brigade. The U.S. Defense Intelligence Agency estimated that in 1978 the personnel strength of the special purpose forces was forty-one thousand.[37]

U.S. Secretary of Defense Harold Brown acknowledged these emerging capabilities of the VIII Special Corps when he testified before Congress in March 1978: "One particularly worrisome aspect is North Korea's significant special warfare capability. . . . " These forces would be deployed by "difficult to detect airlift [to] infiltrate in South Korean rear areas and attack airfields, logistic depots, lines of communications and command posts. South Korea would have to divert forces from their primary mission of repelling an attack on the DMZ to counter special warfare activities of the North."[38]

It is believed that Chang Song-u (also called Choe Sang-uk) became commander of the VIII Special Corps in 1976. Previously he had served as commander of the 16th Light Infantry Brigade during the late 1960s and as head of the KPA military mission to Vietnam in 1973–76. He presumably held his position of commander of the VIII Special Corps until the mid-1980s.[39]

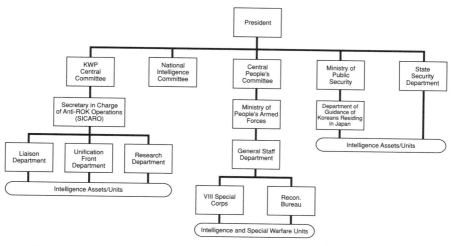

Intelligence and special warfare organizations, 1977.

■ ■ *38th Airborne Brigade*

By 1969 the 38th Airborne Brigade had expanded to twelve airborne battalions, with a total troop strength of approximately 6,700. As part of the activation of the VIII Special Corps, the 38th was subordinated to the new corps. By the mid-1970s the 38th had been expanded to eighteen airborne battalions. At that point (possibly 1976) the brigade was reorganized with six airborne battalions. The remaining twelve airborne battalions were utilized to establish two new airborne brigades: the 48th and 58th Airborne. All three airborne brigades were organized with a headquarters; six airborne battalions (500 troops each); and small combat (i.e., signal company and guard platoon) and service support (i.e., medical and rear service) assets. Average troop strength for each airborne brigade was approximately 3,200.[40]

KPAF airlift capability had improved significantly since 1965 (table 4-1). These capabilities were now consolidated within a transport division directly subordinate to KPAF Command Headquarters. Estimated strength in 1976 was 233 aircraft and 67 helicopters.[41] This force had a theoretical total airlift capability of about 3,700 troops: approximately one airborne brigade, or seven airborne battalions. It should be noted, however, that most of the larger aircraft were utilized solely for governmental support and civilian transport.

109

Table 4-1

KPAF AIRLIFT CAPABILITY, MID-1970s

Aircraft	Est. Number	Est. Capacity (Troops)	Total Lift Capacity (Troops)
An-2 Colt	205	8	1,640
An-24 Coke	7	50	350
Il-14 Crate	1	28	28
Il-18 Coot	2	75	150
Li-2 Cab	14	16	224
Tu-154 Careless	1	167	167
Yak-12 Creek	3	3	9
Mi-4 Hound	54	15	810
Mi-8 Hip	13	32	416
Total	300		3,794

Most notable concerning the KPAF's enhanced airlift capability was the introduction of many An-2 Colt aircraft. These aircraft were introduced as a direct result of the denunciation of Kim Ch'ang-bong at the January 1969 Fourth Plenary Meeting of the Fourth KPA Party Committee for having opposed the introduction of the aircraft. The An-2 Colt held a special place in the minds of Kim Il-song and the KPA's leadership. The leaders' admiration of the Colt dates back to the Fatherland Liberation War, when the KPAF had been initially swept from the skies by the UNC air forces. The only offensive success the KPAF enjoyed during the remainder of the war was the small-scale night bombing campaign conducted by the small Po-2 biplane, which was first manufactured in the late 1920s. The campaign achieved considerable propaganda success by repeatedly conducting nighttime raids against Seoul and Inch'on.[42] Clearly remembering the successes of the Po-2 and his desire to "incorporate old style weapons along with modern weapons," at the January 1969 meeting, Kim Il-song made the acquisition of the An-2 for the KPA's "light infantry forces" a high priority. Large-scale procurement of the An-2 from Poland, the PRC, and the Soviet Union began the following year.[43]

The continued use of the An-2 for the delivery of KPA special forces up until the present day is not as implausible as it might first appear.[44] The An-2 is capable of extremely low-altitude, low-speed flight, which, given the mountainous terrain of the Korean Peninsula, affords it a relatively good chance of infiltrating the ROK undetected at night and under conditions of low visibility. The aircraft has excellent range and short takeoff and landing capabilities, which allow it to operate from unprepared fields almost anywhere on the Korean Peninsula. Furthermore, it has a stable paratroop drop platform, a relatively large cargo capacity, and, because of its construction, a very small radar signature. The An-2 Colt's specifications are as follows:[45]

Crew	2
Payload	12 passengers, 8 troops, or 1,400 kg
Wing span	18.18 m
Length	12.74 m
Height	6.10 m
Takeoff weight	5,500 kg
Maximum speed	250 kph
Cruising speed	185 kph
Landing speed	85 kph
Range	1,000 km

Under conditions of daylight, good visibility, and ROK/U.S. air superiority, however, the aircraft is extremely vulnerable.

During 1979 and 1980, the KPAF acquired approximately 45 additional Y-5s (a license-produced version of the An-2 Colt) from the PRC, bringing the total number of the type to approximately 250 and increasing total airlift capability by 630.[46]

Although the DPRK claimed that it was part of a "meteorological observation team," the recovery of a wrecked balloon and corpses found in the waters west of Sado Island (Sadoga-shima), Japan, on 27 September 1976 may have been a possible indicator of airborne or Reconnaissance Bureau training with hot-air balloons.[47]

▪ ▪ *Light Infantry Brigades*

In April 1969, the KPA established two light infantry brigades under each forward-area army group (soon to be redesignated corps) by disbanding the foot reconnaissance stations and light infantry regiments under the control of each army group and reassigning some of these personnel as cadre members to the light infantry brigades. Subsequently, half of these newly established brigades were subordinated to the VIII Special Corps. Those that remained subordinated to the army groups received administrative and technical support from the VIII Special Corps. During the early 1970s, the rear corps are also believed to have begun the process of establishing light infantry units, but at a reduced level, with each rear corps establishing a light infantry battalion, and subordinate divisions a light infantry company.

Like the light infantry regiments, the new light infantry brigades were from their inception organized as special warfare units. The brigade consisted of approximately 3,200 troops and was organized into a small headquarters staff and seven light infantry battalions. Besides a signal company, there were virtually no organic service support assets and no combat support assets. The headquarters consisted of approximately 50 personnel. The light infantry battalion was the basic tactical unit, all of whose personnel were combat troops. Each battalion consisted of 450–500 troops and was divided into three companies. The light infantry company consisted of 150 troops and comprised three light infantry platoons. Each light infantry platoon consisted of 50 troops organized into ten teams of 5 troops each.

The qualifications for selection of personnel for assignment to the new light infantry brigade included any person previously assigned to a foot reconnaissance station or light infantry regiment who had served in the KPA for longer than one year, and those from the "basic class family members" who were physically strong, healthy, and politically reliable.

The missions for these new light infantry brigades depended upon subordination. When subordinate to the VIII Special Corps, these units were to conduct strategic missions deep within the ROK, including "conducting guerrilla warfare in coordination with local KWP assets [and] . . . establishing 'liberation fronts' and operational bases to expand guerrilla potential. . . . when civilian and military unrest occurs light infantry units are to engage in activities to harass the ROK rear areas."[48]

When subordinate to the forward army group (forward corps) these brigades were responsible for conducting unconventional warfare operations within the army group's area of responsibility. The concept was for light infantry brigades subordinate to the VIII Special Corps to operate in much the same manner as had the 766th Independent Unit during the Fatherland Liberation War. The light infantry brigades under the forward army group would operate as had the divisional guerrilla units.

■ ■ *Amphibious Sniper Brigade*
Details of the organizational development of the KPA's amphibious forces during this period are unclear. The small number of independent naval infantry units (typically of battalion size) established during the late 1950s and early 1960s apparently were combined in the 1970s either into a single brigade or under one operational headquarters. The exact composition and disposition of this new amphibious sniper brigade (also called naval

sniper brigade, navy sniper brigade, amphibious light infantry brigade) at this time is unknown, although it was probably organized along sniper/light infantry lines and had subordinate units on both coasts. Given the disposition of KPN amphibious warfare craft, major elements of this unit are believed to have been concentrated at Namp'o and Sagon-ni.

KPN amphibious lift capability had improved somewhat since 1965 to an estimated strength of twenty dedicated amphibious vessels in 1971 (table 4-2).[49] On the west coast, twelve of these vessels were concentrated at Namp'o and Sagon-ni. On the east coast, the eight vessels were distributed among all the major bases. If concentrated, these twenty vessels had a theoretical total amphibious lift capability of 3,100 troops, which was sufficient to lift the entire amphibious sniper brigade. This force consisted of five *Hanch'on*-class LCM and fifteen LCM formerly from the PRC. The *Hanch'on*-class LCM could carry 60 tons of cargo or vehicles (e.g., two light tanks or one medium tank) or 250 fully equipped troops. The former PRC LCM could carry 34 tons of cargo or vehicles (e.g., one light or one medium tank) or 120 fully equipped combat troops. During the fall of 1973 the KPN is believed to have conducted it first major amphibious combat exercise. This large-scale, joint-service exercise was conducted on the west coast and demonstrated a high level of training and material readiness.

Given the age and characteristics (especially the slow speed) of these vessels, the KPN established requirements for both more capable and faster amphibious warfare vessels. Beginning in 1974–75 the KPN initiated the construction of several new indigenous-designed amphibious assault and support craft: *Namp'o*-class LCPF, *Ch'ongjin*-class PGM (armed with a T-34/8-millimeter tank turret), and *Chaho*-class PCFS

Table 4-2

KPN AMPHIBIOUS LIFT CAPABILITY, 1971

Class	Est. Number	Est. Capacity (Troops)	Total Lift Capacity (Troops)
Hanch'on-class LCM	5	250	1,250
ex-PRC LSM	15	120	1,850
Total	20		3,100

(armed with a 122-millimeter rocket launcher). The *Namp'o*-class LCPF can carry thirty or more fully equipped combat troops and has clamshell bow doors allowing a 1.2-meter-wide personnel ramp to be telescoped out 9.7 meters for landings. An indication of the importance of this new class of craft is that by 1977, a total of 74 *Namp'o* LCPF had been constructed. Thirty were based on the east coast, and 44 on the west coast. Sometime about 1980, construction of the *Hantae*-class LSM began. This class was larger than the *Hanch'on*-class LCM and capable of carrying three to four medium tanks. With the introduction of the *Hantae*-class LSM, the number of former PRC LCM began to decline. By the end of 1982, production of approximately 75 *Namp'o*-class LCPF, 1 additional *Hanch'on*-class LCM, and approximately 2 *Hantae*-class LSM had increased the KPN amphibious lift capability to approximately six thousand. This was sufficient to lift the entire amphibious light infantry brigade plus tanks and additional regular ground troops. The lift capability was complemented by approximately sixty-two *Ch'ongjin*- and *Chaho*-class vessels.[50] The combination of landing and fire support craft provided the KPA with a small but potent amphibious warfare capability tailored specifically to the conditions of the Korean Peninsula (table 4-3).

OPERATIONS

Throughout the 1970s and early 1980s the DPRK continued to conduct infiltration and special operations against the ROK. While most sources

Table 4-3

KPN AMPHIBIOUS LIFT CAPABILITY, 1982

Class	Est. Number	Est. Capacity (Troops)	Total Lift Capacity (Troops)
Hanch'on-class LCM	6	250	1,500
Hantae-class LSM	2	350	700
ex-PRC LSM	13	120	1,560
Namp'o-class LCPF	75	30	2,250
Total	96		6,010

describe these as low level or low intensity, many were quite lethal and aggressive. Overall, however, the climate was distinctly milder than it was during the late 1960s, and the number of operations tended to decline. With two notable exceptions, most operations continued to have as their primary missions the establishment and expansion of KWP cells within the ROK and the acquisition of military and political intelligence. These operations were about equally divided between overland and seaborne infiltrations, with seaborne infiltrations tending to become more prevalent during the later part of this period. Typical of these were the following:[51]

- On 27 July 1970, ROKN and ROKAF units located and destroyed a 50-ton infiltration craft from either the 632nd Army Unit or 448th Army Unit in the East Sea 17 kilometers northeast of the port city of Yongdok, Kyongsang-pukto.
- On 1 June 1971, a 70-ton infiltration craft from the 753rd Army Unit was spotted in the Yellow Sea 120 kilometers southwest of Sohuk-san-do, Sinan-gun, Cholla-namdo. In the subsequent chase and battle, ROKN and ROKAF units destroyed the vessel, killing the fifteen persons aboard.
- On 17 April 1973, two members of an infiltration team were killed while attempting to cross the DMZ north of Yonch'on, Kyonggi-do.
- On 2 July 1974, an infiltration craft, probably from the 753rd Army Unit, approached to within 11 kilometers southeast of Pusan before being spotted and sunk by ROKN vessels.
- On 19 June 1976, a three-man reconnaissance "sniper" brigade infiltration team penetrated 2 kilometers south of the DMZ before they were located and killed.
- On 3 November 1980, an unknown number of infiltrators landed along the southern coast on Hwengan-do, Wando-gun. In the subsequent search and fighting, three infiltrators were killed.

The June 1976 incident presented a noteworthy illustration of the capabilities and missions of sniper brigade personnel. On 8 June a three-man reconnaissance team from the 61st(?) Sniper Brigade in the I Corps successfully infiltrated through the DMZ. It was not until 19 June that the team was discovered and subsequently killed in a firefight with ROKA troops. Maps and photographs recovered from the reconnaissance team gave what appeared to be a chronological listing of reconnoitered targets along the route they followed. The route began on the west side of the Pukhan River just south of the DMZ and proceeded south past Hwach'on and Ch'unch'on. From here the agents moved northwest toward

Yanggu and on to the point where they were discovered just south of the DMZ. It should be noted that even though the reconnaissance team covered considerable distance (approximately 90 kilometers) through extremely difficult terrain, they still conducted a thorough reconnaissance of the area. Units and facilities reconnoitered included ROKA headquarters from battalion to corps level; airstrips and air defense sites; industrial facilities and electric power plants in and around the cities of Ch'unch'on, Hwach'on, and Yanggu; and the Soyang Dam northeast of Ch'unch'on. In addition to these targets, the reconnaissance team appeared to be interested in the ROKA's use of camouflage, the status of the roads, troop movements, friendly reaction capabilities, the distance of facilities from roads, and suitable observation points. Of particular interest was a captured brevity code, which indicated that the reconnaissance team could request a rescue team or artillery support. This was the first known instance of infiltrators presumably being able to request artillery fire. Although the ability to request artillery support did not insure response, it did raise the possibility of a confrontation occurring if a fleeing reconnaissance team approached, or proceeded beyond, a predetermined rescue line.[52]

The two notable exceptions to this generally declining level of operations and their focus on intelligence and subversion were the second and third assassination attempts (the first being the "Blue House" raid) against ROK President Park Chung Hee. In June 1970, the DPRK conducted its second attempt to assassinate the ROK president. Little detailed information is available concerning this incident, since all three agents involved were killed by ROK security personnel. Although it has not been confirmed, it is believed that these agents were sniper brigade personnel. In early June, three DPRK agents infiltrated Seoul. Their mission was to conceal a large remote-controlled bomb at the gate of the National Cemetery, in advance of a speech to be given by President Park on 25 June, commemorating the twentieth anniversary of the Korean War. On 22 June, three days before the anniversary celebrations, the three agents entered the National Cemetery to install the bomb. Something went wrong, however, and the bomb was accidentally detonated, killing one of the agents. The surviving agents quickly fled. Because of the rapid response by ROK security forces, the capital area was sealed off and thoroughly searched for the missing agents. Two weeks later, on 7 July, ROK security personnel located and killed the two agents on a mountain 10 kilometers west of Kimp'o International Airport. The agents were apparently attempting to leave via the coast. Among the possessions of the agents were a DPRK-manufactured machine gun, a pistol, a dagger, a radio, and $150 in U.S. currency. This assassination attempt displayed a remarkable number of similarities with the 1983 assassination attempt against President Chon Tu-hwan in Rangoon.[53]

Four years later, on 15 August 1974, the DPRK conducted its third and final assassination attempt against President Park Chung Hee, this time while he was delivering an Independence Day address before an audience of 1,500 at the National Theater. Although the president escaped unharmed, his wife and a choir girl were killed. Mun Se Kwang (Moon Se-kwang), the assassin, was shot in his hip by President Park's bodyguards and captured. During the subsequent interrogation by ROK security officials, Mun revealed the details of his life and the assassination attempt.[54]

Mun was a twenty-three-year-old Korean national, born and raised in Osaka, Japan. He was recruited as a DPRK operative by a member of the Osaka chapter of Chosen Soren in 1972. He subsequently traveled to the DPRK, where he was apparently trained by the 940th Army Unit. In November 1973, he was assigned the mission to assassinate President Park. Mun was apparently assisted in his mission by a another Japanese national, Mikiko Yoshii. She traveled with Mun to Hong Kong in the fall of 1973, where he attempted to purchase a gun. Having no success, he returned to Japan, where he was able to steal a pistol in July 1974. Mun confessed that he received the final order in May from his controller, Kim Ho Ryong, aboard the DPRK cargo ship *Mang Yong Bong-ho,* berthed in the Japanese port of Nigata. On 6 August, Mun arrived in the ROK using a forged passport in the name of Mikiko Yoshii's husband, Yukio Yoshii. He smuggled the pistol into the country by disassembling it and distributing its pieces among his luggage.[55] In Seoul, on 15 August, he traveled by taxi to the National Theater, where, posing as a Japanese diplomat, he entered the theater and attempted to assassinate President Park.

It appears that Mun was nothing more than an unstable person whom the DPRK easily influenced into attempting to assassinate President Park. They provided no real assistance, other than money, encouragement, and promises of glory, which was enough for Mun. Although the DPRK must have realized that there was little likelihood of success, for them it was a no-lose situation. If he did not succeed, no assets were lost. If he did succeed, a stubborn enemy was dead, also without the expenditure of any real effort. In either case, the DPRK could maintain that it was an act of the Korean people against the oppressive ROK government, since Mun was not a DPRK national. The DPRK did, in fact, deny any involvement in the assassination attempt, saying that it was a manifestation of the will of the ROK people "to overthrow the Park Chung Hee fascist dictatorial regime and establish a democratic coalition government. . . . "

The primary cause of the declining number of operations during this period was the implementation of the new anti-ROK policy based upon long-term political subversion and the diplomatic isolation of the ROK at the international level. Additionally, there were a number of secondary factors, including

- ROK security forces had attained a level of scale and proficiency that dramatically increased the danger of neutralizing most infiltration and subversive operations.
- The DPRK was severely hampered by increasing fiscal troubles; at the same time, it was heavily committed to a major KPA reorganization, modernization, and expansion program, as well as increased support for terrorist and revolutionary organizations in the third world.
- Kim Il-song was committed to consolidating the position of his son Kim Chong-il within the government and assuring his eventual assumption of the presidency itself.

KIM CHUNG-NIN

The eight months between August 1974 and March 1975 were ones of acute embarrassment to the DPRK because of several very visible failures, including the August 1974 failed assassination attempt upon ROK President Park Chung Hee; the November 1974 discovery of the DPRK's first infiltration tunnel under the DMZ; and the March 1975 discovery of a second DMZ infiltration tunnel (a third tunnel was discovered in October 1978; see appendix). As the SICARO, Kim Chung-nin was deemed responsible for these failures, and in October 1975, he was dismissed from all the public offices and the KWP. Within a year he had partially redeemed himself and in September 1976 he was reinstated into the KWP and appointed as director of the Research Department.[56]

During late 1979 and early 1980, the DPRK was once again caught off balance by rapidly changing political events within the ROK much as it had been in the early 1960s. In October 1979, President Park was assassinated by the director of the Korean Central Intelligence Agency, and Chon Tu-hwan assumed power and reinstated martial law. May 1980 witnessed widespread demonstrations throughout the ROK, demanding Chon's removal and the restoration of democracy. Chon responded by imposing further martial law measures, including the closing of all universities. In what was the ROK's worst postwar violence, ROKA troops were dispatched to the southern city of Kwangju to subdue a six-day, armed antigovernment uprising. In the resulting operations at least nineteen people were killed and three hundred arrested. The inability to take advantage of these events is believed to have been the prime factor in Kim Chung-nin's being reinstated as SICARO at the Sixth KWP Congress held in October 1980.

ORGANIZATIONAL DEVELOPMENTS, 1982–89

Sometime during 1982–83 a new series of organizational changes were initiated within DPRK's intelligence and internal security services, as well as with the Ministry of People's Armed Forces.[57] Within the intelligence community, the reorganization efforts were overseen by Kim Chung-nin. While some of these changes can be viewed on the surface as having further delineated responsibilities and having provided for better coordination and more streamlined operations, they were in fact politically motivated and actually resulted in a significant overlapping of responsibilities. Most significantly, the organizations directly subordinate to the SICARO were increased from three to four. The effects, if any, of this reorganization upon the National Intelligence Committee, State Security Department, and Ministry of Public Security are presently unclear.[58] The Ministry of Public Security retained its responsibilities for internal security and some foreign espionage and subversive operations, while the State Security Department continued its mission of political security and the protection of the regime. Both agencies, however, expanded their operations considerably during this period, especially within the Soviet Union and Eastern Bloc countries. These operations were generally restricted to internal security and not positive intelligence or special operations. The State Security Department's involvement with foreign terrorist and revolutionary organizations, as well as with smuggling operations (most notably narcotics), increased significantly during this period.

The Special Operations Division (known as the 563rd Army Unit or 563rd Unit) of the General Political Bureau was reportedly responsible, during peacetime, for establishing clandestine contacts with ROKA troops, kidnaping, planning crossings into the ROK, DMZ loudspeaker broadcasts, and distributing propaganda publications. During wartime the division is responsible for civilian population control in "liberated" areas, identification of subversive elements, and assessing the political and military strength of the ROK.[59]

In 1982 the Ministry of the People's Armed Forces was separated from the State Administration Council and placed under the Central Military Committee.[60] Concurrent with this was the initiation of a program to mechanize and modernize the KPA. To cultivate the KPA's special warfare assets, the capabilities of the Reconnaissance Bureau and VIII Special Corps were significantly developed, and more units were made subordinate to the VIII Special Corps. Personnel from these two organizations would play an expanding role in foreign military assistance and in supporting international terrorist and revolutionary groups.

■ SECRETARY IN CHARGE OF ANTI-ROK OPERATIONS

The overall responsibilities of the SICARO remained essentially unchanged during this period. The intelligence organizations directly subordinate to the SICARO, however, were reorganized into the Liaison Department, Unification Front Department, Operations Department, and Research Department for External Intelligence (RDEI).

Despite the numerous organizational changes that occurred during this period it is important to note that each of these organizations maintained its own individual staffs and operatives, as did the Ministry of Public Security and the State Security Department. Additionally, each organization continued to conduct operations in the ROK and overseas. These operations frequently displayed overlapping, and sometimes conflicting, areas of responsibilities. The major difference was that it was now the operatives from the Liaison Department and RDEI that were most frequently encountered both in the ROK and overseas. In support of their overseas operations most of these organizations maintained various trading companies as "covers" and to generate financing for operations. As noted above the State Security Department became increasingly involved in narcotics smuggling during this period. The Liaison and Operations Departments also operated a small fleet of oceangoing cargo

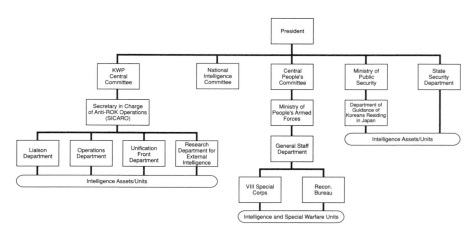

Intelligence and special warfare organizations, 1982–89.

vessels in direct support of their operations and trading companies. The most infamous of these was the *Tong Gon Ae Guk-ho* (see below). In 1988 the DPRK owned seventy-six oceangoing cargo vessels. Of these, eight were operated by the KWP: the *Choong Seong-Ho Number One* (1,000 tons), *Choong Seong-Ho Number Two* (1,000 tons), *Choong Seong-Ho Number Three* (1,000 tons), *Dong Geon Ae Gook-Ho* (or *Tong Gon Ae Guk-ho)* (10,000 tons), *Dong Hae-Ho* (8,000 tons), *Hae Gum Gang-Ho* (20,000 tons), *Song Rim-Ho* (20,000 tons), and *Soo Gun-Ho* (8,000 tons).[61]

▪ ▪ *Liaison Department*
Although the Liaison Department retained overall responsibility for the establishment and maintenance of an espionage and KWP infrastructure within the ROK, it underwent a dramatic reorganization. The most significant aspect of this was the loss, in the early 1980s, of the Liaison Section and its subordinate escort units, which were utilized to establish the Operations Department. Some of the training functions formerly exercised by the 695th Army Unit and 940th Army Unit were probably retained by the Liaison Department. Additionally, the Liaison Department became the primary organization for exercising control over the Chosen Soren. Apparently, the department assumed many of the responsibilities for this organization formerly exercised by the Ministry of Public Security's Department of Guidance of Koreans Residing in Japan. It should be noted, however, that the Unification Front Department also exercised control over some aspects of the Chosen Soren.

▪ ▪ *Unification Front Department*
The effects, if any, of the 1982–83 reorganization upon the Unification Front Department (also called the Unification Front Bureau, United Front Department, or Department of Projects for the United Front) are presently unknown. This department remained responsible for all issues relating to "north–south dialogue," including all anti-ROK psychological warfare operations such as propaganda, anti-ROK radio broadcasts, the spread of Chu'che theology in the ROK and abroad, balloon-pamphlet operations, and so forth. Through its Chosen Soren Affairs Section, the Unification Front Department continued to work very actively within both Japan and the ROK. Sometime during the mid-1980s, Yo Yon-ku resigned as director of the Unification Front Department.[62]

▪ ▪ *Operations Department*
The Operations Department was a newly established organization responsible for basic and advanced training, escort training, and escort operations. The KPA formed the department apparently by separating

the Liaison Section from the Liaison Department and combining it with assets from the Research Department. The Operations Department evidently absorbed many responsibilities formerly under the jurisdiction of the Liaison (e.g., the Foreign Operations Section) and Research Departments, including the training and support of foreign terrorist and revolutionary organizations. Subordinate to Operations were the four seaborne escort and two overland escort units formerly under the Liaison Department. According to Chun Chung-nam and Lee Sang-kyu, infiltrators captured in 1983, each of these escort units had approximately 400 trained agents, for a total of 2,400, not including administrative and other operational personnel.[63] In 1989, Suh Yong-chul, a defector from the overland escort unit headquartered in Kaesong, stated that each unit had approximately 200 personnel.[64] The only known organizational changes within these units themselves was the possible relocation of one overland escort unit headquarters from P'yonggang to Sariwon and the assignment of new unit designations to all its various subordinate components. Only one designation change from this period is currently known: the 632nd Army Unit became the 313th Army Unit.

Notable during this period was the purchase and indigenous development of a number of swimmer delivery vehicles and infiltration craft. These craft were utilized by both the Operations Department and the Reconnaissance Bureau's seaborne escort unit. One such infiltration craft was a high-speed semisubmersible, with a crew of two and capable of carrying three passengers. An example of this craft was captured by the ROK in 1983.[65]

■ ■ *Research Department for External Intelligence*
Continuing its turbulent history for organizational restructuring, the Research Department was reorganized once more in 1982–83. The new organization was named the Research Department for External Intelligence (RDEI, also called the External Information Research Department and External Information Department). The RDEI had as its primary function the collection of external intelligence and foreign operations. It was organized into geographic subsections (e.g., North American Affairs and Japan Affairs). The RDEI's newly assigned foreign intelligence responsibilities overlapped those of other departments and organizations, including the Reconnaissance Bureau and the Information Bureau of the State Security Department.[66] More significantly, the RDEI was placed under the direct control of Kim Chong-il.

One interesting organizational change during this period was the direct result of Kim Hyon-hui's failure to successfully commit suicide after she was detained for her role in bombing Korean Airlines flight 858.

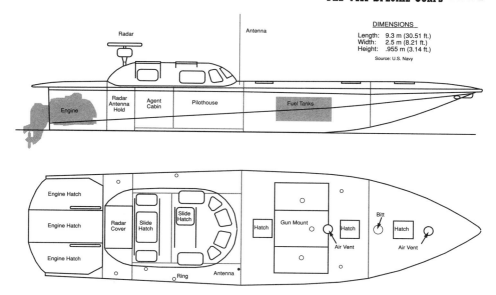

High-speed, semisubmersible infiltration craft.

A recent defector recounts that because her suicide attempt failed, Kim Chong-il "made a decision that 'women agents are no good' and all 20 female agents, who were working at the [RDEI], were discharged from the service. After this incident, no [female] agent was again involved in a special mission."[67] Whether this still holds true is uncertain.

▪ RECONNAISSANCE BUREAU

The primary missions of the Reconnaissance Bureau continued to be the collection of tactical and strategic intelligence within the military sphere, and strategic special operations throughout the ROK and overseas. Although the effects of the 1982–83 reorganization on the Reconnaissance Bureau are presently unclear, its responsibilities and capabilities for strategic special operations continued to expand. The only exception to this was apparently the relinquishing of any remaining control over the DMZ police units. These units evidently were now under the control of the Forward Corps reconnaissance staffs. Coordination between these units and the Reconnaissance Bureau, however, is believed to have continued.

The underlying organization of the Reconnaissance Bureau remained essentially unchanged during this period. The three subordinate sniper brigades continued to develop their special warfare capabilities with expanded training and new equipment. During the mid to late 1980s an expansion of the sniper units subordinate to the Reconnaissance Bureau occurred. The exact nature of this expansion is unclear, however, two alternatives suggest themselves. First, a fourth sniper brigade (possibly identified as the 62nd or 63rd Sniper Brigade) was initially established and then disbanded. The remaining personnel were then used to establish five reconnaissance battalions. Second, there was no fourth sniper brigade and five independent reconnaissance battalions were simply established subordinate to the Reconnaissance Bureau.[68] The bureau also experienced an expanding role in foreign military assistance and in supporting international terrorist and revolutionary groups. The Foreign Language College probably expanded its operations to adjust to these expanding Reconnaissance Bureau responsibilities. Concurrent with this, the emphasis of foreign language training within the DPRK was changing. With the collapse of Communism within the Soviet Union and Eastern Europe in the late 1980s and the resulting deterioration of relationships with the DPRK, the importance of Russian language training was gradually reduced.[69] The bureau's seaborne escort unit (formerly the 448th Army Unit) continued to expand its capabilities with the continued introduction of new specialized swimmer delivery vehicles, midget submarines, semisubmersible infiltration craft, and cargo ships.[70]

During 1982–83, the DPRK obtained a surplus civilian *Seahorse II* midget submarine from Germany. This was accomplished using forged end-user certificates through Singapore. A few prototype craft were quickly built, based upon the German submarine, but no mass production was undertaken. About the same time, production of the *Yugo*-class midget submarine probably ended with a total run of approximately forty-five boats having been built in several versions. By the end of the 1980s the Maritime Department's 137th Squadron (although it may not have still been identified as such) was joined by two additional squadrons to conduct midget-submarine operations against the ROK.

Like the organizations subordinate to the SICARO, the Reconnaissance Bureau also operated a small number of trading companies as covers and to generate financing for operations. Additionally, the KPN operated two oceangoing cargo vessels, which are believed to have supported both these trading companies and operations by the Reconnaissance Bureau and VIII Special Corps. In 1988 these were the *Jang Soo Bong-Ho* at 8,000 tons and the *Hae Yeon-Ho* at 5,000.[71]

One final development concerning the Reconnaissance Bureau occurred during this period. In 1989, Lt. Gen. Kim Tae-sik was appointed director of the Reconnaissance Bureau, replacing Lt. Gen. Chang Song-u.[72]

▪ ▪ *VIII Special Corps*

By far the greatest changes during this period occurred within the VIII Special Corps, which grew dramatically in capabilities, size, and number of subordinate units. By 1984 the special purpose forces (including the three sniper brigades of the Reconnaissance Bureau) had increased in size to eighteen brigades, and personnel strength had risen to approximately eighty-one thousand.[73] Five years later, in 1989, this personnel strength had risen to approximately eighty-five thousand organized into twenty-two brigades (including the three sniper brigades of the Reconnaissance Bureau). Accompanying this was the conversion of a number of standard light infantry brigades into "sniper" brigades and the establishment of light infantry battalions subordinate to most KPA divisions and brigades. While these division- and brigade-level light infantry battalions were not part of the VIII Special Corps there was some level of coordination between their parent units and the corps. If the manpower from these light infantry battalions were added to that of the VIII Special Corps it would have reached approximately one hundred thousand in 1989.

▪ ▪ *Airborne and Airborne Sniper Brigades*

Although the number and organization of regular airborne brigades would remain unchanged at three, during the mid-1980s the KPA began the formation a new type of airborne unit, the airborne sniper brigade (also called Air Force sniper brigades). These were essentially light infantry brigades that received primarily air assault training, although some additional airborne training is believed to have been given. The organizational details of the new airborne sniper brigades are unclear, but they probably followed that of the airborne brigades. The differences between the two units appear to be centered around their missions and mode of employment. The airborne brigades had a conventional mission of assaulting and holding strategic targets within the ROK/U.S. rear areas in company- and battalion-sized units. For such operations they would utilize An-2 and Li-2 transports. On the defense, these units were assigned the counter-airborne and counter-invasion mission. The airborne sniper brigades had offensive special operations as their primary mission. For these missions they would operate in team-sized units and utilize Hughes MD-500 and Mi-2 helicopters. It is believed that the airborne sniper brigades were initially established under the command of the KPAF, although they were soon subordinated to the VIII Special Corps.[74] Apparently, at least some elements of these units received training with sailplanes, ultralights, and hot-air balloons.

In 1981–82, the KPAF acquired approximately fifteen to twenty additional Y-5s (An-2 Colts) from the PRC. These, however, are believed to have been replacement aircraft and did not necessarily increase the total number of the type in service.[75] Sometime during the early 1980s the KPAF began receiving approximately sixty Mi-2 Hoplite helicopters from PZL in Poland.[76] This was followed by a remarkable covert operation in 1984–85, in which the DPRK acquired eighty-seven Hughes MD-500 (twenty model 500Ds, sixty-six model 500Es, and one model 300C) helicopters. These were civilian versions of the MD-500 Defender antitank helicopters used in large numbers by the ROKAF. The KPAF subsequently armed these MD-500s and painted them with ROKAF markings.[77] Thus configured, these helicopters would prove extremely useful to the KPA in any renewed conflict. This was especially true in the areas of special operations and air base assault. The following year, 1986, the helicopters were formed into a special task force at Pakch'on Air Base, 70 kilometers north of P'yongyang.[78] Airborne sniper units have actively trained with these helicopters, sometimes near the DMZ, reportedly with occasional penetrations of ROK airspace.[79] The details of the organizational relationship between the airborne sniper brigades and the MD-500 and Mi-2 units is presently unclear. The helicopter units are controlled by the KPAF, and the airborne sniper brigades by the VIII Special Corps.

Also acquired during the mid-1980s were approximately fifty Mi-24 Hind attack helicopters.[80] While these are optimized for their attack mission, they also have a transport capacity of four troops.[81] Preliminary indications are that both airborne sniper and sniper brigade personnel have trained with the Mi-24 Hinds.[82]

By the late 1980s the KPAF's airlift capability had improve significantly (table 4-4). These capabilities were now organized into three helicopter regiments, three An-2 Colt regiments, and a transport regiment. Estimated strength was 286 aircraft and 257 helicopters. Many of the aircraft in the transportation regiment were utilized solely for governmental support and civilian transport and were thus unavailable for combat operations. This force had a theoretical total airlift capability of about 5,700 troops, or approximately 1½ airborne or airborne sniper brigades.

▪ ▪ *Light Infantry Brigades*

As noted above, sometime during 1982–84 the KPA initiated a major reorganization and redeployment program. The major points of this program were the forward deployment of various General Headquarters and second-echelon assets; the reorganization of several infantry or motorized infantry divisions as brigades (thus making them similar to the combined arms brigades); and the expansion of the VIII Special Corps.[83] The conversion of the infantry and motorized infantry divisions into brigades was accomplished by splitting a division in half, into two brigades, with

Table 4-4

KPAF AIRLIFT CAPABILITY, LATE 1980s

Aircraft	Est. Number	Est. Capacity (Troops)	Total Lift Capacity (Troops)
An-2 Colt/Y-5	250	8	2,000
An-24 Coke	10	50	500
Il-14 Crate	5	28	140
Il-18 Coot	4	75	300
Il-62 Classic	1	175	175
Li-2 Cab	14	16	224
Tu-154B Careless	2	167	334
MD-500D/E Defender	87	4	348
Mi-2 Hoplite	60	4	240
Mi-4 Hound/Z-5	40	15	600
Mi-8/-17 Hip	20	32	640
Mi-24 Hind	50	4	200
Total	543		5,701

the excess units being reorganized at corps level. The expansion of VIII Special Corps was accomplished by the establishment of additional light infantry brigades. Some of these new light infantry units went to the creation of the airborne and amphibious units.

The early 1980s had begun with the Forward Area Corps having a light infantry brigade and an attached sniper brigade from the Reconnaissance Bureau, while most of their subordinate brigades/divisions possessed an organic light infantry battalion. The IV Corps, located in the southwest corner of the DPRK and facing the maritime portion of the DMZ, had two light infantry brigades. Most of IV Corps' subordinate brigades/divisions apparently had no organic light infantry battalions. By 1989, this had changed significantly. The Forward Area Corps now had two light infantry brigades and an attached sniper brigade from the Reconnaissance Bureau, and all their subordinate brigades/divisions possessed organic light infantry battalions. The IV Corps still had two light infantry brigades, but most of its subordinate brigades/divisions now also had organic light infantry battalions. The process of establishing light infantry units within the Rear Corps that had begun during the 1970s continued throughout this period. These light infantry personnel and units established within the Rear Area Corps, however, went to the establishment of light infantry brigades, rather then to brigade/division-level light infantry battalions.

Although the organization of the light infantry brigades remained essentially unchanged, there were apparently some minor differences among brigades in the number of organic light infantry battalions. Details on the numbers, however, are lacking.[84]

The brigade/division-level light infantry battalions were organized identically to the battalions subordinate to the light infantry brigades. They functioned in the reconnaissance or ranger role for their parent units and generally only received administrative and training support from the VIII Special Corps.

■ ■ *Amphibious Sniper Brigades*
Considerable efforts were made during this period to expand the size and capabilities of the KPA's amphibious warfare forces. Although the organizational developments are unclear, by 1982–84, the single amphibious sniper brigade under the control of the VIII Special Corps had been expanded into two brigades.

The headquarters for these two brigades were located at Wonsan and Namp'o. Each brigade consisted of approximately 2,000 troops and was organized into a small headquarters staff, five understrength battalions, and a signal company. Each battalion consisted of approximately 380 troops and was organized into five companies of 75 troops each. The brigade deployed on the east coast had its subordinate battalions dispersed in the Wonsan and Sinch'ang areas; the west coast brigade deployed its subordinate battalions in the areas of Ch'o-do, Namp'o, and the Ch'ongch'on River estuary. On the surface these units appeared woefully understrength. It is important to understand, however, that this "brigade" was more correctly a collection of elite naval commando "teams" and not a traditional naval infantry type of combat unit. Some amphibious sniper battalions were undoubtedly the equivalent of "combat swimmer" (similar in capabilities to Soviet naval commandos or U.S. SEAL units), and "special boat" units (similar to the U.S. SEAL special boat units and SEAL delivery vehicle teams). Elements of this brigade also probably worked closely with the Reconnaissance Bureau's and Operation Department's sea escort units.[85]

By 1988, the amphibious sniper brigades had expanded to seven battalions and approximately 3,500 troops. One brigade remained headquartered and deployed in the Wonsan area. The west coast brigade was headquartered at Hakkye and Pip'a-got, presumably with two battalions deployed in the Hakkye area and four battalions in the Pip'a-got area. Each brigade also had a signal company, an engineer company, and rear services elements. It is believed that a few women were assigned to the signal and rear services elements of the brigades. The brigades also possibly contained a small "combat swimmer" unit. Each subordinate battalion had a personnel strength of approximately 500 and was organized into a headquarters element, four or five companies, and combat support and rear services elements.[86]

As noted above, during the mid-1970s the KPN had established requirements for both more capable and faster amphibious warfare vessels.[87] This had led to the *Namp'o*-class LCPF in 1974–75 and the *Hantae*-class LSM about 1980. Construction of these classes continued through the 1980s and was supplemented by new craft. In 1983 construction began on the *Hungnam*-class LSM, which was larger than the *Hantae*-class LSM and capable of carrying four or five medium tanks. More significantly, in 1987, construction of the high-speed *Kong Bang I/II* LCPA (landing craft, personnel, air-cushion) began. This class was based on commercial technology imported from the United Kingdom and western Europe. These air-cushion vehicles had a top speed of 52 knots and could carry forty to fifty troops. The *Kong Bang I/II* added tremendously to the KPN's amphibious assault capabilities since they could quickly and easily navigate the large mudflats and tidal pools on the west coast of the Korean Peninsula and could deliver troops onto almost any beach within the ROK. More significantly, the KPN could now deliver not only amphibious units, but also regular ground troops, artillery, and armor to a landing site. The augmented landing capabilities greatly improved their chances for initial success and sustainability and raised the threat to the ROK rear. Notably, this increased capability now extended the threat of KPA amphibious assault out of the coastal areas of the ROK and into its interior, especially in the western portion of the country with its relatively flat terrain.

The introduction of the *Kong Bang I/II* had two interesting effects on the KPN. First, the commitment of scarce resources (especially shipyard capacities) to the construction of the *Kong Bang I/II* apparently hurt the production of several classes of missile-armed fast attack craft. Second, although the number of *Namp'o* LCPF increased slightly during this period to about one hundred, only eighty were capable of amphibious operations. With the introduction of the *Kong Bang I/II,* approximately twenty of the oldest *Namp'o*s were modified for other duties. These older craft had their bow doors welded shut and were thereafter used for patrol duties.[88]

With all the above taken into account, by 1989, production of new *Hungnam*-class LSM and *Kong Bang I/II* LCPA had increased the KPN's

Table 4-5

KPN Aᴍᴘʜɪʙɪᴏᴜs Wᴀʀғᴀʀᴇ Cᴀᴘᴀʙɪʟɪᴛɪᴇs, Eᴀʀʟʏ–1980s

	Amphibious Warfare Craft				Submarines			
	LCPF	LCU	LCM	Total	SSc	SSm	SS	Total
West Sea Fleet								
Tasa-ri	23			23				
Namp'o	11		10	21				
Pip'a-got							5	5
Ch'o-do			8	8				
Sa-got	9	2	4	15		1		1
East Sea Fleet								
Ijin-dong	20	2		22	1			1
Ch'ongjin	6			6				
Kimch'aek			2	2				
Cha-ho		2	2	4			4	4
Mayang-do	5	2	4	11			10	10
Wonsan		2		2				
Changjun						5		5
Total	74	10	30	114	1	6	19	26

amphibious lift capability to approximately fourteen thousand troops (table 4-6).

Eꜱᴄᴀʟᴀᴛɪᴏɴ ᴏғ Oᴘᴇʀᴀᴛɪᴏɴꜱ ᴀɢᴀɪɴꜱᴛ ᴛʜᴇ ROK, 1983

In 1983, the DPRK stepped up their operations against the ROK, both at home and abroad. That year, ROK security forces thwarted four infiltration attempts, and in the process, at least eleven infiltrators were killed and two captured. Although the exact reasons for this escalation are unclear, a number of sources attribute this to the growing influence of Kim Chong-il.

On 19 June, ROKA troops intercepted and killed three heavily armed commando frogmen (believed to be from a Reconnaissance Bureau sniper brigade) attempting to cross the Imjin River near Munsan, 32 kilometers northwest of Seoul. The commandos' equipment included ROKA combat

Table 4-6

KPN AMPHIBIOUS LIFT CAPABILITY, 1989

Class	Est. Number	Est. Capacity (Troops)	Total Lift Capacity (Troops)
Hanch'on-class LCM	7	250	1,750
Hantae-class LSM	8	350	2,800
Hungnam-class LSM	16	400	6,400
Kong Bang I/II-class LCPA	25	40–50	1,000–1,250
Namp'o-class LCPF	80	30	2,400
Total	136		14,350–14,600

fatigues, civilian clothes, and a sophisticated silencer-equipped pistol typically employed by DPRK infiltrators on assassination missions. ROK authorities believed that these infiltrations were part of an effort to disrupt the increasing number of international meetings being held in Seoul, including a general meeting of the Inter-Parliamentary Union scheduled for October.

The next month, during the early morning hours of 29 July, ROK coastal guard police spotted a DPRK high-speed infiltration craft and opened fire as it approached the coast near Wolsung, approximately 300 kilometers southeast of Seoul.[89] It is believed that the craft had been dropped off by a larger vessel late on the twenty-eighth and had then approached the coast under cover of darkness. ROKN and ROKAF units were immediately alerted, and at approximately 0100 hours, the infiltration craft was located and sunk. Five infiltrators in scuba gear, believed to be from the Reconnaissance Bureau, were killed on the beach. Much of their equipment, including a variety of photo reconnaissance equipment, was recovered. Additional personnel may have been on board the infiltration craft, since bits of human flesh and diving gear were found in the area. A total of 318 items were recovered in the area of the

131

infiltration attempt, including a rubber boat, communications equipment, compasses, M-16 rifles, film, and ammunition. Most ominously, this incident occurred within 5 kilometers of the Canadian-built 680-megawatt nuclear power plant, which raised considerable concern among ROK officials as to the target of the infiltrators: "Judging from the equipment we seized, and the circumstances in which the incident occurred, we have come to the conclusion that their target was the nuclear power plant."[90]

Two weeks later, on 13 August, an ROKN helicopter sank another infiltration craft in waters off the island of Ullung-do, approximately 160 kilometers off the east coast. At approximately 1000 hours, the ROKN helicopter spotted a suspicious boat, disguised as the Japanese vessel *Asahi-Maru,* in waters east of Ullung-do. The 60-ton, 28-meter-long vessel was equipped as a "mother ship" from which smaller craft could be launched. A signal was sent ordering the boat to halt, which was ignored. The boat then began to flee at 40 knots. The ROKN helicopter next fired several warning shots across its bow. The boat returned fire, and the helicopter attacked and sank the vessel at 1140 hours. The bodies of three crewmen, underwater gear, three machine guns, reconnaissance equipment, two diving suits, two life jackets, and three wallets carrying the picture of Kim Il-song were recovered from the scene of the sinking.[91]

In September, four ROK civilians were killed and two others wounded in an explosion at the U.S. Information Service offices in Taegu. No suspects were arrested at the time, but ROK authorities suspected that the explosion was the work of a DPRK operative. Six years later, in October 1989, a Liaison Department defector, Suh Yong-chul, revealed that the bombing was conducted by a Liaison Department operative, Yi Chol, who received a "hero's homecoming" and was awarded a medal for the Taegu mission.[92]

On 3 December 1983, ROK coastal guard troops spotted a 5-ton DPRK semisubmersible high-speed infiltration craft off Pusan. The troops waited until the craft had reached shore and two infiltrators disembarked. When the DPRK agents were close enough, the ROK troops fired a flare and then jumped and overpowered the infiltrators. Approximately 20 minutes after their capture, ROKN and ROKAF units located, attacked, and sank the infiltration craft, killing its three-member crew. Over four hundred items of equipment, including pistols, hand grenades, and night-vision equipment, were seized from the infiltrators. The two infiltrators, Chun Chung-nam and Lee Sang-kyu, were members of the Liaison Department's 313th Army Unit (also called the 313th Liaison Unit, 313th Liaison Station, and 313th Liaison Department), based in Wonsan. They later provided information on their training and mission (Chun had originally tried to commit suicide by biting off his tongue): "We were isolated on an island off Wonsan for 45 days for the infiltration training. We were confident of success in the mission on December 3rd because we infiltrated the same area in October last year." They stated that they underwent simulated infiltration training twenty-five times in the DPRK before the Pusan mission. Their mission was to rendezvous with an agent already in the Pusan area and bomb important public facilities there with the help of the agent.[93]

RANGOON BOMBING

Clearly the most aggressive act committed by the DPRK in 1983 was the Rangoon, Burma, bombing on 9 October. It was an assassination attempt on ROK President Chon Tu-hwan in which twenty-one people, including four ROK cabinet ministers, were killed. Enough information concerning this operation has come to light to provide a relatively detailed account of how Reconnaissance Bureau sniper brigade personnel conduct external assassination missions.

Sometime in mid-1983, the Liaison Department conceived a plan to assassinate President Chon Tu-hwan during his October six-nation tour of Australia, Brunei, Burma, India, New Zealand, and Sri Lanka. Because of logistical and political considerations, possible sites for the assassination attempt were limited to Burma and Sri Lanka. Strongly influencing the DPRK decision was the conviction that the blame for an assassination attempt in either of these two countries could be easily placed upon domestic insurgents. This assumption was born out in the immediate wake of the Rangoon bombing, when analysts speculated that the attack had been mounted by allies of the former Burmese intelligence chief, Brig. Gen. Tin Oo, recently removed from power, or any of a number of guerrilla groups fighting against the Burmese government, including the Burmese Communist Party.

Arrangements were made to insert an assassination team into the country using the cargo ship *Tong Gon Ae Guk-ho*. Upon completion of the mission, the *Tong Gon Ae Guk-ho* would recover the team. In August 1983, a team composed of three members from the Reconnaissance Bureau (possible the 62nd Sniper Brigade) was assembled under the operational control of the Liaison Department.[94] The team consisted of Maj. Zin Mo (commander), Capt. Kim Chi-o (demolition specialist), and Capt. Kang Min-chul (demolition specialist). Although details of their pre-mission training are incomplete, it is known that the team received intensive mission-specific training in the city of Kaesong in the II Corps. Additionally, they could speak Chinese, Russian, English, and Korean. After receiving a final mission briefing by their unit commander, Kang Chang-su, the team boarded the *Tong Gon Ae Guk-ho* at the port of Ongjin, on 9

September. On 17 September, the vessel entered Rangoon with a cargo of construction materials. The ship unloaded its cargo on 21 September at a Rangoon wharf. The ship's captain then requested permission to stay until 28 September to make engine repairs before heading for Alexandria, Egypt, its next port of call. Although the captain offered to keep the vessel moored at midstream in the Rangoon River, port authorities ordered the ship to move approximately 22 kilometers upriver until 22 September.

On 22 September, the team dressed as crew members and left the vessel by motorboat. Upon entering Rangoon, the team was met by a woman (possibly a Liaison Department agent) who guided them to the home of a counselor from the DPRK embassy. Two days later, on 24 September, the team received its final orders, weapons, remote-control devices, and explosives from the counselor. The same day, the *Tong Gon Ae Guk-ho* quietly slipped out of Rangoon, to minimize the possibility of being connected with the assassination, and sailed to Sri Lanka. The Rangoon team remained at the counselor's home until 6 October, when it conducted a reconnaissance of the Aung San Martyrs' Mausoleum.[95] The following evening, at 2000 hours, the team members bribed the mausoleum caretaker to allow them and three prostitutes to use the grounds on the pretext of a date.[96] While here, they planted three bombs and then left. Each bomb was approximately 25 centimeters long and consisted of a charge of plastic explosive embedded with steel balls and an electronic detonating device powered by Hitachi batteries.[97]

On 9 October, the team made at least two trips to an automobile service station near the mausoleum to verify that the bombs had not been detected. It was from here that they detonated the bombs by remote control at 1025 hours, after a second trip to the service station. The explosion was felt over 3 kilometers away. Two fortuitous events kept the number of casualties low and prevented the death of President Chon Tu-hwan. First, only one of the three bombs was successfully detonated. Second, the team had mistaken Ambassador Lee Kae-chul's motorcade for that of President Chon Tu-hwan, who had been delayed in traffic. After the explosion, the team had planned to return to the counselor's home. Because of the presence of Burmese security personnel, however, the team split into two and headed for the Rangoon River, where they were reportedly to be picked up by the *Tong Gon Ae Guk-ho* on 12 October.

After the explosion, the Burmese security authorities initiated a massive search operation to locate and capture the assassins. That night, Maj. Zin Mo was arrested after being spotted swimming across a creek in east Rangoon, about 10 hours after the blast. He lost one eye and an arm when he detonated a grenade in an attempt to kill himself to avoid capture. Two days later, on 12 October, while waiting to rendezvous with the *Tong Gon*

Ae Guk-ho, Captains Kang Min-chul and Kim Chi-o were discovered hiding along a river bank. In the subsequent pursuit and firefight, Captain Kim was killed. Captain Kang was arrested after being wounded when he too detonated a grenade in an attempt to kill himself to avoid capture.

On 4 November 1983, the Burmese government announced that the DPRK was behind the assassination attempt and ordered the DPRK embassy closed and all diplomats out of the country within 48 hours. On 6 November, Burmese troops escorted the twelve DPRK diplomats and eight dependents to the Rangoon airport in two minibuses provided by the Soviet embassy. The foreigners boarded a DPRK Tu-154 airliner for P'yongyang. The official DPRK response to the findings of the Burmese investigation was given at the 422d meeting of the Korean Military Armistice Commission by Maj. Gen. Lee Tae-ho: "As a matter of fact, the Rangoon incident has nothing to do with us. The southern puppet [ROK] regime fabricated it."

After ten trial sessions the Rangoon Division People's Court, on 10 December 1983, sentenced both Maj. Zin Mo and Capt. Kang Min-chul to death. The official Burmese report that was submitted to the Legal Committee of the U.N. General Assembly on 2 October 1984 indicated that key prosecution evidence was provided by the confession of Captain Kang. Major Zin reportedly kept silent during the trial. Both Zin and Kang then appealed for clemency. Following the rejection of Maj. Zin Mo's appeal the Council of State, Burma's highest court, sentenced him to death by hanging. The following month, on 6 April 1985, this sentence was carried out at Insein Prison, near Rangoon. The Council of State, however, sustained Captain Kang's appeal and indefinitely postponed his death sentence.[98]

Interestingly, fragmentary information indicates that a backup attempt was planned for Kandy, Sri Lanka, by a second team aboard the *Tong Gon Ae Guk-ho* if the assassination team could not complete its assignment in Burma. Following its departure from Rangoon, the *Tong Gon Ae Guk-ho* proceeded west across the Bay of Bengal to Colombo, Sri Lanka. Here the ship docked in Colombo on 29 September, and the captain requested permission to stay and conduct engine repairs, just as he had done in Burma. While the ship was docked in Colombo, twenty-six of the thirty-nine crew members visited the city of Kandy, one of the scheduled stops on ROK President Chon Tu-hwan's itinerary. It is believed that the ship was going to wait in Colombo until the results of the Burma team's attempt were known. If the Burma team was unsuccessful, the *Tong Gon Ae Guk-ho* would leave the Sri Lanka team to make an attempt in Kandy and sail back to Rangoon to pick up the Burma team. The Sri Lanka team would then be recovered, successful or not, at a later time. This plan was foiled, however, when the ROK ambassador to Sri Lanka expressed his concerns over the ship's presence. The Sri Lankan government, having had several negative experiences with DPRK ships in the past, quickly agreed, and the *Tong Gon Ae Guk-ho* was ordered to leave. This Sri Lanka team might have been able to stay behind had it not been for the thoroughness of the Sri Lankan government. On 6 October, before allowing the ship sail, Sri Lankan policemen boarded the vessel and verified the cargo and crew manifests. Three days later, on 9 October, the Burma team detonated their bomb in an attempt to assassinate President Chon Tu-hwan. Even if the Sri Lanka team had been able to complete preparations, they would have been superfluous, since the ROK president canceled the remainder of his six-nation trip, which was to have taken him to Sri Lanka on 14–16 October. On 10 October, Sri Lanka's National Security Council ordered an investigation to determine whether the visit of the *Tong Gon Ae Guk-ho* was linked with the Rangoon bombing.

Sri Lanka was not the last of the *Tong Gon Ae Guk-ho*'s troubles during its late 1983 voyage. After its calls at Aden, People's Democratic Republic of Yemen; Alexandria, Egypt; and Calcutta, India; the ship proceeded to Singapore. On 10 November, Singapore barred the vessel from entering Singapore harbor, indicating its concerns that the ship might be involved in terrorist operations such as the Rangoon bombing. The ship remained anchored at Sultan Shoal, 10 kilometers off the Singapore mainland, for several days before traveling onto the DPRK.

One final result of the failed Rangoon assassination attempt was that Kim Chung-nin was removed from his position as SICARO in March 1984 and demoted to candidate member of the KWP's Political Committee. He was replaced by Ho Tam. In January 1985, the demoted Kim was even further humiliated by being dismissed from his position on KWP's Political Committee. Amazingly, one month later, in February, he was reappointed as SICARO. The reasons for this remarkable turn of events are unknown, but it would appear to be a powerful testament to his political skill.[99]

Disrupting the Olympics

The ROK's winning the honor of hosting the 1988 summer Olympics was a tremendous blow to the prestige of the DPRK. Most of the DPRK's operations from 1984 to 1988 were conducted with one goal in mind: disrupting the 1988 Seoul Olympics by making the world believe that the ROK was unsafe to visit. That these operation extended over a four-year period and varied in intensity from nuisance raids to the destruction of Korean Airlines flight 858 is a clear indication of the DPRK's dedication and intensity of its animosity toward the ROK. These operations also witnessed the expanding power of Kim Chong-il.

On 24 September 1984, several days before the dedication of the

Olympic Stadium in Seoul, a DPRK operative forcibly entered a private dining room at a restaurant in Taegu and shot and killed two ROK women. Approximately a half hour later, he entered a nearby beauty parlor and wounded a woman there, before being overpowered by three men. Before ROK police could arrive, however, he swallowed a capsule of poison he had been carrying. ROK authorities seized forty items from the man's body, including a pistol, ammunition, and a radio transmitter. ROK security officials later identified the pistol as one of the hundred pistols that the DPRK had imported from the Browning Company in Belgium on 8 January 1975. Other examples from this same Browning order were seized from the three Reconnaissance Bureau personnel responsible for the Rangoon bombing.[100] The exact reasons for the shootings are unclear, but they were probably in response to a threat to the agent's "cover," and not related directly to the objectives of his mission.

On 13 September 1984, Chung Hae Kwon was arrested while loitering near construction sites in Seoul, where he was seeking work. During the routine investigation following Chung's arrest, he unsuccessfully tried to swallow a poison capsule that he had hidden on his body. When this failed, he tried to kill himself by biting off his tongue. Authorities quickly realized that Chung was a DPRK agent and searched his apartment. The search recovered a Browning pistol, ammunition, grenades, two radio receivers, and code books. Chung later admitted that he was a DPRK operative and that his mission was to assassinate ROK government leaders and destroy government facilities (e.g., broadcasting stations and foreign diplomatic missions). He further stated that his instructions came directly from Kim Chong-il and that he had been provided with the poison capsule to swallow if he were captured.[101]

In early 1985, the Reagan administration had made international terrorism a foreign policy priority, and issued a number of policy statements condemning it. These statements implicated not only Cuba, Iran, Libya, Nicaragua, and Syria, but also the DPRK as supporters of international terrorism. In a July 1985 speech, President Ronald Reagan described the DPRK's potential for international terrorism: "The extent and crudity of North Korean violence against the United States and our ally, South Korea, are a matter of record. . . . What is not readily known or understood is North Korea's wider links to the international terrorist network."

For reasons that are presently unknown, in February 1986, just one year after he was reinstated, Kim Chung-nin was once again dismissed as SICARO. This dismissal was, however, different from previous incidents since Kim continued to function in relatively high political positions.[102]

DPRK anti-Olympic activities continued, and on 14 September 1986, a bomb exploded at Seoul's Kimp'o International Airport, killing five people and wounding more than thirty. ROK authorities charged that the explosion was a DPRK-engineered attempt both to disrupt the Tenth Asian Games, opening in Seoul on 20 September, and to cast a shadow over the forthcoming Olympics. Although there is little doubt that the DPRK was involved in the bombing, it should be noted that no additional information has come to light to support the ROK claims.[103]

The most serious effort to disrupt the Olympics was the bombing of Korean Airlines flight 858.[104] The bombing was conducted under direct orders from Kim Chong-il, by two operatives of the RDEI, Kim Sung-il and Kim Hyon-hui. The director of the RDEI, Yi Yong-hyok, gave the orders to the two operatives on 7 October 1987. The substance of these orders was the following:

> The party has decided to bomb a Korean Air plane with the aim of blocking south Korea's attempts to perpetuate the two Koreas and also to host the 1988 Olympics on their own.
>
> This project, to be carried out at a critical juncture in time will pour cold water on the desire of all nations of the world to participate in the Olympics and will deal the south Korean puppet regime a fatal blow.
>
> This project must be accomplished without fail and must be kept in absolute secrecy.[105]

Following a month-long specialized explosives course, the the two agents received their final mission briefing from Yi on 10 November. During the briefing, Yi once again emphasized the importance of the mission and the fact that it was being conducted under orders personally written by Kim Chong-il. Two days later, the day of their departure from P'yongyang, Kim Hyon-hui was administered an oath of allegiance in front of a picture of Kim Chong-il.

They traveled to Europe and then to Baghdad. Here, on the evening of 28 November, they boarded Korean Airline flight 858 bound for Seoul, via Abu Dhabi, and Bangkok. Just prior to boarding, Kim Sung-il set the time fuse on the bomb. Once on board, they placed the bomb and liquid explosive in the carry-on compartments above their seats. When the flight arrived at Abu Dhabi they got off, leaving the explosives on board. The plane then took off for Bangkok, and at approximately 2:05 P.M. Korea standard time on 29 November 1987, flight 858 exploded in midair over the Andaman Sea, killing all 115 persons aboard.

Thanks to quick action on the part of Japanese and Bahraini authorities, both Kim Sung-il and Kim Hyon-hui were detained as possible suspects as they attempted to leave Bahrain on 1 December. During the detention, when the situation seemed hopeless, both operatives swallowed small cyanide capsules concealed within cigarette filters.[106] Kim Sung-il quickly died, but Kim Hyon-hui was unable to swallow her capsule completely when an alert Bahraini policewomen immediately cleaned her mouth and started cardiopulmonary resuscitation. Kim Hyon-hui was then quickly transported to a hospital, where her stomach was flushed out. After an initial investigation by Bahraini officials that indicated a DPRK involvement, all evidence, including Kim Hyon-hui herself, and the body of Kim Sung-il were transferred to the ROK on 15 December.

On 28 December, Kim Hyon-hui confessed that she was an operative of the RDEI and that she and Kim Sung-il had planted a bomb on Korean Airlines flight 858 at the express orders of Kim Chong-il.[107] On 25 April 1989, she was sentenced to death for her role in the bombing. An appeals court upheld the conviction on 22 July, and Kim's lawyers stated that they would appeal the decision to the Supreme Court.[108] She was subsequently granted a special amnesty.

As the repercussions of the DPRK's involvement in the destruction of flight 858 snowballed, and as international pressure was brought to bear, the Foreign Ministry of the DPRK, on 5 September 1988, issued a statement that it had no intention of disrupting the Seoul Olympics: "We hereby make it clear that we do not have the slightest intention to obstruct the progress of the Games or threaten them by force of arms. If anything happens in south Korea during the Olympic Games, it will have nothing to do with us and the United states and the south Korean authorities themselves should be held responsible for it. As for 'terrorism,' it is utterly alien to us and the United States itself is the chieftain of state terrorism as already exposed to the world."[109]

That the threat of both international political and military retaliation eventually became too great for the DPRK to ignore was expressed quite simply and succinctly by Suh Yong-chul, a defector from the Liaison Department's Kaesong office: "Six members of our unit received special training to infiltrate during the Olympics, but the plan was canceled. I later knew that it was because the North feared that the ROK side would retaliate. . . . "[110]

The embarrassment resulting from the bombing of Korean Airlines flight 858 is believed to have been the primary factor leading again to the reinstatement of Kim Chung-nin as SICARO in November 1988.[111]

MILITARY ASSISTANCE AND SUPPORT OF INTERNATIONAL TERRORISM, 1969–89

During the twenty years from 1969 to 1989, the DPRK expanded its foreign military assistance to a number of developing countries and to its support for terrorist and revolutionary groups.[112] Personnel from the VIII Special Corps and Reconnaissance Bureau would provide the majority of the advisers sent overseas on military assistance missions, and would serve as instructors and trainers to terrorist and revolutionary groups both overseas and within the DPRK. To a lesser degree, personnel from the regular KPA, Ministry of Public Security, and the State Security Department were also involved in these operations.

Beginning in the early 1970s, the DPRK expanded its terrorist and revolutionary organization training infrastructure, which then consisted of approximately six to ten training facilities within the DPRK. These were located near P'yongyang (e.g., Wonhung-ri), Yongbyon, Sangwon, Haeju, Namp'o, and Wonsan. Courses were generally divided into two categories by their length. Short-term courses would typically last three to six months and concentrated on basic skills such as marksmanship, communications, map reading, ambush and counter-ambush, explosives, sabotage, intelligence, propaganda, psychological warfare, kidnaping, assassination, and terrorism. Long-term courses would last twelve to twenty-four months and would focus on advanced command and staff skills, communications, intelligence, and medical training. All courses were accompanied by extensive ideological indoctrination.

Typical of the advanced training within the DPRK during this period was the case of Plutarco Hernandez, a Costa Rican, who after attending a seven-month intelligence seminar in Cuba was sent to the DPRK in 1971. Here he participated in a grueling officers command and staff course, where he met Kim Il-song. Hernandez later returned to Central America and became one of the chief military commanders of the Sandinist National Liberation Front in Nicaragua.[113]

Among the countries and organizations represented by those trained within the DPRK during 1969–74 were Egypt, Guatemala, Nicaragua, the Palestine Liberation Organization (PLO), the Popular Front for the Liberation of Palestine (PFLP), Thailand, Somalia, South West Africa People's Organization (SWAPO), Uganda, and numerous others. Although estimates vary considerably over the total number of persons trained within the DPRK by the end of 1974, most estimates fall within the range of three to four thousand.

The DPRK reportedly was providing housing and support for approximately 60 foreign terrorist and revolutionaries and their dependents. They were grouped together in a special housing area located in the Chol Bong-ri District of P'yongyang. Of the approximately 150 residents, nearly half were from the Americas and Africa. The rest were from Arab and Asian countries, including the members of the Japanese Red Army who hijacked a Japanese Airlines airliner to P'yongyang in 1970. These residents were under the strict control of the State Security Department and were reportedly utilized as area specialists and foreign language instructors.

Support for international terrorist and revolutionary organizations increased during the late 1970s and through the 1980s. Most significant were infrastructure developments within the DPRK and the utilization of overseas training facilities. The support infrastructure within the DPRK continued to develop, with more VIII Special Corps personnel being assigned to the program, larger facilities, and more courses. As of late 1989, there were ten known active training facilities within the DPRK. Overseas, the DPRK maintained training facilities at one time or another during this period in Algeria, Angola, Chile, Cuba, Guyana, Lebanon, Libya, Mozambique, People's Democratic Republic of Yemen (South Yemen), Peru, Somalia, and Uganda. More ominously, it still maintains a few of these facilities today. The majority of this training was conducted by VIII Special Corps and Reconnaissance Bureau personnel under the guidance of SICARO and State Security Department staff.

Training had progressed considerably beyond earlier training, with courses now covering every aspect of guerrilla, revolutionary, terrorist, and conventional warfare. Typical of these was a company commanders course held in the DPRK, between 1 April 1979 and 10 October 1979, for twenty-one members of the PLO.

Estimates vary considerably concerning the total number of persons trained by the DPRK by January 1990. The number trained within the DPRK has been variously reported as between 10,000 and 15,000. Estimates of the number trained overseas by January 1990 range between 5,000 and 8,000.

Paradoxically, during this period, the DPRK entered a new role in many African countries by providing counterinsurgency and internal regime support. In this interesting development, the DPRK was now providing support for friendly governments in their struggles against national liberation movements. This assistance has witnessed DPRK advisers conducting not only counterinsurgency training, but actual operations in support of foreign governments. Typical of this have been DPRK operations in Mozambique and Zimbabwe.

- MOZAMBIQUE
Even before Mozambique achieved independence from Portugal in 1975, the DPRK was heavily committed to providing military assistance to the Mozambique Liberation Front (Frente da Libertacao de Mocambique, FRELIMO).[114] This assistance, which began slowly during the mid-1960s, dramatically increased following Samora Michael's assumption of FRELIMO's leadership in 1969.[115] During the late 1960s and early 1970s,

141

a number of FRELIMO personnel traveled to the DPRK for guerrilla warfare training. This support was supplemented by training received by other FRELIMO personnel at the DPRK embassy in Dar es Salaam, Tanzania, where FRELIMO had its headquarters. The DPRK's support for FRELIMO is believed to have been coordinated with the Soviet Union and Cuba. Interestingly, DPRK training and assistance probably played a significant role in FRELIMO's 1972 victory over a rival guerrilla organization, the Revolutionary Committee of Mozambique (Comite Revolucionario de Mocambique, COREMO), which was being backed by the People's Republic of China.

On 25 June 1975, the day Mozambique achieved its independence from Portugal, it also established formal diplomatic relations with the DPRK. Since then, the DPRK has maintained a military advisory team in Mozambique. These advisers have cooperated with their counterparts from the Soviet Union and Cuba to train Mozambican military and People's Militia personnel and have participated in counterinsurgency operations.

Because of the escalating counterinsurgency struggle with the South African–backed Mozambican National Resistance Movement (Movimento da Resistencia Mocambicana, RENAMO), the DPRK increased its support of the Mozambican military. During 1982, DPRK advisers provided instruction to the National Service of People's Security and helped establish an elite counterinsurgency brigade, which became operational late in 1983. This unit, which became known as the "Clean Brigade," was commanded by one of President Michael's top advisers, Fernando Homwana. Homwana, together with other officers of the brigade, had traveled to the DPRK for advanced training. In mid-1982, DPRK advisers participated in a joint Zimbabwean-Mozambican operation against RENAMO guerrillas along the strategic Umtali-Beira Railway. Although this operation was a failure, it was notable as the first combat action for the DPRK-trained Zimbabwean 5th Brigade (see below).

Despite continued Soviet, Cuban, and DPRK military assistance, as well as numerous joint Zimbabwean–Mozambican operations, the war against RENAMO continued with little definitive success throughout the 1980s, with both sides frequently being accused of atrocities. For example, in July 1987, RENAMO accused the elite "Clean Brigade" of massacring 380 people in the town of Homoine, 300 miles northeast of Maputo: "This [massacre] was probably done by the 'Clean Brigade,' a Mozambican army group trained by North Korean advisors in 1982."[116]

The extent of the DPRK's support for Mozambique and its involvement in counterinsurgency operations continued to be substantial through the early 1990s, when in 1992, Mozambique's President Joaquim Chissano and RENAMO leader Afonso Dhlakama signed a cease-fire agreement to end their fifteen-year civil war.[117] Aside from supporting the Mozambican military, the DPRK has utilized the country as a support base for its operations in Angola and Zambia, as well as a conduit to provide assistance to terrorist and revolutionary organizations in Africa (e.g., SWAPO, the National Resistance Army in Uganda, the Zimbabwe African People's Union, and the Zimbabwe African National Union) and Asia (i.e., Revolutionary Front for the Independence of [East] Timor, FRETILIN). Despite economic difficulties, the DPRK and Mozambique have maintained friendly relations until present.[118]

▪ ZIMBABWE

DPRK involvement in Zimbabwe dates to the mid-1960s, when it cooperated with both the Soviet Union and PRC in supporting alternately Joshua Nkomo's ZAPU and ZANU.[119] This support initially consisted of financial assistance and the training of ZAPU personnel in Tanzania and the DPRK.

During February 1966, twenty-four guerrillas were brought to trial in Rhodesia. During the trial, the prosecution revealed that the defendants were among fifty-two persons who had received training in guerrilla warfare, explosives, small arms, political ideology, map reading, and communications between March 1964 and October 1965. This training was undertaken in six distinct programs, four in the Soviet Union, one in the PRC, and one in the DPRK. Two of the accused stated they had been deceived by ZAPU officials into believing that they were being sent abroad on educational scholarships. Another asserted that he was not trained for subversive activities, but for a role in a future African government in Rhodesia.

Through the late 1960s and early 1970s, most DPRK assistance was funneled to ZANU through Ghana, Tanzania, and Zambia (in the capital city of Lusaka, where ZANU had its headquarters). Following the 1975 FRELIMO victory in Mozambique and ZANU's internal troubles in Zambia, DPRK assistance to ZANU began to flow in increasing amounts through Mozambique. Here the DPRK, with the PRC and FRELIMO, jointly established training camps and support bases for ZANU guerrillas. Cuba, Romania, and Yugoslavia are also known to have provided assistance.

With the 1980 guerrilla victory and establishment of Zimbabwe, the DPRK stood firmly behind Robert Mugabe and his ZANU. The transition from guerrilla army to professional army did not go smoothly, and there were numerous incidents between the rival factions. In October 1981, the unannounced arrival of 106 DPRK advisers to train the newly established 5th and 6th Brigades aroused latent suspicions between the rival factions.[120] The reason for this was threefold. First, President

Mugabe neglected to consult Nkomo on his decision to accept the DPRK's offer of assistance. Second, both units were being formed mainly with Mugabe supporters. Finally, the 5th Brigade was designated as the government's counterinsurgency unit, while the 6th Brigade was to be the presidential guard.

Both units received training from the DPRK advisers at the Battalion Battle School at Inyanga. The 5th Brigade was first committed to combat during mid-1982, when it conducted a joint operation with Mozambican troops against South African–backed RENAMO guerrillas, along the strategic Umtali-Beira Railway. The operation was a failure because of inadequate training and a lack of discipline. As a result, the brigade was sent back to Inyanga for further training. Brigadier Parence Shiri, the commander of the 5th Brigade, expressed his disappointment with the DPRK advisers, indicating that while they were respected for their personal toughness, they were more notable for their extravagant living and lack of personal discipline than for their ability to conduct realistic military training.

Soon after the failure of the 5th Brigade in Mozambique, the first group of DPRK advisers was phased out and returned to the DPRK. In early 1983, a second group of advisers arrived in Zimbabwe to train the paramilitary People's Militia. Training for the 5th and 6th Brigades had by this time been placed in the hands of British and Zimbabwean officers. After its second training cycle, the 5th Brigade was deployed to the southern Matabeleland province (the home province of Mugabe's rival, Joshua Nkomo) in January 1983. Here, during a six-month campaign, the brigade distinguished itself because of its viciousness and atrocities against black civilians. The last DPRK instructors, under the command of Maj. Gen. Sin Hyon-dok, left Zimbabwe on 8 March 1986. In mid-1989, unconfirmed reports indicated that both countries may have agreed to a new DPRK training mission for the Zimbabwean People's Army intelligence and counterinsurgency personnel.

Since then relations between the two countries have remained close, despite several incidents of smuggling by the DPRK.[121] There have been exchanges of military delegations between the countries and in 1993 President Robert G. Mugabe visited P'yongyang.[122] Interestingly, in July 1994, Zimbabwe announced the appointment of Maj. Gen. Constantine Chiwenga as the new army commander with the rank of lieutenant general. Chiwenga has been the commander of several army brigades, including the KPA-trained 5th Brigade during its 1983 operations.[123]

LIGHT INFANTRY TRAINING GUIDANCE BUREAU, 1990–PRESENT

During the 1990s, international events beginning in the 1980s exposed the DPRK to a continuous series of external crises that have influenced its international outlook and international policies. Accompanying these developments have been numerous internal situations that have affected the very core of the DPRK.

At the international level the dramatic dissolution of Communist Eastern Europe and the Soviet Union, coupled with efforts to pursue an unmonitored nuclear program, have resulted in the international isolation of the DPRK. The isolation, coupled with the loss of economic assistance from these countries, precipitated an economic crisis within the DPRK. On the internal scene, frequent changes within the leadership structure designed to strengthen the power base of Kim Chong-il have taken priority, to the detriment of all other governmental functions. These efforts, however, were of considerable practical benefit when Kim Il-song unexpectedly died in July 1994 and Kim Chong-il assumed the leadership of the DPRK. Three years later, during October 1997, Kim Chong-il was elected Secretary General of the Korean Workers' Party. These events have been accompanied by several years of extremely poor agricultural production that have forced the DPRK to appeal to the international community for emergency food assistance. Taken as a whole, the events of the past seven years have, in the minds of the DPRK's leadership, reinforced the anxieties of isolation and vulnerability. As a consequence, Kim Chong-il has continued to maintain, at great expense to the country, the strength and capabilities of the KPA as a shield against the DPRK's enemies.

The DPRK's policy during the 1970s and 1980s of utilizing political subversion and selected military special operations to undermine the ROK has proven to be a failure. The meteoric economic growth of the ROK led to its exercising tremendous political and diplomatic influence throughout the world. As a consequence, the ROK used this power to deftly turn the diplomatic tables on the DPRK, which now finds itself the object of diplomatic isolation within the international community. Additionally, the ROK experienced a smooth democratic transition of political power in December 1992 with the election of President Kim Yong Sam. The average ROK citizen is currently enjoying unprecedented political freedom and one of the highest standards of living in Asia. While almost all Koreans have a strong emotional desire for reunification, the vast majority of ROK citizens have absolutely no desire to see this occur under Communist leadership. In essence the KWP's political message to the people of the ROK has virtually no appeal. This in turn has negated any meaningful growth of the KWP within the ROK.

The culmination of these circumstances has not meant that the DPRK has given up on its desire for reunification or its support for terrorism and revolution. It has, however, forced the DPRK to retreat in many areas, selectively allocate its scarce resources, and reevaluate its policies. With regards to the ROK, the DPRK has apparently modified its policy of the past twenty years. Although the DPRK still maintains an active effort of political subversion, military special operations have declined dramatically. On the political front it has successfully engaged the United States in high-level negotiations, to the virtual exclusion of the ROK. This policy seeks to wear down the United States through constant negotiations, punctuated with discreet military threats (e.g., withdrawal from the Nuclear Nonproliferation Treaty and continuing its nuclear weapons program and cruise and ballistic missile testing), to extract maximum political and economic benefits. At the same time, the DPRK avoids all possible contacts with the ROK unless absolutely compelled into them.

During 1989–90, the DPRK apparently decided that in order to succeed with these new policies and for the regime to have any chance of survival, the intelligence services and KPA would not only have to be maintained but would have to be strengthened. Within this context the basic role of the DPRK's special purpose forces has not changed significantly, but their importance to the KPA and the DPRK's military strategy has risen. The 1990s have witnessed the continued growth of the DPRK's special purpose forces, not only in absolute number of units but also in capabilities. Special purpose forces have lessened their involvement in the support of international terrorist and revolutionary groups and military assistance to developing countries. This has primarily been a result of the DPRK's decaying political and economic strength. It should be emphasized, however, that these activities do still continue, albeit at a much reduced level. The majority of these changes that occurred within the

DPRK's intelligence services also reflected these realities, but also focused upon increased internal security and regime survival.

REORGANIZATION OF ASSETS

Beginning in 1990 several organizational changes within the DPRK's hierarchy enhanced Kim Chong-il's control over the KPA and affected both the VIII Special Corps and the intelligence services.[1] The most significant changes during 1990 occurred within the National Defense Commission. At the Eighteenth Plenum of the Sixth Central People's Committee, held on 23 May 1990, the National Defense Commission became established as its own independent commission, rising to the same status as the Central People's Committee. Previously, it had been one of the six commissions subordinate to the committee. Subsequently, the Ministry of People's Armed Forces was transferred to the National Defense Commission. Concurrent with this, Kim Chong-il was appointed first vice chairman of the National Defense Commission.[2] The following year, on 24 December 1991, Kim Chong-il was appointed supreme commander of the KPA.[3] Four months later, Kim Chong-il and O Chin-u were both awarded the title of marshal on 20 April 1992.[4] One year later Kim Chong-il was appointed chairman of the National Defense Commission.[5]

These changes precipitated a number of other changes within the DPRK's intelligence and special warfare organizations. The SICARO (now frequently identified by ROK/U.S. sources as the Central Committee Secretary in Charge of South Korean Affairs, or CCSKA) continued to be one of the most politically powerful positions within the DPRK, while its subordinate organizations underwent organizational changes and expansion. Sometime during the early 1990s (possibly at the Central People's Committee May 1990 meeting) the VIII Special Corps was renamed the Light Infantry Training Guidance Bureau. The reasons for this redesignation are presently unclear. However, it has been suggested that this was an effort to camouflage the true nature of the organization. The DPRK's special purpose forces continued to expand during this period from 85,000 troops organized into twenty-two brigades in 1990 to approximately 100,000 troops organized into twenty-five brigades in 1996. (Both figures include the Reconnaissance Bureau's three sniper brigades and five reconnaissance battalions.) Additionally, the forces under the CCSKA would add approximately an additional 15,000 personnel (although not all were operational).[6]

By 1996 the intelligence community would consist of the National Intelligence Committee, CCSKA, Reconnaissance Bureau, Ministry of Public Security, and State Security Department. Special warfare responsibilities were spread among three groups: the Reconnaissance Bureau, the Light Infantry Training Guidance Bureau, and the KPA's light infantry brigades and battalions. The KPA's General Political Bureau still maintained a limited special operations capability, but this is limited to its propaganda efforts against the ROKA. Any such activities are the responsibility of the bureau's Special Operations Division.

- NATIONAL INTELLIGENCE COMMITTEE
  The National Intelligence Committee is a decision-making body led by Kim Chong-il and composed of four other members: Kim Yong-sun, CCSKA; Chung Kyong-hi, director of the Social-Cultural Department; Im Ho-gun, director of the Investigative Department; and Kim Young-chun, chief of the General Staff of the Ministry of the People's Armed Forces (MPAF). This committee is the primary national-level policy- and decision-making body for intelligence and security matters. It establishes overall policy direction for all intelligence activities (which apparently includes Reconnaissance Bureau operations), as well as overall intelligence objectives and delegates responsibilities to the intelligence community.[7]

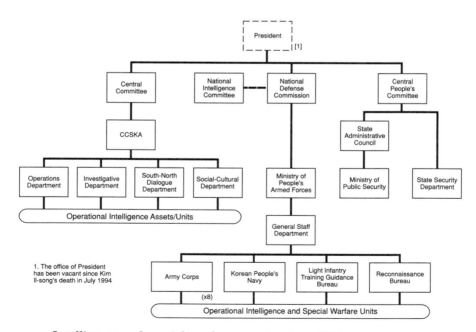

Intelligence and special warfare organizations, 1996.

- CENTRAL COMMITTEE SECRETARY IN CHARGE OF SOUTH KOREAN AFFAIRS
Beginning at the Seventeenth Plenum of the KWP Party Central Committee in January 1990 there began a number of organizational changes within the DPRK's intelligence and special warfare assets. Although the majority of these may be viewed as logical organizational development, some were in direct response to changing policies and evolving doctrines. At the January 1990 meeting Kim Chung-nin was replaced by Yun Ki-pok as CCSKA.[8] Kim was not purged, but was shifted to a new position in an administrative reorganization and remains a party secretary until present. In December 1992, Yun Ki-pok was transferred from his position as CCSKA to secretary for education. This transfer was apparently in response to the much publicized South Korean Workers' Party of Korea espionage case. Yun was replaced by Kim Yong-sun.[9]

The office of CCSKA is responsible for implementing anti-ROK operations, based upon guidelines regarding the operations established by the National Intelligence Committee. It also exercises control over its subordinate agencies and coordinates with the Reconnaissance Bureau, Ministry of Public Security, and State Security Department. It apparently collects information from its subordinate intelligence agencies and other organizations and disseminates finished intelligence products to all DPRK government agencies. In 1996, the office of the CCSKA was located in P'yongyang, as are the headquarters of its four subordinate departments: the Operations, Investigative, South–North Dialogue, and Social-Cultural Departments. In 1996 there were an estimated fifteen thousand personnel (although not all were operational) subordinate to the CCSKA.[10]

▪ ▪ *Liaison Department, Social-Cultural Department*
By the early 1990s the Liaison Department was renamed the Social-Cultural Department (also called the Socio-Cultural Department, Social and Cultural Department, or Department of Socio-Cultural Affairs), although many routinely still refer to it by its former name.[11] Its primary missions remain the establishment and expansion of the KWP within the ROK (i.e., underground KWP cells), and the collection of political intelligence within the ROK and Japan. Operational control over intelligence operations utilizing the Chosen Soren is believed to have been primarily vested within the Social-Cultural Department by the early 1990s. Other agencies (particularly the Operations Department), however, still routinely operated with and through the organization. In 1996 the Social-Cultural Department had a personnel strength of approximately fifteen hundred and was organized into the following groups: administration and training sections; world regional sections; four regional sections dealing with the ROK; political/cultural sections for the ROK (e.g., ROKA, industry); and trading companies

149

(e.g., Dae Song Trading Company). Through its trading companies, the department continued to operate several oceangoing cargo vessels. In 1995 the director of the Social-Cultural Department, Yi Chan-song (also known as Yi Chang-son), was reportedly replaced by Chung Kyong-hi.

■ ■ *Unification Front Department, South–North Dialogue Department*
Although the South–North Dialogue Department is routinely identified as the Unification Front Department, it is believed to have been renamed during the late 1980s or early 1990s.[12] This came about as a result of the increasing level of contacts between the ROK and DPRK. It appears that the CCSKA, at least under Yun Ki-pok and Kim Yong-sun, was not only responsible for all the KWP's intelligence organizations but personally headed this department. The South–North Dialogue Department is responsible for all open and covert issues relating to "South–North Dialogue" and the reunification of the fatherland. The department also conducts all anti-ROK psychological warfare and propaganda operations. Throughout the 1980s and 1990s the department dramatically expanded its open and covert contacts with Koreans living overseas (especially within the United States and Canada). If it succeeds in recruiting a Korean living abroad, the department apparently refers him or her to the Social-Cultural Department.

Much of this department's work was conducted through its Chosen Soren Affairs Section, and the department remains actively involved within the ROK and Japan. The South–North Dialogue Department is organized into thirteen divisions, or sections. Some of these are organized along geographic lines, much as the Investigative Department is, while others are functional. For example, Division Six supervised the Committee for the Peaceful Reunification of the Fatherland, the Central Committee of the Democratic Front for the Reunification of the Fatherland, the Chondoist Chongu Party, the Korean Christians Federation, and the Korean Buddhists Federation.

■ ■ *Operations Department*
The Operations Department remains the primary organization responsible for basic and advanced training, escort training, and escort operations (i.e., covert infiltration of agents throughout the world).[13] This department is organized into a headquarters, a basic training section, an advanced training section, two seaborne escort training centers, four seaborne escort units (also called maritime liaison offices), and two DMZ escort units (also called liaison offices). The seaborne escort units are headquartered in Haeju, Namp'o, Wonsan, and Ch'ongjin. The DMZ escort units are headquartered in Kaesong and P'yonggang (or possibly Sariwon). One of these,

in 1993, may have been the 715th Army Unit (also called the 715th Liaison Unit).[14] Overall personnel strength (students, operatives, and staff) of this organization is estimated to be over five thousand in 1996.

Basic and advanced training generally occurs within a system of safe houses located throughout the DPRK, although most are in the P'yongyang area. This training was previously known as the Central Committee Political School, or 695th Army Unit, and may now go under the name of Central Committee Political and Military Academy. Safe houses are isolated so that students know only the members, operations, and training of their own team to prevent compromise if captured. Instructors and people working within the Operations Department generally have little or no contact with members of other departments. Courses can last from six months to two years and cover an extremely wide range of subjects. Agents or agent teams live alone except for a housekeeper, are generally permitted to leave the house only once a week or month, and may be allowed to visit their families only once a year.

The Operations Department has also been involved in kidnaping operations throughout the world. The primary objective of these operations is to secure persons who can serve as language and cultural instructors for operatives (sometimes being forced to serve as housekeepers for trainees) and to allow a previously trained operative to assume the victim's identity. These later operations have generally occurred within Asia, particularly Japan. As of early 1997, O Kuk-yol was the director of the Operations Department. He has held this position since his appointment in 1989.

▪ ▪ *Research Department for External Intelligence, Investigative Department*
As part of the general reorganization of intelligence assets during the 1990s the Research Department for External Intelligence became the Investigative Department (also called the Investigation Department, or Foreign Intelligence and Investigations Department).[15] In 1996, the director of the Investigative Department was Kwon Hui-Kyong. The Investigative Department retained the responsibilities for the collection of external intelligence and conducting foreign operations. It was organized into a headquarters and six primary sections (along geographic lines): Chosen Soren, Japan, the Americas, Europe, Africa and Asia, and the ROK.

During 1993, the element of the Investigative Department reportedly responsible for training foreign terrorist was separated and subordinated to the MPAF (most likely the Reconnaissance Bureau).[16]

On 3 July 1996, Chong Su-il, an agent of the Investigative Department, was captured while operating within the ROK. Chong's case is interesting as it illustrates the lengths to which the DPRK will go to infiltrate operatives into the ROK.

Chong was born in China of ethnic Korean parents. He graduated from the Arabian Language Department of Beijing University in the late 1950s and joined the Chinese diplomatic corps. He emigrated to the DPRK with his family in June 1963 after serving as a second secretary at the Chinese Embassy in Morocco. Here he worked as an Arabic professor at P'yongyang University of Foreign Studies and served as an interpreter when Kim Il-song met with Arabian dignitaries. Chong was recruited as a potential intelligence operative by the SICARO in September 1974. After undergoing training (most probably with the Central Committee Political School—the 695th Army Unit) for four years and five months, Chong was assigned to conduct operations within the ROK. He used his language skills to pose as an Arab. Prior to his arrival in the ROK he first operated within seven Middle Eastern countries (including Lebanon and Tunisia) for five years and four months before traveling to the Philippines. Here he assumed a Filipino nationality and in 1984 traveled to the ROK on a student visa as Muhamad Kansu. To further improve his cover he married a nurse in Seoul in 1988 and in February 1990 obtained a position as an assistant history professor at Tankook University.

From the time of his initial entry into the ROK he began to collect and transmit to P'yongyang a wide range of military and political intelligence. During his career he received instructions from his superiors via shortwave radio on 161 occasions, and provided refined military and political reports on 80 occasions. These reports were transmitted as both letters and fax transmissions from major Seoul hotels to third-party contacts in other countries. Among the reports he filed were the "latest moves of Sin Sang-ok," the ROK film director who was kidnaped by the DPRK in 1978 but later escaped in Vienna, "check points and anti-tank barriers between Seoul and Panmunjom"; "analysis of April general elections"; "production of K1A1 tank"; and "military equipment procurement program." During his life in the ROK Chong returned to the DPRK four times, traveling by way of China, Australia, and other countries. Here he received awards for his meritorious services and was provided with additional espionage equipment and operational funds.

When he was captured, the ROK authorities confiscated eighty-one different pieces of espionage equipment, including three short-wave radio receivers, a code book, poisoned needles, a decoding book, a bank account book with 110 million won, $4,800 U.S. dollars in cash, and instructions from his headquarters in P'yongyang.[17]

▪ RECONNAISSANCE BUREAU
The primary missions of the Reconnaissance Bureau continued to be the collection of tactical and strategic intelligence within the military sphere,

and strategic special operations throughout the ROK and overseas. The effects of the early 1990s reorganization of intelligence assets on the Reconnaissance Bureau are presently unclear. It is known that by early 1993, the director of the Reconnaissance Bureau, Lt. Gen. Kim Tae-sik (also called Kim Dae-sik), was promoted to the rank of colonel general.[18] Another development was the reported establishment in 1993 of the 198th Army Unit (or 198th Liaison Office). This unit was formed from elements separated from the Research Department for External Intelligence and is headquartered on the outskirts of P'yongyang. It is assigned the training and support of "special terrorist commandos" in infiltration and demolitions using mock-ups of major ROK facilities.[19] It is unclear whether these reports are correct, or if this unit has any relationship to the 198th Army Unit from the 1970s, which operated safe houses around P'yongyang to train espionage and subversive agents.

In 1996, the Reconnaissance Bureau was headquartered in P'yongyang and was organized into a headquarters, several departments, the Foreign Language College, three sniper brigades, and five reconnaissance battalions. The departments were Political, Intelligence, Special, Technical/Radio (responsible for signals intelligence—SIGINT—collection), Training/Plans, and Maritime (also called the Maritime Office, Special Seaborne Operations Unit, Fourth Office or Fourth Department). Additionally, the Reconnaissance Bureau still operated a number of trading companies as covers and to generate financing for operations. The MPAF is known to operate twenty-four such companies.

The Technical/Radio Department operates a number of collection sites throughout the DPRK. These are believed to be located both along the borders with the PRC and Russia and along the DMZ. It is believed that each forward corps deployed along the DMZ has a primary SIGINT collection center staffed by members of the Technical/Radio Department, each with a number of subordinate stations. In addition to these land-based assets the Technical/Radio Department in cooperation with the KPN operates a number of trawlers dedicated to the collection of SIGINT and occasionally will employ oceangoing cargo vessels in a similar role. Likewise, the KPAF has operated a small number of relatively unsophisticated airborne collection platforms based upon the IL-28 and cargo aircraft (e.g., An-2/Y-5 or An-24).

In June 1991, reflecting the realities of the post–Cold War era, the Russian language was downgraded to a category-two language, leaving English and Japanese as the only category-one languages. As the DPRK and United States became increasingly engaged over a number of significant issues during the 1990s, English apparently assumed even greater importance than Japanese. The Foreign Language College is believed to have reflected these changes within its curriculum.[20]

The Maritime Department is reportedly headquartered in P'yongyang and is responsible for infiltrating Reconnaissance Bureau personnel by sea using *Yugo*-class midget submarines (SSm), *Sang-o*-class coastal submarines (SSC), and a variety of support ships and high-speed infiltration craft. The department is organized into a headquarters and three (possibly four) operational bases, identified as the First Base, Second Base, and Third Base. Known base locations are Nagwon-up on the east coast, and Namp'o and P'yongwon on the west coast. Each base is composed of a headquarters and several numbered (e.g., 1st, 2nd, etc.) "formations," which are orgainized into teams. For example, during 1994, the Third Base's 1st Formation is known to have consisted of at least six subordinate teams.[21]

It is presently unclear how the declining inventory of *Yugo*-class SSm and the introduction of *Sang-o*-class SSC affected the organization of the Maritime Department's subordinate units. Yi Kwang-su (also called Li Kwang-su), a captured infiltrator from the *Sang-o*-class SSC that ran aground near Kangnung in 1996 (see below), has stated that during 1994, the department reorganized its subordinate operational units, separating submarines from infiltration craft and support ships. On July 22, 1995, a further reorganization occurred when the Third Base at Nagwon-up (Toejo-dong, 23 kilometers east of Hamhung) detached one of its three formations to form the 22nd Squadron (also called the 22nd Combat Squadron, 22nd Naval Squadron, 22nd Combat Unit, and 22nd Army Unit). It is believed that this new unit consolidated all the Reconnaissance Bureau's submarines into one organization. In September 1996, the 22nd Squadron consisted of approximately three hundred personnel, four *Sang-o*-class SSCs, and one midget submarine (presumably a *Yugo*-class SSm).[22] The *Sang-o*-class SSCs are identified as the *No. 1, No. 2, No. 3,* and *No. 4* submarines or reconnaissance submarines. At this time, one was operational, one was undergoing repairs, one was being "disassembled," and one was captured off the ROK city of Kangnung in 1996 (see below).[23]

The KPN evidently first began production of the 35-meter *Sang-o*-class SSC in 1989 or 1990. This design is believed to have developed from the experimental *41-Meter*-class SSAG built in the 1970s, combined with information obtained from the Yugoslav designs and experience gained on the production of the *Romeo*-class submarines (SS) throughout the 1980s. The *Sang-o* class is built in both standard and reconnaissance versions (see below).[24] By the end of 1990 a total of two *Sang-o*-class SSC had been launched. Currently, the KPN and Maritime Department deploy twenty-two to twenty-four *Sang-o*-class SSC, twenty-two *Romeo*-class SS, and two *Whiskey*-class SS. In May 1996, the DPRK began construction of a 1,000-ton reconnaissance submarine at the Bong Dae Bo factory (also called the Pongdae Boiler Plant) in Sinp'o on the east coast. This factory is subordinate to the 6th Bureau of the 2nd Economic Committee and has been involved in the production of the *Sang-o*-class SSC. The new 1,000-ton reconnaissance submarine is apparently based upon the *Romeo*-class SS and will have the capacity to carry eighty personnel, a crew of about twenty and forty commandos. This project was precipitated when the Maritime Department requested a vessel capable of greater range, endurance, and capacity. Recruitment and training of crew for the new vessel has already begun.[25]

▪ LIGHT INFANTRY TRAINING GUIDANCE BUREAU

As noted, sometime during the early 1990s (possibly at the Central People's Committee May meeting) the VIII Special Corps was renamed the Light Infantry Training Guidance Bureau (also called the Light Infantry Training Guide/Bureau or Light Infantry Instruction Guidance Bureau).[26] Although the reasons for this redesignation are presently unclear, the Light Infantry Training Guidance Bureau has retained its responsibilities as the primary organization for the training and conducting of unconventional warfare and special warfare operations within the KPA. In 1996 the commander of the bureau was Lt. Gen. Yim Tae-yong.[27]

During the 1990s the bureau continued to expand, albeit slowly, so that in 1996 its personnel strength had increased to approximately 88,500 troops organized into twenty-two brigades (this excludes the Reconnaissance Bureau's three sniper brigades and five reconnaissance battalions). Three of these new brigades were airborne sniper brigades.

An interesting development during the 1990s has been the establishment of special forces units staffed exclusively with women, including "long-range seaborne infiltration" and "airborne surprise infiltration" units. In August 1995, Kim Chong-il visited a "maritime special training facility" to observe an infiltration exercise being conducted by a female "long-range seaborne infiltration" unit and praised its performance. Whether these units are subordinate to the Reconnaissance Bureau or the Light Infantry Training Guidance Bureau is presently unclear.

The decline in the DPRK's political and economic strength during the early 1990s affected the training conducted by the Reconnaissance Bureau and Light Infantry Training Guidance Bureau. This general trend reversed itself in 1993 with an increase in airborne and amphibious exercises. In March 1995 the KPAF and KPN conducted their largest exercises since 1991, which included a number of airborne drops.[28] This higher level of special purpose force training continues today.

As previously discussed, the political and economic troubles during the late 1980s and through the 1990s witnessed a steady decline in the DPRK's support of international terrorist and revolutionary groups, and military assistance to developing countries. This, in turn, caused a decline in the number of Light Infantry Training Guidance Bureau personnel involved in such activities throughout the world. Such activities still continue, but at a much reduced level. Reconnaissance Bureau and some Light Infantry Training Guidance Bureau personnel still assist in such training activities both overseas and within the DPRK.

▪ ▪ *Airborne and Airborne Sniper Brigades*

The number and organization of the regular airborne brigades remain unchanged at three, up through 1996.[29] Some minor organizational changes within these units apparently occurred with the introduction of new or different weapons (e.g., the SA-16 and 60-millimeter mortars). The number of airborne sniper brigades increased to three by 1994.

As discussed, it is unclear if the all-female "airborne surprise infiltration" units are part of the airborne sniper brigades. It is interesting to note, however, that a "women's parachute platoon" has existed within the 38th Airborne Brigade since its formation, while no such unit existed within the 48th and 58th Airborne Brigades through the early 1990s. References to the all-female "airborne surprise infiltration" units may thus actually refer to this unit.

Beginning in 1990, the number of airborne training exercises that included training jumps decreased to about one a year as a result of fuel shortages within the DPRK. To compensate for this the brigades expanded ground training, jumping from 80-meter-high steel towers or cables extended across valleys. Beginning in 1993, however, a reversal of this situation developed as the number of airborne exercises steadily increased.[30] These exercises have also included a larger number of special nighttime jumps. A typical exercise involving a squadron of KPAF An-2s was conducted on 4 October 1996 off the islands in the Yellow Sea, within the area of responsibility of the IV Corps. The An-2 planes departed from a base near Kaesong, flew north of Paengnyong-do, then proceeded to a base near the DMZ, where they landed. Shortly afterward they took off and returned to Kaesong.[31]

By 1996, the KPAF's airborne lift capabilities had shown a slight increase in maximum possible lift capacity. Some interesting changes, however, developed in the composition of the transport forces. Most notable were the indigenous production of an improved An-2 variant and the Hyokshin-2 helicopter (a variant of the Mi-2). During the 1990s the KPAF was reported to employ its An-2 Colts in a variety of new and unexpected roles, including jamming, SIGINT, and as carriers of laser-guided bombs to be used with special purpose forces units using laser designators.[32] The total number of An-2 variants within the KPAF increased to approximately 300, while the indigenous production of the Hyokshin-2 helicopter brought the total of Mi-2 variants to approximately 140. Both these aircraft are ideally suited to lift the new airborne sniper brigades. Additionally, it is believed that the KPAF began to introduce small numbers of Mi-26 *Halo* helicopters in 1996, but details are unavailable. The KPAF's theoretical total airlift capability is approximately 7,900 troops, or approximately two airborne or airborne sniper brigades.

▪ ▪ *Light Infantry Brigades*
With the exception of the gradual establishment of several new light infantry brigades during the 1990s, no significant developments occurred with light infantry brigades or the brigade/division-level light infantry battalions. At present it does not appear that light infantry battalions were established within Rear Area Corps brigades/divisions. Rather, as in the 1980s, newly trained light infantry personnel within the Rear Area Corps were utilized to establish new light infantry brigades.

▪ ▪ *Amphibious Sniper Brigades*
Little is known concerning developments within the amphibious sniper brigades during this period, although it is believed that they were subordinated to the Korean People's Navy.[33] This may partly be the result of the introduction of the *Kong Bang* LCPA and the need to conduct intensive training and develop new tactics with the new vessels. The number of amphibious training exercises utilizing *Kong Bang I/II/III* LCPA and midget submarines expanded significantly during 1993–96. It is presently unclear whether the all-female "long range seaborne infiltration" units created during the early 1990s are attached to the amphibious sniper brigades.

By 1996, the production of new *Hungnam*- and *Hantae*-class LSM and *Kong Bang I/II/III* LCPA, had been offset by the conversion of *Namp'o*-class LCPF to patrol boats so that the KPN's amphibious lift capability remained at approximately fifteen to eighteen thousand troops. The capabilities of the *Kong Bang I/II/III* LCPA, however, significantly increased the survivability and viability of the amphibious warfare forces. By 1994, the KPN is believed to have begun construction of a second class of LCPA, the *Namp'o A/B,* but details concerning this are presently unavailable.[34]

▪ STATE SECURITY DEPARTMENT AND MINISTRY OF PUBLIC SECURITY
Both the Ministry of Public Security and the State Security Department retained their respective responsibilities during the 1990s.[35] The Ministry of Public Security (equivalent to the ROK National Police Agency), however, apparently suffered a number of political setbacks, whereas the State Security Department apparently increased in power and influence. The changes that occurred within the State Security Department and

Ministry of Public Security during the 1990s appear to have been directly related to the desire to maintain strict control over the DPRK's population and to prevent any possible coup attempts.

As a result of an increasing number of defectors crossing over the PRC border in the early 1990s, the Ministry of Public Security initiated a redeployment of forces and stepped up its border security operations. After Kim Il-song's death in 1994, border security operations of the Ministry of Public Security were apparently placed under the operational control of the MPAF. Subsequently, control over entry and exit to P'yongyang, which had been Ministry of Public Security responsibility, was placed under the control of the MPAF. In early 1996, the MPAF is believed to have assumed overall responsibility for border security from the Ministry of Public Security.

Within the State Security Department (comparable to the ROK National Security Planning Agency) several significant changes occurred during 1994–95 at the direction of Kim Chong-il. These included the establishment of the "February 16 Unit" and a "special mission group." The "February 16th Unit" is a special bodyguard unit charged solely with the protection of Kim Chong-il, whose birthday is February 16. This unit is reportedly composed of approximately two thousand members selected primarily from orphans from the Fatherland Liberation War and bereaved children of revolutionaries. The "special mission group" is charged with conducting surveillance of and investigating high-ranking officials in the KWP and Administrative Council and general-grade officers of the MPAF. These developments were precipitated by an increase in coup attempts originating within the MPAF. For example, in March 1993 it was reported that an attempt by the commander of the 7th Infantry Division and approximately thirty other officers was detected by the State Security Department before it could be implemented. In April 1995, an alleged coup attempt by officers within the VI Corps headquartered in Ch'ongjin was exposed.

With the DPRK's declining economic, political, and economic strength in the 1990s, both agencies increased their involvement in smuggling (most notably narcotics) and counterfeiting (especially U.S. hundred-dollar notes) operations. It is clear, however, that the vast majority of such activities are within the jurisdiction of the State Security Department. This organization's involvement with terrorist and revolutionary organizations declined during this period but still continues.

MILITARY ASSISTANCE AND INTERNATIONAL TERRORISM, 1990–PRESENT

As discussed previously, the 1990s saw a steady decline in DPRK military assistance and material support for international terrorist and revolutionary groups, because of the DPRK's decaying political and economic strength.[36]

The DPRK nevertheless continued some international efforts. In September 1995 KPA military advisers had been reportedly training the Burundian Army.[37] Earlier, in 1991, the DPRK dispatched intelligence operatives and special purpose force personnel (possibly from the Reconnaissance Bureau) to train members of the Abu Nidal terrorist organization. It also invited members of Abu Nidal to the DPRK. Despite promises to the Philippine government to the contrary, the DPRK has continued its support for rebel groups in the Philippines throughout the 1990s. In July 1994, DPRK operatives met with leading members of the Moro National Liberation Front (a Philippine revolutionary group) in Thailand. The DPRK also provided limited support to groups operating in Cambodia, Indonesia, Iran Jaya, and Pakistan. The primary route for supplying weapons to groups in Southeast Asian countries is through the Maebong Trading Company office in Guangzhou, PRC. This company is one of several directly subordinate to the MPAF.

OPERATIONS

Following the 1988 bombing of Korean Airlines flight 858, infiltration operations against the ROK decreased dramatically and remained low during the 1990s. The reduction in operations stemmed both from the international outcry at such activities and from DPRK's entering into high-level negotiations with the ROK concerning the improvement of relations between the two countries. These negotiations culminated with the conclusion of agreement on reconciliation and nonaggression in 1992. Additionally, the DPRK was conducting protracted negotiations with the United States concerning the former's nuclear program.

Typical of those infiltration operations that did occur was an abortive infiltration attempt on 17 October 1995. At 0220 hours, ROKA troops opened fire on an infiltration team believed to be from a reconnaissance battalion as it attempted to cross the Imjin River south of the DMZ. This team is believed to have consisted of three personnel. In the initial firefight one infiltrator was killed and two escaped. At dawn, ROKA troops located the dead infiltrator's body, which was clothed in an ROKA uniform, and retrieved two M-16 rifles, three hand grenades, two pistols, some ammunition, binoculars, and a pair of flippers. A second infiltrator was later spotted approximately 4 kilometers away moving toward a KPA guard post on the north side of the DMZ. On 20 October ROKA troops located another rifle and some miscellaneous equipment from the third infiltrator further down on the shore of the Imjin River. It is believed that this infiltrator was also successful in returning north.[38]

Substantially more notable have been the subsequent activities of two Social-Cultural Department agents in the Puyo area of the ROK in October 1995,[39] and the infiltration and subsequent grounding of a *Sang-o*-class coastal submarine near Kangnung in September 1996.

- PUYO, OCTOBER 1995
On 29 August 1995, two operatives, Kim Tong-sik and Pak Kwang-nam, from the Sixth Section of the Social-Cultural Department left the port city of Namp'o aboard an infiltration boat camouflaged as a fishing vessel.[40] They arrived at the village of Onpyong-ri, Cheju-do, on 2 September.[41] Their mission had several objectives, including guidance and inspection of Social-Cultural Department operatives actively operating within the ROK, provision of funds and equipment to these operatives, contacting prospective recruits chosen from among ROK dissidents, and finally to escort back to the DPRK an agent who had been dispatched to the ROK ten years ago. They carried an assortment of equipment and operating funds worth 56 million won (including $65,000 U.S. dollars).

From Cheju-do they traveled to the mainland via the city of Mokp'o. Subsequently they rented a room in Songnam and later in Taejon. From these two locations they branched out through the ROK, purchasing supplies and equipment (e.g., shortwave radios, cameras) and contacting at least seven dissident leaders (specifically, former student activists, now in their thirties). Interestingly, whenever they met with these leaders, Kim would identify himself without hesitation as "a party liaison man coming from the North."

About 15 September they traveled to Puyo, 140 kilometers south of Seoul, to scout the Chonggak-sa Temple, where they intended to contact the agent whom they were to escort back to the DPRK. After a preliminary reconnaissance of the temple and the town, both operatives left Puyo. They arrived back in Puyo on 24 October to make the actual contact. While scouting the temple again they aroused the suspicions of local residents, who reported them to the authorities. When the police arrived at around 1420 to question them, a firefight occurred. In the subsequent two-hour-long firefight one police officer was killed and one was wounded, and Kim was wounded and captured. Pak was successful in escaping into the Sok-san mountains. Three days later, on 27 October, ROKA troops located Pak hiding in a mountain quarry. In the ensuing firefight, he was wounded and captured. After being transported to an Army hospital, he later died of his wounds.

Two aspects concerning this incident are of particular interest. First, the equipment carried by the operatives was of significantly better quality

than those used by previous operatives. In addition to the almost standard Belgium-made Browning pistol fitted with a silencer, they carried a
13-centimeter-long fountain-pen-shaped poison gun and darts. This gun
was powerful enough to penetrate a 7-millimeter-thick wooden panel at
a distance of 3 meters. The radio used to contact their headquarters was
a Japanese-made high-performance shortwave radio. In their communications with headquarters, the operatives used a combination random
number table and one-time pad. The resident's registration cards, which
both operatives possessed and which more than anything else allowed
their free movement within the ROK, were described as "exquisitely
forged." Unlike in the past, the names appearing on the cards were real
people and the forgery was almost perfect. Complementing this was the
excellent and extensive training both operatives underwent to allow their
easy adaptation to the lifestyle within the ROK. According to one ROK
official, "They looked smart just like ordinary urban youths in the South
and on the strength of the familiarization training, they could mingle
freely with South Koreans." The second item of interest was that this was
Kim Tong-sik's second infiltration into the ROK. He was first dispatched
to the ROK in May 1990, when he escorted two operatives back to the
DPRK. In the earlier mission, Kim had entered the ROK via Cheju-do.
He had then contacted Yi Son-sil (a high-ranking member of the KWP's
Political Bureau and director of the Central Region Chapter of the South
Korean Workers' Party) and conducted espionage activities with her until
October. They subsequently contacted a second operative, Hwang In-o. In
October the three traveled north to Seoul and exfiltrated on 17 October
through Kanghwa-do, northwest of Seoul. In recognition of his meritorious service, Kim was awarded a medal and a hero's certificate. Upon
returning to P'yongyang, Yi Son-sil was accorded a hero's welcome in
recognition of her successful organization of underground KWP cells
within the ROK. Hwang In-o met with a less glorious fate. After subsequently returning to the ROK, he was arrested in September 1992 and
convicted of violating the National Security Law.[42]

▪ KANGNUNG, SEPTEMBER 1996

On the evening of 13 September, Capt. Chong Yong-ku, commander of the
No. 1 Reconnaissance Submarine of the Second Team of the 22nd Squadron,
Maritime Department of the Reconnaissance Bureau, called his crew
together and held a conference of KWP party members to discuss their
forthcoming reconnaissance mission.[43] During the conference a resolution
was unanimously adopted pledging the precise execution of their mission.
After several short speeches, the operatives read an oath of allegiance
pledging to return only "after fulfilling the order of Gen. Kim Chong-il."

All participants signed it. Following the conference Captain Chong, his crew, and several dignitaries attended a banquet arranged by Lt. Gen. Kim Tae-shik, director of the Reconnaissance Bureau. Kim encouraged his men to perform their reconnaissance mission with courage. The following morning, at 0500, the *No. 1 Reconnaissance Submarine* left its base at Nagwon-up and set sail for Kangnung. Kim Dae-shik saw them off.

The *No. 1 Reconnaissance Submarine* was a *Sang-o*-class SSC specifically modified for reconnaissance operations.[44] All torpedoes, torpedo-handling equipment, and tubes had been removed. The forward area was then converted to carry a reconnaissance team, and a floodable diver lock-out chamber was installed. The only armament aboard the submarine were small arms and a 107-millimeter recoilless rifle. On this mission the submarine carried a total of twenty-six people: twenty-one crew members (of which at least two were qualified as reconnaissance team escorts), the director and vice director of the Maritime Department, and a three-man reconnaissance team.[45] The specifications of the reconnaissance version of the *Sang-o*-class SSC follow:[46]

Displacement, tons	275 surfaced; 350 dived
Dimensions, meters	35 × 3.5 × 3 (with sail, height is about 7 meters)
Main machinery	1 diesel generator; 1 motor; 1 shaft
Speed (maximum), knots	7.5 surfaced, 8 dived
Speed (economical), knots	2.5 surfaced, 3 dived
Range, nautical miles	At least 1,500 surfaced
Complement	Maximum of 30: 5 officers, 15 crew, 10 passengers
Armament	No torpedoes are carried. External storage points along both sides of the hull are used to carry naval mines, special operations equipment, and other miscellaneous equipment. (The attack version reportedly has four 533-millimeter torpedo tubes.)
Independent operational period	20 days

The mission of the three-man reconnaissance team was to collect information and photographs of military-related facilities in the Kangnung area while the submarine was to photograph the beach and shore facilities.[47] This was to be the second operational mission into ROK territorial waters for 22nd Squadron. The first was a successful reconnaissance mission off the ROK city of Kangnung on 15 September 1995.

In preparation for the current mission the submarine and reconnaissance team conducted a total of five training exercises, two of which were conducted in July and August under operational conditions. On both occasions the three-man reconnaissance team boarded the submarine at night, led by an instructor assigned to the Reconnaissance Bureau. They would then sail out of port, submerge and return to a point approximately 300 meters from the shore. The reconnaissance team accompanied by a two-member escort team then left the submerged vessel, swam to shore and then returned. The infiltration portion of the training exercise required one to one-and-a-half hours to conduct. This differed from routine training which typically consisted of two to three exercises a month with just the escort team swimming to shore and returning.

Once the *No. 1 Reconnaissance Submarine* left Nagwon-up, it submerged to periscope/snorkel depth and, cruising on its diesel engines, turned south toward the Military Demarcation Line separating the two Koreas, thus maintaining a full charge on its batteries. At a point approximately 8 kilometers north of the Military Demarcation Line, power was transferred from the diesels to electric motors and the periscope and snorkel were lowered. The submarine submerged to 60–70 meters, and it entered ROK waters. At approximately 1930 hours on 15 September, the submarine arrived at a point approximately 8 kilometers off Kangnung. This involved a voyage of approximately 135 nautical miles from Nagwon-up. When the submarine arrived here, it rose to periscope depth to determine its exact location and then approached land. At 2000 hours, it approached to about 300–400 meters from shore and settled onto the seabed in 15 meters of water. Here it sat while the reconnaissance team and two escorts donned scuba gear, exited the lock-out chamber, and swam to shore.[48] When the team reached 30–40 meters from shore, the escorts continued to the beach and secured the landing area. This was completed quickly and the three-man reconnaissance team came ashore at 2100 hours. The members removed their equipment and quickly proceeded inland. The escorts, possibly with the extra scuba gear, then returned to the submarine. When they were recovered, the submarine moved to a waiting area in international waters.

On 16 September, the submarine reentered ROK territorial waters and attempted to recover the reconnaissance team. This attempt was not successful, and the submarine returned to the waiting area in international waters.[49]

The following night, a second attempt was made, which ended in disaster. At approximately 2100 hours on 17 September, while approaching the shore to recover the reconnaissance team, the submarine ran aground 200 meters off An-in Beach, 9 kilometers south of Kangnung. The submarine sustained serious damage, and the crew could not control it. Unable to free themselves, despite numerous attempts, and with sunrise coming in a few hours, Captain Chong realized that the situation was hopeless. After radioing a message detailing the situation to the Maritime Department headquarters, Captain Chong ordered the ship abandoned. Unable to scuttle the submarine because of the shallow water, a fire was started to destroy as much equipment as possible. The crew then abandoned ship. By 2350 all twenty-six crew and passengers on board the submarine had reached the beach carrying all available weapons and equipment.

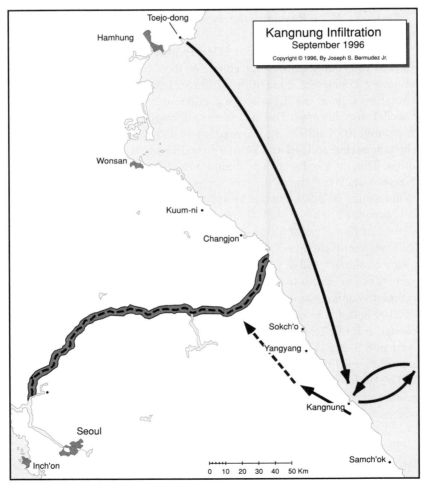

Kangnung infiltration, September 1996.

The abandoned submarine was first spotted at 0100 hours the next day by a taxi driver on the coastal road south of Kangnung. In response, ROK authorities immediately initiated standard counter-infiltration procedures, placed ROKA units on alert, and rushed other troops and National Police units to the Kangnung area. Blocking positions were established north of the city to prevent the North Koreans from reaching the DMZ, and search operations were initiated. Additional security precautions were taken nationwide, particularly in Seoul.

Although it is presently unclear what transpired once the crew reached shore, it is known that they headed inland into the mountains and eventually separated into several groups. At 1630 hours on 18 September, ROKA troops captured Yi Kwang-su, a helmsman, who began to provide information on the submarine and its mission.

The largest group of eleven members moved inland to a mountain clearing approximately 8 kilometers southwest of the grounded submarine. At approximately 1700, ROK forces found the bodies of these eleven men. Ten were together, and the eleventh was a short distance away. ROK authorities speculate that the eleventh killed his companions (all had been shot in the head) and then shot himself (a handgun was found on his body). It appeared to be a case of mass suicide to prevent capture. Among the bodies were those of the director and vice director of the Maritime Department, the submarine's political officer, and the leader of the reconnaissance team. The reconnaissance team leader was apparently the one who carried out the mass execution and suicide.

A gruesome but standard operating procedure for North Korean infiltrators is to commit suicide rather than be captured alive. The families of captured infiltrators are typically stripped of their jobs and homes and sent to work camps.

Between 19 and 30 September ROKA and National Police forces conducted a major cordon and search operation to capture the remaining infiltrators. During this operation eleven additional infiltrators were killed in a series of firefights. The search operations for the three remaining infiltrators, two of whom were from the reconnaissance team, continued through October and into November. On 5 November, two reconnaissance team members were located northwest of Kangnung and, in a short firefight, were killed. The last member of the submarine crew, Ens. Li Chul-jin, is believed to have escaped.

On 29 December, after considerable international diplomatic pressure, the DPRK issued the following apology for the failed infiltration attempt:

A spokesman for the DPRK Foreign Ministry has been authorized to express deep regret over the submarine incident in the sea off Kangnung,

South Korea in September 1996, which caused severe casualties. The DPRK will make efforts to prevent the recurrence of such an incident and make joint efforts with the sides concerned for durable peace and security on the Korean Peninsula.[50]

The next day the cremated remains of the crew, passengers, and reconnaissance team were returned to the DPRK at Panmunjom.[51] On the same day, ceremonies were held rewarding six civilians who had actively assisted in locating the infiltrators.[52]

The *Sang-o* submarine, however, remained under ROK control. On 22 September, after basic salvage operations had been completed, the ROKN towed the *Sang-o* to the port of Tonghae, where more complete repairs and a through examination of the vessel were completed.[53] The recovery of the submarine has proven to be a technical intelligence windfall, as ROK and U.S. specialists have had an opportunity to examine at length a recently DPRK-manufactured submarine, including its navigation and communication equipment; oil/fuel, optical, and radar systems; and much more.

Several more interesting aspects of this incident deserve mention. According to the sole captured infiltrator, Yi Kwang-su, it was unusual that the director (Kim Dong-won) and vice director of the Maritime Department would accompany an operational mission. To have such high officials on the mission may have been an indicator of its importance. What that importance may have been, however, is presently unknown. Next, according to ROK sources, through the end of September the Reconnaissance Bureau was able to contact the two reconnaissance team members still evading ROKA searchers by radio "from two to five times a day." What is remarkable is the reconnaissance team's ability to successfully elude a massive cordon and search operation for forty-nine days before being located and killed. It is a testimony to their training, skill, and determination. It may also be indicative of what to expect from these elite troops in wartime. A diary recovered from a team member detailed their activities during this period and provided insight into reconnaissance team escape and evasion operations.[54] Even more impressive, the sole escapee, Ens. Li Chul-jin, was a crew member aboard the submarine and not a reconnaissance team member. All members of operational Reconnaissance Bureau units must undergo special training, including extensive escape and evasion, but to expect this level of proficiency from a sailor is noteworthy.

This entire operation needs to be placed in perspective. This was a relatively routine reconnaissance operation, of the type that the Reconnaissance Bureau has been conducting for years. It was not a deliberate attempt to land a large guerrilla unit to conduct armed operations as in the 1960s. Nor was it a precursor to an imminent invasion. Such missions as this routine reconnaissance mission of September 1996 have the potential for great success or catastrophic failure. Unfortunately for the submarine crew and passengers and the DPRK, it was a failure.

Finally, contrary to what might be expected, the Kangnung failure did not have a negative effect upon the career of Col. Gen. Kim Tae-sik, director of the Reconnaissance Bureau. Since the incident, he has been a regular companion of Kim Chong-il on his visits to various military units.[55] The effect of the incident upon the career of Lt. Gen. Yim Tae-yong, director of the Light Infantry Training Guidance Bureau, is unknown.[56]

Three-ton, three-man, 18.7-foot long DPRK midget submarine captured after its grounding on a mudflat during a receding tide at the confluence of the Imjin and Han Rivers, 5 July 1965. *(Author's collection)*

Romeo-class submarine (P/N 15) operating on the surface off the east coast of the DPRK. *(Author's collection)*

Dismantled submersible capable of being transported to the scene of operations by high-speed infiltration boats. *(Author's collection)*

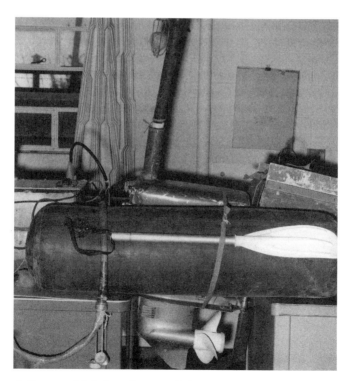

Swimmer delivery vehicle found concealed in a small rock crevice on Hoenggan-do Island, ROK, 4 November 1980. *(UNC Military Armistice Commission)*

Wreckage of a DPRK high-speed agent infiltration boat captured after a high-speed chase off the northeast coast of the ROK on 21 July 1979. *(Author's collection)*

Swimmer-delivery vehicle captured on beach at Mijo-ri, ROK, 1 December 1980. *(UNC Military Armistice Commission)*

Captured high-speed, semisubmersible infiltration craft. *(David Stiegman)*

Captured *Sang-o*-class coast submarine, Kangnung, ROK, September 1996. *(Author's collection)*

Chapter 6

SPECIAL PURPOSE UNITS TODAY

COMMAND AND CONTROL

Command and control of the DPRK's various special purpose forces can be broken down into two broad categories, the military and the party.

- MINISTRY OF PEOPLE'S ARMED FORCES
  In principle, the top military policy-making body in the DPRK is the KWP's Central Military Committee (identified as the Military Committee prior to 1984), which had been chaired by Kim Il-song until his death in July 1994. Since then the Central Military Committee has hardly been mentioned by the DPRK. In reality the National Defense Commission, chaired by Kim Chong-il, has been in control of military policies and their implementation and the military since April 1992. At that time, an amendment to the DPRK's constitution separated the National Defense Commission from the Central People's Committee and elevated it to a position equivalent to that of the committee's.

  Subordinate to the National Defense Commission is the Ministry of People's Armed Forces. The ministry consists of the General Guards Bureau; General Political Bureau; General Rear Service Bureau; General Staff Department; Military Armistice Commission; Military Police Bureau; Military Prosecution Bureau; Military Tribunal Bureau; Party Committee of the Korean People's Army; and the Political Security Bureau.

  The General Staff Department, headed by the chief of the general staff, directly controls twelve army corps; the Korean People's Air Force; the Korean People's Navy; four commands (Air Defense [or Antiaircraft Artillery], Artillery, Capital Defense, and Mechanized); and fifteen bureaus (Cadres, Classified Information, Communications, Engineering, Geological, Inspection, Light Infantry Training Guidance, Military Development, Military Mobilization, Military Training, Nuclear Chemical

Defense, Operations, Ordnance, Reconnaissance, and Replacement).

Thus command and control of all the military special purpose forces flows from the National Defense Commission through the Ministry of People's Armed Forces to the General Staff Department. From here it flows in four directions: to the Light Infantry Training Guidance Bureau, the Reconnaissance Bureau, the Korean People's Navy, and the light infantry units subordinate to the various army corps.

▪ CENTRAL COMMITTEE SECRETARY IN CHARGE OF SOUTH KOREAN AFFAIRS
The Korean Workers' Party (KWP) is the most politically significant entity within the DPRK. The general secretary position left vacant by the death of Kim Il-song was filled when Kim Chong-il was elected in October 1997. Control of the KWP is exercised through the party's executive decision-making body, the Central People's Committee, which is controlled by Kim Chong-il. Subordinate to the Central People's Committee are the National Intelligence Committee and the office of the Central Committee Secretary in Charge of South Korean Affairs (CCSKA). The National Intelligence Committee is chaired by Kim Chong-il and serves as the primary national-level policy- and decision-making body for intelligence and security matters. The CCSKA controls four subordinate intelligence-related departments: Operations, Investigative, South–North Dialogue, and Social-Cultural. These organizations have a significant number of operatives who are trained and sometimes employed for special operations.

▪ COORDINATION
There is considerable overlap in the command and control of all special purpose and intelligence organizations at the national and policy-making levels. The degree of this overlap decreases at each subordinate level. Coordination between the various organizations at the operational level, as well as administrative and technical support, varies according to mission and the immediate political agenda of the individual organizations. In general, coordination between intelligence services is fair to poor. Between intelligence agencies and Ministry of People's Armed Forces (MPAF) special purpose organizations, it is poor (the possible exception being with the Reconnaissance Bureau, where coordination is fair to poor). Coordination between special purpose organizations within the MPAF is good to fair.

LIGHT INFANTRY TRAINING GUIDANCE BUREAU

The Light Infantry Training Guidance Bureau is the single largest organization within the MPAF charged with the training and conducting of unconventional and special warfare operations.[1]

169

■ MISSIONS

The primary responsibilities of the Light Infantry Training Guidance Bureau commander and his staff are the following:

- Preparation of doctrine, and planning and organizing the mobilization readiness and tactical preparedness of KPA special purpose units.
- Planning the tactical and strategic employment of special purpose units and advising the chief of the general staff.
- Administrative and specialized technical support to all special purpose units.
- Organizing and supervising the tactical training of subordinate special purpose units and the training of support personnel.
- During wartime to function as the primary headquarters coordinating all special purpose operations.

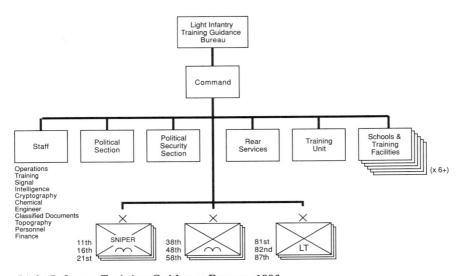

Light Infantry Training Guidance Bureau, 1996.

■ ORGANIZATION

The Light Infantry Training Guidance Bureau is organized like the other KPA branch commands. Its principle components consist of the Command Group (in 1996 the commander of the bureau was Lt. Gen. Yim Tae-yong); Staff Department, headed by the chief of staff; the Political Security Section; Political Section; Rear Services Section; special purpose force training facilities; and subordinate special purpose units. The chief of the Staff Department controls the various sections in the department: operations, training, signal, nuclear-chemical defense, topography, engineering, cryptography, intelligence, personnel, finance, and classified documents.

Directly subordinate to the Light Infantry Training Guidance Bureau are political and political security sections; a training unit; a rear services element; several schools and other training facilities; and nine special purpose brigades totaling approximately 31,500 troops (table 6-1). The nine special purpose brigades are the 11th, 16th, and 21st Airborne Sniper; 38th, 48th, and 58th Airborne; and 81st, 82nd, and 87th Light Infantry Brigades. There are also reports that the bureau also controls a hot-air balloon unit, but this remains to be confirmed. During wartime it is believed that operational control of the eleven light infantry brigades currently subordinate to the army corps (primarily within the I, II, and V Forward Corps and IV Corps) may revert to the bureau, who would delegate operation control to an army corps for specific missions.

Table 6-1

SPECIAL PURPOSE BRIGADES OF THE LIGHT INFANTRY TRAINING GUIDANCE BUREAU

Type	Brigades	Manpower	Total
Airborne brigades	3	3,500	10,500
Airborne sniper brigades	3	3,500	10,500
Light infantry brigades	3	3,500	10,500
Total	9		31,500

LIGHT INFANTRY BRIGADES AND BATTALIONS

- MISSIONS

In general the primary missions assigned to the light infantry brigades and division/brigade light infantry battalions are tactical or operational, with operations normally limited to within the corps area of operations.[2] The battalions focus their operations in the forward zone, from a point some 15–30 kilometers in the ROK/U.S.'s rear, back toward the forward edge of the battle area (FEBA), whereas the light infantry brigades focus

171

their operations from this point out to the edge of the corps area of operations (i.e., deeper into the ROK/U.S. rear area). Operations in the area beyond the edge of the corps area of operations (the ROK/U.S. strategic rear) will be the responsibility of the airborne, airborne sniper, amphibious sniper, and sniper brigades. The standard light infantry units have the capability, training, and equipment to execute the following missions:

- Enveloping or flanking attacks in support of the brigade, division, and corps.
- The seizure or destruction of nuclear, C^3I, chemical, and missile assets, and sensitive facilities, especially airfields and petroleum, oil, and other lubricants (POL) storage sites, within the forward areas.
- The interdiction, seizure, or control of forward area lines of communications, primarily those employed for the reinforcement or resupply of forces deployed on the DMZ.
- Seizure and control of important topographic features (mountain passes, hills, rivers, etc.), and civilian facilities (dams, power plants, etc.).
- Augmenting corps and division reconnaissance assets.
- Unconventional warfare operations.
- Rear guard and delaying operations.
- Counter-special operations.

The missions assigned to the three light infantry brigades directly subordinate to the Light Infantry Training Guidance Bureau are presently unclear. Available evidence suggests that their mission is a combination of the strategic defensive and counter-special-operations missions assigned to the airborne brigades and, on the strategic offensive, to operate in the ROK/U.S. strategic rear by establishing a "second front."

- COMMAND AND CONTROL

  The 81st, 82nd, and 87th Light Infantry Brigades operate under the control of the Light Infantry Training Guidance Bureau. They may, however, be attached to army corps commanders for specific operations. During peacetime the remaining eleven light infantry brigades operate under control of the army corps commander in whose area they are deployed. The army corps commander may delegate a subordinate division commander with operational control of a light infantry brigade, depending upon the situation. As noted, during wartime, control of these light infantry brigades may revert to the bureau. The deployment of the eleven light infantry brigades subordinate to army corps is presently unclear, although it is believed that they are primarily deployed with the forward corps (table 6-2).

Table 6-2

Deployment of the Eleven Light Infantry Brigades Subordinate to Army Corps

Designation	Location
U/I Light Infantry Brigade	I Forward Corps?
U/I Light Infantry Brigade	I Forward Corps?
U/I Light Infantry Brigade	II Forward Corps?
U/I Light Infantry Brigade	II Forward Corps?
U/I Light Infantry Brigade	II Forward Corps?
U/I Light Infantry Brigade (75th?)	V Forward Corps?
U/I Light Infantry Brigade (80th?)	V Forward Corps?
U/I Light Infantry Brigade	IV Corps?
U/I Light Infantry Brigade	IV Corps?
U/I Light Infantry Brigade	IV Corps?
U/I Light Infantry Brigade	VII Corps?

Table 6-3

Deployment of Light Infantry Brigades Subordinate to the Light Infantry Training Guidance Bureau

Unit	Location
81st Light Infantry Brigade	Huich'on (Hyangsan)
82nd Light Infantry Brigade	Huich'on (Hyangsan)
87th Light Infantry Brigade	Hamhung

The deployment of the light infantry brigades subordinate to the Light Infantry Training Guidance Bureau is shown in table 6-3. The 87th Light Infantry Brigade is reported to be both a bicycle and a ski unit: the troops ride bicycles in long-distance marches and receive ski training.[3]

▪ ORGANIZATION AND EQUIPMENT

All light infantry brigades follow a standard organization. The brigade is typically commanded by a major general and has a personnel strength of 3,200–3,700. It is organized into a headquarters and rear services, signal company, and six or seven light infantry battalions.[4]

The headquarters is organized into command, staff, political, political security, and rear services elements. There is presently no detailed

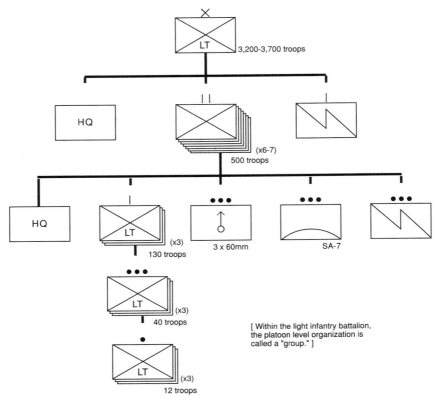

Light infantry brigade, 1996.

information concerning the particular functions performed by the light infantry brigade headquarters staff. However, it is believed that what follows is a reasonably accurate estimate.[5] The commander and operations staff perform essentially those duties attributed to the S1, S2, and S3 in U.S. Army military organizations. The chief of staff is responsible for the indoctrination of all personnel and supervises implementation of policies and procedures of subordinate battalions. The deputy brigade commander, political security, investigates political offenses, criminal activities, and suspicious acts or statements. The deputy brigade commander, rear services, not only performs S4-type duties but is also responsible for conduct of support activities. The communications officer provides communications for the headquarters.

The light infantry battalion is the brigade's basic element for combat operations. Each battalion, including the division/brigade light infantry battalions, is typically commanded by a colonel and has a personnel strength of approximately five hundred. It consists of a headquarters and rear services, signal platoon, and three companies of three "groups" (i.e., platoons) each. Each "group" is composed of three squads.

Although the division/brigade light infantry battalion is organized identically to those organic to the light infantry brigades, its headquarters and rear services elements may be slightly larger.

In general the combat equipment found within all special purpose units is highly flexible and varies considerably, depending upon specific mission requirements. Small teams carry only personal equipment, light arms, and mission-specific equipment; larger teams also carry crew-served weapons.

During training, light infantry personnel are apparently provided with standard KPA infantry uniforms. During combat operations, they may typically wear civilian clothing (e.g., women's clothing, including wigs, and civilian clothing with temporary camouflage); ROKA uniforms (typically with officer ranks); mottled camouflage uniforms in summer; and an all-white overgarment in winter.

Combat arms and ammunition typically include a dagger or bayonet; pistols, primarily carried by officers (types include a 7.62-millimeter Type-64/68, silenced versions of a 9-millimeter Browning automatic, and Soviet Tokarev 7.62-millimeter automatics); rifles (Type-46/68 AK-47/AKM, Czechoslovak Skorpion, M-3, M-16 with serial numbers removed, and others); machine guns (7.62-millimeter Type-62 RPK/RPD light machine gun); hand grenade/demolitions (from the KPA, PRC, ROK, and United States); antipersonnel and antitank mines; recoilless rifles (82-millimeter B-10 or 107-millimeter B-11); RPG-7 and AT-3 Sagger; 60- or 82-millimeter mortars and the appropriate ammunition.

Other gear usually carried by light infantry personnel includes a compass and map; flashlight; watch; binoculars; gas mask (ShM "k" series or its Czech or Polish versions); knapsack, poncho, and blanket; canteen and mess kit; first aid kit; entrenching tool; mission rations (often carried on an ROK-type web belt); and a rope and hook (the hook is used not only for climbing but for digging).

In addition to the normal gear, personnel on special missions often carry ROK/U.S. currency, 35-millimeter cameras with 400-millimeter telephoto lenses and fifty to one hundred rolls of film (including infrared), electronic intelligence and signals intelligence equipment, and encryption/decryption devices (depending upon the mission).[6]

▪ OFFENSIVE OPERATIONS
Generally speaking the division/brigade light infantry battalions conduct unconventional warfare operations within 15–30 kilometers of the FEBA

and are concerned with assisting the operations of their parent division. Operating in "group"- and company-sized units, the battalions concentrate on targets of immediate tactical importance, to isolate ROK/U.S. units deployed along the FEBA from their tactical rear. Tactical targets include the following:

- Division, brigade, and battalion command posts. It is hoped that by the destruction or disruption of these headquarters, those enemy units deployed along the FEBA will be isolated from each other and their fire support assets. They can then be reduced individually.
- Important terrain features such as mountains, passes, rivers, bridges, and tunnels. Control of such terrain features will prevent ROK/U.S. units from being reinforced or from shifting forces laterally.
- Military/civilian airfields and heliports. These will be seized to deny their use by the ROK and the United States, which will limit air operations over the FEBA and provide forward operating bases for the DPRK airborne units, thus extending the distance to which they can be deployed in the ROK.
- Artillery assets and antitank defensive positions. The ROK/U.S. defense of the area north of Seoul is based upon the use of successive lines of extensive antitank obstacles and the employment of concentrated artillery fires. These antitank obstacles are not to be manned by the withdrawing troops, but rather by mobilized reserves. If they are not properly manned they are ineffective. The light infantry battalions and brigades would attempt to occupy these positions before the mobilized reservists, thus denying them their use, or at minimum, forcing them to fight for their own defensive positions. Such a situation would likely have a significant effect on reservist morale. ROK/U.S. strategy also calls for the employment of concentrated artillery fires, yet they have limited numbers of medium and heavy artillery systems. The loss of any artillery will significantly degrade the ability of ROK/U.S. ground force units to hold their positions.

In addition to being responsible for the aforementioned tactically important targets, teams from the light infantry battalion can augment the division's reconnaissance assets, provide the primary forces for any envelopments attempted by the division, and conduct extended operations deeper within ROK territory. These teams, however, will probably not be detached from the division or operate outside of the division's area of operations.

The light infantry brigades' responsibilities are similar to those of the battalions, but differ in scope. The brigades conduct unconventional warfare operations in an area further (between 30 and 70 kilometers,

SPECIAL PURPOSE UNITS TODAY ■ ■ ■ ■ ■ ■

i.e., out to the edge of the corps area of operations) from the FEBA than do the battalions, and assist with the operations of the corps. Operations beyond this are the responsibility of the other special purpose units. Like the battalions, the brigades operate in "group"- and company-sized units to concentrate on targets of tactical/operational importance. The aim is to isolate ROK/U.S. units deployed along, and immediately behind, the FEBA from their operational/strategic rear. Targets for light infantry brigade attacks go beyond the light infantry battalion's targets and are at a higher level (i.e., army, corps, division) and at a greater depth into the ROK/U.S. rear. The targets will include the following:

- Army, corps, and division command posts and C³I facilities. The objective would be the capture or destruction of these elements to limit the ability of the ROK and United States to identify the major KPA avenues of approach and initiate appropriate responses. Another object would be to isolate the ROK/U.S. corps deployed along the FEBA from their strategic rear. Attacks on these facilities, especially theater/global C³I installations, could have a significant effect on the initial stages of a war.
- Lines of communication. These will be severed at "choke points," thus isolating the ROK/U.S. units deployed along the FEBA from their strategic rear. This in turn would significantly hurt the ability of these enemy units to conduct a protracted defense, and would facilitate their being divided into small pockets of resistance, which could then be destroyed piecemeal. This interdiction would also have a serious effect on the ROK mobilization effort and the morale of mobilized units. These attacks also represent an effort to create the conditions necessary for an envelopment or double envelopment.
- Military/civilian airfields and heliports. These facilities would be seized in a combined action with airborne and reconnaissance units. The objective would be the on-ground destruction of a significant portion of ROK/U.S. aircraft, or rendering the airfields inoperable,[7] thus limiting the extent of ROK/U.S. air superiority during the initial stages of an attack. Since the United States also plans to conduct theater reinforcement by airlift, the loss or interdiction of any major air base would significantly affect this reinforcement.
- Antitank defensive positions and corps-level artillery/rocket assets of the army. Elements from the light infantry brigades will help, at a greater depth, the light infantry battalions seize the successive lines of artillery positions and antitank obstacles along the approaches to Seoul before they can be manned by mobilized reservists. This would facilitate a rapid KPA armored advance on the capital and the

177

envelopment of ROK/U.S. units deployed along the DMZ. Army, corps-level artillery/rocket assets (175 mm, MLRS, LANCE, etc.) would be sought out and destroyed. The importance of these enemy units is their ability to direct long-range fires on the KPA's operational rear. More importantly, however, are their nuclear and chemical delivery capabilities.

- Army-, corps-, and division-level POL, ammunition, supply, storage, and mobilization facilities. The capture or destruction of these facilities within the forward areas will deny ROK/U.S. forces the means to conduct a protracted defense or to shift their reserves. It could also have a significant effect upon the mobilization of reservists.

Like the light infantry battalions, the brigades will augment the corps' reconnaissance assets, provide the primary forces for any envelopments or double envelopments attempted by the corps, and have the capability to conduct extended operations deeper within ROK territory. A light infantry brigade can, and most likely will, detach units to operate beyond the corps area of operations.

The size of a light infantry or special purpose unit employed against a specific target depends upon a number of considerations, including the importance of the target, the type of target, and the tactical situation. A tactically unfavorable condition, however, does not preclude an attack. Quite the contrary, all special purpose units can routinely conduct attacks under completely unfavorable tactical conditions, depending upon surprise, firepower, and speed to offset such conditions. It should also be noted that if the target was important enough, these units will not hesitate to conduct attacks that would be considered "suicide" in other armies. The typical size of an attacking unit can range from a platoon to a battalion-plus (table 6-4).[8]

As regular ground forces advance, elements from the light infantry battalions and brigades would continually be pushed forward, seeking to destroy or disrupt ROK/U.S. headquarters, C[3]I assets, and lines of communication. The forces would always be attempting to create the conditions necessary for the envelopment and destruction of ROK/U.S. units.

- DEFENSIVE OPERATIONS
  During defensive operations or—worse—withdrawals, light infantry units will operate as either a "rear-guard/delay" or a "stay-behind" force. The rear-guard/delay force will harass the ROK/U.S. forces as they advance by conducting ambushes and destroying bridges, tunnels, power grids, telephone poles/towers, and so on. The stay-behind force will attempt to establish guerrilla bands to harass ROK/U.S. forces and provide intelligence to

Table 6-4

TYPICAL SIZE OF A LIGHT INFANTRY UNIT ATTACKING A PARTICULAR-SIZED TARGET

Target	Unit Size
Air base	Battalion plus
Missle, C³I, or radar site	Squad to "group"
Division-level command element	"Group"
Corps-level command element	"Group" to company
Field army-level command element	Company to battalion
Bridge, tunnel, railroad bridge, etc.	Squad
Government facilities (radio or TV station, telephone central office, etc.)	Squad to "group"

General Headquarters, corps, or division commanders. They will also serve as a counter-special-operations force for local commanders.

AIRBORNE AND AIRBORNE SNIPER BRIGADES

▪ MISSIONS

The airborne and airborne sniper brigades have different missions; a major difference is where each brigade focuses its operations.[9]

▪ ▪ *Airborne Brigades*

The airborne brigades (also called airborne assault, airborne infiltration, or airborne light infantry brigades) operate within the ROK/U.S. strategic rear areas and have the capability, training, and equipment to conduct battlefield infiltration in order to execute the following missions:

- Support strategic and operational ground force operations by seizing and holding critical geographic features (e.g., mountain passes) or portions of the ROK infrastructure (e.g., tunnels and dams).
- Support strategic and operational-level amphibious landings.
- Block strategic lines of communication and reinforcement.
- Conduct raids and ambushes against reinforcements, mobilizing reserves, and reserve mobilization and storage facilities.
- Establish a "second front" within the ROK's strategic rear.
- Conduct raids and assaults on high-value targets.

The airborne brigades also serve as a vital part of the KPA's strategic

179

reserves and are charged with the following defensive missions:

- Defensive operations within the strategic rear areas, including counter-airborne and counter-invasion operations.
- Provision of guidance and training in counterguerrilla operations to regular army and paramilitary reserve units.[10]
- Guerrilla operations, if the brigade is deployed within the ROK/U.S. rear during a KPA strategic defensive operation.

The missions of the 38th, 48th, and 58th Airborne Brigades are presented in table 6-5. This information was provided by a recent DPRK defector.[11]

■ ■ *Airborne Sniper Brigades*
The missions of the airborne sniper brigades (also called air force sniper brigades or airborne infiltration brigades) are similar to those of the amphibious sniper brigades. The airborne sniper brigades will operate throughout the entire ROK, including within the FEBA. They are responsible for

- Seizure or destruction of ROKAF/USAF-related facilities, especially air bases and C^3I and missile and radar sites.
- Seizure or destruction of strategic/theater C^3I, missile, and NBC (nuclear, biological, and chemical) warfare assets.
- Targeting reconnaissance for DPRK weapons of mass destruction.

Table 6-5

Missions of the 38th, 48th, and 58th Airborne Brigades

Unit	Offensive Missions	Defensive Missions
38th Airborne Brigade	Special warfare throughout ROK	Counter-airborne or counter-invasion operations in P'yongyang area; serve as a reserve force of the Light Infantry Training Guidance Bureau
48th Airborne Brigade	Infiltration and special warfare in western sections of ROK	Counter-airborne or counter-invasion operations in Hwanghae Province (southwestern section of DPRK)
58th Airborne Brigade	Infiltration and special warfare in eastern sections of ROK	Counter-airborne or counter-invasion operations in Kangwon Province (southeastern section of DPRK)

- Assassination or abduction of ROK political leaders and senior ROK/U.S. military commanders.
- Support of airborne brigade operations.
- Support of amphibious sniper and sniper brigade operations.
- Deception and special operations throughout the ROK.
- Special operations in Japan and Okinawa.

The exact nature of the defensive missions assigned to the airborne sniper brigades is presently unknown. In all likelihood the missions are similar to those of the airborne brigades.

The missions and capabilities of the airborne and airborne sniper brigades approach those of U.S. airborne and ranger forces and the Russian airborne and raydoviki. However, they are by no means as heavily equipped as any of these units, and they have a guerrilla/counterguerrilla training role as part of their unconventional warfare mission.

- COMMAND AND CONTROL

Command and control for airborne and airborne sniper brigades, like that of the amphibious sniper brigades, is not entirely clear. It extends from the MPAF, through the General Staff Department and Light Infantry Training Guidance Bureau, to the individual brigades. The nature of airborne and airborne sniper operations, however, requires that these units work closely with the KPAF, which provides transportation and logistical support for all such operations. The extent of the control exercised by KPAF Command Headquarters over these brigades, if any, is unknown.

The KPA currently possesses three airborne brigades and three airborne sniper brigades, which have a total personnel strength of twenty-one thousand. These brigades are presently deployed as follows:

Table 6-6

DEPLOYMENT OF AIRBORNE SNIPER AND AIRBORNE BRIGADES SUBORDINATE TO THE LIGHT INFANTRY TRAINING GUIDANCE BUREAU

Unit	Location
11th Airborne Sniper Brigade	Kwail
16th Airborne Sniper Brigade	Yangdok
21st Airborne Sniper Brigade	Kwail
38th Airborne Brigade[12]	Sangwon (Chunghwa)
48th Airborne Brigade	Yonsan
58th Airborne Brigade	P'an'gyo (Pankyo)

A direct relationship between airborne units and air bases (or air bases of a specific type) has yet to become evident. Many of these units are located near jet fighter bases, whereas some are further away. Other units are located near transport air bases, and a few are located near highway strips.[13] As with air bases, no direct relationship between airborne units and helicopters, sailplanes, ultralights, or hot-air balloons is presently evident, other than the fact that some airborne units train in their use. The exception to this is that airborne units are generally associated with An-2s and Li-2s, while airborne sniper units are generally associated and train with MD-500s and Mi-2s. Taech'on Air Base, which is the location of one of the KPA's two airborne training facilities, is a MiG fighter base.[14]

- ORGANIZATION AND EQUIPMENT
- ■ *Airborne Brigades*

The organization of the individual airborne brigade is similar to that of the light infantry brigade. The airborne brigade has a personnel strength of approximately 3,500 men and is organized into a headquarters element, a signal company, six airborne battalions, a guard platoon, a medical unit, and a maintenance and repair unit. Since its establishment, the 38th Airborne Brigade has also had a "directly subordinate women's parachute platoon" of 25 troops, whose mission in peacetime is to provide support to major training events of the Paramilitary Training Units and 38th Airborne Brigade. During wartime, this female platoon uses An-2 aircraft to infiltrate enemy territory, where the women pose as ROK civilians for reconnaissance missions. It is unclear whether the 1990s references to an all-female "airborne surprise infiltration" unit were referring to this unit, or to newly established units subordinate to the Reconnaissance Bureau or airborne sniper brigades.

Each battalion has a personnel strength of approximately five hundred and is organized into a headquarters element, four airborne companies, a mortar company (nine 60-millimeter mortars), an antitank platoon (four recoilless rifles), an air defense platoon (SA-7/-16), and a signal platoon. The airborne company has approximately seventy-five troops and is composed of three platoons of about twenty-five troops each. Each platoon is composed of three squads of eight troops. The squad consists of the following troops: squad leader (automatic rifle); assistant squad leader (automatic rifle); machine gunner; rocket launcher operator; first grenade launcher operator; second grenade launcher operator; first automatic rifleman; and second automatic rifleman (also the radioman). Each company also possesses three M-16s. These are not fired, but used for training. In KPA service the RPG-7 is called the "number 7 rocket launcher," and the SA-7 is called the "Hwasung-ch'ong." The battalion is the tactical

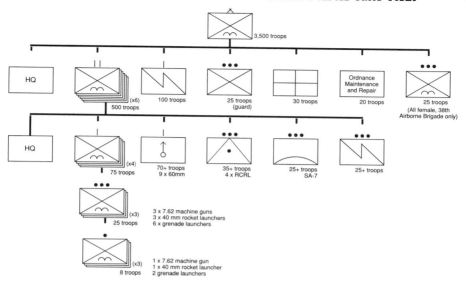

Airborne brigade, 1996.

unit normally employed for independent operations, although companies, platoons, and even squads are also capable of independent operations.

In addition to the aforementioned weapons, airborne brigades utilize long-range communications equipment manufactured in the People's Republic of China (PRC) and will make extensive use of any captured enemy weapons and equipment. Airborne unit signal operations are under the control of the 9th Signal Brigade, subordinate to the MPAF Communications Bureau.

■ ■ *Airborne Sniper Brigades*

The organization of the airborne sniper brigade is similar to that of the airborne brigade. The airborne sniper brigade has a personnel strength of approximately 3,500 men and is organized into a headquarters element, a signal company, six airborne sniper battalions, a guard platoon, a medical unit, and a maintenance and repair unit.

The airborne sniper brigade differs significantly at the battalion level. Each battalion has a personnel strength of approximately 500 and is organized into a headquarters element, six companies, and a signal platoon. The airborne sniper company has approximately 80 troops and is composed of three platoons of 25 troops each. Each platoon is composed of six teams of 4 troops each. Sometime during 1992–95 the KPAF tested

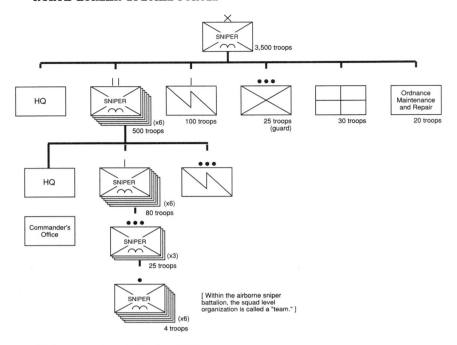

Airborne sniper brigade, 1996.

the capability of KPAF An-2s to carry laser-guided bombs in support of special purpose forces using laser designators. These may be employed by the airborne sniper units.[15]

The KPA airborne battalion organization, with 500 troops, is significantly larger than comparable Russian air assault (300 troops) and air mobile (250) battalions, but smaller than PRC (605) and U.S. airborne infantry (687) and air assault infantry (733) battalions. The KPA battalion is always considerably "lighter" in equipment.

Airborne and airborne sniper personnel are trained in both medium- and low-altitude jumps. With the development of a new parachute in 1991, however, low-low-altitude jumps have become the standard mode of employment. These airborne and airborne sniper units utilize two indigenously manufactured parachutes: the Chayu-914 (or Freedom-914, so named because it was developed on 14 September) and Chayu-91 (or Freedom-91, so named because it was introduced in 1991). Most airborne personnel prefer the newer Chayu-91 because of its reliability and low-altitude performance.

A Chayu-914 opens after 150 meters of free fall; therefore, a jump was typically conducted at a minimum altitude of 300 meters. The Chayu-91 opens after 40 meters, so jumps are now carried out from a minimum altitude of 80 meters. According to defectors, the Chayu-91 is comparatively lighter and easier to operate than the Chayu-914. When the chute is opening, there is little shock and it is easier to handle the suspension lines. Finally, it is easier and takes less time to fold up the parachute after use. Table 6-7 compares the two parachutes. It is believed that a small component of each brigade is qualified in HALO (high-altitude, low-opening) and HAHO (high-altitude, high-opening) operations.

Airborne/airmobile training is known to be conducted at three or more known locations: Taech'on and P'yongyang East Air Bases and several other airborne training facilities around the country.[16] Located at Sinyang, P'yongan-Pukto Province, is a specialized training area that includes mock-ups of the DMZ area, ROKA division command posts, tank positions, artillery gun positions, and an airfield.[17]

The primary means of transport for airborne brigades is the An-2. Called the "Antuggi," it carries eight airborne troops in KPAF service. When there is a shortage of An-2s, Li-2s (called "Lidul," carrying sixteen airborne troops in KPAF service) are used. The primary means of insertion for airborne sniper brigades are MD-500s, Mi-2s, and An-2s.

▪ DOCTRINE

Although KPA airborne doctrine is generally based upon Soviet/Russian doctrine, it is believed to have been strongly influenced by the airborne operations conducted by UNC forces during the Fatherland Liberation War. The KPA has taken this body of experience and doctrine, combined it with lessons learned in more recent conflicts (e.g., Grenada, Falklands war, and Operation Desert Storm), and modified it to meet its own unique

Table 6-7

A COMPARISON OF THE CHAYU-914 AND CHAYU-91 PARACHUTES

Designation	Chayu-914	Chayu-91
Size (square meters)	75	50
Number of suspension lines	28	24
Length of suspension lines (meters)	9	6
Weight (kilograms)	19 (when a reserve parachute is included, 25)	10
Minimum jump altitude (meters)	300	80

requirements. This doctrine apparently divides airborne operations (as they do amphibious operations) into three broad categories: strategic, operational, and sniper/special operations.

■ ■ *Strategic-Level Operations*

Strategic-level operations are conducted by a brigade or one or more battalions and are confined to targets of extreme military or political importance. In all likelihood, strategic operations will be carried out either at the beginning phases of any new conflict, or when they are needed as a strategic catalyst. These operations are not intended to be conducted independently, but rather in coordination with other special purpose or regular ground force operations. Likely missions for strategic operations include the following:

- Seizure and control of vital geographic regions and features (e.g., mountain passes), cities, and economic facilities (e.g., nuclear and hydroelectric power plants) throughout the ROK's strategic rear.
- Establishment of a new front within the ROK's strategic rear.
- Assisting the advance of corps-level units by outflanking, or assisting in the double envelopment of, ROK/U.S. positions.
- Combined operations in support of strategic amphibious landings.

Although the KPAF does possess the airborne lift capability to conduct a brigade-level strategic airborne landing, such an operation would probably exhaust the resources of the KPAF and would be extremely costly because of probable ROKAF/USAF air superiority. An operation of this size would be expected to alter the course of the war and, almost assuredly, be conducted in combination with a strategic amphibious landing or major ground forces attack. Most of these operations would be of battalion or reinforced battalion size.

■ ■ *Operational*

These operations are conducted by units of battalion, company, or platoon strength. They will concentrate on raids, ambushes, assaults, and reconnaissance, with company- or platoon-strength operations being the norm. Battalion-strength operations can be expected when the objectives are of considerable value. Although these operations may be conducted independent of other special purpose or regular ground force operations, they will typically have such support. Objectives for these operations will include

- Combined operations with, or in support of, other special purpose units, especially those amphibiously landed within the ROK strategic rear (including the seizure of a beachhead in advance of an assault by amphibious sniper units).

- Assisting the advance of ground force units by outflanking, or assisting in the double envelopment of, ROK/U.S. positions.
- Assisting the advance of ground force units by seizing bridges, river crossing points, and other important terrain features.
- The interdiction, seizure, or control of ROK/U.S. strategic/theater-level lines of communications.
- Deception and unconventional warfare operations.

▪ ▪ *Sniper/Special Operations*

Sniper/special operations cover a wide range of missions and will be conducted by units of company, platoon, squad, or section size. Their operations will frequently be conducted independent of other special purpose and regular ground force units and will have the following objectives:

- Seizure or destruction of ROK/USAF air bases, C³I facilities, NBC and missile assets, and other sensitive facilities within the strategic rear.
- Maintaining pressure on retreating ROK/U.S. forces.
- Intelligence operations to seize enemy documents, weapons, and equipment.
- Assassination or abduction of important military or political personnel.
- Deception operations (typically conducted over a wide area).

- AIRBORNE LIFT CAPABILITY

The KPAF presently possesses approximately 695 transport aircraft and helicopters capable of conducting airborne operations. These have a theoretical capability to airlift a total of 8,000 troops (table 6-8). This figure, however, is extremely optimistic, as it assumes that the KPAF would commit all possible aircraft (including VIP transports) and helicopters to this mission and would achieve a 100 percent "in-service" rate. It also assumes that ROK/U.S. forces do not have air superiority.

A more realistic estimate would be that the KPAF can airlift four to five thousand troops, or eight to ten airborne sniper battalions, which could be employed anywhere on the Korean Peninsula. Nevertheless, even at this lower level it is doubtful that the KPAF could support them solely with air assets.

The airborne brigades are made even more effective by their use of the An-2 Colt. The An-2 is a single-engine multipurpose biplane that first

Table 6-8

KPAF PRESENT-DAY TRANSPORT HELICOPTER AND OTHER AIRCRAFT AIRLIFT CAPABILITY

Aircraft*	Est. Number	Est. Capacity (Troops)	Total Lift Capacity (Troops)
An-2 Colt/Y-5	300	8	2,400
An-24 Coke	8	50	400
Il-14 Crate	5	28	140
Il-18 Coot	4	75	300
Il-62 Classic	6	175	1,050
Li-2 Cab	14	16	224
Tu-134B Crusty	2	72	144
Tu-154B Careless	4	167	668
MD-500D/E Defender	87	4	348
Mi-2 Hoplite/Hyokshin-2	140	4	560
Mi-4 Hound/Z-5	48	15	720
Mi-8/-17 Hip	27	32	864
Mi-24 Hind	50	4	200
Mi-26 Halo	n.a.	80	
Total	695†		8,018

*Interview data; *Jane's Sentinel: North Korea (DPRK)* (London: Jane's Information Group, 1995), pp.16–18; "DPRK Domestic, International Air Routes Noted," *Yonhap*, 11 February 1993, as cited in FBIS-EAS-93-027, 11 February 1993, pp. 22–23; Paul Beaver, "Equipment: Mi-2 Armed and Ready," *Jane's Soviet Intelligence Review* 1(2): 76–77; Aviation Advisory Service, *International Air Force and Military Aircraft Directory* (Aviation Advisory Service, 1987), pp. 181–82; and "North Korea to Import Hungarian Helicopters," *North Korea News*, 8 December 1986, p. 4.

†This number is probably too low, since Sharpe, in *Defense White Paper 1995–1996*, gives figures of 480 transport aircraft and 290 helicopters, a total of 770. If this is correct, the total airlift capability of the KPAF would be even greater.

went into production in 1947. The aircraft normally cruises at 100–125 miles per hour (160–201 kilometers per hour) and has a 550-kilometer operating radius with a normal payload of eight airborne troops or 1,020 kilograms. The An-2 is, however, capable of slower speeds (to 57 miles per hour [91 kilometers per hour]) and more payload (up to thirteen passengers) if required.[18] As noted in the previous chapter, instead of the

An-2's age and slow speed being a drawback, they are actually an asset. The advantage is that these aircraft can fly below the mountaintops down the valleys leading from the DPRK to the ROK, and can thus evade detection by ROK air defense radars. Airborne personnel would then parachute into military installations to wreak as much destruction as possible from within.[19] To counter this threat, the USAF began a program in 1985 to modify the radar on its E-3 AWACS aircraft to track the slow- and low-flying An-2.[20] Even with this modification, however, it is unlikely that most An-2s could be detected and even less likely that they could be effectively intercepted by ROKAF/USAF aircraft in a nighttime attack. During daytime operations the An-2s would suffer heavy losses, but many would get through ROK/U.S. defenses.

The covert acquisition, during the late 1980s, of approximately eighty-seven Hughes MD-500D/E helicopters has had a significant effect upon the ability of the KPAF and airborne sniper brigades to conduct special operations. The MD-500D/E are civilian versions of the Hughes MD-500 Defender antitank helicopters used in large numbers by the ROKAF. The KPAF has "heavily armed" and painted these helicopters in ROKAF colors.[21] Airborne sniper units are actively training with these helicopters and have conducted this training near the DMZ, with occasional penetrations of ROK airspace. Another recent acquisition, since at least 1981, has been the importing of Soviet sport sailplanes manufactured in the city of Arsenyev, north of Vladivostok. ROK sources indicate that the DPRK does not engage in sailplane sports and that these sailplanes have been used to train "members of the Airborne Infiltration Brigade under the Special 8th Corps."[22] Airborne training for sniper units may now include sailplane, ultralight, and hot-air balloon operations.

■ OFFENSIVE OPERATIONS

Because of the importance of the three airborne brigades as a major portion of the strategic reserve forces, their vital rear-area security mission, and the KPAF's limited airlift capabilities, probably no more than the equivalent of one or two airborne battalions would be employed for offensive operations during the initial stages of a renewed conflict. The remaining elements of these brigades may be employed when sufficient reserves become available to assume the rear-area security mission (after approximately thirty to sixty days) and if the KPAF can maintain its airlift capabilities. The three airborne sniper brigades, however, would be fully utilized from the very onset of a renewed war. The type and size of the target determines the size of attacking airborne or airborne sniper force. The current target/unit allocations for missions not requiring the holding of the target are presented in table 6-9.[23]

Table 6-9

TYPICAL SIZE OF AN AIRBORNE OR AIRBORNE SNIPER UNIT ATTACKING A PARTICULAR-SIZED TARGET

Target	Unit
Air base	Company
Command post	Company
Corps HQ	Two companies
Division HQ	Company
Missile base	Platoon
Nuclear facility	Company, battalion
Port facility	Company

For missions requiring the holding of an air base or port facility the KPA will employ a multicompany- or reinforced-battalion-sized force from the airborne brigade, depending upon size and importance of the target. The estimated number of aircraft required to carry specific airborne or airborne sniper units are shown in table 6-10.

Airdrops and air landings will typically be conducted at dawn, dusk, or night and under unfavorable weather conditions. On rare occasions, however, (e.g., when conducting special operations or employing MD-500D/E helicopters for air base assaults) they may be conducted during

Table 6-10

ESTIMATED NUMBER OF AIRCRAFT REQUIRED TO CARRY SPECIFIC AIRBORNE OR AIRBORNE SNIPER UNITS

Unit	An-2	Li-2
Airborne sniper team	$1/2$	$1/4$
Airborne sniper platoon	3	2
Airborne sniper company	10	5
Airborne sniper battalion	63	32
Airborne squad	1	1–2
Airborne platoon	3	2
Airborne company	10	5
Airborne battalion	63	32

daylight hours. A typical drop zone for an airborne battalion is 1,000–2,000 meters wide and 2,000–3,000 meters long. Suitable locations include airfields, golf courses, sports fields, parks, and the like. An air landing zone for the An-2 Colt (primary transport for airborne units) is typically at least 30 meters wide and 350 meters long. Highways are excellent air landing zones. Mi-4/8 helicopters need a 50-meter-diameter circle.[24] Airdrops will typically be conducted at approximately 100 meters altitude. The estimated times to drop an airborne unit into a single drop zone range from 5 to 90 minutes (table 6-11).[25]

Table 6-11

ESTIMATED TIME (IN MINUTES) TO DROP AN AIRBORNE UNIT INTO A SINGLE DROP ZONE

Unit	Daytime	Nighttime
Battalion	30–45	45–90
Company	10–15	15–30
Platoon	5–10	10–15

Airborne operations will rarely employ sailplanes, ultralights, or hot-air balloons as a primary means of transportation because of both the limited load-carrying capabilities of these craft and their sensitivity to weather conditions. It should be noted, however, that these craft are useful for some types of infiltration and reconnaissance missions because of their minimal radar signatures.

When conducting a combat drop, a reconnaissance team drops first and guides the aircraft in from the ground. If time is constrained, or the combat situation dictates, the airborne force drops directly into the target area. If there is sufficient time or if the combat situation otherwise permits, the force drops into a mountainous area away from the target and then force-marches to attack. Airborne and airborne sniper units typically carry seven days' worth of food during combat operations. Once the troops exhaust these rations they are to "resolve the situation themselves by any means necessary." If airborne brigade forces are expected to hold a position of strategic importance for any length of time, the KPAF may attempt small resupply operations of ammunition and food at night.[26]

One of the primary objectives of the airborne sniper brigades is ROK/U.S. air bases. Notably, all 109 active ROK airfields, including

191

Cheju International (on Cheju Island, 473 kilometers from the DMZ), are within the operating radius of the An-2.

A typical airborne sniper raid on a major ROKAF/USAF air base would be conducted by a reinforced company or reinforced-company-sized unit, possibly supported by sniper or Social-Cultural Department elements. The conduct of the attack would include the following actions:

- Pre-mission training on mockups of the air base and pre-mission reconnaissance will be conducted by Social-Cultural Department or Reconnaissance Bureau personnel.
- Two to three days before the attack, airborne sniper or sniper teams will be inserted into the area (possibly by MD-500D/E helicopters) to verify the enemy situation and reconnoiter or mark the landing zone. Just prior to the attack, these units will establish blocking positions along all these routes and cut all known communications links.
- At dusk the airborne sniper unit would arrive over the air base in a combination of An-2s and helicopters (most likely MD-500D/Es painted in ROK markings, but possibly including Mi-2s and Mi-24s). The helicopters, armed with rockets, machine guns, or missiles, will commence the assault by neutralizing the control tower and airfield defenses. The airborne sniper troops will parachute directly onto the air base.
- As soon as the helicopters commence their attack, those units previously deployed outside the air base will attack its perimeter defenses.
- As the airborne sniper troops land they will form up into a headquarters, communication, and security subteam and a number of general and special assault teams. The general assault teams will each be assigned a specific target within the air base. Priority targets include aircraft, pilots, the control tower, hangers, communications facilities, and ammunition/fuel storage areas. The special assault teams will be tasked with seizing any nuclear or chemical munitions stored on the base and the capture of classified documents and senior officers.
- With their mission complete the airborne sniper troops will attempt one or a combination of the following five actions: (1) withdraw using helicopters and An-2s that land to retrieve them; (2) advance to a remote location to await the arrival of helicopters or An-2s to retrieve them; (3) advance to a remote coastal location to await retrieval by KPN or Maritime Department assets; (4) withdraw into the mountains and form a guerrilla unit to harass the ROK/U.S. rear; or (5) if the objective is important enough, fight to the death, with no relief or retreat expected or intended.

It is conceivable that the KPA would attempt to seize and hold an air base for a variety of reasons. If such a mission is executed it will likely follow the above outline, but probably also include the following:

- Additional airborne sniper, airborne, or even regular ground force troops will either be airdropped or be air landed as conditions permit. These operations will be conducted using An-2, or possibly even An-24, transports.
- The defensive positions will be reinforced by the airdrop or air landing of additional SAMs and ATGMs, as well as larger-caliber crew-served weapons (e.g., ZPU-2/4, ZU-23, 120-millimeter mortars, and 76.2/85-millimeter guns).
- The airborne sniper unit will wait until the arrival of KPA ground forces or fight until it is eliminated.

Other major targets for airborne sniper units will include the ROKAF/USAF tactical air control center at Osan Air Base and the auxiliary tactical air control center at Taegu Air Base; the P'ohang-Uijongbu Army Petroleum Distribution Pipeline and its pumping stations (a major supply conduit of POL for ROK/U.S. units); the Pusan–Uijongbu fiber-optic communications system; and other rail, power, and communication

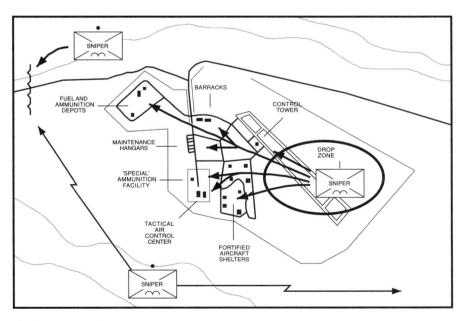

Air base assault.

networks (including the Tango C³I facility).²⁷ The attack against the pipeline and fiber-optic systems will in all probability be a combined operation. Light infantry units will be responsible for the northern terminus at Uijongbu; sniper and airborne sniper units for the stations throughout the interior; and sniper and amphibious sniper units for the terminals in the ports of P'ohang and Pusan.

During a prolonged war, airborne units will be employed to conduct unconventional warfare (especially guerrilla warfare) and special operations throughout the ROK against strategic targets.

▪ DEFENSIVE OPERATIONS
The ability of the airborne brigades to conduct effective defensive operations while deployed within the ROK/U.S. strategic rear is severely limited by the absence of heavy weapons, and the brigades' dependence on extraordinary means of logistic support. This is especially true when defending against an armored or combined arms attack. If forced into an untenable defensive situation, airborne brigades are likely either to attempt exfiltration and form small guerrilla units or to fight to the death.

During defensive operations within the DPRK the airborne brigades' primary responsibilities are counter-airborne, counter-invasion, and counterguerrilla operations. They will also participate in the defense of strategic installations or areas. Additionally, they are assigned general rear-area security responsibilities (e.g., instructing regular army and paramilitary reserve units in counter-airborne operations). If the need arises, the airborne brigades may also be employed as standard light infantry units. Depending on the situation, the airborne sniper brigades may be employed to counter any ROK/U.S. special operations within the DPRK.

KOREAN PEOPLE'S NAVY, AMPHIBIOUS SNIPER BRIGADES

The unique geographic and demographic characteristics of the Korean Peninsula all but ensure that the amphibious sniper brigades (also called navy sniper brigades, naval sniper brigades, or amphibious light infantry brigades) will play a significant role in any future conflict.²⁸ Some of the more salient characteristics particularly affect the importance of amphibious operations. Of the Korean Peninsula's 8,700 kilometers of coastline, approximately 6,800 kilometers is within ROK territory. This long coastline is almost impossible to completely seal or defend. Furthermore, the Korean Peninsula is surrounded by more than three thousand islands, the majority of which are likewise within ROK territory. These islands could provide shelter or forward bases of operations for assaulting or infiltrating amphibious sniper units.

The ROK's coastal plains are quit narrow and vulnerable to interdiction. The eastern plain is 3–5 kilometers wide; the western plain is 15–20 kilometers wide. A majority of the ROK's north–south lines of communications and strategic targets (both military and political) lie within these narrow coastal plains.

- MISSIONS
The amphibious sniper brigades are trained to conduct offensive amphibious assault, unconventional warfare, and special operations along the ROK coast. What separates them from the other special purpose brigades is their specialized amphibious warfare training, equipment, and manner of employment. The amphibious sniper brigades will conduct the following offensive missions:

  - The seizure, disruption, or destruction of key installations within coastal areas.
  - Assisting the advance of standard ground force units by enveloping coastal flanks.
  - Assault landings to seize and control a beachhead to allow the landing of standard ground force units.
  - Assisting standard ground force units during river crossing and bridging operations within coastal areas (e.g., the Han River estuary).
  - The establishment of a new front within the ROK's strategic rear.
  - Reconnaissance and special operations.
  - Defend against ROK/U.S. special operations.

The amphibious sniper brigade are also charged with thefollowing defensive missions:

  - Security and defense operations within the strategic rear areas.
  - Assisting base security units in the defense of KPN bases.
  - Limited island or coastal defense operations.

These missions are roughly comparable to U.S. Marine and SEAL (sea, air, and land special forces) units or to Russian naval infantry and naval commandos. The difference is that the amphibious sniper brigades are neither trained nor equipped to force a landing against a heavily defended beach.

- COMMAND AND CONTROL
Command and control for the amphibious sniper brigades is not entirely clear. It is believed to extend from the MPAF through the General Staff

Department to the KPN Command Headquarters at Namp'o. The day-to-day administration of the KPN and the supervision of its operations are delegated to the commander of the navy. His directives are passed down to the fleet and the attached amphibious sniper brigades, through the commanders of the Yellow Sea Fleet Headquarters at Namp'o, and the East Sea Fleet Headquarters at Wonsan. Administrative and technical support is also provided by the Light Infantry Training Guidance Bureau. During wartime, control of these amphibious sniper brigades may revert to the bureau.

The KPN's two amphibious sniper brigades have a total personnel strength of approximately seven thousand. These brigades are presently headquartered on the west coast at Hakkye (south of Namp'o and across the Tae-dong River) and on the east coast at Wonsan. It should be noted that while the brigade headquarters and most subordinate battalions are deployed at these locations, a number of battalions are detached and located at other navy bases or facilities:

Table 6-12

DEPLOYMENT OF AMPHIBIOUS SNIPER BRIGADES SUBORDINATE TO THE KOREAN PEOPLE'S NAVY

Unit	Location
U/I Amphibious Sniper Brigade	Wonsan (east coast)
U/I Amphibious Sniper Brigade	Hakkye (west coast)

■ ORGANIZATION AND EQUIPMENT

The organization of the amphibious sniper brigade is apparently derived from that of the light infantry brigade, although the amphibious sniper brigade is somewhat smaller. It consists of a headquarters element and rear services element, a signal company, an engineer platoon, and six battalions. Although there is no hard evidence, each brigade organization is also believed to contain a "combat swimmer" unit (similar in capabilities to Russian naval commandos or U.S. SEAL units), and a "special boat" unit (similar to the U.S. SEAL special boat units and SEAL delivery vehicle teams).

Each amphibious sniper battalion has a personnel strength of approximately five hundred and is organized into a headquarters and rear services element, a signal platoon, five companies, and a mortar company. Each company is organized into a headquarters element and four platoons.[29]

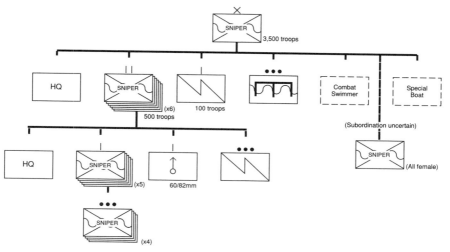

Amphibious sniper brigade, 1996.

The KPA amphibious sniper battalion is slightly larger than the Russian naval infantry battalion (409 troops), and is smaller than the U.S. Marine infantry battalion (867). Additionally, compared to both the Russian and U.S. units, the KPA amphibious sniper battalion is considerably "lighter" in equipment. The types of weapons and equipment likely to be found within the amphibious sniper brigades are the same as those for the light infantry brigade, although they might also include the following:

- 120-millimeter mortars, which may replace the 60/82-millimeter mortar.
- 107-millimeter B-11 recoilless rifles, which may replace the B-10.
- Engineer equipment (including flame throwers and mine- or obstacle-breaching equipment).
- Amphibious tanks and armored personnel carriers.
- ROK/U.S. weapons and equipment.
- Specialized high-speed infiltration craft, midget submarines, and swimmer delivery vehicles.[30]
- Specialized underwater equipment (SCUBA, etc.) and weapons.[31]

It is believed that amphibious sniper brigade personnel receive amphibious warfare training at the Ijin-dong naval base on the east coast (VI Corps) and Tasa-ri on the west coast (VIII Corps).[32] This is tentatively confirmed by the geography of the areas, and the unusually large numbers of amphibious warfare craft based nearby. In addition to this amphibious warfare training, some amphibious sniper brigade personnel may be airborne qualified.

- Dᴏᴄᴛʀɪɴᴇ

The KPA based its amphibious warfare doctrine on experiences gained during amphibious operations along the east coast at the beginning of the Fatherland Liberation War and later during the November 1951–March 1952 "island-hopping" campaign along the west coast. Additional influences were the major UNC amphibious operations and small raids during the war; the lessons learned by the Soviet Union during World War II; and the PRC experiences during the 1950s, early 1960s, and 1990s.[33] The KPA has modified these experiences to meet its own unique requirements. KPA doctrine apparently divides amphibious operations into three broad categories: strategic, operational, and sniper/special landings.

- ■ *Strategic Landings*

Like strategic airborne brigade operations, amphibious strategic landings are multibattalion-level operations against targets of great military or political importance. Also like their airborne counterparts, amphibious sniper operations will probably only be conducted at the beginning phases of any new conflict, or until they are required as a strategic catalyst. Strategic landings are conducted in coordination with other special purpose or regular ground force operations. Likely objectives for strategic operations include the following:

  - Assisting the advance of regular ground forces along the coastal plains on the ROK's western coast by conducting landings in the Inch'on/P'yong'taek area; or on the eastern coast by conducting landings in the Kangnung or Samch'ok areas.
  - The seizure and control of vital geographic features such as the islands and straits along ROK's west coast.
  - The seizure and control of a beachhead as a first echelon to allow the landing of regular ground force units. Such operations would include the landing of small numbers of light tanks and armored personnel carriers.
  - The disruption, seizure, or control of major naval bases, ports, airfields, and so forth, located within the coastal zone.
  - The establishment of a new front within the ROK/U.S. strategic rear.

- ■ *Operational Landings*

Battalion-, company-, or platoon-sized units will conduct the operational-level amphibious landings. When the objective is of considerable value, a battalion-strength unit will conduct the operation. Otherwise, company- and platoon-sized units are the norm. Like airborne and airborne sniper brigades, the amphibious sniper brigades typically are supported by other special purpose or regular ground forces during operational-level amphibious landings. The objectives of operational landings include the following:

- The seizure or destruction of sensitive facilities (especially air bases, POL storage and mobilization) within coastal areas.
- The interdiction, seizure, or control of ROK/U.S. operational/strategic lines of communications within the coastal areas.
- Assisting the advance of ground force units by outflanking or assisting in the encirclement, or envelopment, of ROK/U.S. positions along the coasts.
- Combined operations with, or in support of, airborne and reconnaissance units landed deep within ROK territory.
- Preinvasion beach reconnaissance, including the seizure of a beachhead in advance of an assault by other amphibious units.
- Deception operations.

▪ ▪ *Sniper/Special Operations*
Sniper and other special operations are conducted during both peacetime and wartime by company-, platoon-, squad-, or team-sized units. Operations will typically be conducted independently of other special purpose and regular ground force units. Objectives for these operations include

- The seizure or destruction of nuclear, chemical, C³I, and missile assets within coastal areas.
- The destruction of ROK/U.S. surface combatants, auxiliaries, and civilian shipping located within ROK naval bases and ports.
- Seizure or destruction of strategic facilities (i.e., railroad tunnels, dams, submarine telecommunications cables, and nuclear and conventional power plants).[34]
- Intelligence operations to seize documents, weapons, or equipment.
- Assassination or abduction of important military or political personnel.
- Preinvasion beach reconnaissance.
- Deception operations (typically conducted over a wide area).
- Raids against U.S. theater/global facilities (such as U.S. bases in Japan, Okinawa, and Pearl Harbor).

▪ AMPHIBIOUS LIFT CAPABILITIES
The ability of the KPA to employ the amphibious sniper brigades depends

199

upon the amphibious lift capabilities of the KPN. During the past ten years the KPN has made significant advances in the construction and deployment of amphibious warfare craft. As of 1996, the KPN has approximately 193 amphibious warfare craft, with a theoretical amphibious lift capacity of approximately nineteen thousand troops (table 6-13).[35] This includes 135 of the *Kong Bang I/II/III* LCPAs, whose high speed and ability to traverse large mudflats and ride up onto the beach significantly increase the survivability and viability of amphibious sniper forces.

A more realistic estimate of amphibious lift capability is seventeen thousand troops. This amphibious lift capacity easily exceeds the combined personnel strength for both amphibious sniper brigades (seven thousand troops) and allows the KPA to quickly reinforce any amphibious assault with regular ground troops and heavy equipment (e.g., tanks, artillery, multiple rocket launchers).

- AMPHIBIOUS LANDING OPERATIONS
- - *Organization*
  The organization and conduct of a strategic amphibious landing or a battalion-sized operational amphibious landing are described below. Other landings will be similar but proportionally smaller and may include some modifications. In smaller operations, the "outer screen" would be eliminated;

Table 6-13

KPN AMPHIBIOUS LIFT CAPABILITY, 1996

Class	Est. number	Est. Capacity Troops	Total Lift Capacity Troops
Hanch'on-class LCM	7	250	1,750
Hantae-class LSM	10	350	3,500
Hungnam-class LSM	18	400	7,200
Kong Bang I/II/III-class LCPA	135	40–50	5,400–6,750
Namp'o A/B-class LCPA	n.a.	n.a.	
Namp'o-class LCPF	23	30	690
Total	193		18,540–19,890

the "fire support" force would double as a "coastal screen"; and the "landing force" would consist solely of *Namp'o* LCPF or *Kong Bang* LCPA.

Landing sites will typically be selected from isolated coastal areas away from naval bases, ports, and towns. Consideration is given to the time required to arrive at the landing site, coastal defense measures, weather, and tide conditions, which can vary as much as 10 meters in the Yellow Sea. The tides are less of a consideration when *Kong Bang* LCPA are employed.

The landing force, consisting of various landing craft or air-cushion vehicles and amphibious sniper brigade personnel, will concentrate at forward naval bases (e.g., Sagon-ni on the west coast and Kosong on the east coast). Prior to the actual landings, squad-sized units will conduct beach reconnaissance and establish ambush positions, possibly with the assistance of sniper and airborne sniper units. In addition to the actual landings, deception landings and raids will be conducted.

The landing force will embark and be joined by an escort force. The combined invasion force will be under the command of an operations team and is likely to be organized into the following components:

- An outer screen, responsible for isolating the invasion fleet from ROK/U.S. surface combatants and for acting as scouts for the inner screen. The outer screen will consist of *Romeo*-class patrol submarines or *Sang-o*-class coastal submarines. These will arrive on station several days before the amphibious phase of the operation begins.
- An inner screen, which consists of fast attack craft—missile *(Soju, Osa I, Sohung,* or *Komar),* will engage at long range any vessels that are sighted by, or pass through, the outer screen.
- A coastal screen, which will provide protection from any attacks originating from the shores, along the invasion force's line of approach. Additionally, it may conduct preemptive raids against enemy naval facilities. This screen consists of fast attack craft—torpedo *(P6, Sinp'o,* and *Sinhung).*
- An escort, composed of large patrol craft *(So I, Taech'ong,* etc.) and gun-bearing fast attack craft—gun *(Chodo, Mo IV,* etc.). It will provide limited antiaircraft defense, deal with any enemy craft that penetrate the screening forces, and provide limited fire support to amphibious sniper units once they have landed.
- Fire support units, which will accompany the landing force into the beach and will provide fire support if required. These units will consist of fast attack craft—gun (e.g., *Chaho* or *Ch'ongjin).*
- A landing force, which will typically consist of at least two groups. The first group will be composed of *Namp'o*-class LCPF; the second or following groups, additional *Namp'o, Hantae,* and *Hanch'on.* If the land-

ing force instead primarily uses *Kong Bang* LCPA, then the escort forces will probably depart base before the *Kong Bang*s and most of the coastal screen will likely utilize *Sinhung*-class fast attack craft.

The main bodies will approach at night or under conditions of limited visibility. The actual landings will occur at night or first light.

Company- and battalion-sized units will assault in the first wave and secure the beachhead, possibly with the assistance of amphibious light tanks or armored personnel carriers. Upon landing, units will assume frontages similar to those of ground forces, with a battalion having a frontage of approximately 1000 meters. The battalion landing sites will be 800–1,000 meters apart. Once the beachhead is secured, follow-on echelons could include standard ground force units, possibly reinforced with additional armor and artillery.

■ ■ *Command and Control*

Until the amphibious sniper brigades have established themselves ashore, overall operational control of an amphibious operation is believed to be exercised by the Operations Team located at the respective fleet headquarters or forward naval base. This team also exercises control over the movements of all ships. This awkward chain of command reduces the status of the commander of the naval group and his subordinate captains to "conning officers" who merely maneuver their ships according to orders from base headquarters. Once the amphibious sniper brigade has established itself ashore, control is transferred back to the respective amphibious sniper commanders, who are now directly subordinate to the Light Infantry Training Guidance Bureau or to the General Staff Department. There is a remote possibility that this chain of command may be modified if the landing force includes a *Najin*- or *Soho*-class frigate, which may have a limited command and control capability.

■ ■ *Fire Support*

Fire support will not be employed unless the enemy has detected the landing force, or in attacking areas known to be fortified or occupied by enemy units. Under these circumstances, the escort and fire support forces will provide traditional, albeit limited, naval fire support. The KPA will also use standard artillery units, which will be inserted on nearby islands. Although the primary mission of the KPAF is air defense, additional fire support may be realized prior to a landing from a limited number of KPAF ground attack sorties. It is important to note, however, that neither ground attack sorties nor air superiority are prerequisites for amphibious operations. Most operations will be conducted without KPAF assistance. To coordinate fire support assets, amphibious landings may also include a fire support coordination team.

▪ ▪ *Augmentation*

Depending on the size and location of a landing operation, the amphibious sniper brigades may be augmented by attached amphibious light tank, artillery, and air defense elements. The KPA presently fields a small number of light tank battalions (amphibious) equipped with PT-76/Type-63 light tanks.[36] These battalions are apparently subordinate directly to the Armor Command Headquarters, but are attached to the IV and II Corps (Forward) to support amphibious operations along the west coast and Han River estuary, respectively. Other of these battalions are attached to the III Corps for coastal defense along the western coast. Augmentation by artillery units will typically include 76.2/85-millimeter guns, 107-millimeter multiple rocket launchers, or 120-millimeter mortars. Air defense units will be equipped with SA-7/-16, ZPU-2/4, or ZU-23.

▪ SNIPER/SPECIAL OPERATIONS LANDINGS

Special operations landings are not only employed by small teams from the amphibious sniper brigade for prelanding reconnaissance, raids, and so forth, but are also employed to insert Reconnaissance Bureau and Operations Department personnel.[37] The majority of these landings are conducted with the guidance and assistance of the Reconnaissance Bureau's Maritime Department. The landings employ a wide variety of highly specialized infiltration craft and submarines, which can be divided into three categories based upon their distance from the port of embarkation: short range, long range, and global.[38] Short-range operations typically employ *Yugo*-class midget submarines or high-speed infiltration craft. Long-range operations employ *Sang-o*-class coastal submarines or specialized agent transfer ships (i.e., "mother ships") carrying *Yugo*-class midget submarines or high-speed infiltration craft. Global operations use oceangoing cargo vessels, but during wartime may also use *Romeo*-class submarines.

For short-range infiltrations, the infiltration team (typically two to four persons) will embark upon a high-speed semisubmersible infiltration craft or *Yugo*-class midget submarine at a forward port or naval base. The infiltration craft normally then proceeds well out to sea to minimize detection from ROK-held islands or shore patrols, before turning south and making a high-speed approach toward the shore. The operation is normally done under the cover of darkness or inclement weather. Immediately prior to landing, the infiltration craft will halt approximately 500 meters from the shore to evaluate the situation. If security is lax and the water is deep, the vessel will rapidly approach the coast. If the water is shallow, the landing is accomplished by individual swimmer delivery devices or small rafts. If the high-speed semisubmersible infiltration craft are used, the engines are silenced approximately 200 meters from the landing site, whereupon the craft is paddled into shore. The infiltration team will be preceded to shore by a two-man escort team that secures the landing site. Once secure, the infiltration team proceeds ashore, and the escorts return. Both groups use swimmer delivery devices, SCUBA equipment, small rafts, or swimming to get ashore.

Up until the 1990s, longer-range infiltrations employed agent transfer ships that acted as "mother ships" for specialized high-speed semisubmersible infiltration craft or *Yugo*-class midget submarines. Typical operations proceed like this: The mother ship (usually a vessel of 50–100 tons) departs from its home base with a landing craft and swimmer delivery vehicle. At a designated point in the open sea, the mother ship deploys the landing craft and swimmer delivery vehicle. The landing craft then transports the swimmer delivery vehicle into ROK territorial waters to the infiltration point, approximately 5–10 kilometers from shore. Here the swimmer delivery vehicle separates from the landing craft and carries the infiltration team toward shore. As it approaches shore, the vehicle submerges and carries the infiltration team of three to six men up onto the beach. A *Yugo*-class midget submarine would function much like the landing craft. Even though mother ship operations are embarked in the open ocean, where detection is less likely, the size of the mother ship and its inability to submerge make these operations more susceptible to ROK/U.S. detection. Several mother ships were lost to ROKN and ROKAF operations. Additionally, a number of specialized infiltration craft were damaged and lost when being deployed or recovered by the mother ship. Of interest with regards to mother ship operations in the 1990s have been the repeated sightings of white (gray?) high-speed craft operating along the Japanese coast in the Sea of Japan. Because of the distance from the DPRK, these have been conducted using mother ships. These operations are directly related to special purpose operations in Japan including smuggling and narcotics trafficking. Beginning in the 1990s, the DPRK began construction of the *Sang-o*-class coastal submarine, which has sufficient range to cover the entire Korean Peninsula without the assistance of a mother ship. Operations with the *Sang-o*s follows the same general pattern as other infiltrations.

The west coast of the ROK is generally more suitable for special operations landings, as it has an irregular coastline and numerous offshore islands that render surveillance difficult while affording concealment for beach approaches. The extreme tidal range (as much as 10 meters) and associated currents, coupled with shallow offshore gradients, however, constitute a major drawback. Along the east coast, tides are not an inhibiting factor. The relatively straight coastline, while devoid of adequate cover, offers a wide choice of landing sites. Additionally, the steep drop-off of the shore allows infiltration submarines to approach close to shore while remaining submerged. The primary east coast debarkation port is Wonsan; on the west coast, Namp'o.

Global operations, of necessity, utilize oceangoing cargo vessels and, during wartime, possibly *Romeo*-class submarines. The KPN's *Romeo*s, however, are not known to have ever operated in open oceans, thus making it problematic as to whether they could effectively accomplish a global special operations mission.

■ OFFENSIVE OPERATIONS

In the event of renewed hostilities the amphibious sniper brigades would include the following:

- One strategic landing on the west coast in the Inch'on-P'yong'taek area. This landing represents an effort to outflank and envelope both the capital city of Seoul and the ROK/U.S. forces deployed along the DMZ. A landing in this area would also significantly threaten the port of Inch'on and the USAF bases at Osan and Suwon, as well as the Suwon Highway Airstrip, P'yong'taek Airport, and the P'yong'taek Highway Airstrip. The loss or disruption of any of these facilities could have a significant effect on ROK/U.S. air superiority, close air support, and theater reinforcement. This landing would be conducted in concert with an IV and II Forward Corps attack toward Seoul, and a V Forward Corps attack to outflank the city. The V Forward Corps attack would attempt to join up with the amphibious landing and complete a strategic envelopment of Seoul and ROK/U.S. forces deployed north of the capital. The landing would also receive support from airborne and sniper units.
- One or two operational landings on the east coast near Kangnung or Samch'ok in an effort to outflank and envelope ROK/U.S. forces deployed along the eastern half of the DMZ and to isolate the northeast section of the ROK from the rest of the country. These landings will be conducted in conjunction with an I Forward Corps thrust south along the coast, and a V Forward Corps attack south from the DMZ and then east to the coast.
- One or two operational landings on the west coast of Kangdwa-do Island or the Kimp'o peninsula northwest of Seoul. These landings would not only threaten Seoul, but would outflank a significant segment of the defensive lines north of the city.

205

- Numerous tactical landings of company and platoon size, and special operations against naval bases (e.g., P'ohang, Mukhojin-ni,
  Masan, Mokp'o), ports (e.g., Inch'on, Pusan), coastal airfields (e.g.,
  Suwon, Osan, Kwangju, Kunsan), and important targets located in
  coastal areas (e.g., the P'ohang-Uijongbu Army Petroleum Distribution Pipeline and the Pusan-Uijongbu fiber-optic communications
  system).[39] These operations will be conducted in cooperation with
  airborne sniper and sniper brigade personnel.
- Special operations against U.S. facilities in Japan (e.g., Yokota and
  Misawa Air Bases), Okinawa (Kadena Air Base), and others.

Strategic and operational landings, however, are not necessarily limited to wartime operations. If the DPRK leadership believed that the political climate was favorable, they could again initiate limited escalation.
Such escalation could take the shape of strategic/operational landings to
seize the ROK island of Ullung-do or, more likely, one of the United
Nations–controlled islands of Paengnyong-do, Taech'ong-do, Soch'ong-do,
and others. If successful in seizing one of the islands, the KPA would then
petition the United Nations for a truce. Such operations would place both
the ROK and U.S. governments in extremely difficult positions. The ROK
would either have to escalate and risk full-scale war by attempting to
recapture the island(s), or lose credibility by doing nothing. Similarly, the
United States would be thrust into the awkward position of deciding
whether to be drawn into a costly conflict over a few small islands.

- DEFENSIVE OPERATIONS
  Like the defensive operations of the airborne brigades, those of the
  amphibious sniper brigades within the ROK/U.S. rear are restricted by
  the lack of heavy weapons and the need for extensive logistic support.
  The needs are even greater when the brigades are defending against an
  armored or combined arms attack. The amphibious sniper brigades' reaction to an untenable defensive situation is the same as the airborne reaction: troops will either attempt exfiltration, form small guerilla units
  behind enemy lines, or fight to the bitter end.[40] During defensive operations within the DPRK the amphibious sniper brigade may participate
  in coastal defense operations to protect naval bases, ports, and islands;
  may construct and man beach defenses and obstacles; and may function
  as standard light infantry units. These units probably are responsible
  for operations against ROK/U.S. special operations forces.

- GLOBAL OPERATIONS
  Besides its traditional amphibious warfare fleet, the DPRK possesses a

significant theater/global amphibious lift capability with the KPN's 22 *Romeo*-class submarines and its merchant marine fleet, which in 1996 consisted of 143 vessels.[41] Although the *Romeo*-class submarines are old, they are capable of inserting and supporting small amphibious sniper brigade teams anywhere in the southwest Pacific (and conceivably even in Hawaii and the U.S. mainland).

The KPA has a long history of employing its civilian merchant fleet for special operations. Examples are the 25 June 1950 attempted landing of the 766th Independent Unit northeast of Pusan; the continued use of small coastal vessels to insert agents along the ROK coastline; the use of merchant ships to supply revolutionary groups in Africa; the employment of the *Tong Gon Ae Guk-ho* to transport three Reconnaissance Bureau members to Rangoon for the 9 October 1983 assassination attempt on ROK President Chon Tu-hwan; the attempt to establish a SIGINT post in the Gulf of California; and more.

The *Tong Gon Ae Guk-ho* is a DPRK merchant ship that has been frequently employed to support KPA special operations throughout Asia.[42] According to U.S. intelligence sources, it is the only merchant ship in the world identified as an instrument of state-sponsored terrorism.[43] The vessel first came to the public's attention in October 1983 for its role in the DPRK's attempted assassination of ROK President Chon Tu-hwan in Rangoon. Later, in 1985, the *Tong Gon Ae Guk-ho* made two voyages to Japan, the first during the early summer and the second on 14 August, when it remained for three days. What was particularly disconcerting about both these visits was that the crew manifest disclosed that a majority of the approximately thirty-one crew members, including most of the key officers, were the same crew who had participated in the 1983 Rangoon voyage.[44]

The *Tong Gon Ae Guk-ho* apparently is well prepared for covert operations. In assessing the operations of the vessel, U.S. intelligence sources in 1985 conclude that the ship has a "previous history of involvement in covert transport of terrorist-related personnel and arms" and a "history of involvement in North Korean agent and smuggling activities in Japan and possibly other Asian countries." The vessel is "equipped with sophisticated communications devices, heavy machine guns, small firearms, grenades, a larger than normal crew and special 'training' facilities." The *Tong Gon Ae Guk-ho* has undergone "periodic subordination" to the KWP for special operations "while disguised as a trade ship." It has most likely become "part of the North Korean merchant marine [which] was recently organized into 'suicide squads' in order to become the fourth defensive force of North Korea."[45]

The KPA's use of its merchant fleet is apparently not confined to a few ships. At least ten or eleven ships have been identified as being involved in such activities.[46] For example, in January 1982, Capt. Kang Dokun, of the *Changsan-ho,* a 14,000-ton DPRK merchant ship, defected when his ship became grounded in the approaches to the Malacca Strait.[47] The grounding necessitated immediate hull repairs to make the vessel seaworthy, and Capt. Kang Dokun feared that he would be punished when he returned home. Captain Kang claimed that his ship was one of twenty-seven oceangoing merchant vessels, ranging in size from 3,000 to 20,000 tons, supporting international terrorist activities. He further claimed that his ship had made a series of voyages since December 1980, secretly delivering arms, ammunition, and supplies to leftist guerrillas in Asia, Africa, and the Middle East.[48] An interesting aspect of the DPRK's involvement in the Middle East has been its purchase and resale of PRC-manufactured Silkworm coastal defense missiles to the government of Iran. With the DPRK acting as go-between, the PRC could thereby technically deny selling arms to Iran. The United States took the threat of the Silkworm missiles and their transfer by the DPRK so seriously that in January 1988, the Americans considered intercepting DPRK cargo vessels in transit to Iran.[49] This again became a concern during the 1990s, when the DPRK endeavored to ship Scud ballistic missiles to Syria and Iran.

One of the more intriguing incidents concerning global special operations was the 1983 attempts to conduct SIGINT operations and possibly establish a SIGINT post in the Gulf of California.[50] In January 1983 at least four DPRK "shrimping trawlers" entered the Gulf of California. One vessel of DPRK registry, but flying a Mexican flag, proceeded north toward St. Jorge Bay, off the town of Rocky Point, where it remained at anchor for approximately one week. The ship, identified by U.S. intelligence with the codename *Clomax 71,* was seized by Mexican authorities on 21 January for "fishing illegally in the gulf." U.S. intelligence sources, however, indicate that it was actually conducting SIGINT operations and supplying covert terrorist training camps established in the remote areas of northern Baja California and in the mountains around Culiacan, Sinaloa, in central Mexico. These sources further state that the ship was "bristling with antennas" and had a crew of twenty-eight DPRK and seven Mexican nationals. The Mexican nationals all carried false passports, and the DPRK nationals were believed to have been "soldiers or commandos" involved in training Central American terrorists and revolutionaries.[51]

In May of that year, another DPRK ship reportedly attempted to establish a SIGINT position on the small island of San Ildefonso, in the Gulf of California. Equipment deployed on the island included radio-monitoring and communications devices, which were allegedly powerful enough to allow direct communications with the DPRK. All this equipment was removed by the crew when it was feared that their security had been compromised. Such a position allowed the DPRK to intercept U.S. communications both with Central America and from a host of important U.S. military facilities in southern California and Arizona.[52] The information gathered by these operations was allegedly supplied to the Sandinista government, among others. U.S. intelligence sources indicate that DPRK intelligence-gathering ships have maintained a significant presence within the Gulf of California since early 1982.[53]

These SIGINT operations are not isolated incidents connected solely with North and Central America. DPRK ships are also reported to have been operating in the Persian Gulf during the summer of 1987, providing "early warning, long-range reconnaissance and targeting data to the IRGC [Islamic Revolutionary Guard Corps]."[54]

RECONNAISSANCE BUREAU SNIPER BRIGADES

The Reconnaissance Bureau's three sniper brigades (also called reconnaissance brigades or reconnaissance sniper brigades) remain the DPRK's most elite special operations forces.[55] They are well trained and equipped to perform a wide range of strategic special operations within the ROK and throughout the world. These brigades are complemented by five reconnaissance battalions.

MISSIONS

The operations of the Reconnaissance Bureau's sniper brigades may be conducted during peace and wartime and include, but are not limited to, the following missions:

- Strategic reconnaissance and the provision of timely and accurate intelligence to the General Staff Department and corps commanders.
- Seizure or destruction of strategic/theater and global C³I, missile, radar, and NBC warfare assets.
- Assassination or abduction of ROK political leaders and senior ROK/U.S. military commanders.
- Special operations, including assassination, kidnaping, and diversionary operations.[56]
- Targeting reconnaissance for DPRK weapons of mass destruction (ballistic missiles, chemical weapons, etc.).
- Covert delivery of biological weapons.
- Establishment of military and political intelligence nets within the ROK and fostering the growth of guerrilla forces.
- Assisting other special purpose units with the interdiction, seizure,

or control of strategic targets (air bases; POL facilities; lines of communications; etc.).

- Assisting other special purpose units with the seizure of critically
  important topographic features (mountain passes, tunnels, bridges,
  etc.) and civilian facilities (railroads, highways, power plants, etc.).
- Providing military training to foreign governments, revolutionary
  organizations, and terrorist groups.
- Foreign internal security and defense operations.

The five reconnaissance battalions are believed to have DMZ infiltration as their primary mission, functioning much like the Operations
Department's DMZ escort units.

- COMMAND AND CONTROL
  The chain of command for the sniper brigades extends from the MPAF
  through the General Staff Department's Reconnaissance Bureau, to the
  individual sniper brigades. Because of the sensitive nature of sniper
  brigade operations, there exists a direct relationship between these units
  and the Operations Department. The Light Infantry Training Guidance
  Bureau provides coordination with other special purpose units and
  administrative and technical support.
      Subordinate to the Reconnaissance Bureau are three sniper brigades
  and five reconnaissance battalions. These sniper brigades are presently
  believed to be deployed within the I, II and V Forward Corps. The deployment of the reconnaissance battalions is unknown, but believed to be
  within the Forward Corps (table 6-14).

- ORGANIZATION AND EQUIPMENT
  The organization of the sniper brigade is unclear.[57] At present, it appears
  to have a personnel strength of 3,300–4,600, depending on the number
  of subordinate sniper battalions. It is organized into a headquarters and
  rear services element, a signal company, and seven to ten sniper battalions. Each battalion has a personnel strength of approximately 450 and
  is organized into a headquarters and rear services element, a signal platoon, and five companies of three platoons each. Each platoon has six
  teams of three to four troops each. Unlike other special purpose brigades
  where the battalion is typically the basic element for combat operations,
  the reconnaissance team is the basic operational unit within the sniper
  brigades. Each sniper brigade is theoretically capable of deploying approximately six hundred four-man reconnaissance teams.
      It is believed that each brigade has an organic all-female platoon-sized
  unit (popularly called the "Mata Hari" platoon). These women are trained

Table 6-14

Deployment of Reconnaissance Bureau Sniper Brigades

Designation	Location
17th Sniper Brigade	Sinwon
60th Sniper Brigade	IV Forward Corps?
61st Sniper Brigade	I Forward Corps?
U/I Reconnaissance Battalion	IV Forward Corps?
U/I Reconnaissance Battalion	II Forward Corps?
U/I Reconnaissance Battalion	II Forward Corps?
U/I Reconnaissance Battalion	V Forward Corps?
U/I Reconnaissance Battalion	I Forward Corps?

to the same exacting standards as regular sniper troops and are expected to conduct combat missions. In addition to this unit each brigade is believed to have specific elements specially trained and organized for "direct action" and diversionary operations. "Direct action" operations are primarily concerned with the assassination or abduction of enemy personnel and occur during both peace and wartime. Such operations will almost always be conducted with support from agents of the Social-Cultural Department or the State Security Department. Diversionary operations seek to seize strategic objectives before they can be destroyed, to destroy strategic objectives that cannot be destroyed by conventional means, and to create confusion and panic in rear areas. These operations will be carried out while sniper brigade personnel are disguised partially or completely in ROKA uniforms and civilian clothing. Diversionary units are trained in the use of, and are supplied with, ROK/U.S. uniforms and equipment. This equipment is believed to include M-16 assault rifles, M-60 light machine guns, and a small numbers of M-113 armored personnel carriers painted like ROKA vehicles.[58] Although not equipped with M-48 tanks, elements of the diversionary troops are believed to be qualified in their operation. A few personnel in each brigade are believed to be qualified in HALO (high-altitude, low-opening), HAHO (high-altitude, high-opening), and combat swimmer operations.

The organization of the five reconnaissance battalions subordinate to the Reconnaissance Bureau is presently unknown, but is believed to be similar to that of the battalions subordinate to the sniper brigade. The five reconnaissance battalions of the Reconnaissance Bureau probably have a larger headquarters and rear services element.

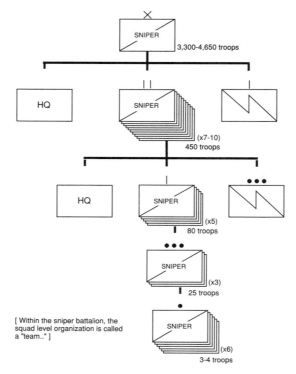

Reconnaissance Bureau, sniper brigade, 1996. The sniper brigade also has an organic all-female, platoon-sized unit, and specific elements of the brigade are believed to have specialized training in diversionary and assassination operations.

The weapons and equipment within the sniper brigades and reconnaissance battalions are probably the same as those for the standard light infantry brigade, although it is unlikely that any weapons heavier than the 60-millimeter mortar or ATGMs will be carried. Furthermore, communications equipment will be more sophisticated (i.e., long-range encrypted burst-transmission radios). All reconnaissance personnel will make use of ROKA uniforms, civilian clothing, civilian transportation, and other captured equipment.

OPERATIONS

During operations within the Korean Peninsula the sniper brigades are responsible for intelligence gathering for both the General Staff Department and the corps commanders, supporting other special purpose operations, and conducting special operations.

Reconnaissance operations will consists of a sniper team conducting independent long-range patrols. These teams will typically be inserted utilizing Reconnaissance Bureau assets (e.g., Maritime Bureau) or with the assistance of the KPN or KPAF. Aside from traditional reconnaissance duties, these reconnaissance teams will also provide support for other special purpose operations by conducting pre-mission reconnaissance, raids, ambushes, and so forth.

Special operations will primarily consist of "direct action" and diversionary operations. "Direct action" teams will attempt to "decapitate" the ROK political and the ROK/U.S. military command and control systems by the assassination or abduction of senior leaders. Meanwhile, diversionary troops, posing as ROKA troops, will conduct a variety of operations to assist other special purpose operations and to spread confusion and fear throughout the rear areas. Such diversionary operations will include, but are not limited to, the following:

- Posing as military police and routing traffic along the wrong roads and into waiting ambushes.
- Posing as reinforcements to spearhead special operations against air bases, strategic/theater C³I, and NBC warfare assets. Special attention will be paid to tactical air control centers at Osan and Taegu Air Bases, and to the former nuclear weapons storage facility at Kunsan Air Base.
- Capture of militarily strategic objectives, such as bridges, tunnels, dams, and hydroelectric plants, before they can be destroyed by ROK/U.S. forces.

Because of their unique skills and capabilities, it is conceivable that elements of the sniper brigades will also be employed in the strategic counterguerrilla role (i.e., the protection of strategically important facilities from ROK/U.S. special operations).

GLOBAL OPERATIONS
Reconnaissance Bureau sniper brigade personnel comprise the primary element for global special operations. During peacetime these operations have been concerned with direct action and foreign military assistance. During wartime, the sniper brigade's responsibilities will be expanded to include special operations against U.S. theater/global facilities such as U.S. bases in Japan, Okinawa, Subic Bay, and Pearl Harbor. The DPRK would also be expected to attempt to conduct special operations within the continental United States during wartime.

The two most widely known sniper brigade operations conducted outside the Korean Peninsula were both direct action missions. These were the 9 October 1983 Rangoon assassination attempt on ROK President Chon Tu-hwan (see chapter 4) and the 1978 kidnapping of two ROK film personalities.

The 1978 kidnapings of the film personalities—Sin Sang-ok and his wife, Choi Un Hui—were believed to have been conducted by reconnaissance personnel, by the direct request of Kim Chong-il. The two victims were abducted in separate operations. The actual kidnaping operations themselves were not unusual, yet they do present several interesting aspects of an apparently developing pattern of reconnaissance operations. For both operations the kidnaping teams were small, consisting of three to five persons, with at least one member or accomplice a female. The operatives wore civilian clothing and spoke at least Korean and Chinese and possibly Japanese. Both kidnapings consisted of an abduction in a foreign country and a subsequent transfer to a DPRK cargo ship for the voyage to the DPRK.[59]

The 29 November 1987 bombing of a Korean Airlines flight 858 from Abu Dhabi to Seoul, although conducted by personnel of the Research Department for External Intelligence, also fits the developing pattern of KPA direct action operations. For example, it consisted of a small team (at least two known persons); one member was a female; both team members wore civilian clothing; both members could speak Korean, Chinese, and Japanese; and both members attempted suicide when their capture and exposure was imminent.[60]

DPRK foreign military assistance is influenced by the belief that "the Communist countries can obstruct belligerency of the 'imperialists' only when they can fan the revolutionary flame for anti-imperialistic and anti-American struggle of all the people of the world."[61] This belief is manifested through an extensive foreign military assistance policy. This policy includes the provision of military training to foreign governments, revolutionary organizations and terrorist groups, foreign internal security and defense operations, and arms transfers.[62]

Sniper brigade and other Reconnaissance Bureau personnel are believed to constitute most DPRK military advisory teams throughout the world. Since the late 1960s, when KPA anti-ROK special operations peaked, the DPRK has frequently attempted to destabilize foreign unfriendly governments and support friendly governments and organizations. During the late 1980s and throughout the 1990s there has been a steady decline in DPRK material support for international terrorist and revolutionary groups. This has primarily been a result of the DPRK's decaying political and economic strength. In turn, this has resulted in a decline in Reconnaissance Bureau personnel involvement in such activities. These efforts are continuing, albeit at a much reduced level (see chapter 4).[63]

Chapter 7

PERSONNEL AND TRAINING

PERSONNEL

Under guidelines established by the Military Mobilization Bureau of the Ministry of People's Armed Forces (MPAF) and the Personnel Affairs Bureau of the General Staff Department, the Military Mobilization Department of each province, municipality, and county drafts youths into the service twice a year, in March and September.[1] The average recruit is seventeen to twenty-five years old and has completed high school.[2] Exempted from the service are some college students, essential personnel in industry, artists, athletes, and those rejected after a physical examination. Also excluded are convicted criminals, family members of defectors, who are not permitted to "cross the gate of the 'sacred' Army." The new recruit is probably from an urban background, educated, indoctrinated, and motivated by the strict and regimented society of his country. His view of the world has been controlled since birth by the state-controlled information and educational systems. With an average height of only 5 feet, 6 inches, the KPA soldier is generally wiry and well muscled and kept in top physical condition by constant, strenuous physical training.[3] Because of his mental and physical conditioning, the KPA soldier is noted for his stamina and capabilities in all types of terrain and weather. His strength, daring, and endurance are proverbial among those who have faced him in combat. The KPA soldier is taught to be a revolutionary combatant. Strong in DPRK ideology and spiritual combat strength, the KPA soldier is determined not to betray the Korean Workers' Party (KWP) and not to surrender to enemy forces under any conditions.

The special forces soldier excels in all the above attributes and is considered among the elite of the KPA. Only the best are accepted for membership in the special forces. Most members of this force are carefully selected from politically reliable soldiers who are members in good standing of the KWP and who have served four to seven years within the combat branches.[4] Under rare circumstances (such as the recruit's having special language capabilities or other unique skills), members can be recruited directly from civilian status.

Legally mandated service periods for enlisted draftees is forty-two months for the KPA and forty-eight months for the KPAF or KPN. These legal periods of service frequently mean little, however. Draftees who serve in the infantry or artillery are discharged at age twenty-six, irrespective of what age they entered the service. Draftees who serve in special forces units are not discharged until age thirty.[5] All soldiers may be kept on active duty regardless of age if they are deemed necessary to unit performance or security.

Since further detailed information concerning present-day special forces personnel practices is currently unavailable, the following two sections are provided to give the reader insight into the historical development of these practices within the special forces.

■ RECONNAISSANCE BUREAU AND SICARO PERSONNEL, 1971
Personnel assigned to unconventional warfare units of the Ministry of National Defense were politically reliable and in excellent physical condition; most of them were experienced noncommissioned officers (NCOs).[6] They were twenty-three to twenty-seven years old and usually graduates of junior and technical schools. Although they were not exceptionally intelligent, the troops were quite capable of absorbing the training material and following orders. Reconnaissance operatives were often chosen from men whose fathers were killed by United Nations Command forces during the Fatherland Liberation War.

Operatives employed by the secretary in charge of anti-ROK operations (SICARO) represented a much broader cross section of DPRK society. Young and old men and even young and old women were recruited, trained, and dispatched to the ROK and overseas. KWP membership and prior military service were desirable but not mandatory. A preference was shown for personnel who formerly lived in the ROK, because their manners and speech were less likely to betray them. Residents of Kaesong were also considered good risks, because their dialect and customs were like those of the northwest province of the ROK, which includes Seoul. According to captured operatives, greater emphasis was placed on the use of women operatives, since women were known to draw less suspicion and were usually more successful. They were used primarily as couriers rather than as underground cell organizers.

■ ■ *Personnel Sources*
Regular KPA units supplied most if not all personnel for Ministry of

National Defense unconventional warfare organizations. NCOs and enlisted men from infantry companies and DMZ police companies were reassigned to foot reconnaissance stations, bases of the 124th Army Unit, and the 17th Reconnaissance Brigade. Operatives for the KWP Central Committee were drawn from farms and factories throughout the DPRK; some were recruited from prisons. Few of those summoned and interviewed by KWP officials refused to become operatives.

Pay and Benefits

Although exact details are not available, it is known that operatives drew special pay, food, and clothing. Apparently while training, operatives of the Reconnaissance Bureau were given the highest-quality rations and uniforms of the same quality as those issued to field-grade officers, but they were paid the same amount as in their previous assignments. Some operatives, however, who had undergone bivouac training had their pay increased eightfold (to 15 won per month for a senior private). Once an operative successfully infiltrated the ROK, he became a team leader and was paid approximately 70 won per month. One captured foot reconnaissance station member explained that his pay was based upon the number of times he had conducted reconnaissance in the DMZ: 20 won per month after the completion of his first mission, and up to 50 won after the completion of seven missions. Foot reconnaissance station personnel who infiltrated through the DMZ into the ROK drew 100 won per month after their first mission and 120 won after their second and subsequent missions. This is roughly equivalent to the pay of a colonel.

Weapons and Equipment

Operatives dispatched to the ROK were well armed, especially those infiltrating through the DMZ. The weapons most frequently carried were the 7.62-millimeter Sudayev sub-machine-gun M-1943 (PPS), 7.62 Tokarev pistol M-1933 (TT), and a dagger 20–25 centimeters long. Espionage operatives were occasionally armed with U.S. M-1 rifles or M-2 carbines. Members of the 124th Army Unit and foot reconnaissance stations also carried antitank and antipersonnel hand grenades and, when necessary for the mission, antipersonnel mines, antitank launchers, explosive charges, and light machine guns. Sub-machine-guns were replaced by AK-47 assault rifles with folding stocks.

Operational equipment can be categorized as general or specialized. General equipment commonly carried by operatives included a canvas knapsack, a wristwatch, a wrist compass, a commercial radio receiver, a radio transmitter, a radio schedule, a code table, random number charts, maps, binoculars, rope, and a counterfeit ROK registration card and employment certificate. Specialized equipment included flotation bags; an Asahi Pentex camera (with 300- to 500-millimeter lens); a rubber raft; a shovel, pick, and saw; wire cutters; a telescope (20X or 40X); a camouflage net; propaganda leaflets; ROK currency (200,000–500,000 won); and a rubberized, waterproof bag.

Operatives most frequently wore imitation ROKA fatigue uniforms made in the DPRK of material obtained from Japan. They also carried civilian clothes. The style of the civilian clothes and some details of the uniforms occasionally exposed the operatives. Many items of equipment were obtained from Japan and the Soviet Union, and many were produced in the DPRK. The uniforms included imitation fatigue caps, fatigue jackets with ROK insignia and fake name tags, fatigue trousers and web belts, canvas shoes with black rubber soles, and gloves and underwear similar to those worn by ROK soldiers. Items of civilian clothing often carried by the operatives and donned after successful infiltration included dark gray cotton trousers and sport shirts; dark gray waterproof nylon jacket and trousers; vinyl, rubberized cloth, or nylon raincoats; and swimming trunks.

Food supplies carried by the operatives were usually sufficient for only a few days. The amount of food carried by operatives depended on the expected duration of their mission, but the following types and amounts were common: dehydrated rice (2 kilograms), powdered rice (2 kilograms), hot peppered paste (400 grams), rice candy (500 grams), chocolate bars (20 each), cakes (3 each), chewing gum (a few packs), sugar (600 grams), and dehydrated cuttlefish (1 kilogram).

Operatives usually carried other miscellaneous supplies. Toilet articles included soap, toothbrush, toothpaste, comb, pomade, razor, towel, and hair cutters. Medicines commonly carried were iodine, methiolate, bandages, penicillin, tetramycin, digestive tables, seasickness pills, vitamin pills, headache pills, and a tourniquet. Remaining items typically carried were a wallet, a pocket knife with spoon, cooking utensils, solid fuel, a water bag, books, cigarettes, a flashlight, and a tent.

▪ ▪ *Resupply Procedures*
Supplies were limited to what could be carried by team members and included as much as a twenty-day supply of rice. When the supplies had been consumed, the operatives were to live off of the land (which was very difficult in the ROK), return to the DPRK, or buy or steal food and other needed supplies. Many aggressive operatives who had planned to stay in the ROK for a long period were apprehended as a result of contacts made with the population to gain food. There was no evidence of plans to resupply from the DPRK, nor were any large caches ever found. Operatives

were taught how to conceal supplies for retrieval and use in a later stage of their operation. Some were instructed in the selection of cache sites where ROK dissident elements could pick up arms and supplies for antigovernment activities. Captured operatives were found with enough weapons, first aid equipment, and other necessities to suggest that they did not depend on resupply from other sources. The amounts, however, were not enough to serve for subsequent operations or long-range caching.

- SICARO PERSONNEL, 1977
Operatives employed by the Liaison Department during this period represented a broad cross section of DPRK society.[7] Men and women of all ages and from diverse occupational backgrounds were recruited. Former residence in the ROK was preferred but not required. Operatives recruited in Japan included ROK citizens visiting, studying, or working in Japan; ROK seamen who frequented Japanese ports; Korean youths born or raised in Japan who were eligible to pursue their education at an ROK university; and leftist-inclined Japanese who traveled to the ROK frequently. These operatives were given the task of establishing espionage nets in Japan and the ROK. As part of this process, the operatives were provided with the necessary funds for establishing a business or other cover. It is not known how much they were paid or what provisions were made for their family members.

TRAINING

The KPA's training system is designed to produce tough, disciplined, and politically well indoctrinated soldiers, who, by dint of their superior ideological training, physical conditioning, and superior skills in guerrilla warfare, can defeat a numerically and technologically superior enemy.[8] Political and ideological training are stressed, as is the general education of the soldier. Soldiers study the Fatherland Liberation War and the Anti-Japanese Partisan Struggle (the term used by the DPRK for Kim Il-song's activities during World War II) to learn from those experiences. Mountain and night skills are taught, and the soldiers are trained in both conventional and unconventional warfare. During training, the soldier learns to overcome all adverse conditions. Particularly emphasized is proficiency in conducting combined operations.

Special forces training builds upon this basic instruction given to all soldiers. It is designed to produce a fanatical fighter even more disciplined and politically well indoctrinated and capable of accomplishing the most demanding conventional or unconventional missions. The training that the members of the special forces receive, such as infiltration, mountaineering, night combat, swimming, martial arts, airborne skills, intelligence methods, demolition, and rigorous physical fitness, are typical of elite units throughout the world. Discipline is considerably harsher for the KPA's special purpose forces than for other such forces around the world, however, and a much stronger emphasis is placed on intensive physical training and political and ideological indoctrination.

The net results of the KPA's training system are tough, intensively trained fighters who can travel farther and faster with more equipment and less food than almost any other soldiers in the world. They are mentally and physically hardened and disciplined, ready to obey orders and to suffer privations that could cause mutinies in other armies.

- RECRUIT TRAINING

Before and during the Fatherland Liberation War, most basic training was conducted at recruit training centers, with advanced training being conducted at the recruit's assigned unit. By the end of the war, this had changed. Most recruits received only the most basic military instruction at the training centers. The remainder of the recruits' training was conducted within a training company in their assigned unit. After the war, the training centers were abolished, and recruit training was conducted completely within the unit. Today, before entering the army, typical recruits receive basic military instruction in school, in their place of employment, or in the militia. Once inducted, new draftees are assigned to their respective divisions, where they undergo a three-month basic training course within a regiment-level provisional training battalion or company.[9]

The mission of the recruit training unit is to provide instruction in basic military subjects. The recruit training unit normally receives recruits one to three times a year, between March and October. Typical recruit training lasts one month and consists of approximately 180 hours of instruction. The normal size of the class is the platoon, with most subjects being taught by company, platoon, and squad leaders. Subjects taught include political doctrine, physical training, map reading, military order and discipline, military drill and ceremonies, first aid and hygiene, NBC warfare, engineering, weapons training, and tactics.

When recruits complete their training, they take the Soldier's Oath, receive their soldier's identification card, and are assigned to an operational unit having a predetermined need for replacements or reinforcements. The individual serves in the military from the date of taking the oath until he or she is twenty-seven years old. Enlisted personnel are assigned to specific branches of service based upon their talents and educational background. Graduates from technical high schools are typically assigned to the artillery, chemical, or signal corps. Those with relevant civilian experience are assigned to be drivers and repair technicians for vehicles and weapons. Individuals without any specific qualifications are assigned to the infantry or engineers. Recruits with demonstrated exceptional political ability and a good family background are assigned military police duties, such as being part of the DMZ police force.[10]

Private is the first rank a recruit receives after taking the Soldier's Oath. He can become a corporal after completion of a rigorous training schedule and sergeant after completing six months of training in an enlisted men's training unit. From here he can advance from staff sergeant to sergeant first class, to master sergeant before ending his service at the rank of sergeant major. The vast majority of KPA officers except those in special services are selected from among common soldiers. For youths who come from the lower classes like the peasant class, the military life is thus considered a springboard for advancement in life. A few third- or fourth-year-service soldiers who show exceptional talent and political reliability may apply to the Kangdong Military Academy or Kim Il-song Political College to become commissioned officers or political officers.

■ UNIT TRAINING

Since 1959 the KPA has based its combat training program on a yearly cycle.[11] Exceptions include units attached to the technical branches and Light Infantry Training Guidance Bureau, which may require more complex training lasting up to two or three years. The annual training program is formulated by the General Staff Department of the MPAF and the commanders of the various arms and services. Overall guidance is provided by the National Defense Commission. Training programs are published in book form each December. This document not only includes the annual training plan but also includes a summation and critique of the previous year's program. KPA corps and division commanders are free to add such training phases as they consider necessary, but always within the limitations of the original plan. Units at each echelon conduct training ranging from the basic training of troops to field exercises in order to satisfy the requirements set forth in the plan. It is important to note that political indoctrination, to prevent deviation from the KPA's political goals, takes precedence over all other training. The indoctrination is conducted at all echelons down to company level and includes self-study for general officers.

The annual training program begins in December and lasts until October of the following year. It is divided into two cycles, with each training cycle in turn being divided into two or three phases. The first cycle, during the winter, lasts from 1 December until 30 April (five months). The second cycle is during the summer and lasts from 1 June until 31 October (also five months). The training cycle from December to April is divided into two phases: the first phase lasts three months, and the second phase two months. The training cycle from June to October is divided into three phases: the first phase lasts forty days, the second phase about seventy days, and the third phase another forty days.

The training phases for the DMZ police and Light Infantry Training Guidance Bureau are somewhat different. DMZ police units spend two months on sentry duty and two months conducting training (two platoons per company are rotated). This is repeated three times a year.

Each cycle consists of approximately 760 hours of training, which progresses from individual unit exercises to joint service maneuvers. The schedule of activities during a typical annual training is as follows:

- December: Construction of fortifications and preparation for winter training.
- January: Individual and squad training.
- February: Squad and platoon training.
- March: Platoon and company training.
- April: Company field training exercise and recruit training.
- May: Pause in training for agricultural activities and preparation for summer training.
- June: Battalion training.
- July: Battalion field training exercise and recruit training.
- August: Regiment training.
- September: Regimental field training exercise and harvesting crops.
- October: Brigade/division/corps combined or joint maneuvers; recruit training and preparation for winter.
- November: Construction of fortifications and repair of barracks.

- INFANTRY UNIT TRAINING
Infantry unit training emphasizes political education and unit cohesiveness and attempts to motivate the soldier to operate under the most severe conditions. Training subjects and hours are not fixed but are based on the General Staff Department's annual training program and the mission of the unit. The training expands upon the subjects taught during recruit training, including military topography, defense against motorized and mechanized units, communications, enemy doctrine, and bivouacking. Great importance is placed on tactics and live-firing training. Political training is conducted in accordance with the annual political training program established by the General Political Bureau.

- RECONNAISSANCE BUREAU AND SICARO TRAINING, 1966–77
Until late 1966, DPRK operations were mainly oriented toward the

collection of military intelligence, recruitment of operatives, and organization of underground KWP cells.[12] Agents were trained individually or in small groups at safe houses. With the decision to initiate a "revolution in south Korea" during the late 1960s, training took on a paramilitary character. This was emphasized by the reorganization and expansion of the 124th Army Unit and the foot reconnaissance stations. Espionage and subversive operations continued through 1967, 1968, and into 1969 and were again the dominant forms of anti-ROK operations. Training included preparation of individuals and small teams in safe houses, operation of KWP schools of subversion, and the continual training of KPA units (such as the 17th Reconnaissance Brigade and the then-new light infantry units) in the tactics of unconventional warfare.

■ *SICARO*

A system of training centers and safe houses known as the Central Committee Political School (or the 695th Army Unit) provided preliminary training to many prospective operatives. The unit headquarters and most branch centers and safe houses of the 695th Army Unit were located near P'yongyang. More detailed general training and specific mission training were given at the safe houses of the Liaison Department. Most school trainees were reportedly former ROK residents. The main training school could purportedly handle about three hundred operative trainees at one time; courses ranged from six months to four years in duration. The curriculum included extensive training in political theory and dogma as well as in subversion and espionage. During the late 1960s, the school began teaching guerrilla warfare and tactics. Students received detailed classroom instruction and practical field application in the methods of tactical movement, land navigation, selection and establishment of bivouacs, security measures, ambush, assault, and demolition.

Beginning in 1970, advanced specialized training for graduates of the 695th Army Unit and other selected individuals was provided by the 940th Army Unit. Conducting six-month- to two-year-long courses, the 940th Army Unit operated several safe houses at various locations throughout the DPRK, mostly in the P'yongyang area. Training conducted by the unit included briefing and preparation of operatives and teams for dispatch on specific missions. During this detailed training, teams lived alone except for a housekeeper and were permitted to leave the house only once a week for bathing and other personal needs. They were visited by instructors and other officials who inspected their progress.

In some cases, eight to sixteen safe house were located in close proximity and constituted a branch school. Safe houses, however, were usually isolated so that operatives would only know the members, operations, and training of their own team and could not jeopardize other missions if captured. Compartmentalization was carried to extremes. When several teams had to be trained in the same lecture room, it was divided into cubicles from which each could see and hear the speaker, but could not observe the other teams. Periods of instruction could last for as little as five days for ROK citizens who had been recruited and brought to P'yongyang for a brief orientation and mission training. On the other hand, many other operatives underwent several months of vigorous studies and exercises.

Political indoctrination consisted of lectures expounding the philosophy of Marx and Engels and the history of social development, politics, economics, historical materialism, dialectical materialism, and the history of the KWP. The memoirs of Kim Il-song on anti-Japanese guerrilla operations were covered extensively. Agent trade craft instruction included methods of establishing an underground party network; map reading; land navigation and infiltration; night marching; swimming; hand-to-hand combat; marksmanship with Soviet and U.S. weapons; and communication by telegraph, dead letter drops, secret writing, telegraph, radio, messages in newspapers, and broadcasts over Radio Pyongyang.

Operatives were also taught a vocation so they could secure a job after infiltrating and thus establish a cover. Training in welding, sheet metal work, sewing machine operation, and fruit and vegetable vending reportedly was provided. Occupational backgrounds already possessed by the operatives (e.g., fishing, farming, and pickpocketing) were put to use.

Members of the sea escort units were thoroughly trained to operate their boats, to land, to escort operatives to specific locations, and to defend themselves. Personnel received instruction in navigation and boat handling, operation and maintenance of engines, operation of communication gear, and map reading. In addition to weapons familiarization and firing (heavy machine gun, anti-aircraft heavy machine gun, light machine gun, assault rifle, pistol, and antitank launcher), personnel practiced hand-to-hand combat, escort tactics, swimming, and forced marching and received political indoctrination. The units underwent considerable training at sea and were subjected to periodic training alerts.

The degree of indoctrination and training of operatives recruited in Japan largely depended upon the individual's capabilities, status, and circumstances in Japan. Those selected for higher-level operations were usually escorted to the DPRK. One double agent, in the DPRK for approximately ten weeks during the summer of 1969, cited some of the instruction he received: history and philosophy, 19 days; revolutionary training, 4 days; cryptography, 2 days; microphotography, 1 day; underground party organization, 2 days; political science and economics, 4 days; ROK political situation, 2 days; and military training, 4 days.

Similar experiences were reported by other operatives trained in the DPRK. Training in Japan was reportedly conducted at individual homes, safe houses, and Chosen Soren schools.

■ ■ *Reconnaissance Bureau and Light Infantry*

Reconnaissance Bureau units were trained for reconnaissance and commando/guerrilla operations. Training given the specialized units could also be applied to conventional KPA units. The training of foot reconnaissance stations and the 124th Army Unit was similar. Little information is available on training within the 17th Reconnaissance Brigade or the light infantry units.

The normal training cycle for foot reconnaissance stations operatives lasted one year and covered political theory, tactics, topography, map reading, land navigation, radio communications, photographic reconnaissance techniques, order of battle of ROK/U.S. divisions, weapons characteristics and firing, demolitions, mountain climbing, physical training, judo, boxing, and karate. During the training cycle, operatives conducted active route reconnaissance in the DMZ. This practice provided a live training environment, and information on infiltration routes and DMZ defenses was collected at the same time. Agents were also exposed to rigorous cold-weather training aimed at enhancing their capability for year-round operations.

In March 1968, the Reconnaissance Bureau directed that 40 percent of training time be devoted to guerrilla tactics to include squad- and platoon-level assault and ambush training, methods of selecting and maintaining platoon-sized operational bases in the ROK interior from which to attack major military targets in division and corps rear areas, and attack training against ROK county seats and governmental facilities. The new training cycle culminated in long-range field training exercises of ten to fifteen days' duration. These exercises included moving to the target area, selecting a bivouac site, reconnaissance, mounting an attack, withstanding a counterattack, and exfiltration. Captured operatives from foot reconnaissance stations have stated that several platoon leaders were given a special course to enable them to train their personnel to conduct platoon-sized attacks.

Typical of the training received in the 124th Army Unit were company-sized ambushes of a battalion convoy and attacks against government facilities. After extensive classroom instruction, training units were moved to the field for practical application of techniques. One field exercise involved a two-company attack against the simulated division command post of the ROKA 50th Reserve Infantry Division; another called for a company-sized attack against an air base. The air base was simulated with mockups of barracks, aircraft, trucks, and defensive installations. The members employed RPG-2 antitank launchers and used gasoline to set fire to the mock structures. Another exercise called for a two-company attack against a simulated missile site. The site had six missile mock-ups, a motor pool with thirty mock trucks, two sentry posts, and a battalion-sized barracks area complete with a barbed wire perimeter fence. The exercise took two days to complete. To add an ingredient of realism, the 124th launched an unannounced two-company attack against an actual DPRK county seat. Assaults were made against the courthouse, post office, a school, and the village bank. A captured operative who partici-pated in this attack described the villagers as being terrified. The 124th conducted ten- to fifteen-day field training exercises in which companies were given sequential problems that required them to reconnoiter the objective, plan the operation, issue operation orders, conduct the attack, regroup, and prepare to receive the next problem. Other 124th training included reconnaissance, use of fishing boats for exfiltration techniques, terrorist techniques, attacks against check points, cold-weather tactics, and the use of TNT to destroy bridges and tunnels.

Personnel of the 17th Reconnaissance Brigade received intensive training in basic infantry and guerrilla tactics, basic engineer and demo-lition techniques, radio communications, marksmanship, reconnaissance, map reading, mine and chemical warfare, boxing, karate, knife throw-ing, mountain climbing, survival methods, and parachute training. Dur-ing the late 1960s, the brigade's reconnaissance battalions underwent a forty-day training cycle that covered basic parachute ground training, tower training, and one airborne jump. The annual training program included a combined field exercise in which members of the 5th Recon-naissance Battalion and other units of the brigade made paratroop drops as aggressor guerrillas.

KPA light infantry units, predominantly regiments, received uncon-ventional warfare training, which was conducted primarily in moun-tainous areas. Emphasis was placed upon long, forced marches, often over mountains and frequently at night. Special training also covered repelling, river crossing, and survival in uninhabited areas under adverse weather conditions, with only meager rations of rice supplied. The mem-bers of the light infantry units were taught how to establish bivouacs and operational bases in hostile territory. Practical exercises were conducted on ambushes and assaults against military and police buildings, ware-houses, convoys, and division and higher-echelon headquarters. This training was apparently quite similar to that of the 124th and foot recon-naissance stations.

■ SPECIAL FORCES TRAINING, PRESENT
Throughout its history, the KPA has valued the individual strength and

endurance of its special forces:[13] "To the [KPA], a squad of men who can march 50 kilometers with a 40 kilogram pack in 24 hours over mountainous terrain is worth more than a battalion of road bound mechanized infantry."[14] Special forces personnel are considered to be among the best-trained soldiers in the KPA. In order to be accepted into the Light Infantry Training Guidance Bureau, a soldier must typically have several qualifications. The soldier must have proven politically reliability and zeal and have served for four to seven years in a combat branch. He must be a qualified enlisted or senior private and have graduated from junior high school or beyond. The soldier needs personal recommendations by his commanding and political officers for excellent duty performance. Last, the candidate must be in excellent physical condition.

Once soldiers are accepted into the Light Infantry Training Guidance Bureau, they are transferred to the training unit, which exercises overall control and responsibility for all training. Here they are further screened for acceptability as members and receive basic special forces training much like their recruit training. The basic special forces training can last twelve to twenty-four weeks or longer, depending upon the skill levels of the trainees and the type of unit to which they will be assigned. This training is designed not only to provide specific skills instruction, but to familiarize the trainee with basic special forces tactics and operations. Additionally, the average length of service for Light Infantry Training Guidance Bureau personnel appears to be eleven to twelve years, as compared with eight to ten years for other military personnel. The bureau is assisted in its training mission by all branches of the KPA (i.e., the KPAF assists with airborne and air mobile training, the KPN with amphibious training, and the Reconnaissance Bureau with intelligence training).

▪ ▪ *Training*
Special forces units receive the same training as do infantry units, but unlike infantry units they receive additional instruction in special combat skills and intelligence operations. Although this special training is typical of elite units throughout the world, discipline within the KPA special forces remains considerably harsher, and strong emphasis continues to be placed upon intensive political and ideological indoctrination. This indoctrination includes instruction in the "educational principles" according to Kim Il-song's teachings for sniper personnel. These principles include maintaining physical strength to overcome adverse conditions, conviction in accomplishing a mission, guerrilla warfare, and lessons learned from the Anti-Japanese Partisan Struggle. Additionally, the study of ROK dialects, customs, politics, economics, and geography is stressed.

Key educational subjects taught to special forces units include the following:

- Political studies: works and virtues of Kim Il-song, KWP ideology and policies, revolutionary traditions, Anti-Japanese Partisan Struggle, inconsistency in capitalistic society, winning spirit, *juche* (the DPRK's version of Marxism-Leninism, stressing self-reliance), proselytizing of the enemy populace and the enemy military personnel.
- Topography: advanced orienteering, map making, geography of the ROK.
- First aid and hygiene: personnel hygiene, seasonal hygiene, advanced first aid.
- Weapons training: infantry weapons, mortars, antitank weapons, antipersonnel/tank mines, recognition of armored fighting vehicles and artillery weapons, enemy weapons.
- Physical training: courage and confidence training, long-distance marching in all terrains,[15] swimming and boating, rock climbing, vehicle qualifications, airborne and air-mobile training, amphibious training, NBC training, ROK dialects and customs.
- Regulations: standard operating procedures (SOPs), garrison SOPs, regulations governing discipline.
- Drill and ceremony: saluting and military courtesy, hand-to-hand combat (including knife fighting), boxing and martial arts, rushing and crawling, combat formations.
- Engineering: demolition, types and capabilities of mines, laying/removing mines (positioning, arming/disarming, etc.), overcoming obstacles (concertina wire, fences, etc.), live fire.
- Intelligence: reconnaissance, intelligence-gathering methods (including SIGINT, etc.), cryptography and photography, use of sophisticated communication equipment.
- Tactics: employment of various types of weapons; weapons capabilities; assembling and disassembling weapons; infiltration and exfiltration; escape and evasion; enemy organization, doctrine, and tactics; live fire; bivouac; covert movement and hideouts; ambush and surprise attack.

Individual training is reportedly grueling, especially within the Reconnaissance Bureau. Although details are lacking, bureau training includes numerous physical highlights. The troops must accomplish the following tasks during training:[16]

- Engage in three hours of hand-to-hand combat daily, except national holidays.

- Throw a dagger so that it can hit a target 8 meters away with 90 percent accuracy.
- Conduct forced marches of 40 kilometers per night and 120 kilometers per day, while carrying a 25-kilogram load.
- Accurately shoot at ground targets 200 meters away, while parachuting from an altitude of 400 meters.
- Use improvised weapons accurately (e.g., hit a target 7–20 meters with a sickle, an ax, or an entrenching tool).
- Swim across the 400-meter-wide Tae-dong River in 30 minutes.
- Receive cold water training, which includes a series of 45- to 50-minute swims during winter.
- Take scuba and diving instruction.

■ ■ *Unit Training*

Unit training for special forces units, from basic training to combined field exercises, is conducted in order to satisfy the requirements set forth in the General Staff Department's annual training plan. Because of the unique nature of special forces unit missions and the resulting demands for highly skilled and motivated troops, however, the yearly training cycle is significantly different from other KPA units. One complete training cycle may actually take one to three years. As with KPA corps and division commanders, the commander of the Light Infantry Training Guidance Bureau is free to add training phases that he considers necessary, within the limitations of the original plan. Unit training generally takes place in one of three areas: the unit's home base, provisional field training areas, or specialized training complexes.

Airborne and air-mobile training is conducted at two known locations, Taech'on and P'yongyang East Air Bases and airborne training facilities. These facilities consist of areas for administration and barracks, paratrooper training, and mockup field training.[17] The paratrooper training area consists of aircraft mockups, rope slides, a jump platform, a parachute tower, and other equipment typical of airborne facilities. Parachute training starts with static line jumps and proceeds up to medium-altitude free-fall jumps. Especially adept students may also receive high-altitude, high-opening and low-opening training. Jumps are made by day and night, over all types of terrain, and in a wider range of weather conditions than in the west. Some airborne troops also receive sailplane, ultralight, and hot-air balloon training.

During airborne recruit training, three drops are conducted, one day and night drop, and one day drop with full equipment (i.e., automatic rifle, entrenching tool, and backpack). Normally, each unit conducts a separate air drop exercise annually. Because of fuel shortages during the past ten years, airborne brigade troops have averaged only one live drop per year. Additional training drops are made from 80-meter towers and from cables strung across valleys. During the late 1980s and early 1990s, annual airborne training exercises utilizing An-2 Colts as drop aircraft were conducted from four air bases: Taech'on, Kangdong, Sunch'on, and Kwaksan. These drops were conducted in company- or battalion-sized units. Combined arms exercises with regular infantry or armored units are sometimes conducted once a year. During field exercises, only one operational map is issued per airborne squad. Airborne brigade personnel do not receive training in riot control or coup d'états, air-mobile skills, or amphibious warfare. They do, however, receive training for urban warfare. Air-mobile training appears to be reserved for airborne sniper brigade personnel. Airborne brigade troops utilize virtually the same radio communications procedures as do light infantry and Reconnaissance Bureau units. Up until 1993 there was no night vision equipment or laser rangefinders in the airborne brigades. Evidently, this equipment is in limited supply within the sniper and airborne sniper brigades. An elaborate training area utilized by the airborne brigades (and possibly other units) is located in the Sinyang area in northern P'yongan Province and is set up with obstacles like those in the DMZ. It has a mockup ROKA division command post, tank positions, artillery gun positions, and air base.[18]

Amphibious warfare training is believed to be conducted at the Tasa-ri (west coast) and Ijin-dong (east coast) naval bases, which purportedly consist of an administrative and barracks area, an amphibious warfare training area, and a general training area. Amphibious warfare training may also be conducted in the Sinp'o or Mayang-do areas on the east coast.

There are approximately 150 training facilities of various sizes for special forces scattered around the DPRK. Each army corps maintains one comprehensive training facility for special forces, which are used for demolition, river-crossing, and commando-type training. These facilities can consist of some, or all, of the following: an administrative and barracks area, a mockup training area, mockup aircraft targets, an air target range, a dummy runway, false building fronts, an obstacle course, a ridge obstacle course, an assault course, a grenade course, a mortar training range, and an infantry combat range. Located at P'yongsan and Gok-san in Hwanghae Province, and in Wonsang in P'yongan Province are elaborate training facilities modeled after the ROK cities and municipal facilities (e.g., the Blue House presidential residence and City Hall).[19]

Pieces of dummy equipment are generally used for training. They normally include replicas of tanks, field artillery, antiaircraft artillery, missiles, and airframes. Tank mockups are used as training devices for antitank training (i.e., with the RPG-7) and as tank crew engagement targets. Artillery and antiaircraft artillery mockups are used like tanks: troops practice demolitions or close-in approach and simulate destruction on the mockups. Missile mockups probably represent specific targets for destruction by direct ground assault. Helicopter and aircraft mockups are used for jump familiarization, identification training, and simulators for demolition. The air target (aircraft silhouettes) range is used as targets for tactical air bombing, helicopter assault, and reconnaissance. The dummy runway probably serves as a decoy to attacking air crews, a practice range for the KPAF, or a rehearsal area for demolition training. False building fronts are for urban warfare training. The ridge obstacle course consists of random, crude obstacles such as log piles, ditches, and walls placed along cleared paths on ridge lines. This course is similar to obstacle/confidence courses found in armies throughout the world. The assault course is used to engage in dry-fire battle drills. It consists of a starting line, obstacles, and bayonet dummies. The infantry combat ranges are small-arms ranges that are used to sharpen marksmanship skills of the troops.[20]

■ ■ *NCOs and Officers*

NCOs for the Light Infantry Training Guidance Bureau are obtained from one of three sources: the corps NCO school, the NCO school of the General Staff Department; and NCOs transferred to the bureau. The NCO schools provide six months of training intended to develop squad leaders. Admission criteria for the schools is the same as for acceptance into the bureau, but also includes demonstrated leadership ability, the potential for growth, membership in the KWP, and the personal recommendation by the KWP.

Officers are typically obtained from recent graduates of the various officer schools. The schools that are believed to provide the majority of special forces officers include Kanggye Military Academy (special training), Kumgang Political Institute (General Staff Department, Reconnaissance Bureau), and the Chunghwa Training School (psychological and guerrilla warfare).[21]

Officer schooling typically requires two to three years to complete, with additional development courses lasting six months to a year. Once a new officer or NCO is posted to the Light Infantry Training Guidance Bureau he is processed through the corps training unit, where he undergoes specialty training, in much the same manner as the ordinary recruit, before being assigned to an operational unit.

Available evidence suggests that once basic special forces training is completed, the trainee is awarded an NCO or junior lieutenant rank and is assigned to an operational unit for the remainder of his career. The

231

rank is probably awarded for pay grade privileges, for the prestige it bestows, and as an indication of professionalism.[22] Some sources indicate that a junior lieutenant rank is employed as a "cover rank" in operational missions. The three sniper personnel who conducted the 1983 assassination attempt on ROK President Chon Tu-hwan were all officers: Maj. Zin Mo, commander; Capt. Kim Chi-o, demolitions specialist; and Capt. Kang Min-chul, demolitions specialist.[23] A KPA defector, Lt. Yu Tae-yun, stated that all personnel positions within the light infantry battalions are filled with men of one rank grade higher than those authorized for comparable positions within ordinary infantry battalions.[24]

■ ■ *Mission Training*

Advanced and target- and mission-specific training is conducted within the operational units. During such training, units utilize a variety of realistic mockups. Frequently, "they construct their own special purpose, widely-scattered, non-permanent type mockups and facilities . . . when convenience and training requirements dictate."[25] This training is made even more realistic by including night airdrops or amphibious assault landings by and conducting "no-holds-barred" raids against other special forces units or militia units defending target mockups. Some training facilities contain full-scale mockups of ROK/U.S. weapon systems and facilities (i.e., aircraft, Lance and Hawk missiles, and communications facilities). To enhance their operational capabilities, some personnel, especially snipers, are believed to travel overseas disguised as tourists, students, diplomats, and economic and military advisers.

The abortive attempt to assassinate ROK president, Park Chung Hee, on 21 January 1968 provides insight into KPA mission training. In preparation for the raid on the ROK presidential residence, the Blue House, a thirty-one-man unit from the 124th Army Unit underwent five days of mission-specific training in the city of Sariwon, starting on 5 January. The provincial headquarters building was used to simulate the Blue House. Elements from the county Workers' Peasant Red Guard (WPRG) regiment were employed to simulate the ROKA and security units.[26]

Troops practiced assaults both day and night and with full equipment and weapons. Although little or no live-fire training was conducted, full use of hand-to-hand combat was permitted and such fighting became progressively more violent. On 9 January, a final practice assault was conducted with a full battalion of WPRG, consisting of approximately five hundred men and women then deployed to protect the building. During the ensuing raid, approximately thirty WPRG members were hospitalized with injuries. Eight days later, the unit was given its final mission briefing and infiltrated into the ROK.[27]

Details of the pre-mission training for the October 1983 sniper team assassination attempt on President Chon Tu-hwan of the ROK are incomplete. It is known that the team received intensive mission-specific training in the city of Kaesong and, because of the nature of the mission, intensive demolitions training. The members of the team could converse in Chinese, Russian, and English, as well as Korean. The team received a final mission briefing by their unit commander before boarding the freighter *Tong Gon Ae Guk Ho'* on 9 September 1983, to sail to Rangoon.

During the 1980s, unconfirmed reports suggested that Soviet SPETSNAZ units had conducted training operations (presumably with special forces units) within the DPRK, and that Soviet SPETSNAZ units operating "in the Soviet Far East . . . include North Koreans and Japanese [personnel]."[28] Although probably true, it has yet to be confirmed. A recent airborne brigade defector has stated that his unit never conducted training with any foreign special forces personnel.[29]

In June 1987, Sgt. Hong Myong-jin, a defector from the 8th Infantry Division (II Forward Corps) DMZ police company, stated that "North Korean soldiers are in training for a raid and destruction at a training field modeled after the Myong-dong streets in downtown Seoul."[30] Another defector, Lt. Yu Tae-yun, stated that nearly all members of the light infantry battalions had infiltrated up to 40 kilometers south of the DMZ in preparation for missions against ROK/U.S. installations and lines of communications within the forward areas.[31]

Some mission training for sniper and airborne sniper personnel is conducted near the DMZ with approximately eighty-seven Hughes MD-500D/E helicopters covertly acquired by the DPRK during 1984–85. These civilian versions of the MD-500 Defender antitank helicopters, used in large numbers by the ROKAF, have been armed and painted in ROKAF colors. Special forces units actively training with these helicopters have, on occasion, penetrated ROK airspace.

One of the most interesting aspects of mission training for special forces and CCSKA (Central Committee Secretary in Charge of South Korean Affairs) personnel has been the use of kidnaped foreign nationals to train direct action teams. Choi Un Hui, the ROK film star who was kidnaped by the DPRK in 1978 and escaped in 1986, recounts that the DPRK has "systematically kidnapped foreigners—mainly women—to serve intelligence functions and other state purposes."[32] This was confirmed by the confessions of Kim Hyon-hui, the KWP operative who placed the bomb on Korean Airlines flight 858. Kim Hyon-hui stated that for two years, she lived with a kidnaped Japanese woman in P'yongyang, to become familiar with Japanese customs and manners.[33] Kidnaped foreign nationals include Chinese, Japanese, Jordanians, French, and others.

They are employed primarily to instruct special forces and CCSKA personnel in the language and customs of their native countries.[34]

■ ■ *Assimilation Training*

Personnel subordinate to the Light Infantry Training Guidance Bureau receive "assimilation" training to allow them pose as ROKA soldiers. For this purpose they attend a one-month course at an assimilation institute in which the instructors are defectors from the ROK who had served in the ROKA. On their first day at the institute, the operatives are issued ROKA uniforms bearing emblems of various ROK divisions, insignia, and names. During the remainder of their training, the DPRK agents wear their ROKA uniforms, use ROK military terms, and generally act as ROK soldiers.[35]

Every effort is made to ensure that time at the institute resembles life in the ROKA. The barracks chief administers ROKA disciplinary actions, and the daily schedule is modeled on that of the ROKA. Troops wake up at 0600, call the roll, and observe a moment of silence while they face the direction of their hometowns. The troops then perform morning calisthenics while they shout ROKA slogans such as "Quick annihilation at the initial stage of war!" and "Let us unite, fight, and win!" While the troops march to the mess hall for breakfast, they sing the ROK song "Real Men." The troops even use the plastic plates and trays typically found in ROK mess halls.

While at the assimilation institute, trainees receive instruction in the use of ROKA M-16 and K-2 rifles and are taught weapons drills in the ROKA manner. The training goes as far as to include ROKA-style disciplinary actions such as the "Wonsan bombing," "rice rolled with seaweed," and "falling back." The students also receive lessons on the ROKA's Nonsan Recruit Training Center, the Defense Security Command, and the military police. They are taught that when they are stopped by ROK military police to tell them what school they graduated from and when they enrolled in the Nonsan Recruit Training Center. They also attend lectures on their counterparts, the ROK airborne and marines units.

After graduation from the assimilation institute, Light Infantry Training Guidance Bureau troops receive eighty hours annually of refresher assimilation training.

■ 38TH AIRBORNE BRIGADE, 1990S

A recent defector from the 38th Airborne brigade has provided details concerning the training activities of his brigade. During the yearly training cycle each brigade member will receive a total of 1,680 hours of training, as outlined in table 7-1.

234

Table 7-1

TRAINING OF THE 38TH AIRBORNE BRIGADE, 1990

Classification	Subject	Hours
Political	Political science (College of Communism, work, study of documents, study of political ideology)	460
Military	Tactics	300
	Marksmanship	240
	Topography	100
	Engineering studies	80
	Ordnance science	20
	NBC warfare	20
	Parachute training	40
General	KPA regulations	40
	DPRK constitution	80
	Drill and formation	60
	Physical training (including fighting techniques, judo, horizontal bar, parallel bar, mountain running, and handsprings)	230
	Personal hygiene	10

These 1,680 hours of training are organized into an annual training schedule of two six-month periods. The first period begins in December. Each period and subperiod builds logically upon the previous one.

▪ ▪ *First Training Period (December through May)*

- *December:* Political science fundamentals (College of Communism); regulations; military science (performance and disassembly of automatic rifle, machine gun, rocket launcher, grenade launcher); formation drill; tactical drill; firing drill; chemical weapons drill; physical training; engineering (emplacement and removal of various mines, enemy mines, performance, emplacement, and removal); 100-kilometer march.

- *January to February:* Prepare for field training, beginning 3 January; movement and field training from January 10 to February 10; movement by march to air base or tower training area (in some years, by drops from An-2 aircraft, or tower and cable drops due to fuel situation); exercise in which forces drop into simulated enemy territory;

taking and holding objectives; assault training against guns, tanks, and missile bases; assault training against air bases, communications centers, and command posts; ambush and counter-ambush training.

- *March to April:* Study of artillery guns and rocket launchers is set up.
- *March:* Political ideology; study of Communism; firing drill; physical training; formation drill; regulations.
- *April:* Political ideology; firing exercises; military science; contests; physical training; engineering; topography; regulations; monthly march, 25–50 kilometers a week (final week, 100 kilometers), secondary work (political science, firing, physical training).
- *May:* Political ideology; supplemental work on farm support; engineering; regulations; tactics; topology; study of the enemy.

■ ■ Second Training Period (June through November)

- *June:* Political ideology; formation; physical training; firing; tactical training (soldier actions in assaulting various objectives and squad training); topography; regulations (preparation for judging when appropriate).
- *July:* Prepare for summer movement and field training based on study of political ideology.
- *15 July to 15 August:* Summer Movement and field training at Chonsan-ri in Sangwon County and Taehung-ri; 10 days of swimming training (after final test, a 600-meter squad river crossing while not armed and a 200-meter squad river crossing while armed; after the 600-meter swim training, training on the move); occupying and holding objectives, and assault and destruction training against objectives, including guns, tanks, missiles, communication centers, and command posts; ambush and counter-ambush training; crossing difficult areas; topography; 200-kilometer continuous march; engineering (techniques for emplacing and removing various mines); techniques for removing and crossing barricades.
- *August:* After movement and field training is complete, study of basic political ideology and physical training.
- *September to October:* Many classes are set up: foreign language, reconnaissance, legal, squad leader, and assistant squad leader.
- *September:* Basic study of political ideology and firing training; unfinished basic annual training; physical training; 50-kilometer march every week.
- *October:* Various training, including study of political ideology, physical training, and tactics; participation in autumn harvest; preparation for Hwamok.

■ *November:* Preparation for winter and preparatory period for winter field training.

The intensive training that the operatives receive during the one-year course of study includes a wide variety of subjects within each discipline.

The **political science** course of study entails ideological training that centers on work, documents, and study. Topics include politics, economics, philosophy, theory of Kim Il-sungism, and revolutionary history.

In **tactics** training, operatives study various soldier actions in the attack, weak points, and breaching obstacles. They also study the commander's ability to command in combat, selection of demolition equipment and explosive charges for various objectives, withdrawal actions, methods of reconnaissance, selection of ambush trenches, main idea of ambush, and mine emplacement. Operatives conduct drills for barrier setup, breaching barricades, passing dangerous areas, forced river crossings, and seizing and holding objectives.

Marksmanship training includes practicing the tempo of fire against moving and retreating targets. For night firing training, operatives fire at lighted targets and at 30- to 50-meter silhouettes. Operatives must fire 100 rounds a year (15 of them must be nighttime firing).

Topography involves the study of the movement, advance, and location of targets by coordinate and azimuth. Operatives also learn techniques for movement and advance by azimuth.

Engineering classes teach mine laying and dismantling (which involves mine capabilities and principles), and operatives learn about ROKA mines.

Ordnance science includes study of various weapons and weapons systems. Operatives learn the capabilities, structure, and operating principles of machine guns, rocket launchers (RPG), grenade launchers, automatic rifles, and pistols. Additionally, they study the capabilities, structure, operating principles, and firing principles of the 60-millimeter mortar and recoilless gun, in accordance with the order to have a thorough knowledge of battalion weapons. There is collective training in artillery classes.

Chemical weapons study concerns the ROKA chemical weapons and their classification. Operatives also learn countermeasures to these weapons.

Parachute training includes the structure, capabilities, and operating principles of parachutes. Operatives learn when to bail out and how to land and drop.

The study of **KPA regulations** includes general soldier tasks, conduct, and ethics; barracks, guard, and individual duties; and the responsibilities of the squad leader and assistant squad leader.

Drill and formation training includes rifle formation, close-order, and marching drill.

Physical training includes many activities, notably fighting techniques, spear fighting, dagger teams, wrestling, boxing, and proficiency on the horizontal bar, parallel bar, and rope ladder. Operatives participate in one 25- to 100-kilometer march per week (each week, the distance increases) and one 100-kilometer march per month. They run two continuous 200-kilometer marches in a year (25-kilometer armed march, carrying weapons and equipment and a 20-kilogram knapsack of sand).

Lessons in **personal hygiene** involve various health treatments and emergency measures.

Several other subjects are taught during this course of study but are not specifically listed in table 7-1. Operatives study the enemy's (including the U.S. Army's) organization and equipment to division level. Operatives also gain mastery of everyday life in the ROKA through language training (recitation of words in the South Korean dialect), by learning South Korean dress, and by studying techniques for passing checkpoints. There are legal, squad leader, and foreign language classes and reconnaissance classes at brigade and battalion. Trainees take automobile, motorcycle, and tank classes at the Training Guidance Bureau.

SUICIDE

It has become both a tragic and an ominous characteristic of DPRK special and intelligence operations that rather than being captured alive, operatives will commit suicide by shooting themselves or blowing themselves up. This policy dates back to at least the 1960s and extends to today. During the 1960s, members of the 124th Army Unit were instructed to kill themselves instead of being captured; on several occasions, different operative carried out these orders. Almost all of the numerous intercepted seaborne infiltrations during the 1970s and 1980s ended with the self-destruction of the infiltrators and their craft. The three sniper brigade members who conducted the October 1983 Rangoon bombing were also instructed to kill themselves, rather than allowing themselves to be captured. Capt. Kim Chi-o was shot and killed, and Maj. Zin Mo and Capt. Kang Min-chul were seriously injured when they attempted to blow themselves up.[36]

More recent, dramatic testament to this policy is the 1996 Kangnung incident, in which eleven Reconnaissance Bureau men allowed themselves to be executed after their *Sang-o*-class coastal submarine ran aground. Much of the dedication to suicide is because of the horrible fate that awaits the extended family of any operative who is captured. Typically, the family is stripped of all rights and privileges and sent to a work camp or coal mine. Here they attempt to scrape out a survival existence while conducting enforced hard labor for the state. The survival rate is low.

That suicide is actually a codified practice, for which operatives train, is evidenced by information from an agent of the Operations Department, An Myong-chin, who defected to the ROK. He has described the four methods of suicide taught to operatives:

- Each member of the team shoots another member while standing in a circle formation.
- Each member pulls the pin of a hand grenade while sitting in a circle.
- One member of the team shoots all the others and then kills himself.
- A separate combat team kills all members of the original team before making its own escape.

If time and situation permit, before any such suicide takes place, a meeting is held to discuss options and to explain to one another the necessity for taking this drastic action. An Myong-chin also stated that in order to desensitize operatives concerning suicide they routinely shout "Let's destroy ourselves for the revolution!" at mealtimes.[37]

LOGISTICS

When deployed for unconventional warfare operations, logistical support is provided by the Light Infantry Training Guidance Bureau or the headquarters to which the special forces unit is attached. There is presently no substantial information as to how units conducting extended operations will resupply themselves. Airborne units are provided with a seven-day supply of rations. After they consume this, they are expected to secure additional rations locally. They are also expected to make use of captured weapons and ammunition. Training literature indicates that the units will live off the land, raid enemy supply depots, purchase food from civilians, or, as a last resort, steal from the local population. It is possible that under special circumstances, a very limited airborne/ amphibious supply is available.[38]

UNIFORMS AND INSIGNIA

A majority of special forces personnel subordinate to the Light Infantry Training Guidance Bureau are provided with two standard KPA uniforms (one for summer and one for winter) and one ROKA uniform. Both the winter and summer KPA uniforms are khaki-colored. The winter uniform contains quilted batting, and when worn inside out becomes a white camouflage uniform. It also has an attached fur collar. Each soldier is also issued an entire ROKA uniform, with name tag, unit insignia, service insignia, rank insignia, combat boots, and field cap. Typically a special forces battalion will maintain a collection of fifteen different ROKA unit insignia. During peacetime, these uniforms are stored inside each individual's knapsack and stored together in the battalion warehouse. These are typically used only during refresher assimilation training, which occurs once or twice a year. At that time soldiers wear their ROKA uniforms and receive training on ROKA close-order drill and on how to pass ROKA military police checkpoints.

During operational missions special forces personnel have been known to wear civilian clothing (including female disguises), ROKA uniforms, mottled camouflaged uniforms in summer, and an all-white overgarment in winter. Airborne units do have a distinctive airborne insignia, but this is almost never worn. Units subordinate to the Light Infantry Training Guidance Bureau are not known to have any other special unit insignia or markings to indicate their special status.

Special forces companies subordinate to the Light Infantry Training Guidance Bureau are provided with three M-16s for familiarization training. Although they do not fire these weapons, they train on them. Consequently, if operatives capture M-16s from ROK/U.S. forces, they can quickly use these weapons.

COMBAT TECHNIQUES, 1960S TO 1970S

Since specific, detailed information about the present-day combat techniques of the various special forces organizations is unavailable, this chapter will discuss what these techniques have historically been and what they might be today.[1]

AMBUSHES AND ATTACKS

The training given from 1963 to 1968 (and possibly into 1970) on ambushes and attacks against barracks, command posts, missile sites, air bases, and county seats reflects possible future tactics.

- AMBUSH

  Considerable training effort was devoted to ambush tactics, which were designed to inflict casualties and to procure uniforms, identification papers, currency, food, weapons, medical supplies, and communications equipment. Company-sized ambush teams included two forward observation teams of four to five men who were placed at vantage points approximately 400 meters in both directions from the ambush site. These forward teams were responsible for sighting the target unit (and any reinforcing unit) and informing the leader of its approach. The remaining elements of the company were emplaced along the ambush site in foxholes at 10-meter intervals, up to 40 meters from and parallel to the road. Ambush sites were usually selected at a mountain pass or a blind curve. Personnel were positioned either on both sides of the site (a two-front ambush) or all on one side (a single-line ambush). Mines were placed in the road, and the team waited. When the convoy or patrol arrived at the ambush point, the leader fired one pistol shot to signal the attack. The ambushers then threw hand grenades and fired their automatic personal weapons (AK-47s or PPS-43s) and light machine guns.

Soldiers of intelligence value were kidnaped and exfiltrated to the DPRK. Withdrawal of the assault elements was covered by security units. The company withdrew in small groups, which reassembled at a predesignated rallying point. The team usually exfiltrated via the approach route because its members were familiar with the terrain. When the KPA unit was being pursued, it prepared another ambush. A small number of troops might pretend to surrender. When U.S./ROK personnel approached to seize the surrendered agents, the remainder of the ambush team opened fire from concealed positions.

- ATTACKS ON BARRACKS

Teams of thirty troops within the 124th Army Unit were trained in the techniques of destroying barracks, killing its occupants, and gathering material and individuals of intelligence value. In a typical attack, the team members were clothed in ROKA uniforms and carried explosive charges, grenades, sub-machine-guns, machine guns, and communications equipment. The team infiltrated the DMZ, moving primarily at night near the target area. A small group of troops reconnoitered the target site during daylight hours to determine the exact locations of barracks, security guards, and avenues of approach. Disguised in civilian clothes, the group conducted its reconnaissance as close to the target as possible. The following night the troops surreptitiously entered the compound through a sewer, culvert, or low area where they could crawl under the fence. Guards were silenced and the team was led to the target buildings by the reconnaissance scouts. Three functional subteams then began their tasks. The attack subteam killed the guards, destroyed the barracks, and killed its occupants by throwing grenades through barracks windows and doors or by setting explosive charges against the external walls. The document-acquisition subteam entered the administrative buildings, located documents, and kidnaped personnel of intelligence interest such as high-ranking officers and NCOs. The protection subteam provided firepower and security for the other subteams while they performed their missions. This subteam also neutralized the motor pool and compound power supply, killing all personnel attempting to escape from the buildings or the compound area, and provided security along approach routes that could be used to reinforce the compound. The document-acquisition subteam was the first to withdraw; the other two subteams provided a rear guard. The unit reassembled at a predetermined rally point, perhaps a rest point used during infiltration. The same route used for infiltration was used for exfiltration unless U.S./ROK troops were encountered. In that case, the team moved by a prearranged alternate exfiltration route. Vehicles were stolen to speed the team's retreat.

■ ATTACKS ON COMMAND POSTS

For attacking U.S./ROK unit headquarters, the 124th Army Unit practiced tactics quite similar to those against barracks. Platoons were
employed against regimental headquarters, and companies were used
against division headquarters. The company-sized units obviously
required greater control measures than those necessary for assault
teams. When preparing to assault a division headquarters, a company of
the 124th established an operational base of well-camouflaged, perhaps
underground, positions approximately 1 hour's march (6–7 kilometers)
from the target. The base was far from villages, roads, and farmhouses.
From the base, a team of three to five men thoroughly reconnoitered the
target. Attack plans were adjusted in accordance with U.S./ROK security measures uncovered during the reconnaissance. The night of the
attack the entire company moved in single file to a staging area very
close to the target. Final adjustments and coordination were made here.
Security squads were dispatched to strategic points to ambush any reinforcing parties. On signal from the commander, one platoon (minus the
security squads) moved surreptitiously to the compound, killed the
perimeter guards, and breached any fences. Another platoon immediately moved through the gap and prepared to attack the barracks. The
final platoon then moved through the gap to the headquarters building,
forced an entry, killed its occupants, and set explosive charges. The barracks were attacked, maximum casualties were inflicted, and the headquarters were destroyed within 5–10 minutes. The company withdrew
in small units, with squads first rallying at predesignated points a short
distance from the target area. Platoons rallied further away (approximately 700 meters from the target), and all surviving members of the
company rallied at a final predesignated point. After a short wait to
assure that all able members had arrived, the team conducted a forced
night march to a bivouac area about 20 kilometers from the objective.
During their exfiltration, the company was not assigned secondary targets but may have ambushed pursuit forces.

■ ATTACKS ON AN AIR BASE

The tactics taught in the 124th Army Unit for attacking an air base were
very similar to those used in the other assault missions. The size of the
attacking unit ranged from one platoon to two companies, depending
upon the size and complexity of the air base. A company-sized team probably consisted of nine squads with the following responsibilities: one
squad to penetrate the fence and to silence the guards; one to attack the
fuel dump; one to assault the radar installation; one to assault the control tower; one to block base personnel who may attempt to counter the

243

attack; two squads to attack aircraft; and two to provide security by ambushing reinforcements. Infiltration, movement to the objective, reconnaissance, and penetration of the perimeter were accomplished as described for other missions. The attack would typically begin at approximately 2300 hours with the destruction of the fuel dump. The explosion drew attention away from other targets that were attacked simultaneously and directly after the fuel dump explosion. The mission and the beginning of exfiltration was to be completed within 30 minutes.

- ATTACKS ON AN ROK COUNTY SEAT

The assault group used to attack a county seat and to assassinate government officials could vary in size from a nine-man squad to a ninety-three-man company. Specific training was conducted by fifteen-man platoons. The mission was accomplished in much the same manner as previously discussed operations. The reconnaissance team, however, might have dressed as common travelers or students and entered the village to gain specific information on the county seat and residences of high-ranking officials. In a violent 5-minute attack, government buildings were to be destroyed, most officials killed, and a few individuals and documents seized and taken to the DPRK.

FOOT RECONNAISSANCE STATION OPERATIONS AND TACTICS

The foot reconnaissance stations normally utilized teams of three to five lightly armed and equipped men in the DMZ area. For targets well below the DMZ, Liaison Bureau teams were usually employed. Reconnaissance teams generally infiltrated during the night hours and attempted to accomplish their mission and exfiltrate without being detected. If discovered and engaged by U.S. or ROK forces, they attempted to break contact and return to the DPRK, but many firing incidents occurred when reconnaissance teams were forced to avoid capture. Reconnaissance teams, however, did attack targets of opportunity when their primary mission was not jeopardized. En route to an objective, reconnaissance teams traveled at night, avoiding villages, main roads, and conspicuous terrain features. The infiltrators preferred to arrive in their operational area in time to prepare a well-camouflaged bivouac, to cache excess supplies, and to reconnoiter the target. Bivouacs usually included dug-in, covered positions with preplanned escape routes. The agents photographed, sketched, and recorded detailed characteristics of the target. Local patrol activity, guard posts, and other security measures were carefully noted.

Foot reconnaissance station raiding teams could often surprise their targets, since they chose the time, place, and type of most encounters.

When discovered by a security patrol, the team's effectiveness was reduced; still they were skillful and tenacious fighters. Although most teams consisted of three to five men, ambush or harassment missions could have involved as much as a reinforced platoon. Weapons included sub-machine-guns, grenades, and occasionally mines, satchel charges, and antitank grenade launchers. Imitation ROKA uniforms were frequently worn by the troops.

Before they were dispatched, teams were thoroughly briefed on mission plans, the characteristics of the objective, and routes. Although they preferred to operate at night, these teams did stage bold attacks on U.S. or ROK outposts and ambushed work parties and security patrols in full daylight. Foot reconnaissance station teams routinely emplaced mines on frequently used roads and then lay in wait to ambush the victims. Attacks on United Nations positions were sometimes planned to draw reaction forces into a killing zone consisting of carefully placed mines and ambush teams. On other occasions, intruder teams have been supported by machine-gun, mortar, recoilless gun, and artillery fire from north of the DMZ.

INFILTRATION TACTICS

■ SEA INFILTRATION

When a boat crew was assigned an infiltration mission, it obtained a boat from the unit repair yard and drew the necessary weapons and navigation equipment. It took a week to complete preparations for the mission. The agent, or team of agents, then boarded the boat but remained isolated from the crew until ready to be put ashore. The large, high-speed boats, capable of speeds in excess of 30 knots, proceeded approximately 100 kilometers out to sea before heading south for the ROK. In the Yellow Sea, an intermediate stop might have been made off the Shantung Peninsula of China to take on fuel from prepositioned vessels. Once the general infiltration area was reached, the craft headed for shore or an offshore island. The boat crew was alerted and ready to man all weapons on a 3- to 5-minute notice. When the boat was about 10 kilometers from the landing site, it proceeded slowly to a point about 450 meters offshore. (Some of the smaller, slower escort boats would make the entire approach slowly, mingling with ROK fishing boats). The crew generally made the final approach between 2200 and 2400 hours by rowing the agent team ashore in a rubber raft or wooden barge. Agent escorts checked the immediate landing area before the team went ashore. Upon completion of the landing, the escort boat immediately cleared the area and returned to the DPRK.

The agent or agent team also cleared the beach quickly. If a large group was landed, members moved in column with point, flank, and rear security elements. Signals and immediate action plans were prepared for any contingency. The unit traveled at night, covering 16–20 kilometers, using terrain for cover and concealment. When moving through hilly country the column traveled parallel to the ridge line about two-thirds to three-quarters of the way to the top. When moving in flat country, double columns were employed. At 0500 to 0600 hours each morning, the unit bivouacked in camouflaged trenches, where the agents remained till dark. Sentries were posted, and contact with indigenous personnel was avoided, if possible.

In one case, a team operated for ten days off the ROK coast from a 26-foot wooden, unpowered vessel. The boat was launched by a mother ship near the operational area, then mingled with ROK fishing boats. From the boat, the team observed coastal defenses. One agent was put ashore to conduct reconnaissance and to capture some laborers for interrogation.

- DMZ INFILTRATION

Agents assigned reconnaissance or assault missions against U.S. or ROK forces deployed near the DMZ usually infiltrated on foot through the zone, sometimes swimming the Han or Imjin Rivers. On the completion of detailed pre-mission training, agents were usually driven to a DMZ guard post. The DMZ police unit at the guard post briefed them on the terrain through which they would travel, the existing security measures employed by the U.S. or ROK units at their front, and on military and civilian activities in the area. Extensive data was available on all likely infiltration routes as United Nations Command lines were constantly observed and probed for vulnerabilities, and every subversive, espionage, and assault team had a secondary mission of reconnoitering the United Nations Command security system for future exploitation. The team was sometimes led by members of the DMZ police unit to the DMZ. Occasionally agents would bivouac in the northern portion of the zone, where they could observe the security elements to avoid and the obstacles to overcome. The agents usually traveled at night and took precautions to avoid ambush positions, guard posts, patrols, obstacles, minefields, villages, and main roads. Infrequently used trails paralleling a ridge line approximately two-thirds of the way up the slope were favored routes of infiltration.

Security discipline was strictly enforced. Smoking and open fires were not permitted; communication was by hand, arm, and body movements. On all missions except assault and ambush, detection had to be avoided. The team posed as ROKA soldiers if they were seen and challenged. If this failed, they killed the challenger(s) silently with a knife or a stone if possible. If necessary, they attacked the challenger(s), as did the assault teams, with hand grenades and sub-machine-gun fire. If ROK civilians were inadvertently encountered, the team may have questioned them, trying to subvert them, warned them against reporting the agents, and possibly even paid them to remain silent. Alternatively, the agents might have killed the civilians outright. During the day the teams bivouacked in a cave or in foxholes dug in the bushy slope of a mountain. A position with good visibility was chosen so the team could reconnoiter military activities, future infiltration routes, installations, checkpoints, ambush and guard posts, road networks, vehicle and pedestrian traffic, and characteristics of the terrain. The bivouac was set up in an area that local residents were not likely to approach and where suitable routes of escape were available. Camouflage nets, tree branches, and grass that blended with the environment were used to conceal the agents during their rest. At certain sites the teams cached weapons, food, ammunition, and clothing so they could travel fast and have bases for replenishing depleted supplies while exfiltrating north.

The following actions were reportedly taken when an obstacle or enemy personnel were encountered.

When a river had to be crossed, agents chose a spot where they could wade across if possible. They removed their clothing and placed it along with weapons and supplies in knapsacks, which they held above their heads. When ice was floating in the river, they would wear a set of long underwear to keep the ice from touching their bodies. If the water was too deep to wade, they swam. A float was sometimes improvised by placing all their clothing and equipment in a waterproof rubber bag. This float and water wings were frequently used to facilitate swimming the river. If the current was flowing in the right direction, agents sometimes would drift downstream toward their objective.

When a U.S. or an ROK observation post or guard post was approached, the team detoured around the position, keeping at least 300 meters away. The positions of these posts were usually known in advance.

If an ambush was discovered, the team detoured, keeping at least 50 meters away. If the infiltration team members were detected they killed the ambushers with grenades and small arms. The mission was then abandoned and the team returned to the DPRK. To avoid detection by an ambush post, the teams made frequent listening stops while crossing the DMZ. Reportedly, an ambush can often be detected by the rattles, rustles, coughing, and whispers made by its members and by the smell of urine.

When an agent team was surprised and challenged by a United Nations Command patrol or guard post, the team members dispersed and the leader responded with a prearranged cover story, stating that they were an ROK unit on some mission or errand. If the team leader felt that the cover story had not been believed, he gave a coded signal prescribing the method to use in attacking UNC soldiers.

When a minefield was encountered, the teams attempted to detour around the area. Agents were taught to recognize U.S. minefield boundary markers. If the team discovered that it was already in a minefield, it would attempt to neutralize the mines in its path. After arranging hand signals for advance or withdrawal and designating a rally point in the event that the group was discovered, the leader moved ahead and the team followed at about 10 meters, keeping the leader in sight. The leader would stick a probe in the ground every 15 centimeters at an angle of 45 degrees. He would make only minimum contact with the surface, allowing only his feet and one knee to touch.

When a wire obstacle was encountered, the team leader determined whether it was electrified, the extent of booby trapping, and the extent of adjoining minefields. A combat plan was devised, and a regrouping point designated before penetration was attempted. The team avoided cutting the obstacle and attempted to pass over it. Ordinarily the primary barrier fence was climbed over or tunneled under. On several occasions, the team would cut the fence to penetrate it. Portions of the fence apparently have been taken to the DPRK.

When pursued by U.S. or ROK soldiers, agents withdrew in unison to the DMZ as fast as possible. They had been instructed to escape through high mountains and to step on rocks and grass to leave no footprints. To mislead pursuers, tree branches or small bushes were broken in a direction other than the escape route. A false trail was sometimes made with footprints and discarded items. If necessary, the agents stopped and fought to destroy or delay pursuing forces. If escape seemed hopeless, agents were instructed to, and frequently did, commit suicide.

▪ OTHER MEANS OF INFILTRATION

Some espionage and subversion agents arrived in the ROK with falsified papers; one means of entry was aboard commercial vessels or aircraft from third countries. Japan was the base for most operations of this type, as it has many Korean residents and a well-organized KWP front, the Chosen Soren. Agents were recruited, dispatched, and supported by the Department for Guidance of the Koreans Residing in Japan, a unit of the Ministry of Public Security. Infiltration was also accomplished by recruiting ROK citizens living temporarily in foreign countries and assigning the missions to be completed on their return to the ROK.

THE DMZ TUNNELS

The tunnels used by the DPRK to infiltrate the ROK are a major tool of the special forces. The U.S. Defense Intelligence Agency has long recognized this: "Until all [tunnels] are located and neutralized, North Korean tunnels represent a potentially significant military threat to the South."[1]

THE DEMILITARIZED ZONE

Most missions assigned to the DPRK's special purpose forces initially require a covert means of insertion into the ROK. The primary obstacle to such infiltration is the DMZ.[2]

At the time of Japan's unconditional surrender on 14 August 1945, elements of the Soviet XXV Army had occupied most of the northern Korean Peninsula and were steadily expanding their zone of control southward. This expansion was halted approximately one month later with the arrival of U.S. forces in the south. By previous agreement, the peninsula was divided at the thirty-eighth parallel into Soviet and U.S. zones. The thirty-eighth parallel provided a convenient line delineating areas of responsibility for the processing of Japanese prisoners of war and assets. From 1945 to 1950, the thirty-eighth parallel increasingly became a political barrier between the Communist Bloc and the Western world. The Fatherland Liberation War altered and reinforced this demarcation, which still stands today.

As a result of the P'anmunjom Armistice Agreement of 27 July 1953, a demilitarized zone (DMZ) of 2 kilometers was established on either side of the military demarcation line (MDL). The armistice suspended active hostilities, withdrew military forces and equipment from the DMZ, and prevented each side from entering air, ground, or sea areas controlled by the other side. Demarcating no specific natural or cultural barrier, this 243-kilometer-long and 4-kilometer-wide (2 kilometers wide on either side of the MDL) DMZ follows a sinuous path across rivers, plains, and mountain ranges. In only a few places does it follow any natural boundary. The western terminus is 42 kilometers northwest of Seoul. Beyond the western end, a neutral zone represented by the Han River estuary extends westward into the Yellow Sea. The eastern terminus is 29 kilometers north of Kansong.

The primary environmental factor of the DMZ is its formidable terrain. With the exception of the major land routes, the terrain consists of hills or mountains whose slopes restrict or channelize vehicular movement. While this type of terrain is favorable for static defense, it almost defies effective defense against unconventional forces. The remote and inaccessible mountain regions have provided havens for KPA infiltrators, providing cover and concealment, safe areas, and numerous routes for evasion and escape.

Vegetation in the DMZ consists primarily of brush and scrub. In the hills and mountains this vegetation provides concealment for small units. The lowlands and principal corridors consist primarily of open fields, many of which have reverted to tall grasses, weeds, and thickets. There is no agriculture within, or adjacent to, the DMZ except for a few local farmers who, for political reasons, have been permitted to cultivate a limited amount of land on the fringes of the DMZ.

Military operations throughout the Korean Peninsula are greatly influenced by the hot, wet summers and cold, dry winters. Most precipitation occurs between June and September, with the heaviest rains in July and August. During rainfall fields and many roads turn into quagmires, and streams become impassable torrents. Summer is also the season of high temperature (90°F or more) and humidity, with fog, low ceilings, and poor visibility. Winter, on the other hand, provides optimum conditions for large-scale ground operations: fields, paddies, and streams are frozen; skies are generally clear and precipitation light; and trees are stripped of foliage. Winter is also the period of extremely low temperatures and strong winds from Manchuria. A surface temperature of 0°F (minus 18°C) and a wind speed of about 20 miles per hour (30 kilometers per hour) produces a wind-chill equivalent of minus 39°F (minus 40°C), a condition not unusual along the DMZ.

After the Fatherland Liberation War, the KPA changed its tactics from overt military aggression to covert subversion, largely accomplished by the infiltration of unconventional warfare forces across the DMZ. The DMZ remained the preferred infiltration route south until the late 1960s, when the ROK, in lieu of adequate manpower to police such a long and hostile border, constructed an integrated barrier system along the southern boundary. A 3-meter-high barrier fence, anchored in concrete and topped by concertina wire, was completed and supplemented with minefields, antitank ditches, and electronic sensing devices. Reinforced watch towers, concrete bunkers, and guard posts were established to overlook the most frequented infiltration routes. Thousands of acres of brush were, and are today, cleared along roads and fences and around military positions within and adjacent to the southern boundary of the DMZ.

During the early 1970s the KPA initiated an extensive program to upgrade and expand its armored and motorized forces. In response to this expanded threat the ROK began to modernize its DMZ barrier system. Included within this modernization was the establishment of an antitank ditch along the length of the DMZ and construction of an in-depth defensive zone behind the DMZ with concrete reinforced positions throughout. All roads and bridges within the defensive zone were prepared for demolition and more. This barrier system was not intended as the sole answer for stemming infiltration into the ROK, or even through the DMZ. However, its effectiveness has resulted in the KPA's being forced to shift to air, sea, and tunnel infiltration. Although more expensive, these methods offer more security. In bypassing the DMZ, special purpose forces personnel can choose landing sites in remote and unprotected places within the ROK rear areas.

THE DMZ TUNNELS

Probably one of the most unusual aspects of the KPA attempts to infiltrate the ROK has been its efforts to tunnel under the DMZ.[3] These tunneling operations began in the early 1960s and proceeded slowly through the late 1960s.[4] Prompted by the fortification of the DMZ, in September 1971, Kim Il-song specifically ordered the construction of infiltration tunnels along the DMZ: "one tunnel can be more powerful than ten atomic bombs put together and the tunnels are the most ideal means of penetrating the South's fortified front line."[5]

The engineer battalion of each infantry division deployed directly on the DMZ was assigned the task of digging two infiltration tunnels. Technical and logistic assistance was provided by the Corps Engineer Department and General Staff Department's Engineer and Rear Services Bureaus. The KPA normally deploys eleven infantry divisions along the DMZ. Based on the estimate that each division is responsible for two infiltration tunnels, there are theoretically twenty-two tunnels. Aside from the four located and neutralized tunnels, ROK/U.S. intelligence currently estimates that there are eighteen suspected active tunnels in various stages of completion along the DMZ.

The first evidence of KPA tunneling operations emerged in November 1973, when ROKA DMZ guards reported numerous explosions that started north of the DMZ and gradually drew closer. Aerial and ground reconnaissance failed to provide any reasonable explanation for these explosions, but road improvements and the construction of fortifications were noted along the northern edge of the DMZ. To keep track of these explosions, seismic equipment was deployed along the DMZ. This equipment soon yielded voluminous information, recording 16,685 explosions on 877 different occasions in the Ch'orwon area alone. Similar numbers were also recorded in the areas of the major north–south routes along the length of the DMZ. However, the majority were located in the west, along the routes that led to Seoul.

In November 1974, a KPA engineer defected and revealed that the KPA was tunneling under the DMZ. More importantly he provided information on the locations of two tunnels, one in the Korangp'o area and one in the Ch'orwon area. Acting on this information, on 15 November, an ROKA patrol found steam rising from the ground in the DMZ near Korangp'o. Five days later, a combined ROKA and United Nations team located what turned out to be a small tunnel. This tunnel, approximately 0.45 meters below the surface, was lined with concrete slabs for roofing and walls and had a small railway along its floor for the removal of spoil. The tunnel had a total length of approximately 2,000 meters (1,000 meters south of the MDL) and measured 1.2 meters high by 1.1 meters wide. Although small, this tunnel would have enabled considerable numbers of light infantry and reconnaissance personnel to pass undetected behind the forward ROK/U.S. positions.[6] Miscellaneous materials found within the tunnel included six boxes of Soviet-produced dynamite, Claymore mines, a DPRK-produced wristwatch, a compass, canteens, telephone sets, pickaxes, light bulbs, and more.

Various methods, including seismic, photographic, and sonic detection, were employed to locate the tunnel in the Ch'orwon area, but met with little success. Finally, a series of exploratory bore holes were drilled on what seemed a likely intercept line in a valley. The bore-hole method ensured that only a minimum amount of drilling would be required and provided cover from KPA observation. Approximately fifty-five bore holes were drilled, of which seven proved to be suspicious. The suspicious holes passed through cavities, or the suspect rock samples contained sand, grass, and other materials (none of which are geological features of granite). In each case, a specially designed camera confirmed the existence of a cavity. Additionally, thousands of gallons of water pumped into the bore holes drained away quickly. It was the KPA themselves, however, who provided conclusive evidence that these bore holes had entered a tunnel. The KPA engineers had placed a cement block under one of the shafts, and cement was obviously a substance not naturally found in 58 meters of granite.

The discovery of the Ch'orwon tunnel was announced on 19 March 1975, and the interception tunnel was completed on 24 March. The tunnel was approximately 50–150 meters below the surface, had a total length of approximately 3,300 meters (1,100 meters south of the MDL), and measured 2 meters high by 2 meters wide. There were three exits toward the south and several wide sections in which troops could be gathered before exiting. Although projections would not allow the passage of a jeep, smaller vehicles and heavy weapons could have passed through it, as well as an estimated eight thousand troops an hour. ROKA/U.S. troops painstakingly cleared the tunnel of three major blocks, all of which had been "booby-trapped." This clearing operation revealed two chambers used to house electric generators and machinery for pumping air and water. On 21 March 1975, Kim Pu-song, a former member of the Liaison Department who had defected to the ROK, stated that the KPA was building other tunnels similar to the Ch'orwon tunnel. These tunnels were designed to have five exits, of which only one or two were to be used during "peacetime," while all the exits were to be used at a "decisive time." He further stated that he had personally participated in the construction of a tunnel 4 kilometers from P'anmunjom.[7] Continued surveillance efforts paid off in mid-1978, when the ROKA located this tunnel, this time only 4 kilometers south of P'anmunjom. On 10 June 1978, the ROKA began digging an interception tunnel, and on 17 October 1978, they broke through into the third KPA infiltration tunnel. This tunnel averaged 73 meters below the surface, was approximately 1,640 meters long (435 meters south of the MDL), and measured 1.95 meters high by 2.1 meters wide.

In December 1989, intelligence indicators detected a possible fourth tunnel. Bore holes were drilled, and an open cavity located. An interception tunnel was then dug, which on 3 March 1990 intercepted a DPRK infiltration tunnel. This occurred approximately 160 kilometers northeast of Seoul in the mountainous region called the "Punchbowl," the scene of heavy fighting during the war. This tunnel, 144 meters below the surface, had a total length of approximately 1,850 meters (1,000 meters south of the MDL), and measured 1.8 meters high by 1.8 meters wide.[8] Table A-1 summarizes the infiltration tunnels discovered thus far.

The road work and construction of fortifications detected along the northern edge of the DMZ were apparently a part of a KPA deception plan to ensure that the huge quantities of spoil produced by these tunnels would not be spotted by ROK/U.S. reconnaissance. Tunnel entries were also located in "dead ground" (ground unable to be photographed) from south of the DMZ. In 1984 there were still eighteen suspected active tunnels in various stages of completion along the DMZ.[9] These tunnels are believed to be the same size as the tunnel found near Ch'orwon. Surveillance of the suspected tunnel entrances and possible exits continues, but their exact

Table A-1

KPA DMZ INFILTRATION TUNNELS DISCOVERED BY ROKA/U.S. FORCES

Tunnel	Discovery Date	Location	Height, Meters	Width, Meters	Depth, Meters	Length, Meters	Distance South of MDL, Meters	Tunnel Lining	Troop Capacity	Invasion Route
1	15 Nov. 1974	8 km NE of Korangp'o	1.2	0.9	0.45	3,500	1,000	Concrete	1 regiment	Korangp'o to Uijongbu to Seoul (total 65 km)
2	19 March 1975	13 km N of Ch'orwon	2	2	50–60	3,500	1,100	None	8,000 troops per hour, plus heavy equipment	Ch'orwon to Poch'on to Seoul (total 101 km)
3	17 Oct. 1978	4 km S of P'anmunjom	1.95	2.1	73	1,640	435	None		Munsan to Seoul (total 44 km)
4	3 March 1990	26 km N of Yanggu	1.7	1.7	144	2,052	1,028	None	1 regiment	Suhwha-Wontong-Yongdong Highway

locations or the extent of construction remains undetermined. Whether interception tunnels will be dug if the infiltration tunnel is positively located is questionable, because of the enormous costs involved.

Abbreviations

AA	Antiaircraft
ATGM	Antitank Guided Missile
C^3I	Command, Control, Communications, and Intelligence
CCSKA	Central Committee Secretary in Charge of South Korean Affairs
COMINT	Communications Intelligence
CPV	Chinese People's Volunteers
DMZ	Demilitarized Zone
DPRK	Democratic People's Republic of Korea (i.e., North Korea)
EUSA	Eighth U.S. Army
EUSAK	Eighth U.S. Army, Korea
FEBA	Forward Edge of the Battle Area
FEC	Far East Command—U.S.
G2	Intelligence section
GHQ	General Headquarters (eqv. General Staff Department)
GPO	Government Printing Office
GRU	Chief Intelligence Directorate, General Staff—Russia
HAHO	High Altitude, High Opening
HALO	High Altitude, Low Opening
HQ	Headquarters
KCP	Korean Communist Party
KFRA	Korean Fatherland Restoration Association
KPA	Korean People's Army
KPAF	Korean People's Air Force
KPN	Korean People's Navy
KVA	Korean Volunteer Army
KWP	Korean Workers' Party
LCM	Landing Craft, Mechanized
LCPA	Landing Craft, Personnel, Air-cushion
LCPF	Landing Craft, Personnel, Fast
LCU	Landing Craft—Utility
LSM	Landing Ship—Mechanized
MDL	Military Demarcation Line

MPAF	Ministry of the People's Armed Forces
MRL	Multiple Rocket Launcher
NBC	Nuclear, Biological, and Chemical
NCO	Noncommissioned Officer
NEAJUA	Northeast Anti-Japanese United Army
OPFOR	U.S. Army Opposition Forces
PC	Patrol Craft
PCFS	Patrol Craft, Fire Support
POL	Petroleum, Oil, and Lubricants
PRC	People's Republic of China (i.e., Communist China)
PT	Patrol boat
PTG	Patrol boat, Guided Missile
ROK	Republic of Korea (i.e., South Korea)
ROKA	Republic of Korea, Army
ROKAF	Republic of Korea, Air Force
ROKN	Republic of Korea, Navy
RPG	Rocket Propelled Grenade
SAM	Surface to Air Missile
SCUBA	Self-Contained Underwater Breathing Apparatus
SEAL	Sea, Air, and Land (the U.S. Navy's special operation force)
SICARO	Secretary in Charge of Anti-ROK Operations
SIGINT	Signals Intelligence
SKGB	South Korea General Bureau
SS	Submarine
SSc	Coastal Submarine
SSm	Midget Submarine
U.S.	United States
U/I	Unidentified
UN	United Nations
UNC	United Nations Command
USAF	United States Air Force
WPNK	Workers' Party of North Korea
WPSK	Workers' Party of South Korea

NOTES

During my research, I had the opportunity to interview numerous military and civilian intelligence experts from a number of countries. Because of the highly sensitive nature of their positions and the subject matter, these experts must remains anonymous. When data from these interviews is utilized to provide the source of information on a subject, or to confirm other sources, the term "interview data" is used.

Chapter 1
OVERVIEW

1. The following publications were used extensively throughout this book and are recommended to anyone interested in the subject. They will only be referenced when specifically required in the remainder of the text. U.S. Defense Intelligence Agency, *North Korea Handbook,* PC-2600-6421-94, Washington, D.C., 1994; U.S. Defense Intelligence Agency, *North Korea: The Foundations for Military Strength,* Washington, D.C., October 1991; U.S. Defense Intelligence Agency, *North Korea: The Foundations for Military Strength, Update 1995,* Washington, D.C., March 1996; Republic of Korea, Ministry of National Defense, *Defense White Paper,* vols. 1990 through 1996–97, Seoul, 1991–97; U.S. Army, *North Korea: A Country Study,* Department of Army Pamphlet 550-81, 1994; and U.S. Army, *North Korean People's Army Operations,* FC 100-2-99, 5 December 1986.

2. U.S. Defense Intelligence Agency, *Military Strength, Update 1995,* pp. 15, 21–22; and Republic of Korea, Ministry of National Defense, *Defense White Paper 1994–1995,* pp. 55–80.

3. U.S. Defense Intelligence Agency, *North Korean Special Purpose Forces,* DDB-1100-475-84, May 1984, p. 1.

4. Since the strictest definition of unconventional warfare operations includes guerrilla warfare involving primarily indigenous personnel, escape and evasion, and subversion, it must be pointed out that these units do not presently employ or train ROK agents for guerrilla warfare. That responsibility is subordinate to the CCSKA.

5. U.S. Defense Intelligence Agency, *North Korean Special Purpose Forces,* p. 1.

6. "Details of Burma Bombing Revealed in Confession," *Korea Herald,* 27 November 1983, pp. 4–5.

7. U.S. Defense Intelligence Agency, *North Korean Special Purpose Forces,* p. 4.

8. Interview data; and Republic of Korea, Ministry of National Defense, *Defense White Paper 1990* through *1995–1996.*

9. U.S. Defense Intelligence Agency, *Military Strength, Update 1995,* pp. 15, 21–22; Republic of Korea, Ministry of National Defense, *Defense White Paper 1994–1995,* pp. 55–80; U.S. Defense Intelligence Agency, *North Korean Special Purpose Forces,* p. 2; and "Why Korea Is Scared," *Foreign Report,* no. 1666, 4 February 1981, 4.

10. U.S. Defense Intelligence Agency, *North Korean Special Purpose Forces,* p. 4.

11. "North Korea—Body Snatchers," Associated Press report, 9 August 1994.

12. U.S. Defense Intelligence Agency, *North Korean Special Purpose Forces,* p. 5.

Chapter 2
BIRTH, WAR, AND RECONSTRUCTION OF THE KOREAN PEOPLE'S ARMY, 1939–61

1. During November 1990 the ROK newspaper *Hanguk Ilbo* carried a nineteen-part story by former KPA Gen. Yu Song-ch'ol. Yu was both a member of the 88th Brigade and the commander of the KPA's Operations Bureau during the Fatherland Liberation War. This valuable firsthand account is translated both in Sydney A. Seiler, *Kim Il-song 1941–1948: The Creation of a Legend, the Building of a Regime.* Lanham, Md.: University Press of America, 1994, and in various issues of the Foreign Broadcast Informations Service, *Daily Reports* (hereinafter cited as FBIS) during November 1990 through January 1991. Seiler's book provides an excellent source for all the events described in this section.

2. Chung Kiwon, "The North Korean People's Army and the Party," in *North Korea Today,* ed. Robert A. Scalapino (New York: Praeger, 1963), p. 108; and Evelyn Becker McCune, *Leadership in North Korea: Groupings and Motivation,* U.S. Department of State, Office of Intelligence Research, 1963, pp. 9–14.

3. U.S. Army, *History of the North Korean Army,* HQ, FEC, MIS, G2, 31 July 1952, pp. 6–7.

4. The Korean Volunteer Army is sometimes identified as the Korean Volunteer Corps.

5. Mu Chong is sometimes identified as Kim Mu Chong. He was the only one of thirty Koreans who set out with Mao Zedong on the Long March and survived, and was rated as one of the best artillery men in the Chinese Communist army and an ardent follower of Mao Zedong. U.S. Army, *History of the North Korean Army,* p. 98.

6. U.S. Army, *History of the North Korean Army,* pp. 90–91.

7. The most notable of the works analyzing Kim Il-song's early life are Dae-sook Suh, *Kim Il Sung: The North Korean Leader* (New York: Columbia University Press, 1988); and Seiler, *Kim Il-song 1941–1948.* See also McCune, *Leadership in North Korea,* p. 9.

8. Seiler, *Kim Il-song 1941–1948,* pp. 19–26, 39.

9. Ibid., pp. 30–36, 45–48; "CPSU Paper Views Kim Il-song's Background," *Chungang Ilbo,* 13 March 1992, p. 1, as cited in FBIS-EAS-92-050, 13 March 1992, pp. 18–19; and "Article Analyzes Armed Forces in North" *Choson Ilbo,* 24 April 1990, as cited in FBIS-EAS-90-082, 27 April 1990, pp. 10–11.

10. Ibid., pp. 45–56, 62–70; and McCune, *Leadership in North Korea,* p. 34. The

number of followers that returned with Kim Il-song varies widely according to the source. It would appear, however, that approximately fifty to sixty were with Kim aboard the *Pugachov,* with others following later.

11. Dae-sook Suh, *Kim Il Sung: The North Korean Leader,* pp. 103–23; U.S. Army 500th MISG, *Full Translation of Military History in Korea,* translation date 5 September 1952, p. 48; and Institute of Internal and External Affairs, *Inside North Korea: Three Decades of Duplicity* (Seoul: July 1975), p. 84.

12. The director of the Kangdong Political Institute is believed to have been Park Byong-yul. See "Kim Il-song Said to Fear Revolt in Military," *Chugan Choson,* 2 December 1993, pp. 32–34, as cited in FBIS-EAS-94-051, 16 March 1994, pp. 21–23.

13. Seiler, *Kim Il-song 1941–1948,* pp. 64–70; and U.S. Army, *History of the North Korean Army,* pp. 8–24.

14. Sometimes translated as the Security Cadre Training Center.

15. Sometimes translated as the Security Cadre Training Battalion Headquarters. Its subordinate units are sometimes translated as Security Cadre Training Centers.

16. U.S. Army, "North Korean Guerrilla Operations," GHQ, FEC, MIS, GS, *Allied Translator and Interpreter Section, Research Supplement, Interrogation Reports* 3 (15 November 1950): 15–22. This report has an interesting contemporaneous account of "CCF" and "North Korean" methods of guerrilla warfare.

17. One of the best studies on this subject is Samuel B. Griffith, *Mao Tse-tung on Guerrilla Warfare,* (Garden City, N.Y.: Anchor Press/Doubleday, 1978).

18. Ibid., pp. 27–28.

19. U.S. Army, "Soviet Partisan Warfare," *Intelligence Review* 173 (October 1950): 13–22; U.S. Army, *The Soviet Partisan Movement 1941–1945,* Department of Army Pamphlet 20-244 (Washington, D.C.: GPO, August 1956); Matthew Cooper, *The Nazi War against Soviet Partisans: 1941–1944* (New York: Stein and Day, 1979); and I. G. Starinov, *Over the Abyss: My Life in Soviet Special Operation* (New York: Ivy Books, 1995). For an informative look at Soviet partisan doctrine see the July 1940 Soviet document issued by the Soviet North-West Front HQ entitled "Instructions Concerning the Organization and Activity of Partisan Detachments and Diversionist Groups," as cited in Cooper, *The Nazi War against Soviet Partisans,* pp. 187–88.

20. U.S. Army, "Communist Guerrillas in South Korea," *Intelligence Review* 166 (March 1950): 41–44; ibid., "The Role of Guerrillas in the Korean War," *Intelligence Review* 181 (June 1951): 17–26; and Larry E. Cable, *Conflict of Myths: The Development of American Counterinsurgency Doctrine and the Vietnam War* (New York: New York University Press, 1986), pp. 33–43; and U.S. Army 500th MISG, *Full Translation of Military History in Korea,* pp. 46–57.

21. U.S. Army, "The Role of Guerrillas in the Korean War," pp. 17–26; ibid., "North Korean Guerrilla Operations," pp. 15-22; U.S. Army, Pacific, *North Korean Army Handbook,* Special Report no. 303, ACS-G2, 1 July 1957, pp. 26–27; and Lawrence V. Schuetta, *Guerrilla Warfare and Airpower in Korea, 1950–53* (Maxwell Air Force Base, Ala.: U.S. Air Force, Aerospace Studies Institute, Concepts Division, January 1964), pp. 7–60.

22. The ROK National Police was organized in 1945, but did not expand until the

outbreak of hostilities. By August 1951 it consisted of sixty-three thousand men, as compared to forty thousand in 1945. The National Police, besides guarding fixed installations and conducting counterguerrilla activities was also assigned railroad security. Several thousand National Police were attached to U.S. Corps to control civilian population, screen indigenous personnel, and conduct counterintelligence missions.

23. The Military Section is frequently identified as the Guerrilla Guidance Section (or Bureau) in contemporary U.S. intelligence documents. This appears to be a mistake since the exact roles of this section and the Military Section were often confused. The possibility exists that both organizations were named the same to create confusion.

24. Several sources also identify a "Zennan Unit" (or Zennam Unit), but little is presently known concerning this unit. Given the time and locations of the Zennan Unit's operations it is probable that it was either part of the enlarged 766th or another title for elements of it. U.S. Army, *Enemy Tactics,* HQ EUSAK, 26 December 1951, p. 120; and U.S. Army, Pacific, *North Korean Army Handbook,* pp. 26–27.

25. Dae-sook Suh, *Kim Il Sung: The North Korean Leader,* pp. 103–4; and U.S. Army, "North Korean Guerrilla Operations," pp. 18–20; U.S. Army, *Enemy Tactics,* p. 120; and U.S. Army, "North Korean Guerrilla Operations," pp. 18–20.

26. U.S. Army, *Enemy Tactics,* p. 120; and U.S. Army, Pacific, *North Korean Army Handbook,* pp. 26–27; Dae-sook Suh, *Kim Il Sung: The North Korean Leader,* pp. 103–4; and U.S. Army, "North Korean Guerrilla Operations," pp. 18–20.

27. Dae-sook Suh, *Kim Il Sung: The North Korean Leader,* pp. 103–4. Some sources indicate that O Chin-u was the commander of the 766th, but other sources state that he was the commanding officer of the 3rd Infantry Division. Available evidence suggests that he was not the commander of the unit, but rather, as indicated in the text, commander of the school in which the unit's personnel were trained. See "Choe Kwang's Biographic Data Detailed," *Pukhan,* July 1990, pp. 102–12, as cited in FBIS-EAS-90-187, 26 September 1990, pp. 37–42.

28. U.S. Army, "North Korean Guerrilla Operations," pp. 18–20; ibid., "North Korean Fifth Infantry Division," GHQ, FEC, MIS, GS, *Allied Translator and Interpreter Section, Research Supplement, Interrogation Reports: North Korean Forces* 96 (28 February 1951): 37–45; U.S. Army 500th MISG, *Full Translation of Military History in Korea,* p. 48; U.S. Army, *History of the North Korean Army,* pp. 80–83;U.S. Army, *Handbook on the North Korean Armed Forces,* pp. 33–34; ibid., *Enemy Tactics,* p. 120; and Royce L. Thompson, *Intelligence Factors Underlying Operation Chromite of 15 September 1950,* U.S. Army OCMH, 30 January 1956, pp. 10–11.

29. One source suggests that in mid-June 1950 the Hoeryong Cadres School was ordered to concentrate its forces in the vicinity of Yangyang, and that at the time of the war these forces were designated the 766th Unit. See U.S. Army 500th MISG, *Full Translation of Military History in Korea,* p. 48. The "Zennan Unit" noted above may have been either part of the enlarged 766th or another title for elements of it.

30. U.S. Army, *Allied Translator and Interpreter Section, Research Supplement, Interrogation Reports: Documentary Evidence of North Korean Aggression,* GHQ, FEC, MIS, GS, 30 October 1950, pp. 46–48. Although U.S. intelligence documents identified the 766th as consisting of six battalions (three regular and three guerrilla), the guerrillas actually operated in distinct groups or bands (15th Guerrilla

Unit, 27th Guerrilla Unit, Nam Don Ue Guerrilla Unit, Namdo Guerrilla Unit, etc.). It appears that the U.S. use of the term "guerrilla battalion" was for convenience.

31. Although most sources indicate that the 945th landed in the wrong sector and proved ineffective, this may be incorrect. The 945th may in fact have been the unit assigned to the Pusan landing. If this is correct, then the 945th proved "ineffective" because it was sunk in transit.

32. Most intelligence reports indicate that 3rd Battalion supported the 5th Infantry Division's attack along the coast. One interrogation report suggests, however, that at least some elements of the 766th remained in the Yangyang area until 29 June and then departed by truck.

33. U.S. Army, *Documentary Evidence of North Korean Aggression,* pp. 48–50.

34. James A. Field, Jr., *History of United States Naval Operations: Korea* (Washington, D.C.: GPO, 1962), p. 51.

35. See document no. 14 in Kathryn Weathersby, "New Russian Documents on the Korean War," *Cold War International History Project Bulletin* 6–7 (winter 1995–96): 30–84.

36. U.S. Army, *History of the North Korean Army,* pp. 80–83; Weathersby, "New Russian Documents," pp. 30–84; and *Velikaya Otechestvennaya Voyna 1941–1945 gg.—Entsiklopediya* [The Great Patriotic War 1941–1945 encyclopedia] (Moscow: Izd. Sovetskaya Entsiklopediya, 1985), p. 461. Because the KPA was then closely modeled after the Soviet army the Korean term commonly translated as "Marine" in contemporary U.S. intelligence documents is more correctly translated as "naval infantry." In messages between Stalin and Kim Il-song, these units are referred to as *morskaya pekhota* ("naval infantry"). This term (naval infantry) will be used throughout this book.

37. See documents nos. 17 and 19 in Weathersby, "New Russian Documents," pp. 30–84.

38. U.S. Air Force, "Airborne Training Center in Pyongyang, North Korea," HQ 5th AF, Deputy for Intelligence, A-2, Special Activities Unit, letter dated 6 March 1951.

39. The designation 526th is believed to carry some significance. When the digits for the 526th Army Unit designation are reversed, they reportedly symbolized the date, 25 June, when hostilities commenced.

40. Pak Song-kun, "Weapons Systems of North Korea," *Kukbang Kwa Kisul,* January 1989, pp. 102–13, as cited in FBIS-EAS-89-055, 23 March 1989, pp. 10–16.

41. U.S. Army, "North Korean Army Engineers," GHQ, FEC, MIS, GS, *Allied Translator and Interpreter Section, Research Supplement, Interrogation Reports: North Korean Forces* 104 (1951): 2–40.

42. U.S. Army, *Enemy Tactics,* p. 126.

43. "1951 'Massacre' by South Forces Detailed," *Hangyore Sinmun,* 25 May 1993, p. 13, as cited in FBIS-EAS-93-109, 9 June 1993, p. 13.

44. Dae-sook Suh, *Kim Il Sung: The North Korean Leader,* pp. 128–29; and Schuetta, *Guerrilla Warfare and Airpower in Korea, 1950–53,* pp. 202–3.

45. U.S. Army, *History of the North Korean Army,* p. 26.

46. U.S. Army, *Order of Battle Handbook: Chinese Communist Forces, Korea and the North Korean Army,* HQ, FEC and EUSA, ACS-G2, 1 January 1956, maps 3 and 4.

47. U.S. Army, *Handbook on the North Korean Armed Forces,* p. 35. This source should be compared with Field, *United States Naval Operations: Korea,* pp. 416–29.

48. For a firsthand account of fighting guerrillas during the war, especially Operation Rat Killer see Paik Sun Yup, *From Pusan to Panmunjom* (New York: Brassey's, 1992).

49. Dae-sook Suh, *Kim Il Sung: The North Korean Leader,* pp. 129–30.

50. U.S. Air Force, "FEAF ECM History during the Korean Conflict," HQ FEAF, 3 May 1954, annex 25, p. 8.

51. Interview data.

52. Seiler, *Kim Il-song 1941–1948,* pp. 145–46.

53. Ibid.

54. Kim Tae-hwan, "Military Strategies of Kim Il-sung (IV)," *Vantage Point* 13 (July 1990): 1–10.

55. U.S. Army, "The Role of Guerrillas in the Korean War," p. 21; ibid., *History of the North Korean Army,* pp. 89–90; and ibid., *North Korean Army Handbook,* p. 25.

56. U.S. Army, *North Korean Army Handbook,* p. 25.

57. Ch'oe Hyon had previously been the commander of the KPA's 2nd Infantry Division. With the United Nations Command breakout from the Pusan perimeter, Ch'oe led his unit on the long withdrawal first west and then north back toward KPA lines. Although they suffered substantial casualties, during this withdrawal the 2nd Infantry Division conducted limited guerrilla warfare operations. Ch'oe and the remnants of his division successfully reached KPA lines sometime in November. Shortly afterward, he was given command of the II Corps. There is some confusion about whether his exact rank at this time was lieutenant general or major general.

58. U.S. Army, *History of the North Korean Army,* pp. 80–83; and Field, *United States Naval Operations: Korea,* pp. 423–26, 432.

59. Chung Kiwon, "The North Korean People's Army and the Party," pp. 121–22.

60. It is important to note that this demobilization was not only for economic reasons. Kim Il-song used it to separate a number of his rivals from their power bases within the KPA. See McCune, *Leadership in North Korea,* pp. 7–8.

61. Interview data; U.S. Army, *North Korean Army Handbook,* pp. 28, 73; ibid., *Handbook on the North Korean Armed Forces,* pp. 127–30; U.S. Army, Pacific, *Order of Battle: North Korean Army,* Special Report no. 325, HQ, ACS-G2, 15 January 1958, pp. v, 11; and U.S. Navy, "The Korean Fishing Season and North Korean Propaganda," *ONI Review* 14 (September 1959): 394–95.

62. "North Korean Army Agent Organizations," *Intelligence Digest* 5 (September 1955): 43–49; U.S. Army, Pacific, *Tables of Organization and Equipment of the North Korean Army,* Special Report no. 304, HQ, ACS-G2, 1 July 1957, charts 54, 57, 58; and "Narrative Biographies of DPRK Figures," *Sindong-A,* January 1995 (Supplement), pp. 210–27, as cited in FBIS-EAS-95-015-S. Contemporary U.S. intelligence documents listed Pak Song-ch'ol (also called Pak Song Chul) as major general and director of the Reconnaissance Bureau, and Major General Cho In-ch'ol as director of the Liaison Department, until at least late 1958.

63. McCune, *Leadership in North Korea,* p. 11; and U.S. Army, *Handbook on the North Korean Armed Forces,* p. 34. The National Intelligence Committee has also been identified as a "bureau." In 1955 the KPA's Political Department was described as the organization that maintained control and directed the efforts of these three organizations, with liaison meetings being held by the Political Department to formulate policies. It is presently unclear whether this was incorrect or whether this

organization, or these responsibilities, evolved into the National Intelligence Committee or Cabinet General Intelligence Bureau by the early 1960s. See "North Korean Army Agent Organizations," pp. 43–49.

64. McCune, *Leadership in North Korea,* p. 11. There is still some question whether the Cabinet General Intelligence Bureau was organizationally subordinate to the KWP Central Committee.

65. U.S. Army, *Handbook on the North Korean Armed Forces,* pp. 7–8.

66. Ibid., p. 44; "North Korean Army Agent Organizations," pp. 43–49; and U.S. Army, Pacific, *Tables of Organization and Equipment of the North Korean Army,* charts 54, 57, 58.

67. U.S. Army, *Handbook on the North Korean Armed Forces,* pp. 7–8; "North Korean Army Agent Organizations," pp. 43–49; and U.S. Army, Pacific, *Tables of Organization and Equipment of the North Korean Army,* charts 54, 57, 58.

68. U.S. Army, *Handbook on the North Korean Armed Forces,* pp. 7–8; "North Korean Army Agent Organizations," pp. 43–49; and U.S. Army, Pacific, *Tables of Organization and Equipment of the North Korean Army,* charts 54, 57, 58.

69. U.S. Army, *Handbook on the North Korean Armed Forces,* p. 44; "North Korean Army Agent Organizations," pp. 43–49; and U.S. Army, Pacific, *Tables of Organization and Equipment of the North Korean Army,* charts 54, 57, 58.

70. U.S. Army, *Handbook on the North Korean Armed Forces,* pp. 7–8, 45.

71. "GUNJI KENKYU Looks at Training, Objectives for Spies in North Korea," *Gunji Kenkyu,* April 1988, pp. 98–106.

72. Chung-in Moon, "Between Ideology and Interest: North Korea in the Middle East," in Jae Kyu Park, Byung Chul Koh, and Tae-Hwan Kwak, *The Foreign Relations of North Korea* (Boulder, Colo.: Westview Press, 1987), p. 390.

73. This event is now honored as "the April 19 Revolution."

Chapter 3
GUERRILLA WARFARE AGAINST THE ROK, 1962–68

1. Interview data; Dae-sook Suh, *Kim Il Sung: The North Korean Leader,* pp. 211–31; Han Sung-joo, "North Korea's Security Policy and Military Strategy," in *North Korea Today: Strategic and Domestic Issues,* ed. Robert A. Scalapino and Kim Jun-yop (Berkeley: University of California, 1983), pp. 144–63.

2. U.S. Department of State, "Arms Suspension: A Big Stick or a Weak Reed," INR-22, 12 November 1969; U.S. Defense Intelligence Agency, "North Korean Armed Forces Modernization," *Defense Intelligence Digest,* December 1968, p. 15; U.S. Defense Intelligence Agency, "North Korea, the USSR, Communist China: Operation Tightrope," *Defense Intelligence Digest,* September 1968, pp. 37–40; and U.S. Defense Intelligence Agency, "USSR Continues Military Aid to North Korea," *Defense Intelligence Digest,* June 1963, pp. 42–43.

3. It is unclear exactly when the South Korea General Bureau was established. At present it would appear that this occurred sometime after September 1961, when Yi was appointed to head this organization. Yi is sometimes identified as Yi Hyo-san. The title "director" is used here for convenience, although it might more correctly be "general secretary."

4. "Biographic Information on One Hundred Officials," *Wolkan Kyonghyang,* January 1989, pp. 12–89.

5. Institute of Internal and External Affairs, *Inside North Korea: Three Decades of Duplicity,* pp. 43–45.

6. The primary ROKA units sent to the republic of Vietnam included the "Capital Division," which arrived 29 September 1965 and departed 10 March 1973; the Ninth Infantry Division, which arrived 27 September 1966 and departed 16 March 1973; and the Second Marine Brigade, which arrived 19 October 1965 and departed February 1972. See Shelby L. Stanton, *Vietnam Order of Battle* (Washington, D.C.: U.S. News Books, 1981), pp. 272–73; and Stanley R. Larsen and James L. Collins, Jr., *Vietnam Studies: Allied Participation in Vietnam* (Washington, D.C.: GPO, 1975), pp. 120–59.

7. Han Sung-joo, "North Korea's Security Policy and Military Strategy," 155–56.

8. "South Army Official Looks at DPRK's Weapons," *Kukbang Kwa Kisul,* January 1989, pp. 102–13, as cited in FBIS-EAS-89-055, 23 March 1989, pp. 10–16.

9. Jack Raymond, "North Korea Jets Attack U.S. Plane," *New York Times,* 29 April 1965; and Robert S. Hopkins III, "Close Call for an RB-47H," *Journal of Military Aviation,* May–June 1992, pp. 44–45.

10. "Escape From the Jaws of Death (I)," *Vantage Point* 10 (May 1987): 11–15.

11. Interview data; Dae-sook Suh, *Kim Il Sung: The North Korean Leader,* pp. 211–31; and North Korean Affairs Institute, *Brief History of North Korean Provocations against South Korea: 1945–1977* (Seoul: October 1977), pp. 30–32.

12. Manabu Aota, *Kim Il Sung's Army.* Contemporary Affairs Series, no. 286 (Tokyo: Nyumon Shinsho, 1979), p. 42.

13. "Article Examines KPA's Formation," *Naewoe Tongsin,* no. 688, 20 April 1990, pp. 1A–5A, as cited in FBIS-EAS-90-149, 2 August 1990, pp. 26–27.

14. One source suggests that this purge began in March 1967 during the secret Fourteenth Plenum of the Fifth Party Congress. Here, O Chin-u led the purge of KWP officials, including Yi Hyo-sun, Pak Kum-ch'ol, Han Sang-tu, and Kim To-man. O Chin-u was soon promoted to general and assumed the position of director of the General Political Bureau. See "Monthly Examines Political Hierarchy in the DPRK Following the Ninth Supreme People's Assembly Elections," *Wolgan Choson,* July 1990, pp. 214–27.

15. Dae-sook Suh, *Kim Il Sung: The North Korean Leader,* pp. 230–31.

16. Kim Il-sung, *Selected Works.* P'yongyang: Foreign Language Publishing House, 1965, pp. 540–45.

17. Interview data; U.S. Defense Intelligence Agency, "North Korean Army Training Steadily Progressing," *Defense Intelligence Digest,* June 1968, pp. 29–31; U.S. Defense Intelligence Agency, "North Korean Infiltration Raises Specter of Insurgency," *Defense Intelligence Digest,* January 1968, p. 6; U.S. Defense Intelligence Agency, "USSR Continues Military Aid to North Korea," pp. 42–43; Manabu Aota, *Kim Il Sung's Army,* p. 64; Institute of Internal and External Affairs, *Inside North Korea: Three Decades of Duplicity,* p. 43–45; John G. Hubbell and David Reed, "Mission: To Murder a President," *Reader's Digest,* July 1968, pp. 142–47; U.S. Department of Defense, *Military Assistance Reappraisal: FY 1967–71,* 1 (June 1965): iv–18, and annex 12: 4–7; and U.S. Defense Intelligence Agency, *North Korean Armed Forces Handbook (U),* DIA-210-11-1-71-INT, January 1971, pp. 119–46. Clearly the best study of the ROK/U.S. perspective of the fighting during

this period is Daniel P. Bolger, *Scenes from an Unfinished War: Low-Intensity Conflict in Korea, 1966–1969,* Leavenworth Papers no. 19 (Fort Leavenworth, Kan.: Combat Studies Institute, 1991).

18. Interview data. One report suggests that by the end of 1965, KPA special warfare forces had expanded to twelve regiment- or brigade-sized units. This, however, appears to be incorrect. Not until the late 1970s would such levels be attained. Association of the U.S. Army, *Special Report. The Search for Peace: A Year End Assessment, 1985* (Washington, D.C.: GPO, 1985), pp. 39–40.

19. Interview data; U.S. Defense Intelligence Agency, *North Korean Armed Forces Handbook (U),* January 1971, pp. 119–46; and Institute of Internal and External Affairs, *Inside North Korea: Three Decades of Duplicity,* pp. 43–45.

20. "South Korea Says It Destroyed Band of Northern Agents," *New York Times,* 14 September 1969.

21. "North Korean Terrorism History," *Hanguk Ilbo,* 10 July 1985, p. 4, as cited in JPRS-KAR-85-007, 24 December 1985, pp. 3–4.

22. "Biographic Information on One Hundred Officials," p. 21.

23. This school may also have been called the Reunification University.

24. During this period, there is also mention of another school, the Liberation Training School under the command of Gen. Ch'oe Hyon, who was later to be appointed minister of National Defense. Whether this was another name for the 695th Army Unit or another school is presently unclear. "Korea Reds Shift Military Leaders," *New York Times,* 22 March 1969.

25. Interview data; and U.S. Defense Intelligence Agency, *North Korean Armed Forces Handbook (U),* January 1971, pp. 119–46.

26. Interview data; and U.S. Defense Intelligence Agency, *North Korean Armed Forces Handbook (U),* pp. 119–46.

27. See Bolger, *Scenes from an Unfinished War,* pp. 137–40, for a comprehensive listing of incidents.

28. "Testing by Reds Presumed," *New York Times,* 14 September 1967; and "New Tactics Laid to North Korea," *New York Times,* 14 September 1967.

29. Interview data; Richard Sharpe, *Jane's Fighting Ships 1996–1997* (London: Jane's Information Group, 1996), p. 397, and *Jane's Fighting Ships 1990–1991,* p. 356.

30. In comparison, a regular KPA infantry regiment had a strength of 1,960 and consisted of three infantry battalions (470 men each) and a full complement of combat and service support units.

31. There is a distinct possibility that the number of transport aircraft in the KPAF was higher then the figure presented here and that they included a number of Il-14 Crate transports. Given the most favorable estimates, however, the total KPAF air lift capability could not have exceeded 900. See interview data; U.S. Defense Intelligence Agency, "North Korean Army Training Steadily Progressing," pp. 29–31; U.S. Department of Defense, *Military Assistance Reappraisal: FY 1967–71,* annex 12: 4–7; U.S. Defense Intelligence Agency, "USSR Continues Military Aid to North Korea," pp. 42–43; and Manabu Aota, *Kim Il Sung's Army,* p. 64.

32. The exact evolution of the unit(s) utilizing the designation 283rd Army Unit is presently unclear. What is presented here is the best account based on available information. Both the 124th and 283rd Army Units are frequently identified as "Guerrilla Unit," "Independent Unit," or simply "Unit."

33. At least one source indicates that the 124th Army Unit was established in March 1967. See Hubbell and Reed, "Mission: To Murder a President," pp. 142–47.

34. Ibid.

35. Interview data; and U.S. Defense Intelligence Agency, *North Korean Armed Forces Handbook (U),* January 1971, pp. 18, 35, 67.

36. Interview data. The Foreign Language College should not be confused with the prestigious, yet civilian, P'yongyang Foreign Language University.

37. Interview data; and "English, Japanese Study Given Preference," *Naewoe Tongsin,* 6 May 1993, pp. C1–C4, as cited in FBIS-EAS-93-145, 30 July 1993, p. 22.

38. See the following articles by the U.S. Defense Intelligence Agency: "United Nations POW/MIA Sightings in North Korea (U)," IIR 2 221 0070 92, 31 December 1991; "Reports of Three Former U.S. Prisoners of War Remaining in KN (U)," IIR 2 221 00187 89, 6 July 1989; and "Rumors of U.S. Prisoners of War Teaching English in KN (U), IIR 2 221 0050 89, 2 February 1989.

39. Interview data; U.S. Department of Defense, *Military Assistance Reappraisal: FY 1967–71* 1 (June 1965): iv–18, and annex 12: 4–7; and U.S. Defense Intelligence Agency, *North Korean Armed Forces Handbook (U),* January 1971, pp. 119–46.

40. The possibility exists that light infantry regiments were only established within the army groups deployed along the DMZ.

41. Interview data; U.S. Defense Intelligence Agency, *North Korean Armed Forces Handbook (U),* January 1971, pp. 119–46; Hubbell and Reed, "Mission: To Murder a President," pp. 142–47; and Choi Young, "The North Korean Military: Buildup and Its Impact on North Korean Military Strategy in the 1980s," *Asian Survey* 25 (3 March 1985): 345.

42. It is interesting to note that Lt. Gen. Kim Chung-tae was reportedly the chief intelligence officer for the Ministry of Public Security.

43. Hubbell and Reed, "Mission: To Murder a President," p. 143.

44. These two provinces, especially Kangwon-do, were areas that witnessed significant guerrilla activity during the Fatherland Liberation War.

45. Kim Shin-jo, the one KPA soldier who was captured, was eventually pardoned for his role in the assassination plot. He took up residence in Seoul, where he married, had two children, and became a deacon of his church. See Peter Maas, "Agent Wins Sympathy in S. Korea," *Washington Post,* 25 January 1988.

46. Hubbell and Reed, "Mission: To Murder a President," p. 147.

47. Since its capture the USS *Pueblo* has remained anchored in the port of Wonsan. It is now a tourist attraction.

48. North Korean Affairs Institute, *Brief History of North Korean Provocations against South Korea: 1945–1977,* p. 63.

49. Interview data; U.S. Defense Intelligence Agency, *North Korean Armed Forces Handbook (U),* January 1971, pp. 119–46; North Korean Affairs Institute, *Brief History of North Korean Provocations against South Korea: 1945–1977,* pp. 36–37; Peter Grose, "U.S. Officials Find North Korean Moves Ominous," *New York Times,* 9 January 1969; Bernard Krisher, "A Soldier's Story," *Newsweek,* 30 December 1968, pp. 33–34; Manabu Aota, *Kim Il Sung's Army,* pp. 43–44; U.S. Defense Intelligence Agency, "North Korean Infiltration Raises Specter of Insurgency," p. 6; and Bradley Hahn, "North Korean Navy: Strong and Getting Bolder," U.S. Naval Institute *Proceedings* 108 (July 1982): 113.

50. Interview data; "North Korean Terrorism History," *Hanguk Ilbo,* 10 July 1985, p. 4, as cited in JPRS-KAR-85-007, 24 December 1985, p. 3–4; "Korea Reds Shift Military Leaders," *New York Times,* 22 March 1969.

Chapter 4
THE VIII SPECIAL CORPS, 1969–89

1. Dae-sook Suh, *Kim Il Sung: The North Korean Leader,* pp. 238–42; "Monthly Examines Political Hierarchy in the DPRK Following the Ninth Supreme People's Assembly Elections," pp. 214–27; U.S. Defense Intelligence Agency, *North Korean Armed Forces Handbook (U),* DDI-2680-37-77, July 1977, pp. 6-1 to 6-8; Richard Halloran, "Pyongyang Shift in Tactics Is Seen," *New York Times,* 11 November 1969; and Takashi Oka, "North Korea Held to Shift Tactics," *New York Times,* 21 September 1969.

2. It is interesting to note that both Kim Ch'ang-bong (also called Kim Chang-pong) and Ho Pong-hak had been O Chin-u's seniors during the partisan years and World War II.

3. This quote has been variously translated as "separate light infantry division," "separate light infantry corps," and "separate light infantry forces." It would seem from the context of his speech that Kim was referring to a class of units rather than a specific unit, although he probably had the future VIII Special Corps in mind when he gave this speech. See Pak Song-kun, "Weapons Systems of North Korea," pp. 10–16.

4. Ibid.

5. Kim Chung-nin (also called Kim Chung-rin, Kim Chung-nim, Kim Jung-rin, and Kim Jung-nin) would be the KWP's SICARO intermittently for the next twenty years. Several sources suggest that Kim became SICARO (then known as the South Korea General Bureau) in 1967, but this is incorrect. This may have been when he was appointed director of the Culture Department. See "Kim Chung-nin's Background Detailed," *Pukhan,* January 1992, pp. 91–100, as cited in FBIS-EAS-92-050, 13 March 1992, pp. 21–27. Another source indicates that there have only been six persons who have held this position until 1995: Yi Hyo-sun, Ho Pong-hak, Yu Chang-sik, Kim Chung-nin, Yun Ki-pok, and Kim Yong-sun. The implication here is that Yu Chang-sik preceded Kim Chung-nin. This confusion has yet to be resolved. See "Article Criticizes Kato's Ties to DPRK," *Bungei Shunju,* 10 December 1995, pp. 116–27, as cited in FBIS-EAS-95-238.

6. Interview data; and "Chronology of Purges by Kim Il-song," *Vantage Point* 17 (July 1994): 34–36. The latter source indicates that Kim Kwang-hyop and Sok San were purged in January 1971.

7. Philip Shabecoff, "Twenty Years after War's Outbreak, Korea Still Knows No Real Peace," *New York Times,* 24 June 1970; and Takashi Oka, "North Korea Held to Shift Tactics."

8. Interview data; and Ki-taek Li, "Soviet Military Policy in the Far East and Its Impact of North Korea (II)," *Vantage Point* 12 (May 1989): 7.

9. "Koreans Sink a Boat with Red Infiltrators," *New York Times,* 8 June 1969.

10. "South Korea Says It Destroyed Band of Northern Agents," p. 11; and "Six North Koreans Killed," *New York Times,* 17 September 1969.

11. "A South Korean Destroyer Sinks Spy Boat after Chase," *New York Times,* 25 September 1969.

12. Republic of Korea, *A White Paper on the South–North Dialogue in Korea* (Seoul: National Unification Board, 1982), p. 411.

13. "North Korea on Alert for Any Retaliation," *New York Times,* 16 April 1969; William Beechem, "Nixon Declares U.S. Will Protect Planes off Korea," *New York Times,* 19 April 1969; "A Lesson in the Limits of Power," *Time,* 25 April 1969, 15–16; "The Spy Plane: What They Do and Why," *Time,* 25 April 1969; Cecil Brownlow, "Korea Assignment Strains Carrier Force," *Aviation Week and Space Technology,* 28 April 1969, 18; and Don C. East, "A History of U.S. Navy Fleet Air Reconnaissance: Part I, The Pacific and VQ-1," *Hook,* spring 1987, p. 30.

14. Dae-sook Suh, *Kim Il Sung: The North Korean Leader,* pp. 238–39.

15. U.S. Defense Intelligence Agency, "Korean DMZ: The Challenge of Making It Work," *Defense Intelligence Digest,* July 1969, pp. 12–14.

16. Choi Young, "The North Korean Military," p. 345.

17. Interview data.

18. Manabu Aota, *Kim Il Sung's Army,* p. 43.

19. Ibid., pp. 43–44.

20. Interview data; "Kim Chung-nin's Background Detailed," pp. 21–27; U.S. Defense Intelligence Agency, *North Korean Armed Forces Handbook (U),* July 1977, pp. 6-1 to 6-8; and U.S. Defense Intelligence Agency, *North Korean Armed Forces Handbook (U),* January 1971, pp. 119–46; Han Sung-joo, "North Korea's Security Policy and Military Strategy," p. 157; Manabu Aota, *Kim Il Sung's Army,* pp. 43–44; "Pyongyang Chief Solidifies Rule," *New York Times,* 22 November 1970; "Korea Reds Shift Military Leaders;" and Takashi Oka, "North Korea Held to Shift Tactics."

21. "Kim Il-sung, a Soviet Agent, Turns into 'Great Leader,'" *Vantage Point* 18 (October 1995): 8; and Huh Moon-young, "North Korea's Foreign Policy in Transition," *Vantage Point* 17 (July 1994): 21–29.

22. During the 1960s Chong Kyong-hui was an intelligence operative and successfully conducted operations in Tokyo and Seoul. As a reward for her excellent service she was appointed to full membership in the Central Committee in November 1970. See "Biographic Information on One Hundred Officials," p. 38.

23. "DPRK Intelligence Operations in Japan Viewed," *Foresight,* December 1995, p. 28, as cited in FBIS-EAS-96-053.

24. "Biographic Information on One Hundred Officials," pp. 12–89, as cited in FBIS-EAS-89-189-S, 21 September 1989, p. 24.

25. "Biographic Information on One Hundred Officials," p. 36.

26. For example, the purge of the partisan generals and the reorganization of the Ministry of Public Security coincided with the deactivation of the paramiltary force known as the Guerrilla Training Units, a force of some sixteen thousand KPA veterans organized to defend the DPRK in the event of war. They trained in partisan warfare tactics for fifteen days a month and farmed for the remainder of the month. These units had been strongly supported by the partisan generals. Kim Il-song apparently believed that they could be used in a coup attempt against him.

27. The State Security Department is also known as the Political Security Department and the State Political Security Department. See interview data; "North Korea as Subcontractor," *Early Warning* 4 (August 1986): 14; U.S. Army, *North Korea: A Country Study,* Department of the Army Pamphlet 550-81, 1976, pp. 212–13.

28. The 283rd Army Unit was possibly disbanded prior to this.

29. Interview data; Sharpe, *Jane's Fighting Ships 1996–1997,* p. 397, and *Jane's Fighting Ships 1990–1991,* p. 356.

30. Interview data.

31. Interview data.

32. "Profile on Defecting North Officer," *Yonhap,* 13 October 1995, as cited in FBIS-EAS-95-198.

33. See the following articles by the U.S. Defense Intelligence Agency: "United Nations POW/MIA Sightings in North Korea (U)," IIR 2 221 0070 92, 31 December 1991; and "Reports of Three Former U.S. Prisoners of War Remaining in KN (U)," IIR 2 221 00187 89, 6 July 1989; and "Rumors of U.S. Prisoners of War Teaching English in KN (U), IIR 2 221 0050 89, 2 February 1989.

34. "Direct action" operations are primarily concerned with the assassination or abduction of enemy personnel and occur during both peace and wartime.

35. During this period the 17th Reconnaissance Brigade was sometimes referred to as either the 17th Airborne Reconnaissance Brigade, or 17th Airborne Brigade.

36. "North Korea—Body Snatchers," Associated Press, 9 August 1994.

37. Public estimates for special purpose force personnel strength and composition vary considerably and simply cannot be reconciled with each other or declassified estimates. Whenever possible, declassified U.S. intelligence numbers are used in the text. See interview data; U.S. Defense Intelligence Agency, *North Korean Special Purpose Forces,* p. 2; United Nations Command, U.S. Forces Korea, and Eighth U.S. Army, *1976 Annual Historical Report,* HIST-S-77-6, 1977, p. 51; U.S. Defense Intelligence Agency, *North Korean Armed Forces Handbook (U),* July 1977, pp. 2-4 to 2-6; Institute of Internal and External Affairs, *Inside North Korea: Three Decades of Duplicity,* pp. 73–74; and "Why Korea Is Scared," *Foreign Report,* no. 1666, 4 February 1981, pp. 2–4.

38. "Stronger North Korea Force Seen," *Army Times,* 20 March 1978, p. 26; and "North Korean Commandos Cause Pentagon Concern," *Army Times,* 5 March 1979, p. 8.

39. "Biographic Information on One Hundred Officials," p. 43.

40. This information is based heavily upon interviews with KPA defectors. ROK and U.S. intelligence did not accept three airborne brigades in KPA order of battle until the early 1980s. See United Nations Command, U.S. Forces Korea, and Eighth U.S. Army, *1976 Annual Historical Report,* p. 36, which credits the KPA with having five airborne battalions totaling four thousand troops at this time.

41. These figures are taken from U.S. Defense Intelligence Agency, *North Korean Armed Forces Handbook (U),* July 1977, p. 4-3. A second source, United Nations Command, U.S. Forces Korea, and Eighth U.S. Army, *1976 Annual Historical Report,* p. 36, agrees with the number of helicopters, but indicates a total of 276 transports instead of 233, with a lift capacity of 4,300 troops.

42. For an interesting discussion of the Untied Nations Command difficulties in countering KPAF nuisance raids during the Fatherland Liberation War, see Mike O'Conner, "Coping with Charlie," *Journal of the American Aviation Historical Society* 30 (spring 1985): 2–11; U.S. Navy, "Enemy Light Plane Raids in Korea," *ONI Review* 8 (August 1953): 378–79; and U.S. Navy, "Korea (North Korea): Notes from a North Korean Defector," *ONI Review* 10 (November 1955): 606.

43. Interview data; William J. Williams, "'Bedcheck Charlie' and the An-2," *Air Power History,* winter 1996, pp. 4–13; and Pak Song-kun, "Weapons Systems of North Korea," pp. 10–16.

44. Piotr Butowski, "How to Replace the An-2?" *AIR International,* October 1996; and Georg Mader, "Hrvatske Zrance Snage," *World Air Power Journal* 24 (spring 1996): 140–47.

45. Butowski, "How to Replace the An-2?"; and Mader, "Hrvatske Zrance Snage," 140–47. A KPA defector who was a sergeant in the 38th Airborne Brigade told the author in 1996 that in KPAF service the An-2 carries eight troops and the Li-2 carries sixteen troops.

46. Interview data.

47. Manabu Aota, *Kim Il Sung's Army,* p. 62.

48. Interview data.

49. U.S. Defense Intelligence Agency, "North Korean Navy: Compact, Capable, Growing," *Defense Intelligence Digest,* November 1971, p. 5.

50. Interview data; United Nations Command, U.S. Forces Korea, and Eighth U.S. Army, *1976 Annual Historical Report,* p. 37; U.S. Defense Intelligence Agency, *Unclassified Communist Naval Orders of Battle,* DDB-1200-124-81, May 1981, pp. 17–18, and *Unclassified Communist Naval Orders of Battle,* DDB-1200-124B-82, November 1982, pp. 19–20.

51. Republic of Korea, *A White Paper on the South–North Dialogue in Korea,* pp. 411–17.

52. United Nations Command, U.S. Forces Korea, and Eighth U.S. Army, *1976 Annual Historical Report,* pp. 5–53.

53. Interview data; "Two Korean Red Agents Killed on Peak Near Seoul Airport," *New York Times,* 8 July 1970; "Park Terms U.S. Troops Vital to the Security of South Korea," *New York Times,* 24 June 1970; "A Korean Red Agent Dies in Seoul Blast," *New York Times,* 23 June 1970.

54. Interview data; "Chongryon, P'yongyang's Advance Guard in Japan," in *Some Facts about North Korea* (Seoul: Naewoe Press, 1984), pp. 90–93; and the following articles by Richard Halloran, "Seoul President Escapes Assassin," *New York Times,* 15 August 1974, "Assassin's Bullet Kills Mrs. Park," *New York Times,* 16 August 1974, "Seoul Connects Suspect to Communists," *New York Times,* 17 August 1974, "Seoul Says North Ordered Park Slain," *New York Times,* 18 August 1974, "Charge by Seoul Irks North Korea," *New York Times,* 29 August 1974, 7; and "South Koreans Open Trial of Man Held for Attempt on Park," *New York Times,* 8 October 1974.

55. One result of Mun's smuggling the pistol into the country was a national program of heightened security at airports and ports.

56. Readers are cautioned that the details of Kim Chung-nin's career are shrouded in considerable confusion. What is presented here is an attempt to sort through this confusion and to tie it into contemporary events. For further details (and confusion) see "Kim Chung-nin's Background Detailed," pp. 91–100; "Narrative Biographies of DPRK Figures," *Sindong-A,* January 1995 (supplement), pp. 210–78, as cited in FBIS-EAS-95-015-S, 24 January 1995, pp. 1–36; "Biographic Information on One Hundred Officials," *Wolkan Kyonghyang,* January 1989, pp. 12 and following, as cited in FBIS-EAS-89-182-S, 21 September 1989, pp. 1–51; and "Article Criticizes Kato's Ties to DPRK," pp. 116–27.

57. Interview data.

58. There is some speculation that the National Intelligence Committee had by this time been disbanded and replaced by a more informal grouping of senior power holders. Until this is confirmed this book assumes that it is still functioning.

59. Interview data; and Kin Motoyoshi, "Political Structures," *Gungi Kenkyu,* March 1986, as cited in JPRS-KAR-86-045, 23 October 1986, pp. 1–13.

60. "North Ministry of Armed Forces Said 'Downgraded,'" *Chosen Ilbo,* 23 March 1995, p. 2, as cited in FBIS-EAS-95-056; "State Administration Council Powers Said Expanded," *Nihon Keizai Shimbun,* 23 March 1995, p. 8, as cited in FBIS-EAS-95-057; Chong Sang-yong, "Resurgence of the First-Generation Revolutionaries and Choe Kwang," *Pukhan,* July 1990, pp. 102–12, as cited in FBIS-EAS-90-187, 26 September 1990, pp. 37–42; and "Comparison with NPRK," *Seoul Sinmun,* 30 December 1989, p. 3, as cited in FBIS-EAS-89-027, 10 February 1989, pp. 23–24.

61. Interview data; and U.S. Defense Intelligence Agency, *Ocean-Going KN Vessels and Other Information,* Intelligence Information Report, September 1988.

62. "Biographic Information on One Hundred Officials," *Wolkan Kyonghyang,* January 1989, pp. 12–89, as cited in FBIS-EAS-89-189-S, 21 September 1989, p. 24.

63. "International News: Korea," United Press International, 14 December 1983.

64. "International News: North Korea—Olympics," Associated Press, 12 October 1989.

65. Interview data; and U.S. Navy, *Cluster Osprey (U),* Naval Intelligence Support Center, NIC-1223X-002-85, August 1985.

66. The Information Bureau may be the same organization that has been previously identified as the "Fourth Bureau" of the State Security Department.

67. "Former North Korean Agent Discloses DPRK's Spy Activities," *Mainichi Shimbun,* 9 May 1996, p. 6, as cited in FBIS-EAS-96-093.

68. Interview data.

69. Interview data; and "English, Japanese Study Given Preference," *Naewoe Tongsin,* 6 May 1993, pp. C1–C4, as cited in FBIS-EAS-93-145, 30 July 1993, p. 22.

70. During this period, the Reconnaissance Bureau reportedly had a subordinate unit identified as the 595th Army Unit or 595th Unit. The organization and mission of this unit is currently unknown. It is possible that this designation was actually for a component of the Reconnaissance Bureau already identified. Interview data; and Kin Motoyoshi, "Kim Chong-il's Army," *Gungi Kenkyu,* April 1986; as cited in JPRS-KAR-86-045, 23 October 1986, pp. 14-24.

71. Ibid.

72. "Daily Profiles Head of DPRK Reconnaissance Bureau," *Choson Ilbo,* 26 September 1996, p. 3, as cited in FBIS-EAS-96-188.

73. U.S. Defense Intelligence Agency, *North Korean Special Purpose Forces,* p. 2.

74. "Weekly Details DPRK Special Operations Forces," *Sisa Journal,* 19 September 1996, pp. 56–58, as cited in FBIS-EAS-96-181.

75. Interview data.

76. PZL has produced several armed versions of the Mi-2, including the Mi-2T, which is used by their special operation forces. See Paul Beaver, "Equipment: Mi-2 Armed—and Ready," *Jane's Soviet Intelligence Review* 1 (February 1989): 76–77. In December 1986 there were reports that the DPRK had concluded an agreement to purchase helicopters from Hungary, although the number and type are unknown.

See "North Korea to Import Hungarian Helicopters," *North Korea News,* no. 351, 8 December 1986, p. 4.

77. "North Military Personnel, Arms Double in Decade," *Korea Herald,* 27 July 1985, pp. 1–2; as cited in JPRS-KAR-85-059, 30 August 1985, pp. 7–8.

78. Interview data; and "Special Force Formed in DPRK with U.S. Helicopters," *Kyonghyang Sinmun,* 24 March 1986, p. 1; as cited in JPRS-KAR-86-015, 14 April 1986, p. 5.

79. Interview data; and Jack Anderson, "N. Korea Penetrates S. Korean Airspace with U.S. Choppers," *Newsday,* 29 April 1985, 54.

80. Aviation Advisory Service, *International Air Force and Military Aircraft Directory* (London: Aviation Advisory Service, 1987), pp. 181–82; and Institute for Strategic Studies, *The Military Balance: 1987–88* (London: Jane's Publishing Company, 1987).

81. Jon Lake, "Mil Mi-24 'Hind' Variant Briefing," *World Air Power Journal* 18 (autumn 1994): 110–35.

82. Interview data.

83. The reasons for this reorganization are uncertain. However, some evidence suggests that the KPA was not satisfied with its mechanization program. One of the primary reasons for this dissatisfaction was the inability of the division-level staffs to adequately handle the increased responsibilities of mechanized operations.

84. This may refer to the possibility that light infantry brigades within the Rear Area Corps may have had one or two fewer organic battalions than those within the Forward Area Corps.

85. Interview data; and U.S. Defense Intelligence Agency, *North Korean Special Purpose Forces,* p. 2.

86. Interview data.

87. Bradley Hahn, "The Democratic People's Republic of Korea: Maritime Power," *Combat Craft,* January/February 1985, 10–19.

88. Ibid.; Sharpe, *Jane's Fighting Ships 1989–1990;* and Sharpe, *Jane's Fighting Ships 1990–1991.*

89. Interview data; United Nations Command, U.S. Forces Korea, and Eighth U.S. Army, *1983 Annual Historical Report,* 1984, p. 27; and Paul Shin, "International News: Boat," United Press International, 7 August 1983.

90. Ibid.

91. Interview data; and James Kim, "International News: Korea," United Press International, 13 August 1983.

92. Interview data; and "DPRK Blamed for U.S. Cultural Center Bombing," *Korea Times,* 13 October 1989, as cited in FBIS-EAS- 89-179, 13 October 1989, p. 26.

93. Interview data; "International News: Korea," United Press International, 14 December 1983; and James Kim, "International News: Korea," United Press International, 3 December 1983.

94. The parent unit for the team had recently received the "Red Flag of Three Revolutions" award. This may have been the 62nd Sniper Brigade. During 1995 a DPRK defector stated that the personnel dispatched to Rangoon were from the "Ch'ongjin Liaison Office of the Department of Operations." See "Articles by Defector Kang Myong-to Reported: ROK-Watching Spy Agencies, Activities," part 8 of 12, *Chungang Ilbo,* 28 April 1995, p. 3, as cited in FBIS-EAS-95-097.

95. The "Aung San Martyrs' Mausoleum" honors seven Burmese leaders assassinated just before Burma gained independence from Britain in 1947.

96. The mausoleum was frequently used for such purposes by young Burmese couples due to the privacy it offered.

97. ROK investigators flown into Rangoon said the three bombs were similar to equipment captured from DPRK agents attempting to infiltrate the ROK. Other equipment recovered from the commandos included a compact radio transmitter, a silencer-equipped pistol, a remote-control device, and batteries. The silencer-equipped Browning pistols were later identified by Interpol as being part of a hundred-gun lot that was sold to a DPRK trading company.

98. "Former North Korean Commando Executed in Burma," in *Some Useful Clues for Understanding North Korea* (Seoul: Naewoe Press, 1986), pp. 111–12.

99. Readers are cautioned that there is considerable confusion concerning the details of Kim Chung-nin's career. Likewise there is confusion about when Ho Tam assumed the position of SICARO and the details of his involvement in anti-ROK operations. See "Kim Chung-nin's Background Detailed," *Pukhan,* January 1992, pp. 91–100; "Monthly Examines Political Hierarchy in the DPRK Following the Ninth Supreme People's Assembly Elections," pp. 214–27; Nam-shik Kim, "The Changing Power Hierarchy of North Korea Since the Sixth KWP Congress (I)," *Vantage Point* 10 (February 1989): 7, 9; and "Chon Byong-ho Promoted to Regular Workers' Party Politburo Membership," *North Korea News,* 12 December 1988.

100. Interview data; James Kim, "International News: Korea," United Press International, 25 September 1984; and "International News: Korea—Agent," Associated Press, 24 September 1984.

101. Interview data; and "International News: South Korea—Spy," Associated Press, 19 October 1984.

102. "Kim Chung-nin's Background Detailed," *Pukhan,* January 1992, pp. 91–100.

103. Interview data; James Kim, "International News: Explosion," United Press International, 15 September 1986; and James Shin, "International News: Explosion," United Press International, 14 September 1986.

104. There are many sources of information concerning the destruction of Korean Airlines flight 858. The best by far (despite some internal inconsistencies) is the official Korean Central Intelligence Agency statement, which was later released as Korean Overseas Information Service, *Investigation Findings: Explosion of Korean Air Flight 858,* January 1988. The brief account presented here is based primarily upon that report and supplemented by interview data. Kim Hyon-hui subsequently wrote a personnal account of her life and this operation. See Hyun Hee Kim, *The Tears of My Soul* (New York: William Morrow and Company, 1993).

105. Korean Overseas Information Service, *Investigation Findings;* and Hyun Hee Kim, *The Tears of My Soul.*

106. The cyanide capsules were later identified as chemically identical to those found on DPRK agents captured in earlier incidents.

107. "Sigur Says DPRK Admits KAL Incident," *Hanguk Ilbo,* 1 November 1989, as cited in FBIS-EAS-89-210, 1 November 1989, p. 25.

108. "Court Upholds Death Sentence for Terrorist," *Yonhap,* 22 July 1989, as cited in FBIS-EAS-89-156, 15 August 1989, p. 41; and "KAL Bomber Receives

Death Sentence," *Yonhap,* 25 April 1989, as cited in FBIS-EAS-89-078, 25 April 1989, p. 34.

109. Terril Jones, "International News: North Korea—Olympics," Associated Press, 5 September 1988.

110. "International News: North Korea—Olympics," Associated Press, 12 October 1989.

111. "Kim Chung-nin's Background Detailed," *Pukhan,* January 1992, pp. 91–100.

112. Interview data; Maxine Pollack, "The Selling of Terrorism: Profit from a Lucrative Export," *Insight,* 20 July 1987, pp. 30–31; "North Korean Terrorism History," pp. 3–4; "Special Housing Area in Pyongyang for Foreign Guerrillas," *Vantage Point* 6 (May 1983): 18–19; and "Data on North Korea's Terrorism Exports," *Kunkje Munge,* September 1983, pp. 123–33.

113. James LeMoyne, "The Guerrilla Network," *New York Times,* 6 April 1986, section 6.

114. Extracted from Joseph S. Bermudez, Jr., *Terrorism: The North Korean Connection* (New York: Taylor and Francis, 1990), pp. 123–24. See also interview data; "North Official Explains Defection in Mozambique," *Korea Herald,* 26 August 1989, as cited in FBIS-EAS-89-165, 28 August 1989, p. 28; "North Korea's Military Involvement in Africa," in *Some Useful Clues for Understanding North Korea* (Seoul: Naewoe Press, 1986), pp. 100–107; Pascal Chaigneau and Richard Sola, "North Korea as an African Power: A Threat to French Interests," *Strategic Review 146* (December 1985: 52–75; "North Korea in Africa," *Africa Now* 40 (August 1984): 28–30; and "Data on North Korea's Terrorism Exports," 123–33.

115. Samora Michael had been FRELIMO's foreign affairs director and was responsible for the initial contacts with the DPRK.

116. "International News: Mozambique Massacre," Associated Press, 22 July 1987. The Mozambican government accuses RENAMO of the massacre.

117. Dennis Redmont, "Mozambique," Associated Press, 7 August 1992.

118. "Mozambique Embassy Closes 'for Economic Reasons,'" Radio Mozambique, 17 April 1995, as cited in FBIS-EAS-95-074; "Mozambican President Meets DPRK Agrotechnical Group," *KCNA,* 4 April 1993, as cited in FBIS-EAS-93-065, 7 April 1993, p. 22; "Mozambican Party Delegation Arrives in Pyongyang," *KCNA,* 9 September 1992, as cited in FBIS-EAS-92-176, p. 17; and "O Chin-u Greets Mozambican Defense Minister," *KCNA,* 24 September 1990, as cited in FBIS-EAS-90-188, p. 24.

119. Extracted from Bermudez, *Terrorism: The North Korean Connection,* pp. 131–33. See also interview data; Jonas Bernstein, "Rival Factions Pave the Way to Unity under One Umbrella, *Insight,* 9 January 1989, p. 28; "North Korea's Military Involvement in Africa," 100–107; "North Korea in Africa," 28–30; Anthony Lewis, "Mugabe, Sensing Victory, Declares He Ought to Rule Rhodesia Alone," *New York Times,* 7 February 1979; and "Trial of Twenty-Four Blacks Begins in Rhodesia," *New York Times,* 8 February 1966.

120. A large number of these advisers were regular KPA troops.

121. "Korean Smugglers," Associated Press, 8 January 1992; and Donald G. McNeil, Jr., "New C-Note Is Awaited in the Land of Fake Bills," *New York Times,* 3 December 1995.

122. "Military Delegation Leaves for Zimbabwe Visit," *KCNA,* 2 August 1990, as cited in FBIS-EAS-90-150, 3 August 1990, p. 15; and "Zimbabwe's Mugabe Begins

Visit to Pyongyang," *KCNA,* 11 May 1993, as cited in FBIS-EAS-93-090, 12 May 1993, pp. 17–18.

123. "Zimbabwe Names New Supreme Armed Forces Commander," Reuters, 6 July 1994.

Chapter 5
LIGHT INFANTRY TRAINING GUIDANCE BUREAU, 1990–PRESENT

1. Interview data.

2. This organizational change was subsequently formalized by an amendment to the DPRK's constitution in April 1992. See "The North Korean Armed Forces," *Vantage Point* 18 (February 1995): 40–42; "Monthly Examines Political Hierarchy in the DPRK Following the Ninth Supreme People's Assembly Elections," pp. 214–27; Chong Sang-yong, "Resurgence of the First-Generation Revolutionaries and Choe Kwang," *Pukhan,* July 1990, pp. 102–12, as cited in FBIS-EAS-90-187, 26 September 1990, pp. 37–42.

3. "BRF—North Korea—Kim," Associated Press, 28 December 1993.

4. "Kim Il-song's Son Gets Title of Marshall," Reuters, 20 April 1992; "North Korea Confers a Top Military Title on Kim Jong Il," United Press International, 21 April 1992; and "Kim Chong-il's Military Support Described," *Sin Tong-a,* June 1993, as cited in FBIS-EAS-93-134, 15 July 1993, p. 12.

5. "Kim Il-sung, a Soviet Agent, Turns into 'Great Leader,'" *Vantage Point* 18 (October 1995): 8; and Huh Moon-young, "North Korea's Foreign Policy in Transition," *Vantage Point* 17 (July 1994): 21–29.

6. Interview data; and Republic of Korea, Ministry of National Defense, *Defense White Paper 1990* through *1995–1996.*

7. Interview data; Oh Il-hwan, "The Aims and Characteristics of North Korea's United Front Strategy," *Vantage Point* 19 (March 1996): 27–29.

8. "Kim Chung-nin's Background Detailed," *Pukhan,* January 1992, pp. 91–100.

9. "Article Criticizes Kato's Ties to DPRK," *Bungei Shunju,* 10 December 1995, pp. 116–27, as cited in FBIS-EAS-95-238; "North Fires Southern Affairs Chief Yun Ki-pok," *Chungang Ilbo,* 27 January 1993, p. 9, as cited in FBIS-EAS-93-041, 4 March 1993, pp. 31–32; and "Transfer of DPRK Official for ROK 25 Affairs Discussed," *Chungang Ilbo,* 25 February 1993, p. 2, as cited in FBIS-EAS-93-037, 26 February 1993, p. 20. Kelly Smith, in "Korea," Associated Press, 7 September 1992, explains that the ROK National Security Planning Agency uncovered a major DPRK espionage group whose leader had worked for the DPRK for 36 years. The DPRK had financed the group with $2.1 million for propaganda activities, which included the founding of a pro-P'yongyang political party.

10. Interview data; Republic of Korea, Ministry of National Defense, *Defense White Paper 1990* through *1995–1996;* Oh Il-hwan, "The Aims and Characteristics," 27–29; and "Former North Korean Agent Discloses DPRK's Spy Activities," p. 6.

11. Interview data; Oh Il-hwan, "The Aims and Characteristics," pp. 27–29; "Articles by Defector Kang Myong-to Reported: ROK-Watching Spy Agencies, Activities," part 8 of 12, p. 3; and "Former North Korean Agent Discloses DPRK's Spy Activities," p. 6.

12. Interview data; Oh Il-hwan, "The Aims and Characteristics," pp. 27–29;

"Articles by Defector Kang Myong-to Reported," part 8 of 12, p. 3; "Former North Korean Agent Discloses DPRK's Spy Activities," p. 6; and "North Fires Southern Affairs Chief Yun Ki-pok," *Chungang Ilbo,* 27 January 1993, p. 9.

13. Interview data; Oh Il-hwan, "The Aims and Characteristics," pp. 27–29; "Articles by Defector Kang Myong-to Reported," part 8 of 12, p. 3; "Former North Korean Agent Discloses DPRK's Spy Activities," p. 6; and "North Fires Southern Affairs Chief Yun Ki-pok," p. 9.

14. Interview data; and "Data: Testimonies by Defectors From North Korea," *Vantage Point* 26 (September 1993): 24–27; and "North Korea Still Bent on Training Armed Agents to Be Sent to the South," *North Korea News,* 20 September 1993, no. 701, p. 4.

15. Interview data; Oh Il-hwan, "The Aims and Characteristics," pp. 27–29; "Articles by Defector Kang Myong-to Reported," part 8 of 12, p. 3; and "Former North Korean Agent Discloses DPRK's Spy Activities," p. 6.

16. "Article on Composition, Mission of DPRK 'Operation Agents,'" *Choson Ilbo,* 23 September 1996, p. 4, as cited in FBIS-EAS-96-185; "NSP Presumes Consul's Murder Work of DPRK Terrorists," *Yonhap,* 4 October 1996, as cited in FBIS-EAS-96-194; and "NSP Urges Bolstering Security Measures against Terrorism," *Chollian Database,* 4 October 1996, as cited in FBIS-EAS-96-208-A.

17. Interview data; "ROK Agency: DPRK Agent Served as Professor in Pyongyang," *Yonhap,* 22 July 1996, as cited in FBIS-EAS-96-143.

18. "Daily Profiles Head of DPRK Reconnaissance Bureau," p. 3.

19. Ibid. This unit has been incorrectly called the "Cultural Liasion Department." The term "special terrorist commandos" apparently refers to foreign terrorist who will operate against the ROK for the DPRK.

20. Interview data; and "English, Japanese Study Given Preference," *Naewoe Tongsin,* 6 May 1993, pp. C1–C4, as cited in FBIS-EAS-93-145, 30 July 1993, p. 22.

21. "Agency Releases Videotaped Testimony by DPRK Infiltrator," *Yonhap,* 29 October 1996, as cited in FBIS-EAS-96-210.

22. It is unclear whether the terms "Base" and "Squadron" (e.g., Third Base and 22nd Squadron) are synonymous.

23. "Captured Infiltrator Cited on DPRK Submarine Operations," *Korea Herald,* 3 October 1996, p. 3, as cited in FBIS-EAS-96-193; "DPRK Has Four Submarine Bases for 'Infiltrations' of South," *Digital Chosun Ilbo WWW,* 30 September 1996, as cited in FBIS-EAS-96-191; and "Captured Agent on DPRK's 1995 Espionage, New Submarine Base," as cited in FBIS-EAS-96-187.

24. Interview data; U.S. Navy, *Worldwide Submarine Challenges: 1996* (Washington, D.C.: Office of Naval Intelligence, 1996), pp. 30–31; Sharpe, *Jane's Fighting Ships 1996–1997,* p. 397; and Sharpe, *Jane's Fighting Ships 1990–1991,* p. 356.

25. "YONHAP Reports on Infiltrator, Defector News Conference," *Yonhap,* 29 October 1996, as cited in FBIS-EAS-96-210.

26. Interview data; and Yu Yong-won, "Wolgan Choson Views DPRK Military," *Wolgan Choson,* December 1990, pp. 166–87, as cited in FBIS-EAS-91-073-S, 16 April 1991, pp. 1–14.

27. "Daily Views Possible DPRK Measures Following Infiltration," *Tong-a Ilbo,* 25 September 1996, p. 1, as cited in FBIS-EAS-96-187.

28. "North 'Largest-Scale War Exercise Since 1991,'" *Yonhap,* 17 March 1995, as cited in FBIS-EAS-95-052.

29. Interview data; "South, U.S. Experts on North's Warfare Units," *Yonhap,* 18 November 1994, as cited in FBIS-EAS-94-223; "General Warns of 'Serious Military Threat,'" *Yonhap,* 29 September 1995, as cited in FBIS-EAS-95-189; and "Joint Chiefs Chairman: Combined Army Expected," *Yonhap,* 20 January 1993, as cited in FBIS-EAS-93-013, 22 January 1993, p. 23.

30. Interview data; and "Joint Chiefs Chairman: Combined Army Expected," p. 23.

31. "DPRK Planes Appear near ROK Air Space 4 October," KBS-1, 4 October 1996, as cited in FBIS-EAS-96-195; and "Defense Ministry Calls DPRK Air Maneuvers Routine Training," *Korea Herald* 7 October 1996, p. 3, as cited in FBIS-EAS-96-195.

32. Interview data.

33. Ibid.; and Sharpe, *Jane's Fighting Ships 1996–1997.*

34. U.S. Defense Intelligence Agency, *North Korea Handbook,* PC-2600-6421-94, 1994, p. 6–220.

35. Interview data; "Attempted 1995 Military Coup d'Etat in DPRK Alleged," *Chugan Choson,* 21 March 1996, pp. 34–35, as cited in FBIS-EAS-96-053; "Article on Past Military Coup Attempts in North," *Iryo Sinmun,* 21 May 1995, p. 9, as cited in FBIS-EAS-95-097; and "DPRK 'Intensifying' Internal Control," *Seoul Sinmun,* 6 May 1996, p. 2, as cited in FBIS-EAS-96-088.

36. Interview data; "Eighty Possible Foreign Terrorists in ROK; DPRK Terrorist Ties," KBS-1, 3 October 1996, as cited in FBIS-EAS-96-194; "DPRK Said to Smuggle Weapons into Southeast Asian Countries," *Tong-a Ilbo,* 11 September 1996, p. 1, as cited in FBIS-EAS-96-177; "NSP Presumes Consul's Murder Work of DPRK Terrorists"; "NSP Urges Bolstering Security Measures against Terrorism"; "Philippines-Rebels," Associated Press, 27 February 1992; and William Branigin, "Manila Bomb Said to Expose Iraqi Ring; Baghdad Diplomat Is Expelled as Search for Agents Spreads Through Asia," *Washington Post,* 25 January 1991.

37. "DPRK Military Said Training Burundian Army," *Choson Ilbo,* 15 September 1995, p. 6, as cited in FBIS-EAS-95-179.

38. Interview data; Moon Ihlwan, "Killing of Suspected Spy Latest Cold War Incident," Reuters, 17 October 1995; and Katherine Bruce, "Shooting of Alleged N. Korean Spy Ends Drama," Reuters, 27 October 1995.

39. Interview data; Bruce, "Shooting of Alleged N. Korean Spy Ends Drama"; "Agents Sent for 'Resident Spy,'" KBS-1, 25 October 1995, as cited in FBIS-EAS-95-206; "News Conference Provides Details," *Yonhap,* 25 October 1995, as cited in FBIS-EAS-95-206; "Police Find Equipment Hidden by Infiltrator," KBS-1, 25 October 1995, as cited in FBIS-EAS-95-207; "Government Confirms 'Spies' Sent by North," *Yonhap,* 27 October 1995, as cited in FBIS-EAS-95-208; "Second DPRK 'Intruder' Shot in Gunfight," KBS-1, 27 October 1995, as cited in FBIS-EAS-95-208; "DPRK Infiltrators Part of 'New Generation,'" *Yonhap,* 3 November 1995, as cited in FBIS-EAS-95-213; "Infiltrators Said Sent on 'Mission of Terror,'" *Yonhap,* 9 November 1995, as cited in FBIS-EAS-95-217; "North Korea Spies Dispatched to Kill Key Figures," *Korea Herald,* 10 November 1995; "Pyongyang's Schemes to Undermine South Korea Behind 'Reconciliatory Gestures,'" *Vantage Point* 18 (November 1995): 16–18; "DPRK Agents Carry 'Pen-Shaped Toxic Guns,'" KBS-1, 29 November 1995, as cited in FBIS-EAS-95-229; "Arrested DPRK Armed Agent's

Testimony Noted," *Yonhap,* 8 December 1995, as cited in FBIS-EAS-95-236; and "DPRK Infiltrator Holds News Conference 8 Dec.," KBS-1, 8 December 1995, as cited in FBIS-EAS-95-236.

40. According to Kim Tong-sik, unlike other sections, the Sixth Section engages in direct illegal infiltrations into the ROK and in recruiting ROK citizens.

41. Accounts of their infiltration aboard a midget submarine and arriving at Kanghwa-do, northwest of Seoul, are incorrect.

42. "Worker's Party Leader Given Life Sentence," *Yonhap,* 26 February 1993, as cited in FBIS-EAS-93-038, 1 March 1993, p. 39.

43. Interview data; "Chronology of North Korean Submarine Drama," Reuters, 29 December 1996; "Agency Releases Videotaped Testimony by DPRK Infiltrator"; "DPRK Sub Infiltrator, Defector Interviewed," KBS-1, 29 October 1996, as cited in FBIS-EAS-96-211; Korean Veterans Association, *North Korea Submarine Incursion* (Seoul: Korean Veterans Association, 1996); Sharpe, *Jane's Fighting Ships 1996–1997,* p. 397; "Recon Photographs Taken by DPRK Espionage Agents Found," *Kyonghyang Sinmun,* 24 September 1996, p. 1, as cited in FBIS-EAS-96-186; "DPRK Makes Radio Contact Daily with Five Remaining Agents," *Joong-Ang Ilbo WWW,* 23 September 1996; "Identities of Twenty DPRK Infiltrators Revealed," KBS-1, 18 September 1996, as cited in FBIS-EAS-96-182.

44. According to earlier reports, Li Kwang-su identified his submarine as the *No. 2 Submarine* of the 22nd Squadron. In a news conference held later Yi stated, "I am combatant Yi Kwang-su of the *No. 1 Reconnaissance Submarine* of the 2nd Team, the 22nd Squad of the Maritime Department of the Reconnaissance Bureau of the Ministry of People's Armed Forces." See "DPRK Sub Infiltrator, Defector Interviewed."

45. The crew and passengers consisted of the following:

- *Supervisors:* Senior Col. Kim Dong-won, director of the Maritime Department; and an unidentified vice director of the Maritime Department.
- *Reconnaissance team:* three unidentified agents.
- *Crew cadres:* Lt. Col. Chong Yong-ku, captain; Maj. Yu Im, deputy commander; Lt. Col. Man Il-chun, chief engineer; Maj. Sin Yong-kil, political instructor; Capt. Won Ung-chol, communications officer; Capt. Pak Tae-hun, deputy chief engineer; and Capt. Yi Yong-ho, navigation officer.
- *Crew:* Combatant Lieutenant Kim Sung-ho; Senior Lieutenants Li Kwang-su, Song Dong-chul, Ham Min-sun, and Kim Chang-bok; Junior Lieutenants Kim Dong-hun and Yang Bong-sun; and Ensigns Byon Ui-jang, Kim Chul-jin, Li Young-chul, Pak Jong-kwan, Li Chul-jin, and Kim Young-il.

46. Interview data; and Sharpe, *Jane's Fighting Ships 1996–1997,* p. 397.

47. Film recovered from the reconnaissance team showed that they had photographed the entire area north and east of Mt. Kwebang. This included an ROK military radar base, the Yongdong thermal power plant, the An-in train station, and the Kangnung area.

48. Interestingly, just five years before, the ROK initiated a policy of removing "antiguerrilla barbed wire" and other obstacles to landing along the east coast. "BRF—Korea-Barbed Wire," Associated Press, 4 January 1991.

49. U.S. Navy, *Worldwide Submarine Challenges* (Washington, D.C.: Office of Naval Intelligence, February 1997).

50. "Foreign Ministry Spokesman Apologizes for Sub Incident," Radio Pyongyang, 29 December 1996, as cited in FBIS-EAS-96-251.

51. "Remains of DPRK Commandos Returned Via Panmunjom," *Yonhap,* 30 December 1996, as cited in FBIS-EAS-96-251.

52. "Government Rewards Those Who Helped during Sub Incident," *Yonhap,* 30 December 1996, as cited in FBIS-EAS-96-251.

53. "Navy Begins Towing Submarine to Port," *Yonhap,* September 1996, as cited in FBIS-EAS-96-185.

54. "Dead DPRK Infiltrator's Diary Reveals Escape Route," *Yonhap,* 7 November 1996, as cited in FBIS-EAS-96-217.

55. "North Korea Promotes Sub Incident Chief," *Chosen Ilbo,* 11 January 1997.

56. "Daily Views Possible DPRK Measures Following Infiltration," p. 1.

Chapter 6
SPECIAL PURPOSE UNITS TODAY

1. Interview data; "Weekly Details DPRK Special Operations Forces," pp. 56–58; U.S. Defense Intelligence Agency, *North Korean Special Purpose Forces*; U.S. Army, "North Korean Army Unconventional Warfare Capability," SRD-8-SC/NOFORN-76, 20 February 1976; and Joseph J. Bermudez, Jr. "North Korea's Light Infantry Brigades," *Jane's Defense Weekly,* 15 November 1986, 1176–78.

2. Interview data; "Weekly Details DPRK Special Operations Forces," pp. 56–58; U.S. Defense Intelligence Agency, "North Korean Light Infantry and Reconnaissance Units," IAR-7-77, January 1978; U.S. Defense Intelligence Agency, *North Korean Special Purpose Forces*; U.S. Army, "North Korean Army Unconventional Warfare Capability"; and Bermudez, "North Korea's Light Infantry Brigades," 1176–78.

3. "Weekly Details DPRK Special Operations Forces," pp. 56–58.

4. Although this is presently the best estimate of the light infantry brigade's organization it is possible that the organization still more closely resembles that of the light infantry brigade during the 1970s (see chapter 4).

5. U.S. Army, "North Korean Unconventional Warfare Capability," p. 9.

6. KPA encryption/decryption devices may, in part, be based upon older U.S. technology, since the KPA seized such equipment (i.e., KW-7) aboard the USS *Pueblo* in 1968. See "Coding Techniques Are Detailed at Navy Spy Trial," *New York Times,* 27 March 1986.

7. Pilots are considered primary targets for special purpose operations, since they are considerably more difficult to replace than an aircraft.

8. U.S. Defense Intelligence Agency, *North Korean Special Purpose Forces*; p. 4; and U.S. Army, *North Korean People's Army Operations,* FC 100-2-99, 5 December 1986, p. 17-8.

9. Interview data; "Weekly Details DPRK Special Operations Forces," pp. 56–58.

10. Interview data; and U.S. Army, "North Korean Unconventional Warfare Capability," p. 8.

11. Interview data.

12. In 1996 the commander of the 38th Airborne Brigade was Maj. Gen. Kim Yong-il. See "Weekly Details DPRK Special Operations Forces," pp. 56–58.

13. U.S. Defense Intelligence Agency, "North Korean Air Assault Forces," IAR-2-78, June 1978, p. 17.

14. U.S. Army, "Imagery Interpretation Key: Korea," TM 30-314, KAC-25/5001-71, June 1971, p. 3.29.

15. Interview data.

16. U.S. Defense Intelligence Agency, "North Korean Air Assault Forces," p. vi.

17. Interview data.

18. U.S. Defense Intelligence Agency, "North Korea: Threat Presented by An-2/Colt," DIAIAPPR-98-80, 12 June 1980, p. 1; and "North Korean Military Threat Assessed," *Aviation Week and Space Technology,* 7 February 1983, 42.

19. "North Korean Military Threat Assessed," p. 42.

20. Deborah G. Meyer, "Does the US Need to Modernize Its Army in the Pacific?" *Armed Forces Journal International,* May 1985, 104.

21. "North Military Personnel, Arms Double in Decade," *Korea Herald,* 27 July 1985, pp. 1–2; as cited in JPRS-KAR-85-059, 30 August 1985, pp. 7–8.

22. "North Korea Imports Gliders from USSR for Military Use," *North Korea News,* no. 340, September 1986, p. 2.

23. Interview data.

24. U.S. Army, *North Korean People's Army Operations,* p. 17-6.

25. Ibid., p. 17-7.

26. Interview data.

27. The Osan facility "serves the same function for South Korea as the North American Aerospace Defense Command complex in Cheyenne Mountain, Colo., does for the U.S. and Colorado." See "Command, Control Capability Upgraded," *Aviation Week and Space Technology,* 7 February 1983, p. 71.

28. Interview data; "Weekly Details DPRK Special Operations Forces," pp. 56–58; U.S. Defense Intelligence Agency, "North Korean Navy: Compact, Capable, Growing," *Defense Intelligence Digest,* November 1971, pp. 4–7; U.S. Defense Intelligence Agency, *North Korean Special Purpose Forces*; U.S. Army, "North Korean Army Unconventional Warfare Capability"; U.S. Army, *North Korean People's Army Operations;* Joseph S. Bermudez, Jr., "North Korean Marines," *Marine Corps Gazette,* January 1987, 32–35.

29. The current battalion organization may also include a mortar battery.

30. These specialized infiltration craft, midget submarines, and swimmer delivery vehicles are under the operational control of either the Korean People's Navy or the Reconnaissance Bureau's Maritime Department.

31. "Military Detains North Korean Citizen on Gun Charges," *ITAR-TASS,* 22 November 1995, as cited in FBIS-SOV-95-225.

32. Amphibious warfare training may also be conducted from the Sinp'o Naval Base or in the Mayang-do Island area.

33. At their peak during World War II, Soviet naval infantry forces totaled "over 350,000 troops in 40 brigades, 6 independent regiments, and a number of smaller units. Five of these brigades were honored with the 'Guards' distinction. Soviet accounts of the war indicate that there were 114 landings carried out by these troops during the war." See Steven J. Zaloga and James W. Loop, *Soviet Bloc Elite Forces* (London: Osprey Publishing, 1985). For a discussion on Communist PRC experiences during the 1950s and early 1960s see David G. Muller, Jr., *China as a Maritime*

Power (Boulder, Colo.: Westview Press, 1983).

34. An indication of the KPA interest in these targets was the unsuccessful infiltration mission near the nuclear power plant at Wolsung on 5 August 1983. See Hahn, "The Democratic People's Republic of Korea: Maritime Power," 16.

35. Interview data; *Jane's Sentinel: North Korea (DPRK)* (London: Jane's Information Group, 1995), pp. 18–19; and Sharpe, *Jane's Fighting Ships 1996–1997,* pp. 396–401.

36. The structure of these light tank battalions (amphibious) is uncertain. They are, however, similar to the standard tank battalion, although they have thirty-one PT-76/type-63 light tanks and a personnel strength of 161 (20 officers and 132 enlisted men). The thirty-one tanks are distributed as follows: one for the battalion commander, and ten for each of the three companies. Of the company's ten tanks, one is for the company commander, and three are for each of the three platoons.

37. Interview data; Massimo Annati, "Underwater Special Operations Craft," *Military Technology,* March 1996, 85–89; "Japan-Spy Boat," Associated Press, 29 October 1990; "Wrecked DPRK 'Spy Ship' Discovered on Coast," *Kyodo,* 29 October 1990, as cited in FBIS-EAS-90-209, 29 October 1990, p. 11; and "Korean Residents Say DPRK Spy Report False," *Kyodo,* 30 October 1990, as cited in FBIS-EAS-90-211, 31 October 1990, p. 9; Richard Compton-Hall, "The Menace of the Midgets," *Submarine Review,* April 1989, 11–17; Peter Maas, "South Korea Accuses North after Agent's Confession," *Washington Post,* 16 January 1988; and U.S. Defense Intelligence Agency, "North Korean Infiltration Raises Specter of Insurgency," pp. 4–6.

38. These categories are not absolutes, but rather reflect an analysis of known operations.

39. For a description of the P'ohang-Uijongbu Army Petroleum Distribution system see Robert E. Wegmann, "Expanding the Line," *Army Logistician,* March–April 1984, 27, "Ministry Says U.S. to Turn Over Pipeline," *Korea Herald,* 7 May 1991, 7; and "U.S. Forces Relinquishing Control of Pipeline," *Yonhap,* 11 June 1992, as cited in FBIS-EAS-92-114, 12 June 1992, p. 13. For a description of the Pusan-Uijongbu fiber-optic communications system see Bernard J. Adelsberger, "Army Fiber-Optic Project Doubles Communication," *Army Times,* 18 May 1987, p. 33.

40. KPA seaborne infiltrators have consistently demonstrated a willingness to kill themselves (typically having large quantities of plastic explosives strapped to their bodies) rather than risk capture.

41. Hahn, "The Democratic People's Republic of Korea: Maritime Power," p. 13; and A. D. Baker III, *Combat Fleets of the World 1986/8* (Annapolis, Md.: Naval Institute Press, 1986), p. 316.

42. The construction of the *Tong Gon Ae Guk Ho* was financed by funds raised by the large community of DPRK nationals and sympathizers living in Japan. See "Details of Burma Bombing Revealed in Confession," p. 4.

43. Jack Anderson, "U.S. Agents Keeping Close Eye on North Korean Terrorist Ship," *Florida Today,* 16 October 1985.

44. Ibid.

45. Ibid.

46. Interview data.

47. The *Changsan-ho* was built at the Namp'o Shipyard and launched at

Namp'o port on 16 September 1981. See "Events in September, 1981," *Vantage Point* 4 (October 1981): 28.

48. "Kang Dokhun News Conference," *Korea Herald,* 15 February 1987.

49. John H. Cushman, Jr., "U.S. Studied Halting Iran-Bound Missiles," *New York Times,* 18 January 1988. The *Tong Gon Ae Guk Ho* has not been involved in these Silkworm operations. Instead it has remained primarily concerned with covert special operations.

50. Jerry Seper, "N. Korean Ship Seizure Off Mexico Described by Valley Businessman," *Phoenix (Ariz.) Republic,* 5 June 1984; Jerry Seper, "N. Korean Spy Ship Tried to Establish Base on Gulf Island," *Phoenix (Ariz.) Republic,* 7 June 1984; and "N. Korean Ships Reported Spying Off Baja Coast," *San Diego Tribune,* 6 June 1984.

51. Seper, "N. Korean Ship Seizure Off Mexico"; Seper, "N. Korean Spy Ship Tried to Establish Base"; and "N. Korean Ships Reported Spying Off Baja Coast."

52. Seper, "N. Korean Ship Seizure Off Mexico"; Seper, "N. Korean Spy Ship Tried to Establish Base"; and "N. Korean Ships Reported Spying Off Baja Coast."

53. The connection, if any, between DPRK and then Soviet SIGINT operations along the western and southern U.S. borders, is unknown.

54. Youssef Bodansky, James Bruce, and Tony Banks, "Iran Exercised Confrontation with US Forces," *Jane's Defense Weekly,* 1 August 1987, 168.

55. Interview data; "Weekly Details DPRK Special Operations Forces," pp. 56–58. The subordination of the sniper brigades to the Reconnaissance Bureau may have changed during the late 1980s or early 1990s. These brigades may now be subordinate to the Light Infantry Training Guidance Bureau. This, however, has yet to be confirmed. In this book, the brigades are assumed to be subordinate to the Reconnaissance Bureau.

56. "North Korea—Body Snatchers," Associated Press, 9 August 1994.

57. For an alternate sniper brigade organization see Joseph S. Bermudez, Jr., *North Korean Special Forces* (London: Jane's Publishing Company, 1988), pp. 127–28.

58. It is interesting that the DPRK obtained significant quantities of damaged and destroyed armored fighting vehicles first from Vietnam in the late 1970s and then Cambodia in 1992. Concerning the Cambodian efforts see "Two DPRK Freighters Reportedly Seen in Cambodian Port," *Yonhap,* 8 December 1992, as cited in FBIS-EAS-92-236, 8 December 1992, p. 18.

59. "Kim Chong-il Analyzed from Tape Recordings," *Yonhap,* 16 September 1995, as cited in FBIS-EAS-95-180; "Tape of Kim Chong-il Conversation Published," *Wolgan Choson,* October 1995, pp. 104–28, as cited in FBIS-EAS-95-181; Bernard Gwertzman, "Two Korean Film Figures Tell of Abduction to North," *New York Times,* 15 May 1986; and William Sexton, "A Rare Peek at N. Korea's Rulers," *Newsday,* 27 May 1987, 9, 13.

60. Republic of Korea, Agency for National Security Planning, *Results of the Invesigation into the Bombing of Korean Air Flight 858,* report, 15 January 1988; "Suspects in Crash Take Suicide Pills," *New York Times,* 2 December 1987; Clyde Haberman, "Seoul Suspects North in Jet Crash," *New York Times,* 3 December 1987; "Seoul Seeks Suspect's Extradition," *New York Times,* 8 December 1987; and "Suicide Victim in Jet Inquiry Termed North Korea Envoy," *New York Times,* 11 December 1987.

61. Hahn, "The Democratic People's Republic of Korea: Maritime Power," pp. 18–22; "The Selling of Terrorism: Profit from a Lucrative Export,"*Insight,* 20 July

1987, 30–31; Clyde Haberman, "North Korea Reported to Step Up Arms Sales and Training Abroad," *New York Times,* 29 November 1987; and "P'yongyang Attempting to Strengthen Its Foothold in Third World," *Vantage Point* 10 (June 1987): 21–23. As cited in Clyde Haberman, "Dilemma for the Mavericks of P'yongyang," *Pacific Defense Reporter,* July 1987, p. 18.

62. Interestingly, Yasser Arafat's personal bodyguards during the 1982 Israeli invasion of Lebanon included two North Koreans presumed to be sniper brigade personnel. Likewise, as of late 1995, the personal bodyguards of Cambodia's King Norodom Sihanouk still include about fifty North Koreans (believed to be from the Reconnaissance Bureau's sniper brigades), originally sent by Kim Il-song. See U.S. Defense Intelligence Agency, *Lebanon / Israel / French / Comments on Beirut Siege,* unnumbered Intelligence Information Report, dated 14 December 1982; and "Phnom Penh," *Jane's News Service,* 7 September 1995.

63. For a detailed examination of the DPRK's involvement in terrorism, revolution, and military assistance see Bermudez, *Terrorism: The North Korean Connection.*

Chapter 7
PERSONNEL AND TRAINING

1. "Article Details Everyday Life in Army," *Chungang Ilbo,* 15 April 1993, p. 1, as cited in FBIS-EAS-93-092, 14 May 1993, pp. 32–33; U.S. Defense Intelligence Agency, "North Korean Army Training: Steadily Progressing," *Defense Intelligence Digest,* June 1968, pp. 29–31; and U.S. Army, "OPFOR: North Korea," TC-30-37, January 1979, pp. 1-1 and 1-2.

2. Although the term of service is officially three and one-half years, most personnel are required to serve until they are twenty-seven years old, with an average term of service of nine years.

3. Personnel are considered unfit for the following reasons: height less than 1.4 meters (4 feet, 9 inches), weight less than 45 kilograms, hypertension, hernia, tuberculosis, heart ailments, psychiatric illness, loss of limb, fingers or more than two toes. Hernia and other correctable deficiencies are often repaired in government hospitals, after which an individual is considered fit for military service. See U.S. Army, "North Korean Paramilitary Reserve Forces," SRD-23-C/NOFORN-76, 1 August 1976, p. v.

4. The politically unreliable category is defined as including former landlords, wealthy farmers, and their families ("families" refer to the extended immediate family, including grandchildren and grandchildren-in-law); former capitalists and their families; families of defectors to the ROK; former Japanese government employees and their families; persons identified as "reactionary elements"; and ex-convicts. Politically unreliable personnel are refused employment at government agencies, important industries, public service facilities, and institutions of higher education, and are discriminated against socially. See U.S. Army, "North Korean Paramilitary Reserve Forces," p. I-15; U.S. Army, "OPFOR: North Korea," p. 3-2; "Escape from the Jaws of Death (II)," *Vantage Point* 10 (June 1987): 16; and "Escape from the Jaws of Death (III)," *Vantage Point* 10 (June 1987): 20–21.

5. Yu Yong-won, "Wolgon Choson Views DPRK Military," *Wolgon Choson,* December 1990, pp. 166–87, as cited in FBIS-EAS-91-073-S, 16 April 1991, pp. 1–14.

6. Since detailed information concerning special purpose forces and intelligence

training is so rare, this section is provided to illustrate how such training has developed and to explain how today's training is conducted. See U.S. Defense Intelligence Agency, *North Korean Armed Forces Handbook (U),* January 1971, pp. 119–46.

7. As with the previous section, this section explains how intelligence training has developed and is conducted today. See U.S. Defense Intelligence Agency, *North Korean Armed Forces Handbook (U),* July 1977, pp. 6-1 to 6-8.

8. "Article Details Everyday Life in Army," *Chungang Ilbo,* 15 April 1993, p. 1, as cited in FBIS-EAS-93-092, 14 May 1993, pp. 32–33; U.S. Defense Intelligence Agency, "North Korean Army Training: Steadily Progressing," pp. 29–31; and U.S. Army, *North Korean People's Army Operations,* FC 100-2-99, 5 December 1986, chapter 16, "Educational and Training System."

9. There does not appear to be a national-level system of separate training centers for new recruits. See "Article Details Everyday Life in Army," pp. 32–33; U.S. Defense Intelligence Agency, "North Korean Army Training: Steadily Progressing," pp. 29–31; and U.S. Army, *North Korean People's Army Operations,* FC 100-2-99, 5 December 1986, chapter 16, "Educational and Training System"; and U.S. Defense Intelligence Agency, "North Korean Armed Forces Modernization," p. 14.

10. The DMZ police are special units responsible for security along the DMZ and the borders with the PRC and Russia. There are approximately ten DMZ police battalions deployed within the I, II, and V Forward Corps. Each battalion apparently attaches one company to each infantry division deployed on the DMZ. These companies are deployed in platoons that rotate every two months. These units perform sentry duty and normal military police functions. They may also be employed to conduct agent escort, scouting, and reconnaissance operations.

11. U.S. Defense Intelligence Agency, "North Korean Army Training: Steadily Progressing," pp. 29–31.

12. U.S. Defense Intelligence Agency, *North Korean Armed Forces Handbook (U),* January 1971, pp. 119–46; and U.S. Defense Intelligence Agency, *North Korean Armed Forces Handbook (U),* July 1977, pp. 6-1 to 6-8.

13. U.S. Army, "OPFOR: North Korea," pp. 1-5 and 5-3; and U.S. Defense Intelligence Agency, "North Korean Infiltration Raises Specter of Insurgency," pp. 4–6.

14. U.S. Army, "OPFOR: North Korea," p. 3-1.

15. One source describes the rigorous training: "We filled backpacks with [30 kilograms] of sand and ran, often in bare feet, over mountain trails until we could cover [65 kilometers] in six and half hours." See Hubbell and Reed, "Mission: To Murder a President," p. 144.

16. "YONHAP Reports on Infiltrator, Defector News Conference,"*Yonhap,* 29 October 1996, as cited in FBIS-EAS-96-210; and "Captured Armed Guerrilla Reveals Training of DPRK Commandos," *Seoul Sinmun,* 25 November 1996, p. 5, as cited in FBIS-EAS-96-229.

17. U.S. Defense Intelligence Agency, "North Korean Air Assault Forces," IAR-2-78, June 1978, p. vi.

18. Interview data.

19. Interview data; and U.S. Defense Intelligence Agency, "North Korean Light Infantry and Reconnaissance Units," IAR-7-77, January 1978, p. vi.

20. U.S. Defense Intelligence Agency, "North Korean Light Infantry and Reconnaissance Units," pp. 9, 17, 28.

21. McCune, *Leadership in North Korea: Groupings and Motivation,* pp. 6–7.

22. Officers and senior NCOs receive privileged treatment in housing, regular leaves, consumer goods, and so forth. There is also a wide disparity in KPA pay grades. A private or private first class receives a salary of approximately 2–2.5 won; senior sergeant or master sergeant, 5.5–7.5 won; junior lieutenant or lieutenant, 75–78 won. One U.S. dollar is equivalent to 2.14 won. As a matter of comparison, a doctor's typical monthly salary is 100–120 won. Special purpose personnel also receive jump, longevity, and hazardous-duty allowances.

23. "Details of Burma Bombing Revealed in Confession," p. 4; and "Terrorists Enter Rangoon as 'Sailors,'" *Korea Herald,* 27 November 1983, p. 1.

24. Institute of Internal and External Affairs, *Inside North Korea: Three Decades of Duplicity,* p. 74.

25. U.S. Army, "North Korean Army Unconventional Warfare Capability," SRD-8-SC/NOFORN-76, 20 February 1976, p. 13.

26. A Workers' Peasant Red Guard regiment can have a personnel strength of 1,000 to 8,000, with the typical regiment having a strength of 3,000 to 4,000. A battalion has a strength of approximately 400. See U.S. Army, "North Korean Paramilitary Reserve Forces," pp. 2–3.

27. Hubbell and Reed, "Mission: To Murder a President," pp. 142–47.

28. David R. Kohler, "Spetsnaz," U.S. Naval Institute *Proceedings* (August 1987): 50.

29. Interview data.

30. "P'yang Wages Propaganda for Armed Revolt in South," *Korea Herald,* 28 June 1987, p. 8.

31. Institute of Internal and External Affairs, *Inside North Korea: Three Decades of Duplicity,* p. 74.

32. Don Oberdorfer, "North Korea Accused of Kidnapping Women," *Washington Post,* 24 January 1988.

33. Republic of Korea, Agency for National Security Planning, *Results of the Investigation into the Bombing of Korean Air Flight 858,* 15 January 1988, p. 5.

34. Ibid.; and Fred Hiatt, "Japan Kidnappings May Lead to N. Korea Spy Case," *Washington Post,* 20 January 1988; and Peter Maas, "South Korea Accuses North after Agent's Confession," *Washington Post,* 16 January, 1988.

35. Interview data; and "Weekly Details DPRK Special Operations Forces," pp. 56–58.

36. "Details of Burma Bombing Revealed in Confession," p. 4; and "Terrorists Enter Rangoon as 'Sailors,'" p. 1.

37. "Defector Comments on DPRK Commando Suicide Methods," *Digital Chosun Ilbo WWW,* 21 September 1996, as cited in FBIS-EAS-96-185.

38. Interview data; and U.S. Army, "North Korean Army Unconventional Warfare Capability," p. 12.

Chapter 8

COMBAT TECHNIQUES

1. U.S. Defense Intelligence Agency, *North Korean Armed Forces Handbook (U),* January 1971, pp. 125–39; and ibid., *North Korean Armed Forces Handbook (U),* July 1977, pp. 6-1 to 6-8.

Appendix
THE DMZ TUNNELS

1. "Why Korea Is Scared," p. 4.

2. Interview data; United Nations Command, U.S. Forces Korea, and Eighth U.S. Army, *1976 Annual Historical Report,* U.S. Defense Intelligence Agency, "North Korean Infiltration Raises Specter of Insurgency," pp. 4–6; and U.S. Defense Intelligence Agency, "Korean DMZ: The Challenge of Making It Work," pp. 12–14.

3. Republic of Korea, *Defense White Paper 1990,* pp. 75–77; Institute of Internal and External Affairs, *Inside North Korea: Three Decades of Duplicity,* pp. 74–76; North Korean Affairs Institute, *Brief History of North Korean Provocations against South Korea: 1945–1977,* pp. 43–44; J. D. Harris, "Under the Land of Morning Calm," *British Army of the Rhine,* no. 54, December 1976, pp. 45–47; David Reed, "North Korea's Secret Invasion Tunnels," *Reader's Digest,* March 1980, 90–94; *Tunnels of War: North Korea Catacombs the DMZ* (Seoul: Korean Information Service, 1978); and "P'yongyang Denounces U.S. for Revealing North Korea's Digging of Invasion Tunnels," *North Korea News,* 6 July 1987, no. 380, pp. 2–3.

4. Sometime during 1961–62, the engineer battalion 26th Infantry Division, then located in Yunan-gun, South Hwanghae Province, began construction on an infiltration tunnel by digging into the side of Yongkak Mountain. See "Escape from the Jaws of Death (I)," p. 13.

5. Republic of Korea, *Defense White Paper 1990,* p. 75.

6. It is quite possible that light infantry and Reconnaissance Bureau personnel had used this tunnel for a considerable period of time before its discovery.

7. Institute of Internal and External Affairs, *Inside North Korea: Three Decades of Duplicity,* pp. 75–76.

8. Republic of Korea, *Defense White Paper 1990,* pp. 75–78. "Korea—Tunnel," Associated Press, 5 March 1990; "U.N. Command Wants Joint Investigation to North Korea," United Press International, 5 March 1990; "Korea—Tunnel," Associated Press, 4 March 1990; "Korea—Tunnel," Associated Press, 3 March 1990; and "Korea—Tunnel Tour," Associated Press, 7 July 1994.

9. Bermudez, *North Korean Special Purpose Forces,* p. 4.

Selected Bibliography

DECLASSIFIED

The following documents have been declassified (either partially or completely) by the U.S. government under the provisions of the Freedom of Information Act.

McCune, Evelyn Becker. *Leadership in North Korea: Groupings and Motivation,* U.S. Department of State. Office of Intelligence Research. 1963.

United Nations Command, U.S. Forces Korea, and Eighth U.S. Army. *1976 Annual Historical Report.* HIST-S-77-6, 1977.

———. *1983 Annual Historical Report.*1984.

U.S. Air Force. "FEAF ECM History during the Korean Conflict." HQ FEAF, 3 May 1954.

U.S. Army. "Communist Guerrillas in South Korea," *Intelligence Review* 166 (March 1950): 41–44.

———. *Enemy Tactics.* HQ EUSAK, 26 December 1951.

———. *Handbook on the North Korean Armed Forces.* Department of Army Pamphlet 30-52, 11 July 1962.

———. *History of the North Korean Army.* HQ, FEC, MIS, G2, 31 July 1952.

———. "Imagery Interpretation Key: Korea." TM 30-314, KAC-25/5001-71, June 1971, p. 3.29.

———. *IPAC Intelligence Summary (U).* PIC 2600-0180-82, October 1982.

———. *North Korean AAA Order-of-Battle (U).* PIC 1140-049A-KS-83, July 1983.

———. *North Korean Antiaircraft Artillery Forces (U).* PIC-1140-058-KS-83, February 1983.

———. *North Korean Armor Force.* SRD-25-S/NOFORN-76, 17 May 1977.

———. "North Korean Army Engineers," GHQ, FEC, MIS, GS, *Allied Translator and Interpreter Section, Research Supplement, Interrogation Reports: North Korean Forces* 104 (1951): 2–40.

———. "North Korean Army Unconventional Warfare Capability." SRD-8-SC/NOFORN-76, 20 February 1976.

———. "North Korean Guerrilla Operations," GHQ, FEC, MIS, GS, *Allied Translator and Interpreter Section, Research Supplement, Interrogation Reports: North Korean Forces* 3 (15 November 1950): 15–22.

———. "North Korean Paramilitary Reserve Forces." SRD-23-C/NOFORN-76, 1 August 1976.

———. *Order of Battle Handbook: Chinese Communist Forces, Korea and the North Korean Army.* HQ, FEC, and EUSA, ACS-G2, 1 October 1955.

———. *Order of Battle Handbook: Chinese Communist Forces, Korea and the North Korean Army.* HQ, FEC, and EUSA, ACS-G2, 1 January 1956.

———. "The Role of Guerrillas in the Korean War," *Intelligence Review* 181 (June 1951): 17–26.

———. "Soviet Partisan Warfare," *Intelligence Review* 173 (October 1950): 13–22.

U.S. Army, Pacific. *North Korean Army Handbook.* Special Report no. 303. ACS-G2, 1 July 1957.

———. *Order of Battle: North Korean Army.* Special Report no. 325. HQ, ACS-G2, 15 January 1958.

———. *Tables of Organization and Equipment of the North Korean Army.* Special Report no. 304. HQ, ACS-G2, 1 July 1957.

U.S. Defense Intelligence Agency. "Korean DMZ: The Challenge of Making It Work," *Defense Intelligence Digest,* July 1969, pp. 12–14.

———. "North Korea: Threat Presented by An-2/Colt." DIAIAPPR-98-80, 12 June 1980.

———. "North Korea, the USSR, Communist China: Operation Tightrope," *Defense Intelligence Digest,* September 1968, pp. 37–40.

———. "North Korean Air Assault Forces," IAR-2-78, June 1978.

———. *North Korean Armed Forces Handbook (U).* DIA-210-11-1-71-INT, January 1971.

———. *North Korean Armed Forces Handbook (U).* DDI-2680-37-77, July 1977.

———. "North Korean Armed Forces Modernization," *Defense Intelligence Digest,* December 1968, pp. 14–17.

———. "North Korean Army Training: Steadily Progressing," *Defense Intelligence Digest,* June 1968, pp. 29–31.

———. "North Korean Infiltration Raises Specter of Insurgency," *Defense Intelligence Digest,* January 1968, pp. 4–6.

———. "North Korean Light Infantry and Reconnaissance Units." IAR-7-77, January 1978.

———. "North Korean Navy: Compact, Capable, Growing," *Defense Intelligence Digest,* November 1971, pp. 4–7.

———. *North Korean Special Purpose Forces.* DDB-1100-475-84, May 1984.

———. *The North Korean Combined Arms Brigades at Namdaechon.* DDB-1100-407-83, May 1983.

———. "Reports of Three Former U.S. Prisoners of War Remaining in KN (U)." IIR 2 221 00187 89, 6 July 1989.

———. "Rumors of U.S. Prisoners of War Teaching English in KN (U)." IIR 2 221 0050 89, 2 February 1989.

———. *Unclassified Communist Naval Orders of Battle.* DDB-1200-124-81, May 1981.

———. *Unclassified Communist Naval Orders of Battle.* DDB-1200-124B-82, November 1982.

———. "United Nations POW/MIA Sightings in North Korea (U)." IIR 2 221 0070 92, 31 December 1991.

———. "USSR Continues Military Aid to North Korea," *Defense Intelligence Digest,* June 1963, pp. 42–43.

U.S. Department of Defense. *Military Assistance Reappraisal: FY1967–71.* Vol. 1. June 1965.

U.S. Department of State. "Arms Suspension: A Big Stick or a Weak Reed," INR-22, 12 November 1969.

U.S. Navy. *Cluster Osprey (U).* Naval Intelligence Support Center, NIC-1223X-002-85, August 1985.

———. "Enemy Light Plane Raids in Korea," *ONI Review* 8 (August 1953): 378–79.

———. "Korea (North Korea): Notes from a North Korean Defector," *ONI Review* 10 (November 1955): 606.

———. "The Korean Fishing Season and North Korean Propaganda," *ONI Review* 14 (September 1959): 394–95.

———. "North Korean Coastal Defenses," *ONI Review* 10 (October 1954): 407–10.

———. *Worldwide Submarine Challenges: 1996.* Office of Naval Intelligence, Washington, D.C., 1996.

UNCLASSIFIED

The following documents are unclassified, although some were obtained from the U.S. government under the provisions of the Freedom of Information Act.

Republic of Korea. Ministry of National Defense. *Defense White Paper 1990.* Seoul, 1991.

———. *Defense White Paper 1991–1992.* Seoul, 1992.

———. *Defense White Paper 1992–1993.* Seoul, 1993.

———. *Defense White Paper 1993–1994.* Seoul, 1994.

———. *Defense White Paper 1994–1995.* Seoul, 1995.

———. *Defense White Paper 1995–1996.* Seoul, 1996.

———. *Defense White Paper 1996–1997.* Seoul, 1997.

U.S. Army. *North Korea: A Country Study.* Department of Army Pamphlet 550-81, 1976.

———. *North Korea: A Country Study.* Update. Department of Army Pamphlet 550-81, 1994.

———. "OPFOR: North Korea." TC-30-37. Draft. January 1979.

———. *North Korean People's Army Operations.* FC 100-2-99, 5 December 1986.

———. *The Soviet Army: Operations and Tactics.* FM 100-2-1, 16 July 1984.

———. *The Soviet Army: Specialized Warfare and Rear Area Support.* FM 100-2-2, 16 July 1984.

———. *The Soviet Army: Troops, Organization and Equipment.* FM 100-2-3, 16 July 1984.

———. *The Soviet Partisan Movement 1941–1945.* Department of Army Pamphlet 20-244. Washington, D.C.: GPO, August 1956.

U.S. Defense Intelligence Agency. *North Korea Handbook.* PC-2600-6421-94, Washington, D.C., 1994.

————. *North Korea: The Foundations for Military Strength.* Washington, D.C., October 1991.

————. *North Korea: The Foundations for Military Strength, Update 1995.* Washington, D.C., March 1996.

————. *Unclassified Communist Order of Battle.* DDB-1200-124-86, April 1986.

U.S. Senate. *Statement of Rear Admiral Thomas A. Brooks, U.S. Navy, Director of Naval Intelligence, before the Seapower, Strategic, and Critical Materials Subcommittee of the House Armed Services Committee in Intelligence Issues.* 22 February 1989.

OPEN SOURCE, ARTICLES

Adelsberger, Bernard J. "Army Fiber-Optic Project Doubles Communication," *Army Times,* 18 May 1987, 33.

Almond, Peter. "That Iran Sub, If Real, May Be N. Korean Model," *Washington Times,* 7 August 1987.

Anderson, Jack. "N. Korea Penetrates S. Korean Airspace with U.S. Choppers," *Newsday,* 29 April 1985, 54.

————. "U.S. Agents Keeping Close Eye on North Korean Terrorist Ship," *Florida Today,* 16 October 1985, 11A.

Beaver, Paul. "Equipment: Mi-2 Armed—and Ready," *Jane's Soviet Intelligence Review* 1 (February 1989): 76–77.

Bermudez, Joseph J., Jr. "North Korea's Combined Arms Brigades," *Combat Weapons* 2 (spring 1986): 26–29, 89–93.

————. "North Korea's Light Infantry Brigades," *Jane's Defense Weekly,* 15 November 1986, 1176–78.

————. "North Korean Marines," *Marine Corps Gazette,* January 1987, 32–35.

————. "The Tank Battalion of the North Korean People's Army," *Armor* 95 (November–December 1986): 16–20.

Chaigneau, Pascal, and Richard Sola. "North Korea as an African Power: A Threat to French Interests," *Strategic Review* 146 (December 1985): 52–75.

"Choe Kwang's Biographic Data Detailed," *Pukhan,* July 1990, 102–12, as cited in FBIS-EAS-90-187, 26 September 1990, pp. 37–42.

Choi Young. "The North Korean Military: Buildup and Its Impact on North Korean Military Strategy in the 1980s," *Asian Survey* 25 (March 1985).

"Chronology of Purges by Kim Il-song," *Vantage Point* 17 (July 1994): 34–36.

"Coding Techniques Are Detailed at Navy Spy Trial," *New York Times,* 27 March 1986.

"Command, Control Capability Upgraded," *Aviation Week and Space Technology,* 7 February 1983, 71–73.

Cushman, John H., Jr. "U.S. Studied Halting Iran-Bound Missiles," *New York Times,* 18 January 1988.

"Details of Burma Bombing Revealed in Confession," *Korea Herald,* 27 November 1983, 4–5.

East, Don C. "A History of U.S. Navy Fleet Air Reconnaissance: Part I, The Pacific and VQ-1," *Hook,* spring 1987, 14–33.

"English, Japanese Study Given Preference," *Naewoe Tongsin,* 6 May 1993, pp. C1–C4, as cited in FBIS-EAS-93-145, 30 July 1993, p. 22.

"Escape from the Jaws of Death (I)," *Vantage Point* 10 (May 1987): 11–15.

"Escape from the Jaws of Death (II)," *Vantage Point* 10 (June 1987): 11–17.

"Escape from the Jaws of Death (III)," *Vantage Point* 10 (June 1987): 20–21.

"Excalibur 180 Surface/Submarine Craft," *Jane's Defense Weekly,* 9 January 1988, 20.

"German Submarine Export to North Korea is Halted," *Wall Street Journal,* 7 December 1987.

Gwertzman, Bernard. "Two Korean Film Figures Tell of Abduction to North," *New York Times,* 15 May 1986.

Haberman, Clyde. "North Korea Reported to Step Up Arms Sales and Training Abroad," *New York Times,* 29 November 1987.

———. "Seoul Suspects North in Jet Crash," *New York Times,* 3 December 1987.

Hahn, Bradley. "The Democratic People's Republic of Korea: Maritime Power," *Combat Craft,* January/February 1985, 10–19.

———. "Dilemma for the Mavericks of Pyongyang," *Pacific Defense Reporter,* July 1987, 18–22.

———. "North Korean Navy: Strong and Getting Bolder," U.S. Naval Institute *Proceedings* 108 (July 1982): 113–15.

Han Sung-joo. "The Political Role of the Military in North Korea," in *North Korea Today: Strategic and Domestic Issues,* Korea Research Monograph no. 8, Institute for East Asian Studies. Edited by Robert A. Scalapino and Jun-yop Kim. Berkeley: University of California, 1983, pp. 133–41.

Harris, J. D. "Under the Land of Morning Calm," *BOAR* (British Army of the Rhine), no. 54, December 1976.

Hiatt, Fred. "Japan Kidnappings May Lead to N. Korea Spy Case," *Washington Post,* 20 January 1988.

Hubbell, John G., and David Reed. "Mission: To Murder a President," *Reader's Digest,* July 1968, 142–47.

"Kang Dokhun News Conference," *Korea Herald,* 15 February 1987.

Kin Motoyoshi. "Kim Chong-il's Army," *Gungi Kenkyu,* April 1986, as cited in JPRS-KAR-86-045, 23 October 1986, pp. 14–24.

———. "Political Structures," *Gungi Kenkyu,* March 1986, as cited in JPRS-KAR-86-045, 23 October 1986, pp. 1–13.

Ki-taek Li, "Soviet Military Policy in the Far East and Its Impact of North Korea (II)," *Vantage Point* 12 (May 1989): 7.

Kiwon, Chung. "The North Korean People's Army and the Party." In *North Korea Today,* edited by Robert A. Scalapino. New York: Praeger, 1963.

Kohler, David R. "Spetsnaz," U.S. Naval Institute *Proceedings* (August 1987): 46–55.

"Korea (North)," *Air International,* October 1985, 163.

Krisher, Bernard. "A Soldier's Story," *Newsweek,* 30 December 1968, 33–34.

Maas, Peter. "South Korea Accuses North after Agent's Confession," *Washington Post,* 16 January 1988.

———. "Agent Wins Sympathy in S. Korea," *Washington Post,* 25 January 1988.

Meyer, Deborah G. "Does the US Need to Modernize Its Army in the Pacific?" *Armed Forces Journal International,* May 1985, 104.

"North Korea Imports Gliders from USSR for Military Use," *North Korea News,* no. 340, September 1986, 2.

"North Korea in Africa," *Africa Now* 40 (August 1984): 28–30.

"North Korea to Import Hungarian Helicopters," *North Korea News,* no. 351, 8 December 1986, 4.

"North Korea to Increase Military Aid to Nicaragua," *Vantage Point* 10 (July 1987): 13–14.

"North Korea's Military Involvement in Africa," in *Some Useful Clues for Understanding North Korea.* Seoul: Naewoe Press, 1986, pp. 100–107.

"North Korea's Temptation," *Foreign Report,* no. 1723, April 8, 1982, 1–4.

"North Korean Military Threat Assessed," *Aviation Week and Space Technology,* 7 February 1983, 42.

"North Korean Terrorism History," *Hanguk Ilbo,* 10 July 1985, p. 4, as cited in JPRS-KAR-85-007, 24 December 1985, pp. 3–4.

"N. Korean Ships Reported Spying Off Baja Coast," *San Diego Tribune,* 6 June 1984.

Oberdorfer, Don. "North Korea Accused of Kidnapping Women," *Washington Post,* 24 January 1988.

O'Conner, Mike. "Coping with Charlie," *Journal of the American Aviation Historical Society* 30 (spring 1985): 2–11.

Pak Song-kun. "Weapons Systems of North Korea," *Kukbang Kwa Kisul,* January 1989, pp. 102–13, as cited in FBIS-EAS-89-055, 23 March 1989, pp. 10–16.

Pollack, Maxine. "The Selling of Terrorism: Profit from a Lucrative Export," *Insight,* 20 July 1987, 30–31.

"Profile on Defecting North Officer," *Yonhap,* 13 October 1995, as cited in FBIS-EAS-95-198.

"P'yang Wages Propaganda for Armed Revolt in South," *Korea Herald,* 28 June 1987.

"P'yongyang Attempting to Strengthen Its Foothold in Third World," *Vantage Point* 10 (June 1987): 21–23.

"Pyongyang Denies Presence of Its Soldiers in Afghanistan," *North Korea News,* no. 372, 11 May 1987, 4.

"Pyongyang Denounces U.S. for Revealing North Korea's Digging of Invasion Tunnels," *North Korea News,* no. 380, 6 July 1987, 2–3.

"P'yongyang Still Denies Any Role in Rangoon Atrocity," *North Korea News,* no. 344, 20 October 1986, 2.

Reed, David. "North Korea's Secret Invasion Tunnels," *Reader's Digest,* March 1980, 90–94.

"The Rise of Kim Jong-Il and the Heir Succession Problem," *Vantage Point* 10 (December 1987): 6.

"ROK Agency: DPRK Agent Served as Professor in Pyongyang," *Yonhap,* 22 July 1996, as cited in FBIS-EAS-96-143.

Schnabel, J. D. "North Korean Artillery, Part 1: Background and Organization," *Field Artillery Journal,* May–June 1978, 18–23.

———. "North Korean Artillery, Part 2: Tactics," *Field Artillery Journal,* May–June 1978, 22–26.

"SEAL Subs," *Gung-Ho Special No. 4: U.S. Navy SEALs,* 1985, pp. 50–57.

"Seoul Seeks Suspect's Extradition," *New York Times,* 8 December 1987.

Seper, Jerry. "N. Korean Ship Seizure Off Mexico Described by Valley Businessman," *Phoenix (Ariz.) Republic,* 5 June 1984.

———. "N. Korean Spy Ship Tried to Establish Base on Gulf Island," *Phoenix (Ariz.) Republic,* 7 June 1984.

Sexton, William. "A Rare Peek at N. Korea's Rulers," *Newsday,* 27 May 1987, 9, 13.

"Suicide Victim in Jet Inquiry Termed North Korea Envoy," *New York Times,* 11 December 1987.

"Suspects in Crash Take Suicide Pills," *New York Times,* 2 December 1987.

"Terrorists Enter Rangoon as 'Sailors,'" *Korea Herald,* 27 November 1983.

Wallace, James N. "New Tensions in Korea: New Risks for U.S.," *U.S. News & World Report,* 24 October 1983, 32.

Weathersby, Kathryn. "New Russian Documents on the Korean War," *Cold War International History Bulletin* 6–7 (winter 1995–96): 30–91.

Wegmann, Robert E. "Expanding the Line," *Army Logistician,* March–April 1984, p. 27.

"Why Korea Is Scared," *Foreign Report,* no. 1666, February 4, 1981, 2–4.

OPEN SOURCE, BOOKS AND REPORTS

Aota Manabu. *Kim Il Sung's Army.* Contemporary Affairs Series, no. 286. Tokyo: Nyumon Shinsho, 1979.

Arkin, William M., and Richard W. Fieldhouse. *Nuclear Battlefields: Global Links in the Arms Race.* Washington, D.C.: Ballinger Publishing Company, 1985.

Association of the U.S. Army. *Special Report. The Search for Peace: A Year End Assessment, 1985.* Washington, D.C.: A.U.S.A., 1985.

Aviation Advisory Service. *International Air Force and Military Aircraft Directory.* London: Aviation Advisory Service, 1987.

Baker, A. D. III. *Combat Fleets of the World 1986/8.* Annapolis, Md.: Naval Institute Press, 1986.

Bermudez, Joseph S., Jr. *North Korean Special Forces.* London: Jane's Publishing Company, 1988.

———. *Terrorism: The North Korean Connection.* New York: Taylor and Francis, 1990.

Cable, Larry E. *Conflict of Myths: The Development of American Counterinsurgency Doctrine and the Vietnam War.* New York: New York University Press, 1986.

Collins, James L., Jr. *Vietnam Studies: Allied Participation in Vietnam.* Washington, D.C.: GPO, 1975.

Collins, John M. *Green Berets, SEALs and Spetsnaz: U.S. and Soviet Special Military Operations.* New York: Pergamon-Brassey's, 1987.

Cooper, Matthew. *The Nazi War against Soviet Partisans: 1941–1944.* New York: Stein and Day, 1979.

Dae-sook Suh. *Kim Il Sung: The North Korean Leader.* New York: Columbia University Press, 1988.

Griffith, Samuel B. *Mao Tse-tung on Guerrilla Warfare.* Garden City, N.Y.: Anchor Press/Doubleday, 1978.

Institute for Strategic Studies. *The Military Balance: 1987–88.* London: Jane's Publishing Company, 1987.

Institute of Internal and External Affairs. *Inside North Korea: Three Decades of Duplicity.* Seoul: 1975.

Isby, David. *Weapons and Tactics of the Soviet Army.* London: Jane's Publishing Company, 1981.

Isby, David C., and Charles Kamps, Jr. *Armies of NATO's Central Front.* London: Jane's Publishing Company, 1985.

Jae Kyu Park, Byung Chul Koh, and Tae-Hwan Kwak. *The Foreign Relations of North Korea.* Boulder, Colo.: Westview Press, 1987.

Jencks, Harlan W. *From Muskets to Missiles: Politics and Professionalism in the Chinese Army, 1945–1981.* Boulder, Colo.: Westview Press, 1982.

Kim, Hyun Hee. *The Tears of My Soul.* New York: William Morrow and Company, 1993.

Kim Il-sung, Selected Works. P'yongyang: Foreign Language Publishing House, 1965.

Korean Information Service. *Tunnels of War: North Korea Catacombs the DMZ.* Seoul: Korean Information Service, 1978.

Muller, David G., Jr. *China as a Maritime Power.* Boulder, Colo.: Westview Press, 1983.

North Korean Affairs Institute. *Brief History of North Korean Provocations against South Korea: 1945–1977.* Seoul: ROK, 1977.

Paik Sun Yup. *From Pusan to Panmunjom.* New York: Brassey's, 1992.

Republic of Korea. Agency for National Security Planning. *Results of the Invesigation into the Bombing of Korean Air Flight 858.* Report, 15 January 1988.

———. *A White Paper on the South–North Dialogue in Korea.* Seoul: National Unification Board, 1982.

Scalapino, Robert A., ed. *North Korea Today.* New York: Praeger, 1963.

Scalapino, Robert A., and Kim Jun-yop, eds. *North Korea Today: Strategic and Domestic Issues,* Korea Research Monograph no. 8, Institute for East Asian Studies. Berkeley: University of California, 1983.

Schuetta, Lawrence V. *Guerrilla Warfare and Airpower in Korea, 1950–53.* Maxwell Air Force Base, Ala.: U.S. Air Force, Aerospace Studies Institute, Concepts Division, January 1964.

Seiler, Sydney A. *Kim Il-song 1941–1948: The Creation of a Legend, the Building of a Regime.* Lanham, Md.: University Press of America, 1994.

Stanton, Shelby L. *Vietnam Order of Battle.* Washington, D.C.: U.S. News Books, 1981.

Sharpe, Richard. *Jane's Fighting Ships 1989–1990.* London: Jane's Information Group, 1989.

———. *Jane's Fighting Ships 1990–1991.* London: Jane's Information Group, 1990.

———. *Jane's Fighting Ships 1996–1997.* London: Jane's Information Group, 1996.

Starinov, I. G. *Over the Abyss: My Life in Soviet Special Operations.* New York: Ivy Books, 1995.

Thompson, Royce L. *Intelligence Factors Underlying Operation Chromite of 15 September 1950.* U.S. Army OCMH, 30 January 1956.

U.S. Army. *Allied Translator and Interpreter Section, Research Supplement, Interrogation Reports: Documentary Evidence of North Korean Aggression.* GHQ, FEC, MIS, GS, 30 October 1950.

U.S. Navy. *Worldwide Submarine Challenges.* Washington, D.C.: Office of Naval Intelligence, February 1997.

Velikaya Otechestvennaya Voyna 1941–1945 gg.—Entsiklopediya [The Great Patriotic War 1941–1945 encyclopedia]. Moscow: Izd. Sovetskaya Entsiklopediya, 1985.

Zaloga, Steven J., and James W. Loop. *Soviet Bloc Elite Forces.* London: Osprey Publishing, 1985.

INDEX

Index

Production of *(cont)*
    Namp'o-class LCPF, 113, 129
    Romeo-class SS, 154
    Sang-o-class SSC, 154
    Whiskey-class SS, 154
    Yugo-class SSm, 124
—*Romeo*-class SS, 206
—Seizure of USS *Pueblo,* 85
—Shipyards, 129
    Bong Dae Bo factory, 154
    Namp'o, 282
    Pongdae Boiler Plant, 154
    Yukdaeso-ri, 78
—SIGINT collection
    Cargo vessels, 153
    Trawlers, 153
—Subordination of amphibious sniper
    brigades, 157
—Swimmer delivery vehicles, 77, 105
—Trading companies, 124
    Cargo vessels, 124
—Training
    Exercises, 155, 157
—*Whiskey*-class SS, 77
—Yellow Sea Fleet, 196
—Yu Chang-kwon purged by Kim Il-
    song, 93
Korean Volunteer Army, 13–15, 21, 258
—1st South Manchurian Brigade, 15
—3rd North Manchurian Brigade, 15
—5th East Manchurian Brigade, 15
—Alternate designations
    Korean Volunteer Corps, 258
—East Chilin Brigade, 15
—Independent Battalion, 15
—Integration into Korean People's
    Army, 23
—Yenchi Brigade, 15
Korean Workers' Party, 6, 20, 28–29,
    40, 42, 62, 93, 161, 169, 215–40,
    273. *See also* Central Committee
    Secretary in Charge of South
    Korean Affairs; Fatherland Lib-
    eration War; Secretary in
    Charge of Anti-ROK Operations;
    and South Korea General
    Bureau
—2nd Economic Committee
    6th Bureau, 155
—Cabinet General Intelligence
    Bureau, 58, 263

Dissolved, 70
Secretariat's General Intelligence
    Bureau, 58
Subordinate to KWP Central Com-
    mittee, 263
—Central Committee, 3, 6, 263
Eighteenth Plenum, 91, 95–96
Fifth Plenum, 65, 70
Fourteenth Plenum, 68
Seventeenth Plenum, 149
Sixteenth Plenum, 69
Third Plenum, 42, 52, 95
—Central Military Committee, 98, 168
Reestablishment of, 65
—Central People's Committee, 58, 103
—Congress
Sixth, 119
—Fatherland Liberation War. *See also*
    Guerrilla operations: Fatherland
    Liberation War
Central Committee attempts to
    expand within the ROK, 47
Independent guerrilla units, 29–41
Liaison Department, 31, 42, 45, 48,
    52; 526th Army Unit, 41, 49, 261;
    567th Army Unit, 50; Branch
    units, 43–44, 49; Eastern Liaison
    Office, 49; Guerrilla Guidance
    Section (Guerrilla Guidance
    Bureau), 31, 41, 49–50, 260;
    Guerrilla Units; Kumgang Politi-
    cal Institute, 46–47, 50, 75, 92;
    Lee Hyon Hang Unit, 49; Military
    Section, 31, 41–44, 47, 49, 50, 57,
    260; Missions, 48; Organization,
    49; People's Guerrilla Command,
    31; Seoul Guerrilla Guidance
    Bureau, 43, 44, 49; Seoul Political
    Institute, 43, 44
—Liaison Department, 60, 69
Cho In-ch'ol, director, 262
Guerrilla Guidance Section, 59; Dis-
    banded, 72
Liaison Section, 59
Military Section, 59; 567th Army
    Unit, 57; 869th Army Unit, 57,
    59; 992nd Army Unit, 57; Cen-
    tral Liaison Office, 60; Dis-
    banded, 72; Eastern Liaison
    Office, 60; Kaesong Liaison
    Office, 60; Missions, 59; Western

310

317

High-speed infiltration craft,
100, 245–46; Mother ships,
245–46; Overland escort units,
100; Semisubmersible infiltra-
tion craft, 100; Swimmer deliv-
ery vehicles, 100; Training Cen-
ters, 100; Training, 224; Used to
establish Operations Department, 121,122; Missions, 99, 121
Organization Section, 99
Personnel Section, 99
Rangoon bombing, 4, 117, 133–36,
207, 213, 232, 238, 272–73;
Training, 233
Rear Services Section, 99
South Korea Exhibition Hall, 99
Suh Yong-chul, 132
Taegu infiltration, 132
Trading companies, 120
Training, 99
Yi Chol; Awarded medal for success-
ful Taegu infiltration, 132
—Missions, 98, 120
—Operations Department, 120, 121–22
313th Army Unit; Established from
632nd Army Unit, 122
632nd Army Unit; Reorganized into
313th Army Unit, 122
Cargo vessels, 120
Ch'ongjin Liaison Office, 272
Established using Liaison Depart-
ment's Liaison Section, 121, 122
Established using Research Depart-
ment, 122
Overland escort units, 122;
Kaesong, 122; P'yonggang, 122;
Sariwon, 122
Seaborne escort units, 122, 128;
High-speed infiltration craft,
122; Semisubmersible infiltra-
tion craft, 122, 132; swimmer
delivery vehicles, 122
Support of terrorist and revolutionary organizations, 122
—Personnel
(1971), 216–19; Pay and benefits,
217; Resupply procedures, 218;
Sources, 216; Weapons and
equipment, 217
(1977), 219
—Rangoon bombing, 136

—Reorganized as CCSKA, 147
—Research Department, 102–3
Establishment of, 98
Kim Chung-nin, 118
Reorganized into Research Depart-
ment for External Intelligence,
122
Reorganized out of Culture Depart-
ment, 98, 102
Used to establish Operations
Department, 122
Research Department for External
Intelligence, 120, 122–23
Alternate designations (External
Information Department, Exter-
nal Information Research
Department), 122
Bombing of KAL Flight 858,
138–39, 159, 214
Established from Research Depart-
ment, 122
Japan Affairs Subsection, 122
Kim Chong-il orders discharge of
female agents, 123
Missions, 122
North American Affairs Subsection,
122
Trading companies, 120
Yi Yong-hyok, 138
—Support of terrorist and revolution-
ary organizations, 139–41, 207,
208
Training infrastructure, 140
—Training
(1966–1977), 222–25
—Unification Front Department,
100–102, 120, 121
Alternate designations (Depart-
ment of Projects for the United
Front, Unification Front
Bureau, United Front Depart-
ment), 121
Chosen Soren Affairs Section, 121
Missions, 121
Seoul, 47, 52, 60–61, 84, 110, 116–17,
130–31, 152, 160–61, 176, 177,
205, 214, 216, 233, 249, 251,
252, 268
—Fatherland Liberation War
Recapture by UNC forces, 45
Third Phase Offensive, 43

About the Author

Joseph S. Bermudez, Jr. is an internationally recognized analyst, author, and lecturer on North Korean defense and intelligence affairs. During the past eight years he has authored two books, and more than fifty articles, reports, and monographs on North Korea. His two books—*North Korean Special Forces* and *Terrorism: The North Korean Connection*—are considered by many to be the definitive open source works on their subjects and have been translated into Korean and Japanese. Bermudez's report, *Military-Technical Observations of the North Korean Nuclear Program,* completed during 1995 for Los Alamos National Laboratory, has quickly become required reading within U.S. Government circles. His work has also appeared in such diverse locations as ABC, NBC, BBC World Broadcasts, Voice of America, the *Financial Times, Japan Military Review,* the *Korea Times, Marine Corps Gazette,* the *New York Times,* the *Washington Post,* and the *Washington Times.*

Mr. Bermudez has lectured extensively in academic and government environments, both in the U.S. and the Republic of Korea. He has also testified before Congress on several occasions as an expert on North Korea's ballistic missile and nuclear, chemical, and biological warfare programs. Mr. Bermudez's work is recognized but not appreciated by the North Korean Government. In 1994, during a private meeting between Mr. Bermudez and North Korea's ambassador to the U.N., Ho Jong, Mr. Ho bluntly stated, "Both I and my government do not appreciate your writings at all and would prefer that you do not write anymore."

The **Naval Institute Press** is the book-publishing arm of the U.S. Naval Institute, a private, nonprofit, membership society for sea service professionals and others who share an interest in naval and maritime affairs. Established in 1873 at the U.S. Naval Academy in Annapolis, Maryland, where its offices remain today, the Naval Institute has members worldwide.

Members of the Naval Institute support the education programs of the society and receive the influential monthly magazine *Proceedings* and discounts on fine nautical prints and on ship and aircraft photos. They also have access to the transcripts of the Institute's Oral History Program and get discounted admission to any of the Institute-sponsored seminars offered around the country.

The Naval Institute also publishes *Naval History* magazine. This colorful bimonthly is filled with entertaining and thought-provoking articles, first-person reminiscences, and dramatic art and photography. Members receive a discount on *Naval History* subscriptions.

The Naval Institute's book-publishing program, begun in 1898 with basic guides to naval practices, has broadened its scope in recent years to include books of more general interest. Now the Naval Institute Press publishes about 100 titles each year, ranging from how-to books on boating and navigation to battle histories, biographies, ship and aircraft guides, and novels. Institute members receive discounts of 20 to 50 percent on the Press's nearly 600 books in print.

Full-time students are eligible for special half-price membership rates. Life memberships are also available.

For a free catalog describing Naval Institute Press books currently available, and for further information about subscribing to *Naval History* magazine or about joining the U.S. Naval Institute, please write to:

Membership Department
U.S. NAVAL INSTITUTE
118 Maryland Avenue
Annapolis, MD 21402-5035
Telephone: (800) 233-8764
Fax: (410) 269-7940
Web address: www.usni.org